FLYING OVER AN OLIVE GROVE

"Fred Spiksley, in my judgement, was unsurpassed both in poise and balance, and in his ability to work the ball with both the inside and outside of both feet."

Herbert Chapman, who managed Huddersfield Town and Arsenal to League title success.

FLYING OVER AN OLIVE GROVE

THE REMARKABLE STORY OF FRED SPIKSLEY, A FLAWED FOOTBALL HERO

Clive Nicholson, Ralph Nicholson, Mark Metcalf

Published in Great Britain by Red Axe Books

© Mark Metcalf, Clive Nicholson, Ralph Nicholson 2016
First Published October 2016

Front and back cover illustrations by Bob Venables

A catalogue record for this book is available from
the British Library.

ISBN 9781911477303

Printed and bound in England by Jellyfish Solutions

Dedicated to Lynda, Megan and Freddie Nicholson

CONTENTS

ACKNOWLEDGEMENTS

Bengt Ågren, Robert Boyling, Trevor Braithwait, John Brodie, Denis Clareborough, Tom Crawshaw, J. Crowell, Mike Davage, Paul Days, Jason Dickinson, Susan Edlington, Keith Farnsworth, Jim Fox, Andy George, Steve Gordos, Mark Harvey, Eva-Kajsa Hedström, John Harvey, Peter Holme and Alex Jackson at the National Football Museum, Krister Malmsten, Roy Massey, Randall Northam, Jonas Nystedt, Tom O'Neill, George Orr, Pascal Bolder Karen Shimmon, Bernd Siegler, Joyce Spicksley, Graham Spicksley, Richard Stonehouse, Andrew Stothard, Jen Sugden, Tom Sutcliffe, Gordon Taylor, Chris Waddle, RD Wells.

The staff at the following libraries: Sheffield, Gainsborough, Glossop, Manchester, Leeds, Fulham, Boston Spa and the British Library. The staff at Gainsborough Heritage Association, the National Archives and Lincolnshire FA.

FOREWORD

BY CHRIS WADDLE

WHEN READING THE various history books written about Sheffield Wednesday Football Club it is impossible to ignore the name Fred Spiksley.

Like me, Fred Spiksley was a winger. It is clear that he was loved by the Wednesday fans for his blistering pace, remarkable ball control, and an eye for goal. With Fred on the field the crowd and his teammates believed anything was possible, and on many occasions they were proven right. I am glad to note that by scoring in the 1993 FA Cup final I was following in Fred's footsteps, as he scored both of Wednesday's goals when Wolves was defeated 2-1 in 1896. The description of the second goal suggests it was one of the greatest goals ever scored in any final during the Victorian era, the shot combined such power, spin and accuracy that it so confused the Wolves keeper that he did not even realise it was a goal until the end of the match!

It is thanks to the years of work by Clive, Ralph and Mark that I have become more fully aware of Fred Spiksley, a player who represented England seven times and was never on the losing side. He scored a hat-trick on his debut and could well – as debated by the authors in this book – have scored three in his second game against Scotland, when he and Billy Bassett destroyed their opponents in a 5-2 success in 1893. It is therefore of little surprise that in 1934 Frederick Wall, who had been secretary of the Football Association for fifty years, selected him as his greatest ever Outside-Left.

I won't comment too much on Fred's life off the pitch except to say it was clearly highly colourful and not without its problems, but to have widely managed and coached abroad, escaped from a German prison at the start of World War I and performed on stage with Charlie Chaplin is quite extraordinary.

INTRODUCTION

FRED SPIKSLEY WAS a gambling addict who would risk his job for the sake of having a bet at the local races. Like all gamblers, he 'felt lucky', but was unlikely to have appreciated that his greatest piece of luck was in being born on 25 January 1870. This was because only fifteen years after his birth football's growing popularity, particularly, amongst the working class, would lead to the Football Association (FA) introducing professional football in 1885. Three years later, the Football League began and football was on its way to becoming the most popular sport in the world.

Spiksley was born in a terraced house in Gainsborough, a small town in Lincolnshire. He was fortunate in being amongst the first wave of thousands of working class teenage lads who could dream of making a living by playing the 'beautiful game'.

After experiencing the thrill of the crowd during FA Cup matches in Gainsborough it is no wonder that he wanted to emulate his heroes by setting up his own junior team. Other youngsters did the same, often sewing their own shirts and paying their subs to raise money to buy a leather football and hire land to play matches on. As is the case today, few of these boys would make it; most ended up working in the booming industrial trades that had developed throughout the north of England. Spiksley's story is different. He would become the first working class lad to be plucked from a life of obscurity and go on to have one of the greatest footballing adventures that any player in the history of the game could boast.

Spiksley's remarkable talent would see him scoring winning goals in an FA Cup final, hat-tricks for England and securing every major honour in the game. It also earned him a place on stage with Charlie Chaplin and saw the future Queen of England waving at him from the touchline.

Although he was forced to escape from a German prison at the outbreak of the First World War, he would make a triumphant return to Germany in 1927, leading 1FC Nuremberg to the championship of Germany. This was to be the highlight of a successful coaching career that saw him become the first professional footballer to coach across three different continents including taking charge of the Swedish national team (where he left a lasting legacy). He later made the first talking film aimed at improving the footballing skills of children.

Not all of Spiksley's life was a triumph, his working class background, gambling addiction and a thin skin, often meant that he would find himself in difficulty, with scandal, bankruptcy, and divorce ultimately tarnishing his good name. Nevertheless he was regarded by many of those that saw him play to be the finest outside left to have played the game right up until the mid-1930s. He had blistering pace and absolute control of the football. He played the game mainly with the outside of his foot. It could be argued that, given the quality of balls and boots that he used, no other footballer has been able to pass and shoot the ball as well as him with the outside of his foot. These talents helped him record the highest average goal ratio of any winger in the history of English football.

He was a player who could have succeeded in any era of the game, an assertion supported by legendary Huddersfield and Arsenal manager Herbert Chapman, who named Spiksley in his best side from the footballing past in his 1934 book 'Herbert Chapman: On Football'.

Fred Spiksley's story has long been forgotten with only

Introduction

dedicated football historians of pre-1900 football having recollections of spotting his unusual name. However the authors of this book have been fortunate, since the popularity and fame of Fred Spiksley meant that he was frequently asked to write about his footballing exploits. Two decades of research has uncovered over 100,000 of Spiksley's own. "Flying Over An Olive Grove" combined Spiksley's own accounts with contemporary match reports and extensive research to reveal the lost story of a boy who was born to a boilermaker in a small terraced house in Gainsborough and became a footballing hero on the local, national and international stage.

CHAPTER 1

ORIGINS OF FOOTBALL AND A FOOTBALL GENIUS
The formative years of the modern game and Fred Spiksley

FREDERICK SPIKSLEY WAS born at 3 Willoughby Street, Gainsborough on 25 January 1870. His father, Edward, was a boilermaker at the nearby Britannia Ironworks. When informed that his third child was imminent he rushed home from work. He found Sarah, his wife of five years, being ably assisted by her mother, Lucy, and a midwife. The baby was born without complications and further boosted England's population, which rose from 7.75 million to 30 million during the nineteenth century.

Fred's brothers, John Edward, who was always called 'Ted', and William, were aged four years and 23 months respectively. Their father had, rightly, celebrated their births lustily. Unfortunately, when he went to record their arrivals at the Register Office his lack of formal education, strong countryside accent and alcoholic stupor combined to make him unintelligible to the registrar.

Ted became a "Picksley" and William a "Spicksley". Fred was correctly recorded as a Spiksley. He was baptised by Reverend R W Charteris on St Matthew's Day, 21 September 1870 at Gainsborough's Holy Trinity Church. Fred later joined his brothers as a pupil at Holy Trinity Church School.

Fred's parents came from Lincolnshire fenland families. A fen is one of four main types of wetland. Fred's grandfather on his dad's side, another Edward, was an agricultural labourer for a local landowner on Metheringham Fen where he occupied a tied cottage with his wife, Rebecca, and five children. Metheringham Fen's main crops were wheat, barley, oats, turnips and potatoes. From an early age all four boys in the family helped till, sow and reap the soil.

Fred's mother's parents, William, a carpenter, and Lucy Porter, an excellent seamstress who made dresses, lived on the Nocton Fen.

It is not known how much schooling Fred's parents had as it was not until the Education Act 1870 that universal education became enshrined in law. The driving force behind the act was Britain's need to remain internationally competitive at a time of rapid industrialisation that in its wake swept up people from the countryside and deposited them in urban locations. These included Sarah Porter who moved to Gainsborough in the early 1860s. In 1800 around a quarter of the UK's population were urban-based and this rose to 77 per cent by 1900.

At nineteen, Edward Spiksley still had to share a bed with his brothers, William and Thomas. His farm labourer's pay was inadequate. Attempts to create a trade union for agricultural workers at Tolpuddle, Dorset in 1833 had led to its organisers being deported under the 1797 Unlawful Oaths Act. As rural workers were unable to unite and organise it meant their wages remained often pitifully low.

There were much higher pay rates within the expanding industrial and manufacturing sectors of the economy. In 1862, Edward's parents helped him load his basic furniture items on to a handcart for the six-mile journey to nearby Lincoln. There he found suitable cheap lodgings before seeking work in the burgeoning engineering businesses. Messrs Ruston, Proctor and Company at the Sheaf Ironworks had a healthy order book that meant they needed good strong workers. The young man became a labourer in the boiler workshop and set out to save some money.

In the meantime, James and Henry Marshall, on inheriting their father William's ironworks business in Gainsborough converted it into a joint stock company. From 1862 to 1864 they extended the existing Britannia Works by installing modern machinery on a 4.5 acre site on which 550 people were employed in various manufacturing workshops that included a plate furnace and facilities for rolling, grinding, drilling and riveting. Finished products included threshing machines for harvesting crops.

Marshall's would eventually employ 6,000 workers on a forty-acre site, and sixteen million bricks were fired in the company's brick kilns, using the red clay excavated from the site when it was first levelled to expand the old ironworks. While the company dominated the small Lincolnshire town there were also other smaller engineering employers such as J B Edlington, which began manufacturing hay-making machines in 1867 and still exists today, and Rose's that manufactured tobacco and sweet-wrapping machinery.

According to Susan Edlington, a local historian and wife of Brian, who today runs J B Edlington, "During the period in which Fred was brought up there was a real buzz in Gainsborough as Victorian entrepreneurs, with very little money in some cases, took considerable risks and started up businesses that in their wake brought full employment."

In the spring of 1864 news reached Edward Spiksley that Marshall's was offering two shillings (10p) a week more than in his current post. This was a significant sum as the average craft weekly wage was four to five shillings (25p) with labourers on under three shillings. (15p).

As the new factory neared completion a steady stream of engineers, platemakers and boilermakers migrated to Gainsborough on the guarantee of better pay and conditions. Many new workers obtained accommodation from the company, the forward-thinking brothers building rows of terraced houses to provide accommodation for them. They later established the Gainsborough Building Society, which existed independently until it merged with the Yorkshire Building Society in 2001. This provided finance at reasonable mortgage rates for employees wanting to buy their own home.

Edward Spiksley moved to Gainsborough to work for Marshall's in 1864 with the added appeal that his childhood sweetheart, Sarah, now aged seventeen, lived in the town with her mother Lucy.

Edward rented 3 Willoughby Street, a terraced house 50 yards from the free-flowing River Trent. Edward swiftly approached Lucy Porter requesting to marry her daughter. When she agreed the pair married on 10 December 1864.

The couple's first child, Ted, was born on 23 December 1865 and William arrived on 30 December 1868.

Their fourth child was born on 12 November 1875. To the Spiksleys' joy it was a girl, who was christened Florence Maud. However, tragedy struck when she died only 36 days later on 18 December 1876. She was buried in Gainsborough's Holy Trinity churchyard. The gravestone is still standing today.

Florence's youngest brother, Fred, began school at five. He would have been unaware but many important things had happened in the world of football in the years surrounding his birth.

By the nineteenth century a very rough and ready form of mass rugby football had been played in Britain for centuries. Games that were played in towns lasted over many days and had goals many miles apart. The authorities had unsuccessfully attempted to prevent what were frequently little more than mass brawls. Now, with the countryside gradually emptying, restrictions could be more easily imposed. The 1829 Metropolitan Police Act heralded the advent of modern policing and in 1835 Parliament banned football on the highways. The annual ritual football matches – some of which still exist today such as at Ashbourne in Derbyshire – was successfully suppressed, often by violent methods.

Around the same time major public schools were pushing ahead with playing football but with far fewer players. It seems reasonable to assume that the impetus must have, in part, derived from the earlier examples of mob football although there is no concrete proof of this. However, with each school playing its own version of the game, which was generally dependent upon the surroundings in which it was staged, problems arose over which rules to use when schools met one another. One of the key points of dispute was the use of hands, which was taboo at Eton but favoured at Rugby. The dispute would eventually be ended when two different games emerged – football and rugby.

The first time that rules were put into written form was in 1845 for the game played at Rugby School. This undoubtedly acted as the impetus for those who favoured a game with the minimum use of hands to put into print their own versions and Eton has a written set of rules dated October 1847. The following year the Cambridge (University) Rules were drawn up and although no written copy exists they appear to have functioned quite well.

Following discussions between representatives from Cambridge University and the public schools of Harrow, Eton, Shrewsbury and Rugby there were new Cambridge rules compiled in 1856 and further refined in 1863. The opening game played under them took place on 20 November that year when Cambridge Old Etonians and Cambridge Old Harrovians met under a set of rules –

including eleven players a side – that remain recognisable over 150 years later.

It would be wrong to pretend this was a seamless transition to a universal playing code as many schools continued to play their own versions of football. Consequently there remained no single body able to command the authority of all those playing the game even after the initiative by Ebenezer Cobb Morley from Barnes football club led to the formation of the Football Association (FA) on 26 October 1863.

In 1867 such was the FA's lack of authority that it had just ten members. Eton and Westminster stayed away. So while the public schools had saved football it also needed some practical men to take it forward.

Derived from the local cricket club, Sheffield Football Club had been established in 1857 when it also drew up its own rules. The club and the rules were the culmination of matches between local teams across South Yorkshire over the previous twenty years or so. The games were crude but unlike earlier forms of football they rarely became riotous. Corners, free kicks and crossbars were pioneered, the use of hands died out quickly and a set of rules was being established that made it possible for teams to face each other on a common front.

Crowds, too, were growing and in 1867 the first knockout cup competition outside the public schools was held with Hallam beating local rivals Norfolk 2-1 in the final. A rival Cromwell Cup, open to clubs under two years old and donated by Theatre Royal manager Oliver Cromwell, came into existence the following year and was won by the newly-created Wednesday FC.

At the FA's 1867 AGM, William Chesterman, Sheffield's FA delegate and secretary of Sheffield FC, was one of six men present. He brought a letter describing the advances made in his locality and expressed strong support for the FA. The previous year, Sheffield had faced, on 31 March, a representative London XI in Battersea Park, an event that signalled that each region was keen to overcome the rules differences. Football was growing in the capital and on 26 January 1867 *The Field* magazine had identified many metropolitan sides that were playing similar games under rules used at Charterhouse and Westminster. These were not too different from the rules adopted in Sheffield.

By the start of 1868 there were 29 clubs within the FA, making it possible to expand the FA committee to include the Old Etonian Arthur Kinnaird aged just 21. As a player, he went on to appear in nine FA Cup finals from 1873–1883. However, he was just as remarkable off the pitch as he served the FA as the treasurer for thirteen years and president for 33 years. Upon his retirement, Kinnaird was presented with the decommissioned FA Cup that was won by Wednesday in 1896.

In 1871 match officials were incorporated into the rules so that an umpire was appointed for each half of the field, although only when a player appealed could they decide if there was an infringement. However, in situations where the umpires disagreed with one another then a referee sitting on the touchline would make the final ruling.

The same year the match duration was set at 90 minutes and the unique position of the 'keeper was introduced as the only player who could handle the ball. In order to prevent abuse of this privilege, he could do so only in his own half. Each team was restricted to eleven players and the football size at between 27 and 28 inches in circumference was standardised. Leather balls, with an internal bladder, were also refined by stitching pre-formed panels together.

The corner, goal kick and free kick were formalised in 1872. Shinguards were invented in 1874 and in 1875 the 8ft-high crossbar was formally introduced.

It was just weeks after Fred Spiksley's birth in 1870, that England played Scotland for the first time ever, at the Oval on 5 March 1870. This game's organiser was FA secretary Charlie Alcock, who, inspired by the Cock House competition at Harrow, the following year created the longest-running cup competition in the world, the FA Cup.

Although the 1870 game is not considered as a full international – only two of the Scotland players, Kinnaird and Robert Smith of Queen's Park, were Scottish-born – the event, and four further games, acted as the precursor to modern international football with the first full game taking place between Scotland and England in Glasgow on 30 November 1872. Interestingly, match reports contain no reference to any player passing the ball. The game was played under Scottish rules and follow-up games in England were under English rules. When the two FAs met with their Welsh and Irish counterparts in 1882 to regularise the rules – or laws, as they were known – it led to the standard two-handed throw-in from behind the head and the clear marking of the touchlines.

With children staying in the infants class until they were seven, Fred spent his first school year at Holy Trinity Church School alongside his brother, William. Despite separate entrances for boys and girls the class was a mixed one. The headmaster was Mr Charles Taylor, appointed to the post in 1875 after eleven years as a teacher there.

Taylor was a keen advocate of football and at his instigation the local Holy Trinity Recreation Society members were persuaded to establish a football section in 1872. Taylor later succeeded in turning the football section team into one of Lincolnshire's finest clubs, Gainsborough Trinity.

From early on, one of Taylor's pupils had a mania for dribbling a ball. Fred Spiksley could rarely be seen without an India-rubber ball as he went between home and school. He tried to keep it under control as he kicked the ball against house walls, dodged pedestrians and trapped the ball just as it seemed certain to enter the road.

These activities would be difficult today when pavements are relatively flat but in the 1870s the task that the youngster set himself was even more of a problem. The path from 3 Willoughby Street to Fred's school was a thoroughfare that consisted of an uneven earthen road in a poor condition. When it rained streets became a morass of clinging mud. There were no paved walkways or gas lamps on Willoughby Street and workers on early shifts needed to tread carefully. Bridge Street near the Trinity School was cobbled and did have gas lamps but it lacked a pavement. The school closed in 1939 and is today occupied by Gainsborough Model Railway Society.

Fred's enthusiasm undoubtedly helped him develop the skills that later earned him great fame although by then dribbling had become less important in football. In the 1870s and into the 1880s football was dominated by the individual approach – in which each forward, of which there were eight with only two backs, ran or dribbled with the ball as far as he could before either losing it to a defender or having it taken from him by a frustrated colleague. However, as players and coaches sought scientifically to refine the sport it didn't take too long to realise that by combining (passing) it was possible to create greater goalscoring opportunities.

Like many of his friends, Fred Spiksley must have been extremely disappointed when Charles Taylor retired in 1877 and was succeeded by John Walker who was more interested in academic exercise than athleticism and sport. Almost immediately football was banned in the school on the basis that it was a danger to the windows. Instead, pupils were encouraged to join the school choir and participate in church services. To compound matters for Fred his practising with the India-rubber ball against his parents' backyard wall had gone slightly awry and his dad was unhappy at having his cold frame for growing cucumbers smashed. The youngster was sent to the local playing field.

Although football remained banned at school, William

and Fred were selected on 8 December 1881 when Gainsborough Grammar School challenged a combined team from the town's middle class schools – consisting of All Saints, Holy Trinity and the Wesleyans – to a football battle.

Both sides adopted a 2-2-6 formation with two centre forwards. The grammar school won 4-1 on a rare occasion when the two Spiksley brothers played football together. It is not known if either scored.

A few weeks later on Fred's twelfth birthday, in January 1882, his father gave him an extra-special expensive gift.

Fred's dad had left Britannia Ironworks in 1878. He had successfully applied for the tenant landlord licence for his local pub, the Crown and Anchor Inn in Bridge Street. This was owned by the rapidly-expanding Hewitt Brothers business. In addition to selling beer, the inn had adjoining lodgings that served as a temporary resting place for travellers. Among them one week were Grace MacGuire and her fifteen-year-old daughter, Nellie, popular professional singers from Ireland. They toured the country performing in provincial music halls. The lodgings were also something more permanent for bricklayers at Edward's last workplace. The new owner employed 18-year-old Eliza Hamilton to assist his wife Sarah in running the lodgings side of the business.

Fred's father had entered a very competitive trade as there were eight pubs in Bridge Street. Even so, the regular ships entering Gainsborough's prosperous, thriving inland port with its own custom house meant there was never any shortage of thirsty customers for strong ale among the seamen who also took advantage of the piano and music hall within the pub, referred to in newspaper adverts as 'Spiksley's Varieties'. Edward Spiksley advertised for a good pianist and vocalist in the *Stamford Mercury* of 24 September 1880 and four years later the entertainment in mid-September featured pedestal skate dancer Mr Fred Williams and comic Miss Minnie Harrington.

Edward Spiksley also had on occasions to deal with some unpleasant customers, including George Dawson, who was sentenced to one month's hard labour after stealing a blanket, an S A Dring who was charged with assaulting the pub landlord and Mary Ann Booth. She was fined 5s (25p) for refusing to quit the pub.

The music hall scene obviously rubbed off on a young Fred Spiksley and it was not long before he was learning to play the piano with some aplomb and was a member of the Gainsborough Music Society at thirteen. During his time at Sheffield Wednesday he became the team's pianist. In 1911 the *Sheffield Daily Telegraph* reported how he had accompanied the musical programme at the annual dinner of the Clarboro' Farming and Gardening Society at the King's Arms, Clarborough, near Retford.

Fred was not the only footballer of his generation to be musically talented. John Southworth finished top scorer in Division One with Blackburn Rovers in 1890–91 and with Everton in 1893–94. After being forced to retire early due to injury he became a professional violinist and played with the Halle Orchestra. Spiksley rated Southworth the greatest centre forward England of his time.

Edward would only stay in business if he kept his pipes clean and pulled a good pint from the wooden barrels used for storage. It was usual to pull and throw away a few beers before the product was good enough to serve each day. The Crown and Anchor became known for the good head on its beer and its music. Edward couldn't read or write, leaving Sarah to tackle any such tasks. The landlord was, though, fully aware of the importance of profit.

From this he bought his son that extra-special birthday present – a Horncastle football. This was every young footballer's dream as it was the ball the emerging stars played with. These included E Rhodes who earlier that month became the first Sheffield Wednesday player to notch four goals in an FA Cup tie as Staveley were beaten 5-1 in a match watched by 2,000 spectators.

Wednesday eventually lost to Blackburn Rovers 5-1 in a replayed semi-final. The losing side included Scotsman James Lang. After impressing in the Clydesdale side that finished runners up in the 1874 Scottish FA Cup, he came south in 1876 to become Wednesday's first – and very probably the first ever – professional footballer, an occupation that under the FA rules then in place was illegal. Amazingly, Lang was blind in his left eye.

In the 1882–83 competition, Blackburn Olympic, bankrolled heavily by local foundry owner Sydney Yates, swept to success in the FA Cup final by beating Old Etonians 2-1. After six final appearances the losing amateur side never returned and their defeat caused apoplexy among football's upper and middle class administrators with the FA immediately threatening to expel any clubs found to be paying their players "over and above legitimate out-of-pocket expenses".

Clubs who did so attempted to keep it hidden until, eventually, over 40 major clubs, including most of the big North West ones, threatened in 1885 to form their own 'British Football Association.' With that, the FA, after losing a few snobbish moralists, capitulated and professionalism became permitted. Working class lads could now view football as a paid occupation.

Fred was so delighted by his present that he dashed to school to show the other boys. No matter that football wasn't allowed, he kicked the ball out of his hands as high as he could and with very little space to work in he instantly brought the ball under control when it re-entered planet earth. The youngster's ball control was such that as he developed as a footballer he maintained he was better with the ball when he was a kid! He delighted in juggling with the ball, a feature he maintained in his professional career to the pleasure of the watching crowd but to the occasional despair of his playing colleagues and coaches who wanted him to cut out 'the fancy skills'.

With their new ball Fred and his mates were now doubly determined to play football. They met in the playground and plotted how to raise funds to start a football club. These were youngsters but their enthusiasm was mirrored ed at higher levels, in 1882 and 1883, by the founding of clubs still in existence today – Burnley, Tottenham Hotspur, QPR, Coventry City and Bristol Rovers.

The children's elders were generous and, armed with the necessary funds, the youngsters were soon up and kicking with Fred appointed as the captain – after all it was his ball! His power extended to him naming the team – Eclipse, an undefeated eighteenth-century thoroughbred racehorse who won eighteen races, including eleven King's Plates. Although the new football team quickly faded the horse remains revered in the racing world with the Eclipse Awards for American thoroughbreds named in his honour. The Sheffield-based Eclipse Tools, named after the horse, is now part of Spear and Jackson.

Matches with other boys were organised. Then the vicar of St John's Church in Gainsborough offered them the chance to play against his own team with the prize of a brand new leather ball for the winners. The offer was accepted but the vicar was taking no chances and appointed himself as referee.

Eclipse bashed home three goals but all three were disallowed so Fred strode across to tell the uncharitable vicar he was clearly not averse to bending the rules. The crimson-faced parson grabbed the Eclipse captain and demanded an apology. None was forthcoming and, shocked at the referee's actions, the better side strode off telling the official to keep his football.

On Easter Monday 1883, the football club in the small Lincolnshire market town of Horncastle, around 38 miles from Gainsborough, had arranged to play Notts Rangers.

The match was at the time Horncastle's biggest and they feared humiliation. They approached Gainsborough for help. After agreeing to play, Charlie Booth from Gainsborough Working Men's Club (WMC) recruited Charlie Howlett, the Gainsborough Victoria 'keeper, who must have known he was in for a busy afternoon.

The WMC had allowed Fred to watch their training sessions and as he became a regular spectator he was gradually allowed to participate in the kickabouts, where his flicks and tricks impressed the older players.

After having less luck finding any outfield players, Booth considered asking Fred to play at Horncastle. A calculated risk was taken and answered in the affirmative. With the two Charlies, Booth softly spoken and Howlett a banjo-playing livewire, Fred Spiksley took the train to Horncastle. Another schoolboy met them. Fifteen-year-old left full back Ambrose Langley, who was already a big raw lad, could hardly hide his disgust on seeing Fred. However, thirteen years later the pair were to share a room on the eve of the biggest game in English football. Despite his stature, Fred played impressively against Notts Rangers.

In October 1883 came a thaw in the school football ban. Canon Hodgkinson, the Holy Trinity vicar with an appetite for sport, successfully persuaded John Walker to allow a side of twelve players to face All Saints Parish School. Holy Trinity won 1-0 and afterwards the football ban was overturned and the canon gave over much of the vicarage garden to a football pitch.

On 15 December 1883 a mismatch was held on the new pitch as Holy Trinity, featuring Fred Spiksley at left wing, thrashed a Marshall's Britannia Ironworks side composed of company employees' children by eight goals to one.

Just over two months later, on 26 February 1884, the fourteen-year-old attended school for the final time. It being Shrove Tuesday it was customary for school children to have a half-day holiday and the scene was set for a football match between Holy Trinity and All Saints Parish School on Mr Cattle's Morton Terrace football field. A brief report subsequently appeared in the Gainsborough News (GN) in which Fred was named the losing side's best player on a day when, despite his efforts, Trinity were beaten 5-2. No goalscorers were recorded.

CHAPTER 2

SACKED!
Early Gambling Exploits

IF FRED SPIKSLEY was fourteen today he would have been signed up by a top football club and his diet, daily routine, education, training and match routine would be well established.

Most major clubs have a huge network in place as they seek to snatch the best talent from their rivals. They liaise with schools and managers of county or district teams. Community schemes help maintain contact with people who organise football at grassroots level. Clubs are looking for talent and attitude from a very early age and most run sides – often through their football academies, which have 9,000 players nationally in their ranks – consisting of players from eight years up to eighteen.

Theo Walcott cost Arsenal £5million when he moved from Southampton in 2006 at aged sixteen. Fred Spiksley was certainly as good.

However, in 1884 there were – openly – no such things as professional footballers and Fred Spiksley needed to find work. Billy Meredith was a coalminer for many years before reluctantly signing for Manchester City.

Fred's burning ambition was to become a jockey like

George Fordham, champion jockey from 1855 to 1863. In Fred's formative years the only regular mode of transport was horse-drawn and Willoughby Street was the primary horse quarter locally. William Robinson, farrier and blacksmith, established his forge at the street top while local ship owners had fine carriages and quality horse stables.

Surrounded by horses, Fred Spiksley delighted in their sights, sounds and smells. His fascination meant he would help muck out stables, put fresh water in troughs and fill the hayrick with fresh sweet fodder. Fred then mastered the art of being able to control horses because they knew he loved and cared deeply for them.

Fred delighted in visiting the White Hart coaching inn in Lord Street to watch the midday arrival of the mail coach from Barton-on-Humber. Railways had replaced mail coaches in most locations but the arrival of these magnificent carriages and four beautiful glossy black stallions still created a stir as the horses were changed before setting out to complete the journey to Lincoln. Passengers who descended to partake of the inn's hospitality returned as the black-capped coachman retook the reins and with a dramatic swish moved the horses steadily forward through the narrow archway into Lord Street before gathering pace up Market Street and leaving the chasing pack of youngsters behind. It was pure theatre.

The Gainsborough Trent Port Steeplechase was on the opposite bank of the River Trent. Everyone wanted to see the action, including Fred Spiksley who would pay his halfpenny toll to cross the Trent Bridge, built by William Weston, to watch the chase. Spectators assembled at key leaping points and the joint start and finish line. Booths selling beer and food enjoyed a lively trade and when the highly colourful horses and jockeys paraded beforehand the crowd roared their approval, especially for their own favourites.

The race was spectacular with horses jumping hedges and ditches in thrilling style. Fred was captivated and was determined to become a jockey when he grew up.

On leaving school, Fred begged his parents for help to become an apprentice jockey. Although they knew nothing about horse racing the couple were willing to make some enquires about what sort of life their son would have if he attempted to become a professional jockey. While undertaking some research they found Fred a temporary stable boy's job with Pellinger's Livery Stables at the White Hart Inn.

Sarah Spiksley bought the *Sporting Life*, a newspaper that was published from 1859 to 1998 and was best known for its horse racing coverage. The paper listed the leading horserace trainers.

According to Fred, his parents wrote to the "leading horserace trainer of the day to enquire about an apprenticeship." This may have been Matthew Dawson of Heath House Stables, Newmarket. Dawson was one of the first trainers to run his own stable rather than relying on a wealthy patron.

No doubt Fred's size, weight, height, commitment and enthusiasm together with his close affinity with horses would have been positives that compensated for not having the strength in his forearms and upper body, which are essential for controlling the horse. The major problem would have been Fred's lack of riding experience.

According to Fred, any plans were scuppered when "as generally happens, friends of the family butted in with their advice and jolly well put the tin lid on it".

Fred was left in despair. It must have been no consolation that his mother then spotted a notice in the *Gainsborough News* (GN) for an 'office boy and messenger.' Instead of featuring within the paper, Fred would be helping fill its pages.

Sacked!

His father accompanied Fred when he met Charles Caldicott, owner of a weekly Friday newspaper that was first published on 12 May 1855. Charles's father, William, had purchased a general printing business in 1846 and had produced a modest newspaper that he gave away free to avoid newspaper taxes.

In the nineteenth century, funding for Britain's protracted overseas wars had meant high taxation on newspapers, with paper, stamp and advertising duties. This boosted government coffers but also raised the price of papers so that their circulation was restricted to reliable society members.

However, in the 1830s all duties were considerably reduced and in 1853 advertising duty was scrapped. Then, on 1 July 1855, stamp duty was abolished with duty on papers finally dropped in 1861. These changes helped establish many more newspapers including the GN covering Retford, Workshop, Isle of Axholme and Gainsborough. With no significant regional competitors, William Caldicott made a very tidy profit, allowing him to buy out the *Doncaster and Pontefract News* and papers in Retford and Epworth.

Distribution of the paper was challenging but the Gainsborough Steam Packet helped with the transport along the River Trent and the mail coach took it to Barton on Humber and Kirton Lindsey. The installation in 1856 of a steam-powered printing press speeded up print runs. The paper was politically neutral, non-religious and allowed freedom of expression with support for good causes such as charities. William died in 1877 and the business passed to his son, who during his subsequent 27-year period in charge expanded it by publishing the *Gainsborough Evening News* to coincide with Tuesday's market day.

Broad-shouldered, full bearded and with bushy eyebrows, Charles Caldicott looked very severe as he examined Fred's school certificate and asked the youngster some questions. The good academic achievements plus Fred's good manners were sufficiently impressive for him to be offered a weekly wage of two shillings (10p) for the office boy post, with the promise that on his sixteenth birthday he would start as a compositor's apprentice if his father could meet the financial requirements. Edward Spiksley accepted the offer and Fred started work in the newspaper industry on St David's Day, March 1, 1884.

When Fred had worked almost two years in the office, his father paid an unknown sum for his indentures – an agreement binding an apprentice to a master – and on 25 January 1886, Fred began a five-year apprenticeship as a compositor, a practice which involved a person inserting each metal letter of a word into frames for printing. Fred's wages rose to three shillings (15p) with a guarantee of ten shillings (50p) a week if he successfully completed the five years.

From Monday to Friday, Fred worked from 8am to 6.30pm with an hour for lunch. On Saturdays he worked from 8am to 1pm. No talking was permitted except on work-related business and any worker arriving late could expect to be sent home with a commensurate pay deduction.

If Fred could apply himself to the work in front of him over the following five years and obtain a qualified skill then his future prospects would be much brighter compared to anyone else who remained as an unskilled labourer. For males, completion of an apprenticeship was a major rite of passage often comparable to marriage.

Being an apprentice could though be dangerous. Apprentice Albert Tune had his left foot crushed. In the nineteenth century, employers and workplaces were subject to few safety regulations. Catching limbs in complex machinery was frequent and Tune got the toe of his boot caught in the gear and cogs of the printing press mechanism. Tune's left toe had to be amputated and in order to walk he required a specially-made boot that was paid for by his employer.

Sacked!

By tradition, the season's first flat race meeting was held in March at Lincoln racecourse. The main attraction was the one-mile Lincoln Handicap but when Fred asked his employer in 1887 if he could be excused work for half a day to go he was met with a blank refusal. With the passing of the Bank Holiday Act 1871 a number of religious festivals had become legally paid holidays but it was not until the 1936 Annual Holiday Bill that an annual paid holiday became a statutory right.

The seventeen-year-old young man was on thin ice if he skipped work to watch the horse racing. But, consumed by his passion for the sport of kings, that is what he did. Leaving work after lunch he bought a rail ticket to Lincoln and thoroughly enjoyed himself. He considered it well worth losing a day's pay.

Coming home, however, he began to have some reservations and these were to prove well founded. The following day he was confronted by his employer and, with no trade union to represent him, was sacked on the spot for gross misconduct. Fred's apprenticeship and the money his dad had paid for it were gone and despite Edward Spiksley's plea for leniency a pompous Charles Caldicott was unmoved. Edward Spiksley was naturally very angry at his son's stupidity, which threatened his work prospects and caused great family concern.

Sadly, the incident also failed to curb Fred's enthusiasm for horse racing and the gambling which goes with it and was merely the beginning of what became a life-long addiction. In the late 1940s Fred was in his 70s when Joyce Spicksley, whose husband, Alan, was his nephew, met him in the kitchen at a family shop in Gainsborough: "He was ironing the old big white £5 notes and he had a large suitcase stuffed with them that he had won at Doncaster Races. Yet when he died a few years later he owed money.

"He was known as a big gambling man and was always betting. It meant he had a lot of money on occasions and nothing on others. I don't think very highly of him, he was consumed by gambling on the horses and he would go all over the country betting."

Out of work, Fred Spiksley, at least, could indulge in his football. In mid June 1887 an under 18s football tournament was organised by Lincolnshire FA as part of Queen Victoria's Golden Jubilee celebrations in mid June 1887. When a Gainsborough side called the Jubilee Swifts was entered Fred happily accepted the invitation to play, with his first match on Saturday 9 April 1887.

While working at the print works, Fred had played in some local club matches. On 17 October 1885 he assisted Trinity Institute (TI) to beat Saint John's 2-1. TI were widely known as the reserves of Trinity Recreationists, Gainsborough's premier football club.

Football was becoming popular. Its simplicity and little need for equipment meant many more young boys were playing the game. B Spooner, a Holy Trinity churchwarden, had overseen the Recreationists' aspiring footballers for many years. He ensured that only physically strong boys with football skills were given trial matches against the senior XI.

Fred Spiksley played at right wing in the TI winning side that lined up in a 2-3-5 formation as follows: Hyde, Spindler, Watson, Musgrave, Scaithe, Leaning, Spiksley, Bingham, Atkinson, Baker, Martin. There are no match reports and while his selection was recognition of his abilities he was not chosen again over the next couple of months. It's possible that his light build counted against him.

On the early evening of 17 December 1885 the then office junior performed for Gainsborough Working Men's Club whose secretary Charles Taylor, Fred's former head teacher, selected him at right wing against Wesleyans FC. A 2-1 success was noted in the GN: "The two Working Men's goals were scored by their centre forward, Mee, who was brilliantly supported by the teenager Fred Spiksley."

Sacked!

In April 1886, playing for Gainsborough Wednesday second XI, he scored in a 3-1 defeat of Morton Saint Paul's second XI. He then played in three drawn matches for Wednesday, later scored in a 4-3 defeat against Gainsborough Victoria, hit two in a 5-1 defeat of Haxey and then netted three goals in three consecutive victories.

When football resumed after the 1886 summer break the youngster scored for Wednesday, named because of the day when they played their games, as Ferry and District was defeated 4-1 and Fred then played his final match for the club in a 3-2 defeat against the Wesleyans in which he failed to net.

On 30 October 1886, Fred was again playing for the Working Men's Club in an important Lincolnshire County Cup-tie with Lincoln Rangers. The match finished 0-0 but there was controversy when Fred, playing very well, narrowly had a goal disallowed for offside.

On 19 March 1887, Fred, recently sacked by Charles Caldicott, was present to watch Gainsborough Trinity first team play Notts Jardines.

The home team faced a crisis with three right-sided team members missing due to illness and injury. Youngster David Brelsford had potential. He was asked to play as he was already stripped as the nominated reserve, a role which once the game started was superfluous as substitutes only became an accepted part of football in the 1960s. Reserve full back David Deitz lived close enough to the ground to be summoned to replace George Vamplew at right half.

Faced with playing with ten men a gamble was taken to allow Fred Spiksley to make his competitive debut at inside right at seventeen years and 54 days. Today we are familiar with players graduating to first team football at the age of sixteen, although this is becoming increasingly rare in the Premier League. In 1876 football was a much rougher and dangerous game and opportunities for youngsters such as Fred would have been limited. Fred was only 190 days older than Wayne Rooney was when he made his Everton debut against Tottenham Hotspur in 2002.

The Jardines were a good side with real strength down the left where the May brothers, Teddy and Billy, were a powerful combination. They quickly exerted control over the young novices and Jardines led 2-0 at the interval. The home side had taken 30 minutes to mount a serious effort on goal when Fred Spiksley hit a fine low shot that skimmed off the muddy surface forcing the Jardine 'keeper to make a smart save.

Having snowed in the morning, the heavy pitch cut up badly as the game progressed. Spiksley switched with Brelsford to take up the outside role in the second half. His pace and trickery quickly began to cause problems only for the away side to score a third against the run of play.

From the restart the ball was played out to the Trinity outside right. He skipped past Robertson, cut back inside the experienced Jardine captain, full back William 'Wiggy' McLeod, named because he wore a wig, before rounding Grundy the 'keeper and then crossing to his unmarked captain Brown who found the net to make it 1-3. This led to a breathless finale but with no further goals the away side were victors.

In 1921, Fred Spiksley recalled: "Much to my surprise McLeod found marking me a constant source of worry. I was constantly swooping down on him, and at the end of each encounter he was at great pains to carefully adjust his wig. The local supporters thought this was hilarious, and doubled up with laughter by his performance, they shouted out: 'Eh up, Wiggy, keep your hair on!'

Before moving south to become a professional footballer, McLeod, capped by Scotland in 1886, had played for Cowlairs, one of the original members of the Scottish League when it started in 1890. He was a very good player. For a youngster to make his afternoon so uncomfortable was some feat.

Sacked!

Afterwards the GN match report by Charles Jennings noted: "Spiksley, considering his young age and light weight, played an excellent game with his shots and screws being very good. His passing was well timed, and the measure of his performance is enhanced when you consider that he was up against two excellent backs in McLeod, the Jardines captain, and Robertson. Spiksley would be a great addition for the team."

Nevertheless, when Trinity beat Brigg Town 4-0 in the Charity Cup final, Vamplew, Tom Smith and Abe Watkin returned to the side in place of the youngsters, leaving Fred to concentrate on guiding the newly-formed Jubilee Swifts towards cup success.

Jubilee Swifts had been the brainchild of successful businessman, Mr Cooke, a football enthusiast who owned a Boston jewellery, watch and clockmakers shop. The knockout competition attracted 82 entries and Cooke donated a prize of a 'Waterbury Pocket Watch' for every boy in the winning team.

Fred Spiksley's side thrashed Lindum Avenue, 13-0 in the first round with him using his blistering pace to score 11. Swifts then crushed Lincoln Mayfield 12-0 with Fred Spiksley hitting nine goals.

The Swifts right winger was a pale youth who was much faster than anyone else. Having spent hours practising with his India-rubber ball, and already giving a full Scottish international a runaround in his senior debut, his brilliance with a football made him simply unplayable for those of a similar age.

Fred then scored six as Gainsborough Wanderers lost 10-0. The following round was a much tighter contest and at the interval it was 0-0 with Lincoln Park Avenue. The two Park full backs, Rawlinson and Collingwood, played very well to restrict Spiksley's opportunities.

After the five-minute interval Park Avenue took the lead, Duce's effort being the first the Swifts had conceded in the tournament. Within a minute the score was 1-1 when Spiksley scored from a free kick. Then Pinning made it 2-1 before Spiksley completed the scoring in a 3-1 victory. The fifth round was comfortably negotiated as the Swifts notched six without reply against Lincoln Wanderers thanks to goals from Spiksley (3), Winn (2) and Pinning.

A special thrill awaited the youngsters as the prestigious location for the semi-final was Grimsby Town's ground at Lee Park, Cleethorpes, where Gainsborough Swifts would meet Grimsby Humber Rovers.

The Grimsby side were much bigger and stronger than their opponents who were accompanied to Cleethorpes by a large following who were surprised when it was announced that the Swifts line-up was radically different from the earlier games with just four players in their settled roles.

Confused by the changes, the Swifts were heavily beaten, 7-0, all the goals coming when they kicked into a strong wind in the second half.

Humber Rovers beat Horncastle Gridirons 3-2 in the final. The crowd included Fred Spiksley who was delighted when his name was shouted out at the presentation ceremony afterwards. For finishing as the cup's top scorer with 31 goals he was awarded a watch made by Waterbury, the American company established in 1880. It was a proud moment.

The competition had been widely reported in the GN whose readers included growing numbers of football fans who delighted in reading an impressive number of local match reports. Spiksley's talent meant that Gainsborough Trinity Football Club could not overlook him.

Trinity had their roots in the year after Fred Spiksley was born. Canon George Langton Hodgkinson was sent back to Gainsborough in 1867 after a three-year curacy at the Holy Trinity Church from 1861 to 1864. On his departure, the church had massively overspent on a new organ and Hodgkinson was charged with repairing the damage.

Sacked!

Along with his wife, Fanny, a linguist in many languages, the 'new' man quickly revived spirituality among his former parishioners, allowing him to pursue his belief in the Muscular Christianity Movement that was promoted by Thomas Hughes, author of Tom Brown's Schooldays.

In 1871 the Holy Trinity Recreation Society was established. Having played first class cricket for Middlesex the canon at first prioritised the summer sport. Then at the first AGM in May 1872 it was announced that a football team was to be started up under the direction of Holy Trinity Church School teacher Charles Taylor and churchwarden James Donson.

Early games were played at the top of Pingle Hill overlooking Marshall's Britannia Ironworks. This meant that whenever the ball was kicked downfield the game was halted to enable it to be recovered from the railway line at the bottom of the hill. The Recreationists were first mentioned in the GN when in a fifteen-a-side game they beat Trent Football Club 2-0 on Boxing Day 1874.

Wearing blue stockinette caps helped the team recognise their own players in muddy conditions in a period when it was not compulsory for sides to wear different coloured shirts, such a change not being formally introduced until after the formation of the Football League in 1888. The colour of the caps meant Trinity became forever known as The Blues.

In 1876 the Recreationists were challenged to a football match by Gainsborough Town Sports Club, which was formed in May 1874 when the cricket and rugby clubs combined. The game was played at the Northolme sports ground, which had been a cricket ground from at least 1840 and probably earlier. The Recreationists won the match 6-0.

In September 1881, Lincolnshire football clubs came together to form the Lincolnshire FA. In addition to membership fees the clubs agreed to make their players available for county matches that were becoming an increasing part of the football calendar.

Trinity played their first Lincolnshire County Cup-tie on 4 February 1882 and after drawing 2-2 they beat Grantham Victoria 3-1 in the replay at Pingle Hill.

Over the following years, Trinity began asserting their superiority as Gainsborough's finest side. Charles Caldicott found that when they won, his newspapers sold in larger numbers, as followers were keen to read about the success of their local team in what was starting to become an engaging pastime for the working classes around the North of England. Realising that his finances might help Trinity to continue to win, Caldicott had himself co-opted on to the club committee. Trinity could now be sure of fielding a competitive side each week.

On 24 October 1885, Trinity Recreationists played their first FA cup-tie when they met Grantham Town at Northolme. Appalling weather restricted the attendance to 1,600, including possibly Fred Spiksley, who lived ten minutes' walk away. Trinity won 4-1 but there was controversy when the defeated club objected to Sammy Pearson appearing for the victors as he had been signed by Lincoln City as a professional.

The appeal was disallowed but Trinity were informed that Pearson could not play for them again without Lincoln City's permission. Gainsborough lost in the following round 2-1 against Middlesbrough.

During the summer of 1885 Trinity Recreationist Football Club joined forces with the Gainsborough Town Football and Cricket Club on the Northolme sports field. Gainsborough Trinity was born.

Combining forces meant there was finance to build a new grandstand for 200 spectators and make other improvements that included a wire fence around the pitch to keep spectators off it. The construction of a 6ft 6in-high wooden perimeter fence that incorporated a substantial pair of entrance gates allowed for an entry fee to be charged for the newly-enclosed ground. This general move towards professionalism was not welcomed by everyone. Feeling it betrayed his Christian principles, Canon Hodgkinson resigned as club president.

The Trinity committee recognised that Fred Spiksley was a special talent and knew this hadn't gone unnoticed elsewhere. There was little option. If they intended retaining his services they needed to act quickly. Charles Caldicott organised a committee meeting at which it was agreed to offer the seventeen-year-old a professional football contract. Fearing the youngster's dad would not allow him to sign it unless he was also offered back his apprenticeship, the businessman invited Edward Spiksley to meet him. The apprenticeship was reinstated on the agreement that Edward consented to his son signing a two-year contract to become a professional footballer. He was to remain one for nineteen years and thereafter remained active in football as a coach for the following 30 years.

Despite this, Fred's passion remained horse racing as in September 1887 he paid a recently-appointed apprentice to rush over shouting that his mother had been taken seriously ill. It was a lie and he skipped work to go to Doncaster and watch the St Leger. When he returned to work only his footballing exploits prevented him being dismissed for a second time.

CHAPTER 3

UNDER MADDEN'S WING
Spiksley's first season as a Trinity Professional

THE SUMMER OF 1887 was marked by riotous celebrations for Queen Victoria's Golden Jubilee. On Wednesday 22 June, Gainsborough shopkeepers decorated their frontages with an undeclared competition breaking out to see who could find the most imaginative, decorative designs. Large crowds walked the streets admiring the displays. At 10pm townsfolk headed for Castle Hill to see the huge beacon set alight. When it was fired, the whole sky seemed to ignite and within minutes other local communities right along the Trent Valley had lit their own bonfires.

The following morning church bells rang out and the Parish Church held a thanksgiving service for the monarch. There was a children's procession and then a massive party for youngsters after which there was a six-a-side football competition, bicycle races, dancing, hot air balloons, games and dancing.

John (Jack) Madden, the new Trinity coach from Dumbarton, captained one of the football sides. The son of Irish immigrants, John Madden, was born on 11 June 1865, the youngest of nine. Money was tight and he received little formal education. At fifteen his brother-in-law, Bill Burgess, secured him a job as a 'catch boy' in a riveters' gang in Denny's shipyard on the River Clyde. The job meant catching red-hot rivets in a metal bucket as part of a team effort that involved precisely inserting rivets in steel plates on a ship's hull so that it was water tight. This hard, noisy and dangerous work was combined with periods when work was scarce.

Football was sweeping across Scotland and, after practising with a tin can at an early age, Madden had developed a real talent for dribbling. He won many 'dribbling with the ball' races. After playing junior football he joined Dumbarton in 1886–87, sparking controversy by becoming the first Roman Catholic to play for 'The Sons of the Rock'. Scoring a debut goal in a victory over Third Lanark dispelled any problems. Dumbarton ended up reaching the Scottish FA Cup final and Jack played in the 2-1 defeat against Hibernian at Hampden Park.

Unlike in England, the Scottish FA were determined to retain the amateur tradition and it was not until 1893 that professionalism was permitted. Between 1872 and 1887 England beat Scotland just twice. Little wonder that English professional clubs sought to recruit good Scottish players by paying them more than could be earned in engineering workshops, mines, mills, shipyards and factories.

Scots gladly moved south and from the 1887–88 season onwards English clubs competed frantically to recruit the best north o' the border. Losing such talent weakened the domestic Scottish game and it led to angry scenes and violence when anyone with an English accent arrived unexpectedly on a scouting mission.

A fine example of the influence of Scottish players during the early years of professional football was the benefit game for Sheffield United captain William Hendry. The first such game for a United player, it featured a team

– with two exceptions – of Sheffield-based Scots against a team of Englishmen playing in the city.

Gainsborough Trinity had a progressive, ambitious committee. Determined to keep up with their Lincolnshire rivals, they recruited Glasgow football agent Mr Wilson to find them a top class centre forward and a full back. John Madden's father had died three years earlier and his income sustained a large family. As a fast, dangerous forward he had the attributes that Gainsborough required. Preventing him signing professionally was the newly-introduced FA rules that any professional not local to a team had to live no more than six miles away over a two-year period if they were to play in FA competitions.

More than anything, Madden was going to be needed for important cup matches. So Gainsborough asked if he minded registering as an amateur, for whom the residential qualification period did not apply, and instead be paid as their football coach. Madden keenly accepted the offer, not realising that the coaching role was a sham.

Meanwhile, the Dumbarton full back Bobby Ferguson also signed for Gainsborough. Madden asked the Gainsborough committee to arrange a competitive pre-season friendly and when both new men turned up it became apparent that the new coach genuinely wanted to be one!

Rather than lose him, Madden was allowed free rein. This proved to be an inspired decision. He quickly impressed on his new charges the need to pass the football along the ground and retain possession. He was an expert in coaching the art of movement off the ball and creating space. He tailored skill sessions to suit each player's role within the team. Madden himself could shoot with great power and a back heel manoeuvre he perfected was pure genius. In addition to being a fine masseur and fitness trainer he impressed on players the need to prepare mentally for a game, to eat properly and restrict their alcohol consumption. Madden was a man way ahead of his time.

He continued working part of the week on the Clyde – earning between £1 and £1 10s shillings (£1.50) – before travelling on the Friday overnight train to Lincolnshire. Gainsborough beat local rivals Lincoln City 1-0 in Madden's first game. As always, before departing north he discussed with the players what had and hadn't worked well. Madden earned £2 10s (£2.50) a week plus his travelling expenses.

On his return south, Madden participated in the Gainsborough Working Men's Club third annual sports day. He won the football dribbling race. In the 440 yards handicap race a young Fred Spiksley won easily despite a 32-yard handicap.

One week later, Fred Spiksley entered the 440 yards race in the Worksop Athletics and Sports meeting. Sheffield's Tom Kinman was one of the England's fastest quarter-milers and yet he was given a fifteen-yard head start on his Gainsborough rival, who thrashed him by eight yards. Weeks later the defeated man won the Amateur Athletics Association (AAA) Northern Counties Championship. Having become a professional sportsman, Fred was prevented from racing at AAA events and he never raced again until his football days were over when, despite a serious knee injury, he was a regular winner.

As a youngster, Fred had been fortunate to meet Charlie Booth, fifteen months his senior, who had got him to play for Horncastle. Booth's mother, Keziah, was just twelve or thirteen when he was born and he never knew his father. He was left with his grandparents and, after his grandfather died, Charlie began working at Marshall's clay-pits when he was eight. The money earned kept his grandmother out of the workhouse.

Charlie loved the outdoors and being on his own. He and Fred were like chalk and cheese but when they were both out one evening honing their football skills they struck up an unlikely friendship. When they ran dribbling the ball the younger man won all the races but when the ball was taken away the power and stride pattern of the bigger man won any sprint race. Fred was unaware that Charlie competed in professional sprint races for money. Spotting that Fred was becoming taller, Charlie asked whether, in return for paying him a fee, he would like some sprinting lessons.

Without an income, Fred agreed that in return for lessons he would bring his new trainer some fresh eggs. He began sneaking into his parents' hen coop and taking half a dozen eggs. One morning he was surprised to find no eggs and he soon discovered why when his parents accused him of stealing. No explanations proved sufficient and he was grounded for a week. When he did escape he found Charlie had entered him for a quarter mile race. When Fred duly won the competition his presentation to his parents of the £6 winnings helped change their attitude. From then on Fred collected half a dozen eggs for the Booth family each week.

Fred was to maintain throughout his life that he would have won the AAA 440 yards race. "From 17 to 22 I experienced a phenomenal increase in my strength, speed and acceleration. It is difficult to compare my pace on the football field with the speed of the amateur quarter milers on the running track, but what is certain is that whenever I got past a defender even when keeping the ball under control at my feet I was never ever caught by anyone when I was at my best."

The start of the new competitive football season saw the introduction of pitch markings including the corner, half way line and centre circle. In addition, two semi-circles, each with a radius of six yards from the posts, were now compulsory, to mark the area from where goal kicks could be taken.

Fred Spiksley played at inside right for the Trinity opening game against Notts Rangers that was played at Morton Lane as Northolme was being used for cricket.

Trinity: Hoodless, Ferguson, Jubb, Smith, Billy Brown (captain), Cater, Vamplew, Spiksley, Madden, Chambers, Robinson.

The home side won 3-1 with the third coming when Cater's fine pass was fired powerfully home by the inside right to jubilant and enthusiastic cheering. Victory had been achieved despite the first-half loss of Madden after a nasty tackle left him with a severe ankle injury. To add insult to injury, when the subsequent free kick was fired home the 'goal' was chalked off as there were no direct free kicks in 1887. The GN match reporter praised Fred Spiksley for his "pretty game and good goal" but expressed some doubts, stating "on several occasions his light weight told against him."

Such concerns appeared to be shared by the Trinity selection committee and, against the wishes of their coach, they rested their youngest professional in the games that followed.

However, the match on 15 October 1887 was the biggest of the season so far, the FA Cup first qualifying round against Boston Town. John Madden wanted Fred Spiksley at inside right and the Trinity selection committee were content to let the coach have his own way.

At half-time the game was effectively over as Trinity raced into a 4-0 lead. Then on the hour mark the home inside right justified his selection by scoring a great goal when he put spin and swerve on the ball so that it curved well away from the 'keeper and into the goal. It was for its era a truly remarkable goal and stunned the 2,000 inside Northolme who had never seen anything like it.

In time, a crucial part of Fred Spiksley's game was his skill in moving the ball in the air. This was virtually impossible in wet conditions when the leather football would become heavy and misshapen. However, on dry days Fred could spin and swerve the ball to score goals, cut out opponents, reach better-placed colleagues and generally confuse opponents. At corners he could use the outside of his right foot to swerve the ball away and conversely he used the outside of his left to spin and swerve the ball so it could dip and bend into the goalmouth under his opponents' crossbar.

Defenders and 'keepers were unnerved. This time the GN reporter had to admit: "If Spiksley maintains the form he showed on Saturday in a 7-0 victory he is well worthy of a permanent place. He is certainly light, but I have not the slightest doubt that Spiksley will live long in the memory of the footballing public, with his speed, agility, and his deadly shooting."

However, on 5 November 1887, the second qualifying round FA cup tie between Lincoln City and Gainsborough Trinity again saw the team selection committee unwilling to risk Fred Spiksley in a fixture with a violent record. Lincoln, passionately backed, won 2-1.

Fred Spiksley returned to the Trinity side for the next few games and scored regularly, including another curling effort in the 5-1 defeat of Sheffield Heeley.

Over the winter months of the 1887–88 season, Gainsborough were able to maintain a good level of success with Madden regularly scoring including three against Kiveton Colliery in a 10-3 win in which Fred Spiksley notched his first senior hat-trick. Keen to ensure the emerging star remained grounded, Madden later told him off for failing to pass to better-placed teammates when Fred Spiksley scored a real beauty against Small Heath Alliance. The scorer was initially most hurt but when he considered things more deeply he realised Madden was correct and resolved not to repeat his mistake. Spiksley would go on to score many goals in his career, but he also became famous for creating chances for those playing inside him. In his 1900 book, Association Football, the great England half back Ernest Needham, wrote the following, which proved that Spiksley had learnt a valuable lesson from Madden and developed to become a greater player:

"When he finds himself in difficulty he will always pass the ball to someone better placed – a form of unselfishness that a good many well-known players might do well to copy. Instead of this, many men would rather lose the ball by trying to beat one or two opponents than pass it to a better-placed partner: not so Spiksley."

When Trinity played Lincoln City away in the Lincolnshire County Challenge Cup there was no chance that Fred Spiksley would not be selected. Confident of success the 5,000 crowd included 1,700 from Gainsborough who saw their heroes win for the first time at their local rivals' steeply-sloping John O'Gaunt's ground. Concerned beforehand that they might lose, the City committee had sent their players away for special training, thus ensuring they also stayed away from heavy drinking before the game. Afterwards a single John Madden goal was likely to have provoked just such bouts among losers and winners alike. It was some goal! Penned in and surrounded, the Trinity centre forward spun round to place the ball accurately just inside the posts.

The second half was a fierce affair and Fred Spiksley came in for some close attention. By emerging unscathed he showed he was more than ready for such encounters. Having played brilliantly, the visiting 'keeper Charlie Howlett, who wore spectacles when he played, was afterwards chaired shoulder high from the pitch by the delighted visiting fans. The victorious side were met by a cheering crowd when they returned to Gainsborough. With the Britannia Ironworks band belting out some fine tunes the team were chaired shoulder high to the club's headquarters at the Sun Inn.

Over the following weeks, Trinity continued to play with aplomb and they beat Derby County and Doncaster Rovers before thrashing Retford Town 15-1 with Spiksley scoring five. In the Lincs Cup semi-final, Trinity won 4-1 at Grantham Town. There was then revenge for the 4-0 early season thrashing when Trinity defeated Grimsby Town 1-0 courtesy of a Dick Sharman effort. Of their last 22 games, Trinity had won nineteen and lost two.

In the GN Charity Cup semi-final game there was a 10-0 destruction of Grantham Rovers with Spiksley hitting four. Sheffield Heeley were then beaten 4-2 in a thrilling final. Spiksley got one goal and also collected his first senior winner's medal. Charles Caldicott was delighted that Gainsborough Trinity had won the trophy, a solid silver one that he had specially commissioned from a top silversmith from Birmingham's jewellery quarter.

All eyes now turned towards the Lincolnshire Charity Challenge Cup final, which Trinity had reached only once before.

In its infancy, football was marked by constant appeals over a whole series of infringements, real and imaginary. Many FA Cup-ties were replayed and sides thrown out. Gainsborough's final opponents were Grimsby, who in early April wrote to the local FA resigning in protest that the final game would take place at the home of Lincoln City, a club with whom, for a multitude of reasons, they were in dispute.

There then followed farce upon farce. Grimsby and Gainsborough played each other in friendlies with Grimsby winning 6-1 and losing 1-0. Grimsby then claimed they should be awarded the cup! Gainsborough wrote to the FA saying they would turn up in Lincoln on 14 April and kick off the game before claiming the cup. The FA responded by moving the final until the following weekend. In the event Gainsborough did not carry out their threat and on 5 May the FA instructed the clubs to play the game in Boston on 12 May. Gainsborough refused and there the matter lay until at the AGM of the Lincolnshire in July a motion was passed that the trophy and medals be withheld.

Angered by the perceived injustice, Gainsborough Trinity wrote to Lincolnshire FA stating they would resign if the Challenge Cup and medals were not handed over to them. When Lincs FA ignored this request, Trinity quit, thus absenting themselves from future Lincolnshire Cup competitions. In the event the absence was only for twelve months.

Worse was to follow for Gainsborough Trinity in the summer of 1888. The club had pursued their Challenge Cup grievance to the detriment of all other affairs and thus forgot to renew John Madden's contract. When they finally got in touch he had re-signed for Dumbarton.

It was a big blow for Gainsborough and a young Fred Spiksley who fully appreciated everything the Scot did for him, stating years later:

"There is no doubt I owe a great debt to Madden as I was placed under his guiding influence, and he became my coach, mentor, and friend.

"On being introduced to senior football there is no doubt that for their future success and welfare young players greatly need the steadying influence of an experienced and talented player close at hand. His advice, if followed, will go a long way towards bringing out any ability that young players may possess. Of course, if the ability is not there in the first place, you cannot bring it out, but if the innate ability is present, there is no doubt that a good coach will develop all that he has to work upon, on the correct lines, and then the player's improvement will depend entirely upon himself.

"When I was introduced into the Gainsborough Trinity first team, I was positioned as an inside forward to Jack Madden our centre forward, and played in this position for most of the season. Now Madden was already a player with a great deal of experience, and his tremendous ability was clear for all to see. The wonder to me was how a player of such exceptional skill came to play his football for Gainsborough Trinity."

Flying over an Olive Grove

After leaving Trinity, John Madden would go on to have a successful playing career with Celtic, who had just played their first match in May 1888, the first ever old firm derby. While at Celtic Madden won three Scottish League titles and represented Scotland on two occasions, scoring five goals. However, it would have been little surprise to Fred Spiksley that it would be Madden's coaching career that was to gain him legendary status. In 1905 he became coach and manager of Slavia Prague, a position he would keep for 25 years, collecting countless trophies. Amazingly, Madden was still coaching teams at the age of 73, from his wheelchair. Honoured with a huge funeral on his death, Madden remains a Slavia legend.

CHAPTER 4

BIRTHDAY DISASTER
A career-threatening injury at Olive Grove

A REVOLUTIONARY MOVE that changed forever the face of football and many other sports marked the beginning of the 1888–89 football season. It was the development of a league system.

Scotsman William McGregor was the man responsible. Following the introduction of professionalism the Aston Villa committee man recognised that clubs needed a guaranteed source of income if they were to have the funds to pay players.

High-profile friendly matches and cup competitions were one thing, but fans were being regularly forced to make do with one-sided contests or left frustrated at not knowing in advance who their side might face at the weekend. Attendances and income consequently suffered.

With support from fellow Villa committee members, McGregor searched for other clubs keen to back his new idea. By early March 1888, McGregor was confident enough to send a formal letter to five clubs: Blackburn Rovers,

Bolton Wanderers, Preston North End, West Bromwich Albion and Aston Villa.

He suggested clubs might overcome their current problems by proposing that "ten or twelve of the most prominent clubs in England combine to arrange home and away fixtures each season." The five were asked to propose other clubs who should be invited to get involved.

On the eve of the 1888 Cup Final, held at the Oval between prospective members Preston and West Brom, representatives of Aston Villa, Notts County, Blackburn Rovers, Wolverhampton Wanderers, Burnley, Stoke and West Brom held a successful meeting and invited Preston, Everton, Accrington, Bolton Wanderers and Derby County to join them, at the Royal Hotel, Manchester, on Tuesday 17 April 1888, in formalising affairs and arranging fixtures for the 1888–89 season.

It is this meeting that marks the birth of competitive league football, though its historic nature didn't stop clubs beginning an ongoing tradition of squabbling among themselves! Even the name proved problematic with McGregor's suggestion of Football Union overruled in favour of William Sudell's Football League.

McGregor wanted clubs to divide gate money but delegates, who felt that a guaranteed sum of £15 for visiting clubs was more preferable, rejected that. Egalitarianism had been swiftly abandoned. McGregor became chairman of the new organisation.

The Wednesday, Nottingham Forest and Halliwell, (the latter claiming to be the second best Lancashire team), were left disappointed when their applications to join the new league were rejected on grounds that there were insufficient dates for any additional fixtures.

So while the merits of some of the clubs were queried – Everton were considered inferior to local rivals Bootle – those present on 17 April were happy to become a select band of pioneers. To their credit they clearly knew what they were doing because eleven of them still play in the Premier League and Football League today, Accrington being the exception (formed 1878 and dissolved 1896).

The clubs were also open to change as they adopted rules requiring the bottom four clubs to face a re-election battle with non-League clubs seeking entry.

So good was McGregor's idea that it was immediately imitated as clubs, left disappointed at not being invited, rushed to form a parallel Football Combination. Twenty clubs, including Gainsborough Trinity, joined up. However, this many clubs proved too many, as there were too few weekends, midweek games being almost impossible to arrange due to many players' work commitments and – in an era where there were no electric floodlights – dark winter nights.

Club secretaries were left to arrange matches between respective clubs and Combination games were badly disrupted by cup-ties and prestigious friendlies. Some teams did not even realise they were members and by the end the league had largely collapsed.

The first Combination games took place on 8 September 1888. On that date, Fred joined his team mates on the 7.45am train from Lincoln that was bound for Manchester and then down to the Potteries to play Port Vale. His elder brother, William, had started up his own pork butcher's business in local rented premises and had already left to begin work before Fred washed and dressed.

Fred was always very particular about his playing kit. As he always changed into a fresh shirt at half time he made sure he placed both of his blue tops into a battered portmanteau. Long knickers (shorts) and blue football stockings, tie-ups and shin guards were also packed with a towel, toilet bag and a bar of carbolic soap. Fred's boots were typical of the time, being largely adapted workmen's boots that were designed for strength with an indestructible block toe and studs hammered into the soles.

Joining the team in their private saloon, Fred was in a good mood and looking to build on his successful first season with Trinity. He had enjoyed every minute and after being capped for Lincolnshire he had been presented with a top hat by a wealthy patron. However, the loss of Madden and his Scottish counterpart, Ferguson, was bound to have an impact and Gainsborough were further weakened by the loss of 21-year-old Harry Chamberlain, the darling of the Northolme crowd and especially the ladies who adored his good looks. Scorer of nineteen goals the previous season he had moved to Lincoln.

Fred's partner on the left, Harry Robinson, had developed diabetes and his absence was another blow. Sadly, he died on 16 September. To compound matters, no pre-season matches had been organised.

Fred was selected at inside left and at 1-0 down his attempted overhead scissors kick almost levelled the scores. By the end of the game, though, the away side had been heavily beaten, 6-1.

The rush was now on to find new players. William Croft was sent back to Scotland and two new Scots were recruited for the match away to Long Eaton Rangers, where on their arrival the home stadium and its world famous cycle track impressed the Gainsborough players. Having travelled through the night, debutants Pollock and Watts were shattered and it was no surprise that their side lost 3-2 with Spiksley scoring once.

The defeated side's poor start to the new campaign continued with a 3-1 defeat at Rotherham Town and there was a growing sense of panic that Trinity may be heading towards a disastrous season. However, William Croft had had some success in recruiting new players and after employing football agent John McCabe of Leith, Edinburgh, Gainsborough were able to sign four new players – Shamrock Coyne, an Irishman from Hibernian, and three Scots, William McKay from Hearts, Alec Brady from Sunderland and John 'Jack' Angus from Newcastle West End. Each new man would earn double the match fee paid to local players. Only Coyne was available for the first Gainsborough home league fixture that Newton Heath won 5-1 before a crowd of 2,000.

After such a disappointing start it was no surprise that club members had not been renewing their membership subs. The gate for the second home fixture fell to 600, who witnessed an improved performance. Coyne scored and Trinity beat Leeds Association 5-0. The following weekend the Scot was joined by McKay and Angus in the team and, with both newcomers playing on the left of the attack, Spiksley was moved to centre forward with instant success. He scored five times in an 8-0 thrashing of Lincoln Ramblers. Angus then scored three times as Lincoln City was beaten 4-1.

Angus and McKay were ineligible for FA matches, as they had not completed the required residential period. Trinity overcame a similar problem for Coyne by registering him as an amateur while secretly paying him a wage.

One player who was not receiving a wage was Fred Spiksley who, along with his father, had no idea that when he signed his two-year football contract with Trinity that he was becoming a professional footballer. As such Fred had never asked for the money he was supposed to be paid and he was well into his second season when Dick Sharman asked why he was not collecting his 2s 6d (12.5p) for home games and five shillings (25p) for away games to compensate for loss of earnings.. Fred calculated that he was owed £6 10s (£6.50). He had, of course, been receiving his apprenticeship wages but he was rightly upset that no-one from the club had informed him about collecting his match fees. Now aware of his value to Trinity, when he finally went to get what he was owed Fred asked for his contract to be amended to a weekly wage of 7s 6d (37.5p) This was agreed.

Trinity beat Notts Jardines 4-0 in the FA Cup second qualifying round, Spiksley netting twice. He then scored three in a 4-4 draw with Grantham Town. The following weekend the four new signings, all forwards, played for the first time together. When Fred Spiksley, again switched to centre-forward, was starved of the ball he was encouraged to leave the field early by some of the Trinity supporters already angry at seeing captain Tom Smith lose his place to the newcomers.

Fred believed the new players were playing for themselves but he was persuaded to play in the FA Cup-tie against Boston Town and he scored twice in a 5-3 win. The game was Coyne's last for Trinity as he then received a letter from Everton inviting him for a trial and he departed hastily. Clearly he had only played for Gainsborough to put himself in the shop window and his leaving angered local players, including Spiksley who refused to play against Notts Rangers and Long Eaton Rangers.

However, having failed to secure a contract with Everton, Coyne returned to Gainsborough in the hope of again playing for the local club.

On Monday 3 December, three strangers with suitcases alighted from the Manchester train on platform 1 at Gainsborough's Great Northern Station. Burnley had started their first season in the Football League very badly and were bottom of the table. Aware that Gainsborough had done well after signing four new players, the East Lancs club's directors sought to boost their hopes of avoiding a re-election battle by obtaining the signatures of some of the four men.

Angus had let slip what was going on and said he was not involved. The station porter was warned to listen out for Lancashire accents, the news of the poachers' arrival immediately swept through Gainsborough as they made their way to hide out in the lodging houses of the three players set to transfer their allegiance to the Turf Moor club.

Britannia Ironworks closed for an hour at dinner time and so when all six men finally emerged to make a dash for the Manchester midday train they were pelted with eggs and tomatoes, then punched and had their clothes torn before they finally reached the sanctuary of their railway carriage.

As the train departed, disgruntled Gainsborough fans threw more eggs. Angus's loyalty pledge to the club later disappeared when he left without warning to go to Everton. He was later converted into a 'keeper during a short spell with Sunderland and returned to play eleven League games in the 1890–91 season when Everton captured the Division One title. He died of typhoid fever in the summer of 1891.

With only nine players to call on, Trinity withdrew from their weekend FA Cup game against Grimsby. Letters to the local paper expressed the hope that Trinity would not sign any more Scots! Arthur Elliott was offered a contract to play at centre forward and this allowed Fred Spiksley to play outside left.

On 22 December a full-strength Sheffield Wednesday side – all Sheffield born and bred – played a friendly at Northolme and Gainsborough acquitted themselves extremely well in a 1-1 draw. The home goal saw Spiksley hit a 40-yard crossfield ball to Tom Smith on the right wing. He combined with George Vamplew to create space for a cross which found the unmarked Spiksley, who had run 80 yards to score easily. Everyone was impressed.

Spiksley continued his fine form with five goals in a 10-2 hammering of Bamford Wanderers before the side lost 1-0 in the return match with Wednesday when Spiksley made his first appearance at Olive Grove.

In the GN Charity Cup, Gainsborough drew Wednesday away in the third round. A special chartered train took 500 supporters to the match in Sheffield. A 6,100 crowd witnessed the home side's captain Billy Betts win the toss and immediately the match started Wednesday swarmed all over the away defence in which full backs Fred Palmer and Charlie Jubb performed heroically. It was 0-0 when tragedy struck as Spiksley, celebrating that day his nineteenth birthday, made a powerful run down the middle. Wednesday full back Teddy Brayshaw was far too late with his reckless sliding tackle and he left his opponent lying on the ground having snapped his leg between the knee and ankle. Brayshaw had got the ball just at the moment that Spiksley had put the outside of his right foot to it and the shockwave created by the collision fractured his shinbone. Attempts to stand up were agony and the Gainsborough physician Doctor Wright confirmed it was a broken leg. The injured player was taken to the Arundel and Surrey Hotel where he had his leg set. Without a key player the away side lost 4-0 but only after Fred's sprint trainer, Charlie Booth, had exchanged blows after being the victim of another reckless Brayshaw tackle. Booth had been given special permission to play for Trinity by his club, Wolverhampton Wanderers. This being 1889 no player was cautioned or dismissed as, after all, it was a man's game! Spiksley's absence was a big blow personally and for his side. Over the following weeks Trinity enjoyed mixed fortunes including defeats at home to Lincoln City (1-0) and Grimsby Town (7-1). In an experiment to draw large crowds the games were played under floodlights. Ten arc lamps were employed and although the attendances were large enough to justify the experiment, borrowed from the Bramall Lane Sports Club in 1878, it proved unsuccessful as a practical exercise as the lights kept failing.

The injured youngster, who must have feared his career might already be over, missed Trinity's final nine matches of the season and was confined to his bed for eight weeks with splints. He required crutches when he got up and with his muscles in his right leg having wasted considerably, he needed to build them back up with a programme of exercises during a period when he also restarted his apprenticeship. Plenty of walks and lots of swimming were a boost and over the summer of 1889 he was able to start practising his ball skills once more.

By the start of the 1889–90 campaign, Fred had not played competitively for almost eight months. The season saw the introduction of a new law which allowed a referee to rule a player 'out of the game' (send him off) for dangerous play or poor conduct.

Fred's return came in a benefit match organised on his behalf by Trinity fans seeking to compensate him for his loss of earnings while he was recuperating. Trinity played a Combined Gainsborough XI consisting of the lesser clubs' best players. Its recipient was humbled that over 1,000 spectators attended and donated £10 to him after expenses. The youngster, however, was disappointed by the lukewarm reception he received for his low-key performance and those of a similar nature that followed. In many ways, Fred had a thin skin and stated many years later: "A player returning from injury doesn't get the sympathy he deserves. Supporters are hard taskmasters." Gainsborough Trinity had written to The Wednesday football club asking them if they would contribute towards Spiksley's benefit fund, but Wednesday were not forthcoming with any donation.

With twenty teams, the Football Combination had proven unmanageable. The Football League, however, with just twelve teams, had proven an unqualified success. It was imitated in 1889–90 with the formation of the Football Alliance, the Northern League and the eleven-team Midland Counties League. The last of these was the brainchild of Jack Strawson, the Lincoln City secretary. Trinity joined it along with Burton Wanderers, Derby Midland, Derby Junction, Leek Town, Lincoln City, Notts Rangers, Rotherham Town, the Sheffield Club, Staveley and Warwick County. This guaranteed twenty competitive games.

Trinity's first game at home to Lincoln City saw them include new 'keeper William Gresham, recruited from Boston, and he was beaten twice in a 2-1 defeat with the winner coming from his brother who was playing for Lincoln. Playing at Burton Wanderers, Fred Spiksley experienced some rough treatment and he was left virtually incapacitated as the home side recovered from two down to score two dubious goals and earn a draw.

There was some relief when Trinity then won 5-4 at the Sheffield Football Club. Although the pitch was a quagmire the conditions did not prevent a real thriller taking place before 1,250 spectators.

As his form started to return, Spiksley notched an early equaliser in a friendly match with Blackburn Rovers only for the Football League side to show their superiority by roaring to a 5-1 success. Earlier in the decade Rovers had won the FA Cup in three successive seasons. The fact that the East Lancs side had been willing to play in Gainsborough nevertheless made it a special day.

On 28 December 1889, Trinity faced Rotherham Town at home in a Midland League match and in the visitors' goal was Arthur Wharton. He was the first black professional footballer. He had travelled to England from Ghana to study in Darlington and soon discovered he had a special sporting talent. In 1885 he won the AAA 100 yards championship at Stamford Bridge, London. He retained the title the following year and became the first man to run 10 seconds dead for the distance.

At football, he took to goalkeeping and was especially noted for his ability to punch the ball long distances. He was persuaded to play for Preston but, being a free spirit, he argued with manager William Sudell.

Arthur joined Rotherham as a professional for the 1889–90 season and played at centre forward where he could use his blistering speed and keep his sprint trainer happy by avoiding the extra risk of injury that went with playing in goal, violence against 'keepers being fair game in 1889. Yet when the Rotherham 'keeper De Ville was injured against Burton Wanderers there was no other option expect to put Arthur between the sticks. He thrilled the crowd with his special tricks that included catching the ball between his knees, picking up opposing forwards and dumping them in the goal and pulling down the crossbar to prevent shots entering the goal. Arthur's actions naturally infuriated opposition fans and players and led to a number of incidents, many of quite a violent nature in which he gave as good as he got.

Playing in goal against Gainsborough Trinity, Wharton, who was commemorated in 2014 with a 16ft permanent memorial at the National Football Centre at St George's Park, was brilliant and as shot after shot rained down on him he performed heroically. Only once was he beaten when Spiksley feinted one way and sent him the other. As the game entered the final minutes the away side led 2-1 when the Trinity scorer broke clear and as he moved to equalise Wharton dashed forward and literally jumped on his right leg.

The 'keeper's actions prevented a goal and ensured his side won the game but left the recipient fearful that he had suffered another serious injury. The home support, aware that Fred had recently returned from a broken leg, roundly booed the 'keeper. When the match ended a number of fans invaded the pitch and after surrounding the 'keeper an unseemly scuffle broke out which was only ended when the police arrived quickly to restore law and order. Thankfully, the Trinity outside left was saved by his shin pad and departed with just a sore shin.

Over the following weeks the pitchside action was much more pleasant for the Gainsborough fans as their team won through to the FA Cup fourth qualifying round and were drawn away to Lincoln City, who despite kicking up the hill took an early two-goal lead. Trinity's 'Tuppenny (2d)

Gods' – so called because they paid a 2d entry fee and were the most fanatical – were taunted by City's most vociferous supporter 'Leather Lungs' who offered odds of 3 to 1 on City.

Fred Spiksley was a gambling man and he must have fancied the odds as soon after he scored with an unstoppable cross shot. The match proved a thrilling one that City won 5-3.

Trinity had more success in the Lincolnshire County Cup. Initially, Grimsby Humber Rovers proved stubborn opponents in the semi-final but four second half goals took Gainsborough into the final.

On 5 April 1890 when Trinity played their final home Midland League game of the season the match with Leek Town was delayed by twenty minutes so that the GN could take a special team photo that was printed in the paper on 2 May 1890. The photograph shows the team with the GN Charity Cup and with Trinity set to face Notts Olympic in the final the feeling was that the game would be a walkover! It was but Trinity still didn't win the cup.

The Leek game attracted a 1,500 crowd and saw Gainsborough win 9-2 with Spiksley and Willcocks both hitting three.

However, no-one was talking of these feats but of an incident which afterwards the GN reporter referred to as 'funny'. Having conceded a seventh goal, a Leek player mistakenly passed the ball on the restart to Elliott who standing on the half way line flicked it up and aimed a low volley that just kept on going and going and going right past a transfixed Critchlow in the away goal to make it 8-2. Was it a fluke or pure genius? We will never know as no-one asked the scorer afterwards but it split the crowd with half laughing and half applauding enthusiastically.

Elliott notched another goal as Grantham Rovers were beaten 6-0 in the final of the Lincolnshire County Challenge

Cup at Lincoln's ground. The trophy was presented when the team returned home to Gainsborough for a celebratory tea at the Sun Inn. When Walter Forrest accepted the trophy on behalf of Gainsborough Trinity he reminded everyone what had occurred in 1888 before stating: "The committee have always been determined not to rest until the County Cup has been won."

The Midland Counties League's first season ended for Gainsborough with a 3-2 defeat at Lincoln City, who were crowned champions with Gainsborough down in seventh place. Gainsborough had scored 47 goals, the second highest, and conceded 32. With 23, Fred scored almost half of Trinity's league goals. During the 1889–90 season he scored 36 goals, twenty more than Arthur Elliott and Taffy Thomas who finished in equal second place in the Gainsborough score chart.

Fred had played particularly impressively in the second half of the season, notching 25 goals in eighteen games. His form had not gone unnoticed as his achievements were chronicled in the *Athletic News*, regarded by many as the leading sports paper of the time. As the season came to a close a number of letters began arriving for him at his parents' pub. One in particular could not be ignored as Blackburn Rovers were prepared to offer him £2 10s (£2.50) per week to play for them. If he accepted he would be playing for the FA Cup holders as on 29 March 1890, Rovers had thrashed The Wednesday 6-1 in the final with William Townley hitting the final's first ever hat-trick.

Football, however, was a precarious business and hadn't Fred broken his leg not so long back? He also had his apprenticeship to complete and with nine months to go he could not let his father down again, especially as it would give him a trade to fall back on if his football failed to bring any future financial rewards.

Fred let everyone know he would be playing for Trinity in the 1890– 91 season and he ended the current campaign on 30 May by creating one of the goals as his side beat Notts Olympic 4-1 in the Gainsborough News Charity Cup final at the John O'Gaunt's ground. However, Charles Caldicott's great pleasure was extremely brief as just two days later the defeated side correctly pointed out that David Brelsford in the Trinity goal had earlier played for the club's reserve side in the competition.

It meant that while the Trinity players were allowed to keep their medals, Notts Olympic were awarded the cup.

CHAPTER 5

TRINITY TRIUMPH
Gainsborough Trinity win the Midland League and Wednesday are lucky to get their man

THE 1890-91 SEASON was to be Fred's last with his local club and it would be a roaring success.

Unlike the previous summer the Trinity outside left was healthy enough in 1890 to participate in the rowing club's regatta. Elitism had been ended at the club's AGM when high entrance and membership fees were dumped in favour of cheaper membership fees. Membership numbers multiplied and the additional income helped to purchase new boats and improve the boathouse.

A full regatta was now possible for the first time in ages with prizes totalling £25. Large crowds packed the river banks for the swimming and rowing events with many witnessing a dramatic rescue on the first day when swimming instructor Professor Bocock plunged into the river to save a young swimmer called Michael Burge who had got trapped by some floating weeds and was choking to death. Amazingly, Burge proceeded to win the open half-mile handicap swimming event!

Also successful was Fred Spiksley who, rowing with Roy Goodall, snatched the novice coxed pairs title in a titanic final in which the pair beat Joy and Schofield. Then, in the scratch coxed pairs event, Spiksley and J R Rawlings won their heat and semi-final before beating Woodhouse and Longmire by 4.5 lengths to take the title and collect a silver cup.

Little over a week later, Gainsborough Trinity played their first practice match and it was announced that the club committee had not repeated the previous summer's mistakes and had strengthened the team.

The injured William Gresham was fit to resume in goal while Harry Walkerdine from Notts County would play centre forward. John Clements had also previously represented Notts County and he had been recruited to play at full back while Scotsman Harry Swinton, previously with Bury, was another new signing for a side whose half back line was to be Steve Carlin, Billy Brown and Fred Palmer. Billy Cooke and Taffy Thomas would form the right attacking flank. Arthur Elliott had been courted by a number of clubs but in the event he also re-signed for the Blues. Hopes were high for a successful season.

The League campaign began with a 5-1 success at Long Eaton Rangers but in the second game there was a shock. After taking the lead through Elliott, Trinity conceded a 'goal' when a Gummer shot that missed by some distance was awarded by the referee, who sitting on the half way line was asked to adjudicate after the Gainsborough and Rotherham umpires failed to agree. Rotherham won 3-2.

The growing number of occasions when the umpires failed to agree was creating increasing demands for the referee to assume full control of games – after all, it would undoubtedly lead to improved decision making, as has proved the case ever since!

Trinity Triumph

On 4 October 1890 the Gainsborough game against Lincoln City in the FA Cup became a landmark match when the referee was given complete control of events. If the experiment and those that followed were successful then there was every chance it would be permanently introduced for the start of the 1891–92 season and also be combined with the introduction of neutral referees and linesmen to end accusations of favouritism against match officials.

The FA decided to appoint for this important occasion the experienced referee, Arthur Kingscott, known as 'The Knight of the Whistle.'

The match clashed with the Nottingham Goose Fair, which was considered to be the 'Carnival of the Midlands' and it meant that many potential spectators were unable to attend. Nevertheless football specials conveyed 1,270 travellers from across Lincolnshire who on a warm day poured into the pubs before the match.

A crowd of 3,200 created a great atmosphere and as the players dressed beforehand the referee entered both dressing rooms and warned them against rough and dangerous play. The match started punctually at 3pm.

The result was a 3-1 victory for the away side who clearly benefited from some inconsistent decisions by the referee. At 2-1 he failed to spot that Elliott's shot had gone over the line before 'keeper Jack Robinson, who was the man of the match, palmed it away. Minutes later, Gresham disputed without success whether a Lincoln shot had crossed the line and then, almost from the restart, Joe Duckworth got away with hacking down Harry Walkerdine as he raced towards the Lincoln goal.

There were also other rough challenges by Lincoln players with the *Athletic News* report stating: "Lincoln City's persistent infringement of the 'laws of the game' should have been penalised with at least two sendings-off." Robinson later became a big football star. He was one of the first 'keepers willing and able enough to make diving saves and he was not afraid to dive at the feet of an attacker and take the ball from him. He went on to play eleven times internationally and must be regarded as one of England's greatest 'keepers.

Trinity drew at Derby Midland in the following match where Spiksley missed when presented with an open goal, following which a wag in the crowd urged him to be given some glasses.

Trinity played their first home League game on 18 October 1890 and it came after the club committee decided to up admission prices from 4d to 6d (2p to 2.5p), with the only concession being that advanced tickets could be purchased for 4d. Having massively improved the ground and invested heavily in new players, the committee needed to increase revenues. Just 550 people turned up to witness a 4-0 success in which Cooke netted three. A letter published in the GN by *A Working Man* blamed the price increase for the small crowd as "the majority are working class and most earn less than 18 shillings (90p) a week out of which they pay six shillings (30p) rent. This leaves very little to keep a wife and family going."

When Trinity faced Sheffield United, who were formed for the start of the 1889–90 season, there was a familiar face in the opposing goal in Charlie Howlett, who always preferred to fist away low shots rather than catch them. He was known to be unable to withstand a heavy charge and before kick-off the players of his former club devised a plan to hit him hard early on.

A disgusted Spiksley wanted none of it. However, when Mr Stringer, one of Gainsborough's wealthy patrons, entered the dressing room and offered "two silver crowns" for the first man to floor the Sheffield 'keeper his attitude swiftly changed and he became determined to win the cash on offer. He did so as well, crashing into his friend and sending the 'keeper's glasses flying into the air. Referee

Jack Strawson seemed certain to caution him but he was let off with a severe telling-off as Howlett donned his glasses and was left stunned at seeing who had dumped him on the floor.

A relieved Spiksley had won the money and he also scored in a 4-1 victory. Howlett excused his friend but had already arranged retribution against Mr Stringer.

Gainsborough had been invited to play a club match against Woolwich Arsenal on the Invicta playing field, a great amphitheatre that could accommodate 15,000 fans. An 8,500 crowd saw Arsenal go ahead when Arthur Christmas scored. Spectators had been left thrilled by the speed and ball control of Spiksley and as he sprinted away from the home full back Peter Connolly and half back David Howat someone in the crowd bawled out "Oh, my goodness! He runs like the wind!"

On 75 minutes the youngster escaped from Howat and met a cross to spectacularly volley the equaliser. Arsenal quickly re-took the lead and then survived fierce pressure to win the match after which cries went up from the crowd "Bravo Trinity". Rough working hands were employed by two men to hoist Fred on to their shoulders and carry him back to the pavilion where he was heartily cheered. Despite the defeat Gainsborough were absolutely delighted when their share of the gate receipts was handed over and totalled £150.

On Boxing Day, Port Vale returned home punch drunk from Lincolnshire as they were thrashed 11-0 at Northolme with Elliott and Spiksley both netting three. In twenty games so far in the season the latter had scored twenty times.

As the new year was entered another letter was posted through Fred's door by a local unidentified man who had been asked by Accrington to observe his performances and who had the previous season written to him stating that the East Lancs Football League club sought his signature. With his apprenticeship shortly to be completed on his 21st birthday, Fred this time wrote to the small, unfashionable but friendly club indicating that their offer was something he would like to take up. Fred agreed to visit Accrington and discuss terms.

Accrington, known as 'th Owd Reds', were battling to avoid having to apply for re-election. Fred could not prevent that happening this season, but Accrington's charismatic secretary Joe Hartley wanted to steal a march on his rivals by recruiting some of the best players around in order to demonstrate that his club should remain in the League as they would subsequently be a force to be reckoned with. In 1891 it was perfectly legal for clubs to approach players before their contracts expired but secrecy was important as once news leaked out that a deal had been agreed then the player and his family might experience resentment and even violence by fans of his current club

Although violence at football was never organised it was not unusual. When Trinity beat Derby Junction 1-0 on 3 January 1891 the referee, Mr West, needed protection by the Gainsborough players. Home fans had attempted to assault West after he blew the final whistle on 80 minutes. They were unaware that it had been agreed to cut the game by 10 minutes because of bad light and thought he had abandoned the match.

Eight days later, Fred, with his overcoat collar turned up as he left Gainsborough by train, travelled to Accrington where he enjoyed lunch with Hartley, club president D. W. Spark and chairman Mr Hargreaves. They outlined how they could find Fred a good job as a compositor with a local printer and also pay him £2 10s (£2.50) a week throughout the year as a professional footballer. The contract was ready to sign but Fred asked if he could take it home to discuss this with his parents before he put pen to paper. Hartley was happy enough with this and Fred departed believing he would soon be returning.

However, when he arrived back in Sheffield he had

missed the final train home. He was directed to the Maunche Hotel by the stationmaster and there he bumped into Fred Thompson, the Wednesday captain. During the conversation that followed, Fred let slip why he was in Sheffield and the Wednesday full back urged him to not to sign the contract in his pocket and wait until he had heard from the Olive Grove club. Thompson departed hastily.

Fred returned home on the early hours train and went to work on a day when the North played the South in an England trial match in Nottingham that saw the first official use of goal nets. They were invented by a Liverpool civil engineer John Brodie, who had taken out a patent for his "net pocket". As they were made on Merseyside then it was appropriate that a player from there was the first to put the ball into them – Everton's Fred Geary scoring for the North after quarter of an hour.

It was widely agreed the nets were a success and *The Football Field* reported on 17 January 1891: "Mr Brodie's goal nets are likely to be generally adopted."

By the start of the following season every major team were using them. Yet goal nets are not compulsory and despite being mentioned as a necessity in all competition rules a game could go ahead without them.

'Nets may be attached to the goals and the ground behind the goal, provided that they are properly supported and do not interfere with the goalkeeper.'
Laws of the Game 2008–09 FIFA

Brodie Avenue in Liverpool is named in John Brodie's honour and an English Heritage blue plaque is positioned at the late Victorian detached villa he occupied in suburban Ullet Road.

After he had finished work on 12 January 1891, Fred was handed by his mother a telegram from Henry Pearson, the Wednesday club secretary, inviting Fred to meet him and John Holmes and Arthur Dickinson, the Sheffield club's president and financial secretary respectively. Dickinson's title was slightly confusing as he effectively picked the side at Wednesday for many years and in 1899 he oversaw the club's conversion to a limited company and actually became the first shareholder. Dickinson's duties included scouting for players in Scotland. He joined the Wednesday committee in 1876 and stayed until 18 May 1920.

Two days after the telegram a return ticket to Sheffield arrived. At the meeting the following Sunday, Fred was offered £3 a week for 40 weeks of the year and the promise of a compositor's job in Sheffield for a further ten shillings (50p) a week after he had completed his apprenticeship. As had been the case with Accrington, Fred asked for some time to discuss the offer with his parents. When he did so they were happy with Wednesday's terms and their son agreed to join a non-League side rather than one from the Football League.

Fred Spiksley had arrived in Sheffield to discuss terms the day after he and Gainsborough had played one of their finest matches – against Staveley. A close-knit community in North Derbyshire, Staveley was steeped in sporting tradition and boasted a very good football team. They included two men who later became England internationals, full back Harry Lilley and Ernest Needham, the latter nicknamed 'Nudger' by his teammates because of his ability to nudge opponents off the ball. The latter was to become a footballing legend at Sheffield United. He joined them when he was eighteen after working as a lad on the pit bank in the local colliery from the age of thirteen.

Due to someone leaving the taps on, the match was played at Pingle Hill as Northolme was only good for water polo. In the event it was Staveley who were all at sea as the local side beat them 10-0 in a match that was played in a snowstorm throughout the second half. The final goal was the best of the afternoon when Gainsborough's outside left dribbled at lightning-fast pace through the bewildered Staveley defence before rounding Bill Lilley to score. Fred never forgot the game and years later wrote: "In this game we had to rely on football science ... our skill and speed simply bewildered our opponents so that we kept them guessing from start to finish."

Ernest Needham also remembered the day when his story appeared in 1912. "Our captain told me to shift from left to right half to stop the outside left. I might as well have tried to stop the wind. The outside left was Fred Spiksley ... the finest outside left I have ever met and whose dribbling was a treat to watch. He could either combine with the others and make openings by lively centres, or cut past the back on the inside to go for goal himself. He could also shoot with either foot.

"Being such a dangerous man, he got a lot of knocking about, but he took it as a rule with very good grace. I shall never forget Freddy's dazzling wing play with Wheldon of the Villa, as the left wing in 1898, when England beat Scotland 3-1. Ah, Fred was a gem of a player in those days!"

Having agreed to join Wednesday, Fred wrote to Accrington thanking them for their offer but declining it. Within 48 hours, Accrington replied by telegram upping their offer to £182 a year, the equivalent of £3.50 a week and more than Wednesday's offer. A few hours later there was a knock on his parents' door. They answered it and found Joe Hartley standing there. He was quickly ushered into the parlour. His character soon won over Fred's parents who also saw a strong business case for their son to play for Accrington.

Hartley stressed to Fred that his club were in the Football League while Wednesday were struggling in the Football Alliance. He then confided that Arthur Elliott, Fred's partner out left for Gainsborough, had agreed to sign for Accrington. As Fred agreed, the offer was a strong one that really could not be refused.

The decision seemed almost straightforward but he turned Accrington down. Fred explained his reason in an article published on 8 May 1920, "I could only blurt out that I preferred Sheffield to Accrington because it was much closer to my home and family." This was very similar to what he had said in an earlier article in 1907.

However, in 1920 he added the following: "You may wonder why I was so keen on this point when Accrington's offer was so superior, and want to know my reasons. I do not care to answer this question, but if you cared to ask Mrs Spiksley I have no doubt that she would suggest that there must have been a woman in this case, and I have been married for too long to enter into any argument with a lady."

Spiksley was obviously deliberately cryptic in his justification for signing for Wednesday and his intentions behind this can be interpreted in different ways. What is clear is that some part of his decision-making was based upon his relationships with women. He seems to be suggesting that if you were to ask Ellen in 1920, the person who knows him best, she would have confirmed that the only factor in Fred's life that would overrule money and gambling would be a woman. Therefore, because Accrington were offering more money than Wednesday and a chance to play League Football, then there must have been a woman in his life at this time.

Knowing that he was set to play for Wednesday in 1891–92 made Fred determined to end his time with Gainsborough by winning the Midland League and he helped his side beat Lincoln City 3-0 with Walkerdine scoring three in five minutes. The following day Fred came of age and he travelled to Sheffield to sign his new contract.

On the next day, Fred came out of his time as an apprentice at the GN. Charles Caldicott presented him with his certificate as a fully-qualified compositor and Fred tendered his resignation to take up a job in the composing room with the Sheffield Telegraph. Wednesday had arranged lodgings at 19 Talbot Street, Sheffield where he shared rooms and rent with accountant Thomas McCabe. Over the following two and a half seasons he worked Monday to Friday at the paper. While he continued playing for Gainsborough in 1891 he travelled there each weekend.

Moving to Sheffield was essential as it was feared that once Gainsborough fans heard that Fred was leaving some would see the move as betrayal. Fred was not keen to face the same treatment as the players poached by Burnley.

Gainsborough's good form continued as Grimsby Town were beaten 2-1 in the Lincolnshire Challenge Cup semi-final. After this win a Grimsby fishmonger delivered to the Hickman Arms in Gainsborough half a ton of fish with instructions to distribute it to the winning team and the deserving poor of the town.

Eating the fish clearly didn't do the Trinity players much good as the following weekend they lost their third League game of the season when beaten 3-1 at Derby Junction. The losers were now a point behind leaders Derby Midland. But when the sides met at Northolme, Trinity moved into first place with a fine display that saw them win 3-0.

Hitting the top was a real pleasure, unlike Fred's journey with his eldest brother, Ted, who was intent on building a new life overseas and had successfully applied for a job in the iron and steel industry in Pittsburgh, USA. Since moving to Sheffield, Fred had visited his brother most nights but on the evening of Friday 6 March 1891 the pair journeyed to Liverpool and booked into a local lodging house.

The following morning, Fred helped Ted to stow away his sea chest and after the final farewells the ship cast off for America at 8 o'clock. The pair didn't know when they might see each other again and must have sorrowfully departed in opposite directions with Fred off to face Sheffield United at Bramall Lane. The venue had first opened as a cricket ground on 30 April 1855 and first class cricket was to continue being played there until 1973. This was long after the Bramall Lane committee had been forced during the late Victorian era to drop its hostility to football in order to generate the income they required to keep it open.

With Wednesday playing away the gate was boosted by fans keen to see their new signing and the 500 Gainsborough fans present were shocked to learn that Fred Spiksley was departing. The away side took an early lead but were pegged back when two of their players failed to take note that the half-time interval had been cut from ten to five minutes. Elliott and Murell were still in the dressing room when the home side netted in the first minute of the second half. Spurred on by their success Sheffield poured forward and Crawford scored a second. The away side were then unfortunate when a goalbound shot ended up inches short of the goal, the bladder in the ball having burst.

After 90 minutes Gainsborough had lost a vital match and their supporters departed doubly disappointed after the news that their outside left was leaving. Wednesday fans were also upset as their new man had played poorly. With hindsight, Fred should not have played as he was exhausted and emotionally drained from a tiring journey to Liverpool and back. Gainsborough's lack of a travelling reserve forced him to play.

More disappointment followed as Trinity lost 1-0 to Lincoln City in the Lincolnshire County Challenge Cup final. However, the following weekend, Gainsborough beat Port Vale 3-1 to capture two valuable points. Two days later, on Easter Monday, Warwick County took a two-goal interval lead when they played Gainsborough at home. Defeat would have ended the away side's title chances and with Spiksley providing a succession of beautifully-weighted crosses and corners the home side were under constant second-half pressure. When County did try to break away they were pushed back by the Gainsborough half back line of Murrell, Carlin and Henrys. Arthur Elliott scored two and after Billy Cooke put his side ahead Fred Spiksley wrapped up the scoring for a 4-2 win.

This was a vital victory. It meant that in the final game of the season Gainsborough knew that as long as they avoided being beaten 11-0 at home by second-placed Long Eaton Rangers then they were certain to finish in top spot as the Lincolnshire club enjoyed a two-point advantage and a far superior goal average. The title was in the bag and it may have been that complacency had set in as Rangers took a 3-1 lead only for the champions-elect to hit back when Spiksley ghosted in to net from a fine Murrell cross. Taffy Thomas then did some splendid work and Walkerdine sent hats up in the air as he made it 3-3.

So it was that on 17 July 1891, Gainsborough Trinity received twelve Midland Counties League championship-winning medals for presentation by the Trinity executive to the players. The medals were designed in silver with a 'gold shield' in the centre and a 'gold scroll' below.

Along with the medals, Gainsborough were presented with the Midland Counties League championship pennant.

Gainsborough's great success in a league where they competed with much bigger sides had nevertheless come at a cost as they were losing some of their top players with Fred Spiksley going to The Wednesday, Arthur Elliott to Accrington, John 'Taffy' Thomas to Sheffield United, Arthur Henrys to Newton Heath, George Murrell rejoining Grimsby Town and Harry Walkerdine rejoining Notts County. The team had been decimated but they had won the title and every man jack of them had earned it.

CHAPTER 6

LEAGUE ASPIRATIONS
An impressive first season playing for The Wednesday in the Football Alliance

FRED'S NEW CLUB, The Wednesday, who became Sheffield Wednesday in 1929, had attracted their record crowd of 16,871 when they lost 2-0 to West Bromwich Albion in the FA Cup on Valentine's Day 1891. In 1890, Wednesday had reached the final against Blackburn Rovers but lost 6-1 against a side from the Football League – a league which the losers had designs on joining. At the end of the 1889–90 season, Sunderland had become the first change to the original League line-up when they were elected to replace Stoke.

The numbers passing through the turnstiles indicated Wednesday would be a healthy addition to the Football League. One problem was the Sheffield club's form as they had slumped from top spot in 1889–90 to the bottom of the Alliance in 1890–91. Out of 22 games just four were won, all of them at home.

Wednesday Football Club had developed out of Wednesday Cricket Club, which was formed in 1820.

Similar to the Gainsborough club for which Fred played a handful of games, it took this name because matches were played on Wednesdays. Four years after its inauguration the club opened Darnall cricket ground and within a few years it had seats for 8,000 spectators. It was considered one of England's finest cricket grounds.

On Wednesday 4 September 1867, John Pashley's proposal to form a football club was accepted by members and a committee was established by the 60 or so who joined the new club that night. In their first game, the Mechanics Club were beaten by three goals and four rouges to one rouge in a game played at Norfolk Park. A rouge was the outer part of the then twelve feet wide and nine feet high goal. It was separated from the middle part – the goal – by posts on either side. One goal was worth any amount of rouges. Rouges were abolished in 1868 when the goal width became eight yards.

In 1877, Wednesday won the first Sheffield Challenge Cup competition, beating Heeley 4-3 in a thrilling final that attracted 8,000 to Bramall Lane. Most of these spectators would have been working in either the steel or cutlery industry. Sheffield has a long industrial history; coal was burned at Templeborough by Roman soldiers, and the Sheffield manorial accounts of 1442–3 refer to coal-pits and charcoal-making; they also say that there were a number of water mills on the rivers.

The list of Sheffield taxpayers in 1297 records a Robertus le Cotelar (Robert the Cutler) although the cutlery trade is probably even older. Sheffield had thus acquired a distinctive character early in the second millennium and although the census of 2 January 1616 recorded 2,207 people – of whom 725 were the begging poor – it was a fact that most provincial towns had populations under 20,000. That was less than a tenth of the size of London, which even then dwarfed the rest of the nation. Sheffield's population, out of which three out of every five men worked in the cutlery trades, was to rise dramatically to reach 10,121 by 1736. Most of the rise was natural, with more births than deaths annually, but there was also immigration from surrounding parishes. Sheffield's weekly Tuesday and Thursday markets attracted many visitors from parts of Derbyshire, Notts and the West Riding of Yorkshire.

Sheffield's population continued to rise throughout the eighteenth century. In 1801, 31,314 lived in the central township with 45,755 in the entire parish. By 1851, Sheffield was a borough with 135,310 people and the numbers continued to rise as it was transformed dramatically by the building in its east end of great steelworks that gobbled up labour.

The manufacturing of iron goods had been replaced by steel after Benjamin Huntsman, a Doncaster clockmaker, invented 'cast steel' in the mid eighteenth century. Key to this was the understanding that coke fuel could reach higher temperatures than charcoal. Coal mined from the Barnsley seam was excellent coke and Huntsman became a full-time steel maker on the east side of Attercliffe Green in 1751, the year when the River Don Navigation was opened at nearby Tinsley.

Over the following century the Sheffield–Rotherham region became the world's number one steel-producing centre. Sheffield also benefited from the ingenuity of Thomas Boulsover who discovered that by fusing silver and copper they could be worked as one metal into the external appearance of silver. Plate silver was much cheaper, Sheffield plated wares sold handsomely and the trade employed thousands. As industry developed more workers were needed and as their wages increased, partly as a result of trade union agitation, and Saturday half-holidays became the norm then the way was open for emerging football clubs to seek support.

Capturing the first Wharncliffe Charity Cup in 1879 cemented Wednesday's place among the local giants of football. By then, Wednesday had begun to embrace professionalism with the signing of James Lang but it was Bob Gregory who was the fans' initial hero especially after notching Wednesday's first FA Cup goal when Blackburn Rovers were beaten 4-0 in December 1880.

The greatest Wednesday player in the pre-league period was left-winger Billy Mosforth, an engraver who played nine times for England. Mosforth was lightning quick, possessed great dribbling ability and could hit accurate screw or spin shots that would change direction as they came in from the corner flag. In an era where individualism was king, Mosforth, known as "The Little Wonder." had a valid claim to the throne. Future Wednesday left wingers would be judged against this marvellous player.

Mosforth also played a vital part in ensuring the club survived when he and Tom Cawley persuaded a reluctant Wednesday president John Holmes that professionalism must be embraced in 1887.

Confusion following the death of secretary William Littlehales in January 1886 saw Wednesday fail to send in their 1886–87 FA Cup entry. Most of the club's best players joined local side Lockwood Brothers and did very well by reaching the fourth round. Without their stars, Wednesday struggled and even lost 16-0 against Halliwell, a result that remains their record defeat.

In April 1887, Mosforth and Cawley, both of whom had previously been banned by Sheffield FA over payment allegations, helped form Sheffield Rovers with the intention of assembling all of Sheffield's best players to fight for the FA Cup the following season. It was felt that if the players needed expenses to play they should have them and it was agreed these would be 5s (25p) and 7s 6d (37.5p) for home and away games respectively. Such payments, much less than at many other professional clubs, really only covered a player's loss of wages when he was absent from work playing football. Rovers only ever played three games but their formation forced Wednesday to hold what proved to be a historic meeting in June at the Garrick Hotel, Sycamore Street. At this it was agreed that their players would from then on be paid, at least, similar expenses – the amounts, in fact, immediately rose to around £2 a week in 1888. If Wednesday had remained an amateur side they would have been overtaken by other clubs prepared to pay the best players to play for them. Professionalism meant Wednesday required a ground where they could be assured of a larger financial return. Bramall Lane was ruled out because the committee there insisted on taking a massive slice of the gate receipts.

Wednesday secured a lease for seven years on a field off Queen's Road and adjacent to the Midland railway line, which often meant the match ball needed rescuing during games. Bill Russell was paid to fulfil the task.

New facilities cost £5,000. The stream which ran through the field was covered over, the ground was enclosed and named Olive Grove.

Professionalism and a new ground ensured that Wednesday became the premier club in Sheffield with old clubs such as the Lockwood Brothers, Heeley and Attercliffe Reds gradually fading away.

In 1888, Wednesday applied unsuccessfully to join the Football League and a year later, after another unsuccessful application, the club helped form the Football Alliance. Wednesday won their first league match 2-1 at home against Bootle on 7 September 1889. The game was watched by a crowd of 2,000. Later in the season, six times that number watched the Notts County FA Cup replay. Despite a poor season, six-thousand gates were common throughout the 1890–91 season.

Yet, if Wednesday were going to become a Football League member then the 1891–92 season required a major on-field improvement. Hoping that the fine form of the 1889–90 season could be recaptured the Wednesday committee chose to augment the squad with just three new players in Fred Spiksley, Gavin Thomson from Third Lanark and the experienced Scotsman Tom Brandon from Blackburn Rovers, who became club and team captain.

In a most unusual move for the times Brandon, who had a well-deserved reputation for head-butting opponents every once in a while, was given a two-year contract that also included the summer months. To Blackburn's disgust, Wednesday lured him across the Pennines with what ultimately proved to be a false offer of a public house. A deeply homesick Brandon returned to his former club in December 1893. His consistency was finally rewarded with a Scottish cap in 1896. Tom's younger brother, Bob, had signed for Wednesday in October 1890 but was released at the end of the season. Another younger brother, James, signed from Preston North End, played briefly for Wednesday in the 1891–92 season before moving on to Chesterfield Town. Cousin Harry Brandon did much better after he arrived in December 1890 from Clyde and the utility player made over 200 competitive appearances for Wednesday, including the 1896 FA Cup final.

In Fred Spiksley The Wednesday had signed a rare talent, despite Fred still only weighing in at just under eight stone. He had four seasons of professional football under his belt and had survived a broken leg and was now stronger than ever. Although the Football Alliance was considered a stronger league than the one Spiksley had just won with Gainsborough Trinity there was not too much between the two leagues, especially the top teams, and Wednesday would have been excited by the prospect of signing a player who had played 126 times for Trinity and had netted 131 goals. Despite his obvious raw talent there still would have been some question marks over Fred Spiksley and if he would fit into 'the mould' of his new team. Selection would have definitely been far more competitive than it was at Trinity. Arthur Dickinson had aspirations of gaining entry into the Football League, which was more of a political challenge than an on-field one. Despite his obvious speed, skill and reputation Fred Spiksley, who was now 21, would have to prove that he had the strength and tenacity to compete against teams that also harboured the same dreams as Dickinson.

Fred first wore a Wednesday shirt on 18 August 1891 in a public trial match – the whites versus stripes at the Sheaf House Ground close to Bramall Lane, which was now being used regularly for football after United were formed on Friday 22 March 1889. He was very roughly treated by opposing right half Ernest Bartlett who continually used his considerable weight advantage in a series of heavy charges.

One Bartlett challenge had his opponent's head scraping along the cinder running track surrounding the pitch. Fred years later commented, "This was the worst game I had to contend with." Bartlett never made a first team appearance but, having been overpowered, Fred Spiksley's name was not on the team sheet for the first friendly match of the season away to Sunderland Albion.

Fred had not turned down League football to play in the reserves and immediately sought out John Holmes to request to be released from his contract. When the Wednesday chairman was joined by Arthur Nixon the pair couldn't persuade the impetuous young man to bide his time and he continued to demand his cards in order to seek another club. A desperate Nixon told the new Wednesday winger that the side wasn't yet officially confirmed, bringing to an end an increasingly acrimonious meeting.

A few days later Fred received a postcard saying he was picked to play at Sunderland. The reason for the change was never clarified but the move proved a wise one as although Wednesday lost 2-1 their goal was scored by debutant Fred Spiksley, who thereafter never had to worry about his place in the Wednesday team when he was fit.

Fred made his competitive debut for Wednesday at home to Grimsby Town in the Football Alliance on 19 September 1891.

Wednesday: Smith, McConnachie, Mumford, Brandon, Betts, Cawley, Gemmell, James Brandon, Thompson, Woolhouse, Spiksley

Five of the side had played in the 1890 FA Cup final. Goalkeeper Jim Smith helped Wednesday to two Sheffield Challenge Cups and two Wharncliffe Charity Cups while also playing in 22 consecutive FA Cup matches. A steel smelter, Smith, was a real character who smoked a clay pipe during games, throwing it away when the ball came towards his goal.

Billy Betts, who was also a fine cricketer, was one of Wednesday's greatest players of the Victorian era and during the three years in the Alliance he missed just a handful of games. Although he became one of Wednesday's first professional footballers, Betts continued working as a stoker at Neepsend Gas Works. He had a reputation for being made of solid steel and played once for England against Wales in February 1889. His grandson Dennis Woodhead played over 200 games for Wednesday during the 1940s and early 50s. Betts was to sit next to Fred Spiksley and Tom Crawshaw when Wednesday last won the FA Cup at Wembley in 1935.

Henry Woolhouse was a versatile forward who netted five goals in Wednesday's club record 12-0 FA Cup win against Halliwell in January 1891. His place in the side was threatened by the arrival of Fred Spiksley although he did play in Wednesday's losing semi-finals in 1894 and 1895.

Tom Cawley made his debut for Wednesday on 5 November 1881 in an FA Cup-tie at Providence. He made his final appearance in the FA Cup over a decade later and in between he earned a reputation for fairness and superb ball control that in an era of 'kick and rush' meant he stood out on a football pitch. Off it, his decision to speak up in support of professionalism was vital in ensuring Wednesday survived. In 1889, Cawley netted four times in an international trial match but still wasn't selected to play for England.

Albert Mumford signed professionally for Wednesday in 1887 and it was his two goals against Bolton Wanderers on 8 March 1890 that helped his club win their FA Cup semi-final 2-1. Incredibly versatile, Mumford later helped the reserves to two league titles before his loyalty was rewarded with a benefit match against Sheffield United in 1896.

The home side beat Grimsby 4-2 with Woolhouse, scoring three times, repeating his feat from an earlier game against the Canadian touring side. Woolhouse was still bearing the scars from the tourists' match in which he and James Dalton tangled in a bout of wrestling during which the Canadian sank his teeth so hard into his opponent's cheek that blood poured from his mouth. The pair were separated with great difficulty but neither was dismissed.

Dalton later played for Sunderland, thus becoming the first Canadian to play first-class football in England and a very early example of the soccer cosmopolitanism common today.

On 17 October 1891, Fred Spiksley created two goals and opened the scoring with his first Alliance goal as Burton Swifts lost 5-2 at Olive Grove. Wednesday then lost 3-2 at Bootle. Following the introduction of the penalty kick at the start of the season, Tom Brandon's goal was the club's first from 'the spot'. In fact the marking of a spot was still some time away and the penalty taker could place the ball anywhere along the twelve-yard penalty line that ran the full width of the pitch and within which any offence meant a penalty.

In late October, Fred played in his first Sheffield derby match against a United side competing in the Northern League. It was a friendly but there was nothing welcoming about Bob Cain's heavy charge early on that left him with double vision. Wednesday were thrashed 5-0 before a crowd approaching 23,000. For days afterwards, Fred feared venturing out and when he did he hid himself away.

The result did, however, prove positive. Wednesday directors had not previously considered the virtues of regular formal training and practice. Thereafter it was agreed that any player not employed elsewhere would train for a minimum of two hours at Olive Grove each morning. Several Scotsmen were also invited south for trials although in the event only Bob Brown was considered good enough to sign. Brown had a good shot, great dribbling ability and became nicknamed 'Sparrow' for his dainty ball skills.

Wednesday won five and drew one of the six games after the heavy derby defeat. They also took revenge by beating United 4-1 in a friendly match with the newspapers stating that Spiksley scored twice when he argued he had, in fact, scored all of his side's goals! The journalists covering the game would have experienced difficulties identifying who was who on the field after heavy rain resulted in the unnumbered players shirts and hair being totally soaked and covered in mud.

The Wednesday outside left did, though, enjoy some fortune because after being the last to enjoy a hot bath he felt a shooting pain in his knee and discovered a piece of flesh the size of a half crown piece (2s 6d or 12.5p today) hanging loose. The player decided to cut it off when he got out of the bath; he was prevented from doing this by one of his teammates who went to get Dr Lockwood. The doctor stitched up the wound but the pain was excruciating and the injured man was given brandy to prevent him passing out. The injury prevented Fred Spiksley from playing over the next four weeks as his knee kept breaking out in abscesses, the result of some foreign substances in the wound. The treatment had worked, though, preventing the potentially fatal tetanus infection from developing.

Flying over an Olive Grove

As 1892 dawned, Wednesday lay in second place and on 9 January they beat Small Heath 6-3 with Spiksley scoring two and Brown three. The winning side had a new goalkeeper in Bill Allan whose enormous feet meant a cobbler needed to work overnight to make a good pair of football boots big enough for him to play for Wednesday. Allan became a regular over the next four seasons, earning the nickname 'William the Silent' for his quiet demeanour.

On 23 January 1892 a 16,500 crowd crammed inside Olive Grove to see Wednesday face Bolton Wanderers in the FA Cup first round. Playing his final game of a long career for the Lancashire side was Kenny Davenport. At 3.47pm on Saturday 8 September 1888, Davenport, an England international, had become the scorer of the first ever League goal as he put his side ahead at Pike's Lane in a game that Bolton eventually lost 6-3 to Derby County.

Wednesday won 4-1 and their outside left scored twice – both from close in – but was left needing to visit the hospital when Sandy Paton's boot inflicted a wound that required ten stitches. Dai Jones scored the single Bolton goal. In 1902 the Welsh international died of tetanus after he suffered a similar knee injury to Fred Spiksley's in the 1891–92 season.

In the FA Cup second round Wednesday overcame Small Heath 2-0 in a rough game that led to Olive Grove being closed for a fortnight by the FA. Then in the last eight of the competition they came up against West Bromwich Albion and were outplayed, losing 2-1. With six league games remaining, the Sheffield club needed a strong finish to have any chance of again winning the Football Alliance. In the event they won twice and lost three to finish in fourth place, five points behind champions Nottingham Forest.

Wednesday, though, had shown they were a force to be reckoned with. In addition to their respectable fourth place they had beaten League side Bolton in the FA Cup and Accrington (6-0), Preston (6-1) and Notts County (5-2) in club games. They now hoped to be accepted into the Football League.

And what of Fred Spiksley's first season at Olive Grove? It had not been easy as in many games he had faced 'big bruisers' all keen to knock the lightweight youngster into the crowd.

Yet the Gainsborough lad ended the season having played sixteen of 22 league games and scored nine goals. He also scored two in the FA Cup as well as many other goals in the numerous club games that were played throughout the season. In all, Wednesday played over 70 games in 1891–92.

Fred's form was so good that he had even been selected as England's first non-playing reserve for the international match in Wales that was won by the away side 2-0.

It had clearly been a good first campaign for Fred Spiksley in the Sheffield Wednesday colours and he later commented: "My workload was a heavy one and to come through it was a tremendous achievement in itself. Having survived my first season, I was extremely proud of myself, and insofar as Wednesday was concerned then my selection as first reserve for England was evidence that Wednesday had little to complain of as to the bargain they had made."

On 22 April 1892 the Football League agreed to form a Second Division. The League had been expanded to fourteen clubs in 1891–92 and two clubs would now be added to form a First Division of sixteen. These would then vote for twelve new members to form the second tier. However, the matter was largely predetermined with the League minutes stating: "It was felt that the Alliance as a body (except St George's) should be admitted to the League." The Alliance, born three years earlier, was to be absorbed.

With twelfth-placed West Bromwich Albion excused from applying for re-election in recognition of having won the 1892 FA Cup, there were five Division One places up for grabs. Applications from newly-formed Liverpool, Newcastle East End and an amalgamated Middlesbrough side were rejected.

This meant the three re-election applicants from Division One in Accrington, Stoke and Darwen competed with Nottingham Forest, Newton Heath and Wednesday from the Alliance in the contest for Division One places in 1892–93. Wednesday won the most votes and Darwen the least. The latter thus dropped down into Division Two where the vast majority of Alliance joined them, plus Burslem Port Vale, Northwich Victoria and Sheffield United. The Football League had expanded to Manchester, Lincolnshire, Cheshire and South Yorkshire.

CHAPTER 7

A NEW HERO RISES
Wednesday's first season in the Football League

HAVING ACHIEVED ENTRY to the Football League, Wednesday sought to improve their team and facilities. Newcomers for the 1892–93 season were Alec Brady, Harry Davis and Alex Rowan. Scotsman Brady had moved south from Partick Thistle in the summer of 1888 and after a short spell at Sunderland he had moved to Gainsborough Trinity before departing within weeks to Burnley. In February 1889 he re-signed for Sunderland. At the start of the 1889–90 season a dispute between Burnley and Everton over his registration delayed his debut for the Toffees until November 1889. He thereafter played for eighteen months at Everton where, as the first of many inside-forwards who could bring others into play with deft, accurate passing, he helped the Toffees capture the newly-minted League trophy in 1890–91. He then sensationally quit England to return home to play for Celtic before joining Wednesday a year later. Brady came south with Fred Spiksley's former coach, John Madden.

This was the second time that Wednesday had tried to sign Madden in a twelve-month period. With Wednesday turning their attentions to north of the border, to pay for first class talent, the club had to resort to their own poaching missions similar to that of Burnley in 1888. The man who took the responsibility upon his shoulders to 'run the gauntlet' was Arthur Dickinson, the club secretary. In 1899 Dickinson was to recall his adventures in Scotland in the *Lancashire Evening News:*

"In 1891 I went up to Ferguson of Arthrlie, and Richardson of Hurlford. Here it was that I had my first experience, for at Barrhead, where an agent and I had gone for Ferguson, we were tackled by a mob. They knew for what purpose we were there and set upon us with the heartiest goodwill. Their sense of appreciation of our presence was forcibly expressed by means of showers of stones. It was no time for argument, so we cut and ran, the mob after us. I never moved more rapidly in my life. Luckily we had provided for some such contingency by having a conveyance drive by as if his mother-in-law were after him. He had a good pair of horses and took them along at a better pace than they had ever done in their lives. Our gentle friends in the rear pursued us for a while, but could not stay the pace. So we escaped in such a to-do. And we had got our players secured, which was everything. This was in February, and next month I was off again, gathering in Gibson R Gemmell and R McConachie. These, however, were secured with comparatively little trouble. In August of the same year we landed Gavin Thompson of the Third Lanark.

"In September of 1891, however, I had a rare adventure. I went up to get Towie, who afterwards came to North End, and left them to play for Derby County. He was playing then with Geordie Dewar's old team – Dumbarton. In the same club was a full back named Spiers, whom I also wanted. John Wilson's agent met me and at Partick we picked up Jack Madden, of the Celtic. Wilson and I got off at Bowling and Jack went straight on to Dumbarton to bring up the two players. We arrived at the appointed rendezvous – Sinclair's Restaurant, a noted football house, and one that every Scotch player is acquainted with – and presently in came Madden, accompanied by Towie and Spiers. We had to use a great deal of persuasive eloquence to effect our purpose and at last seemed to have succeeded. Towie took up a pen to sign the professional form for us, and it was all but done when – the door opened and in stalked the secretary of the Dumbarton club, the trainer and two or three gentlemen with opinions and muscle. We were fairly and squarely trapped.

"Wilson bolted and got clear beautifully. Jack and I were left to face the music and without any preliminaries we prepared to depart. We scrimmaged our way down the stairs and there found a crowd – hundreds of them – waiting for us. The entry of the club officials, and our reception by multitude were partly of the same plan. The crowd yelled like savages and made for us. Now Madden hadn't any interest in me, except that he had seen me landed in a hole. And that was good enough excuse for him, so he stuck to me like a brick. We got our backs against the wall and, by Jove, Jack did fight!

"He was real pluck. Sheer weight of numbers separated us and then it was a case of making a bee line for the station. I don't know how he got along, for the crowd followed, letting go at me at every possible chance. Several times they tried to trip me up and had I gone down it might have proved awkward. As it was I was thoroughly mauled. At last I struggled into the station and rushed into a train standing there. Luckily it was just about to start for Glasgow – my destination. In the same train the agent was seated, spick and span and comfortable without a scratch.

"I was bleeding from my mouth and nose, and felt just about used up. When my face 'developed' I had two blackened eyes and was generally cut and bruised. With such a face as I had, I dare not appear in public, and for two days after stayed in my hotel in Glasgow. Then I had to send for a chemist to paint away the discolouration around my eyes before I dared venture forth as a respectable man.

I never heard how Madden fared after we parted in the crowd, for I did not see him again for another year."

One year on and it looked as though Dickinson had finally got his man. With Madden and Brady in Sheffield, Wednesday were confident that both men would turn out in the blue and white stripes for the club's first season in the Football League.

No-one knew it, but a Roman Catholic priest, acting as a detective, was hot on the two players' trail and had followed them from Glasgow. Two hefty bodyguards accompanied God's man when he located Madden and persuaded him to return to Scotland. Madden was spirited away on the night mail train. Once Wednesday became aware that Brady might be the next to be whisked back north, Arthur Dickinson had him smuggled by train to Boston and locked away in a safe house for two weeks until it was clear that the priest had tired of looking for him. Brady arrived back in Sheffield the day before Wednesday's first Football League match.

Wednesday also signed Harry Davis from Birmingham Saint George's. Davis had done well in fixtures against Wednesday and was seen as the ideal replacement on the right wing for the released Duncan Gemmell, who was fortunate as he gained a place at Royal Arsenal in Plumstead.

Having lost Gavin Thomson with a broken ankle at the end of the previous campaign, Madden's loss left Wednesday short of someone to lead their front line. Dickinson left for Scottish side Albion Rovers, where his target was Alex Rowan who two seasons earlier had struggled when representing Nottingham Forest. Dickinson hoped the homesick teenager with raw talent had matured since returning to Scotland. The change was remarkable; Rowan, who had netted six goals against

A New Hero Rises

Clydebank in October 1891, was now six feet tall and twelve stones. He had the physique to deal with the heavy kicking, charging and elbowing prevalent in the Football League. Rowan gladly signed for Wednesday.

The Wednesday first team pool for the start of 1892–93 was:-

Keepers – Bill Allan, Jim Smith

Backs – Tom Brandon, Albert Corbett Mumford, John Darroch, James Brown

Half backs – Harry Brandon, Billy Betts, Alex 'Sandy' Hall, Bob McConachie

Forwards – Harry Davis, Bob Brown, Alex Rowan, Thomas McIntosh, Harry Woolhouse, Alec Brady, Walter Dunlop and Fred Spiksley

Wednesday's first ever Football League game was at Notts County. With Trent Bridge occupied for cricket the game was at the Nottingham Castle Ground on 3 September 1892. The 13,000 crowd included 2,000 from Sheffield. As kick-off approached and many remained locked out there was a rush to gain entry and once inside fans spilled on to the pitch, resulting in a 25-minute delay while they were relocated to a less crowded part of the ground. The players eventually entered the arena at 3.54pm.

The home side were on the attack in the early stages but Tom Brandon superbly marshalled his defence and Wednesday soon got the upper hand in a fast-flowing game played on hard ground. The surface suited Fred Spiksley well and the Wednesday winger hit a shot that dropped into the crowd off the top of the crossbar. On eleven minutes, Notts conceded the opening goal when, from a Spiksley corner, either Harry Davis or captain Tom Brandon scored. Most records give the goal to Brandon. There was disappointment soon after when Spiksley had an effort disallowed for offside. At the interval two mounted policemen came into the ground to ensure the crowd did not encroach on the pitch. When the match resumed, Brady missed narrowly and with both sides failing to net the match finished Notts County 0 Wednesday 1.

The following Saturday, Wednesday played their first home game in the Football League. Ironically, it was against Accrington, the club for whom Fred had come so close to signing. The match was played in a newly-refurbished Olive Grove. In the summer of 1892 ground improvements had proceeded quickly enough to turn the Wednesday ground, which had staged its first match on Monday 12 September 1887, into one of the finest enclosures in the country.

The pitch had been re-turfed and levelled, thus ending visiting teams' complaints that Wednesday gained an unfair advantage by the peculiarity of their ground. The playing field measured 125 by 86 yards, easily accommodating the pitch measurements required for cup-ties, although Wednesday in fact adopted a medium-sized layout of 115 by 76 yards.

The purchase of an additional piece of land at the 'Heeley End' allowed the stand there to be enlarged and improved. An old wooden stand running down the side of the pitch had been replaced by a brand new brick-built stand capable of hosting 1,000 people at a shilling (5p) each on comfortable seating. Underneath were the dressing rooms and bathrooms that contained a tiny gas stove for the comfort of the players and one slipper bath large enough to accommodate eleven men. Two Wednesday players, Harry Davis and Fred Spiksley, were known for being exceptionally clever in getting stripped after the match and getting into the bath first. "Both of them I am sure would have gone into the bath with their boots on if they thought they would be beaten in the race to the slipper bath," said Langley.

In front of the stand an enclosure costing 6d (2.5p) to enter was to prove popular. The uncovered 'Sheffield End' stand had been taken back and raised. Despite the changes the pitch's proximity to the terracing and seating remained so close that the intimacy and personal bonds between players and spectators remained strong. Wednesday supporters felt they were part of the team. This bond was strengthened because Wednesday never trained behind closed doors and fans watched the training sessions for free. Afterwards it was not unusual for the players to have a beer with fans at the Earl of Arundel and Surrey Hotel where, naturally, the main topic was football.

The ground improvements cost Wednesday around £2,000, a hefty sum but the club committee were confident that the impressive new facilities could be paid for as they were convinced they had assembled a top quality team that the public would want to watch, especially with the guaranteed regularity of top class teams visiting Olive Grove – such as Aston Villa, Everton and League champions Sunderland. Despite the massive improvements there was still the need for Bill Russell to be regularly despatched on to the nearby railway tracks to fetch balls that had been kicked there. Wednesday had to keep half-a-dozen handy on match days.

There were 9,000 people at the Accrington game for which Wednesday made one change, Rowan replacing Walter Dunlop with Davis moving out to the wing to accommodate the new player. The home side were three up by half-time and ran off to great cheers after winning 5-2 with Brown scoring twice and Davis, Rowan and Spiksley one each.

The return match two weeks later at Accrington's Thorneyholme Ground, which is still used today as a cricket ground, saw the East Lancs side win 4-2. In the intervening period, Wednesday had lost at Preston and Bolton.

Victory over Burnley was followed by a draw at Nottingham Forest and then four straight victories, including a 3-2 success against Sunderland that was watched by 20,000, the largest home crowd of the season. The Wearsiders had thrashed Aston Villa at Perry Barr on 17 September 1892 and afterwards William McGregor dubbed them the "Team of All Talents". The week before the game with Wednesday, Sunderland had beaten West Bromwich Albion 8-1 with Johnny Campbell scoring twice. The Scot finished as top scorer in Division One in 1891–92, 1892–93 and 1894–95.

Campbell opened the scoring against Wednesday. After gaining possessions on the halfway line he raced away before beating Allan with a surprise snapshot that gave the 'keeper no chance. Sunderland 'keeper Ted Doig, who always wore a cap because he was embarrassed about being bald, also had no chance when Hall equalised with a long dropping shot. Jock Scott restored Sunderland's lead but after Brady equalised, Hall scored the winner from a free kick that saw the ground erupt. Sunderland's defeat failed to prevent them racing to the title and they finished with eleven points more than second-placed Preston.

Sunderland beat Wednesday in the return match 4-2 on 28 January 1893. Many excursionists from Sheffield made the trip north, including a detachment of young men from Attercliffe who were conspicuous in their blue and white hats. The final goal of the game was scored by Fred Spiksley, who, reported the *Newcastle Daily Leader*, "made several beautiful runs."

The week after beating Sunderland, Wednesday beat Bolton Wanderers 4-2 in a game in which Spiksley scored his first League double. A fortnight later, Jack Southworth notched two as Wednesday lost 3-0 at home to Blackburn Rovers.

The weekend between the two League games marked Fred Spiksley's debut in the annual inter-association match between Sheffield & Hallamshire and Glasgow. Such matches between city teams were a popular feature in football's early years. During his time at Trinity, Fred had made three appearances for the Lincolnshire Association team across four seasons. Although he was to go on and achieve much greater accomplishments it is known that Fred was deeply proud of representing Lincolnshire and cherished the caps that he was awarded.

Fred had made his debut for Sheffield Hallam against the London FA in February 1892 before a crowd of 10,000 at Bramall Lane.

Sheffield & Hallamshire: Lilley, Mumford, Lilley, Howell, Betts, Whitham, Leedham, Dobson, Hammond, Woodhouse, Spiksley

Playing in white jerseys, Sheffield scored on 30 minutes when Spiksley's perfect ball presented Harry Hammond of Sheffield United with an unmissable chance. Hammond and Spiksley continued to combine superbly and the home side won 4-1 with Hammond scoring three. The victors had now won twelve against the London FA's thirteen in the series of matches.

In 1895 Fred and Harry Davis scored in a 2-0 victory in London and the following season the Wednesday outside left scored two as London were beaten 7-4 in a thrilling Monday afternoon game at Olive Grove. Both sides' forwards were in superb form and failed to be hampered by the torrential rain and muddy pitch.

London had their revenge in 1897 when an over-confident Sheffield side lost 4-1 in the capital with the only consolation goal coming from Fred Spiksley. In 1898 and 1899, Sheffield won 3-2 at Olive Grove and 7-0 at Owlerton.

The first Sheffield-Glasgow game had been played at Bramall Lane on 14 March 1874. It ended 2-2, but in the next sixteen times the sides met Sheffield won only once – in 1891 when the Glaswegians were beaten 4-3 at Bramall Lane.

In October 1892, Fred lined up at outside left against Glasgow in the following XI: Massey (Doncaster Rovers), Whitham, Lilley, Howell, Betts (captain), Needham, Davis,

Leatherbarrow (Rotherham), Hammond, Woolhouse, Spiksley.

The game ended 3-3 with Davis scoring twice for the home side and Fred once. Fred made many other appearances against Glasgow and in 1893 he was part of the Sheffield side that thrashed their opponents 7-2. In the next game played in Glasgow in 1895, the away side lost 3-1 as the Scots took advantage of 'keeper Billy Foulke's inability to reach down to fast low ground shots. Foulke showed his class, though, when the teams, without Spiksley, met in Glasgow in 1897 when he played brilliantly in a 0-0 match. Fred Spiksley was later part of the successful Sheffield sides in 1896 (5-1) and 1898 (2-1), as well as playing in the losing games in 1899 (4-0) and 1902 (2-0 at Owlerton).

Games between Glasgow and Sheffield continued annually until 1938 and were briefly revived between 1949 and 1957.

In late November 1892, Goodison Park witnessed a brilliant match in which Everton were beaten 5-3. According to the *Liverpool Mercury*, Fred Spiksley scored the third and fourth Wednesday goals and assisted his inside partner, Brady, a former Evertonian, to two. The Wednesday attacking-left pairing were now becoming a potent force and would remain so until 1899.

In early 1893 attention turned to the FA Cup and a tie with a Derby County side containing John 'the Good' Goodall and youngster Steve Bloomer. Olive Grove was packed with 18,000 inside and they saw the away side take an early lead from a bullet header by Sam Mills. On 65 minutes, Derby scored a second through Goodall after Allan was taken out in a heavy challenge.

With just seven minutes remaining, some disappointed Wednesday fans began making for the exit gates. One who was determined to stay till the end was George Ulyett, who had played once for the club in goal against Notts County in the FA Cup in 1882–83 but was best known as a Yorkshire and England cricketer.

A New Hero Rises

Ulyett was a Spiksley fan and Wednesday fan. He made it very clear he still had faith and when one of his fellow fans said the odds against Wednesday were 50-1 he quickly struck a bet with him. Within seconds it was 1-2 as Davis scored. Soon after the restart the scorer made space for a fine centre that Rowan pounced on to level. Wednesday players, officials and fans jumped for joy. When the referee sounded his whistle after 90 minutes, the home side now had an extra thirty minutes in which to win the tie.

Ernest Hickinbottom had kicked Fred Spiksley black and blue throughout. He was again detailed to do so in extra time. He did so until the last minute. But when Billy Betts swung the ball over his head the Derby half back was left for dead when Fred Spiksley raced away before drawing Jimmy Methven out of position, cutting inside at speed and then rounding 'keeper Jack Robinson and scoring what proved to be a dramatic winner.

Spiksley had won the game and the Wednesday fans now had a hero they could adore. The result was harsh on Derby who for at least 80 minutes had been the better side.

This was to be a defining event in Fred Spiksley's career as a professional footballer and was indeed a 'coming of age' moment. Against top quality opposition and in an FA Cup tie where Wednesday were dead and buried Spiksley had delivered the winning goal. From that moment on, with Fred Spiksley on the field, the Wednesday players and supporters alike knew that no match was ever lost. If Spiksley was not already the darling of the Wednesday supporters he was now and they dubbed him 'The Olive Grove Flyer'.

However, if the victorious side thought that was the end of matters they were quickly disillusioned. It was an era when many clubs, for a variety of reasons, protested after losing an important cup-tie Derby did so. The East Midlanders claimed that Brady, Rowan and recently-arrived half back Bruce Chalmers were ineligible. An FA sub-committee quickly absolved the latter player of any wrong-doing and also decided that was the case with Rowan. Brady was a different matter, signed in the summer he had failed to complete his residential qualification period in Sheffield and was thus ineligible for FA and county cup matches.

The sides were ordered to replay the match at Derby's Racecourse Ground. Sheffield papers accused Derby of poor sportsmanship. In return the *Derby Telegraph* pointed out that after Wednesday had thrashed Notts County 5-0 in 1890, and the latter subsequently had their protest upheld and won the second game 3-2 then Wednesday had then made their own successful appeal. The tie was eventually decided in a third match when Wednesday went through 2-1.

The replay in this latest saga was in Derby on a Monday afternoon. It attracted 14,000 including many away fans who took advantage of football specials laid on by the Midland Railway Company. Woolhouse replaced Brady.

So tightly packed was the crowd that there were frequent interruptions as spectators spilled on to the pitch. In an attempt to push back the crowd, mounted policemen even charged across the field as the game progressed. Hickinbottom was determined to ensure his opponent did not score and Spiksley several times required treatment from the Wednesday trainer. One ridiculously high tackle left him poleaxed and as he lay looking upwards, the Wednesday outside left could see Steve Bloomer looking at him with a hint of disgust for the tactics his own side were employing. Fred asked him after the game what he thought of it and the future star replied: "If this is first class football I don't think much of it."

The game was won in extra time when John Goodall scored a great goal that was totally out of place with the previous poor fare. Derby were through, or were they? It transpired that Bloomer had unknowingly broken the rules by signing two professional contracts – with Derby and Burton Wanderers. When he admitted this was the case at the subsequent FA sub-committee, its chairman Charles Crump rose and said: "That's enough, replay tomorrow."

On 2 February 1893, Wednesday and Derby faced each other for the third time. On a working day a crowd of 10,000 was inside Olive Grove to witness a thrilling encounter that Wednesday won 4-2. Goodall put his side ahead on four minutes. Betts then hit a scorcher on eight minutes to level and within a minute of the restart the ball was sent out to Spiksley. In a repeat of the first tie at Olive Grove, he destroyed his marker and left Robinson with no chance as his powerful shot rocketed home to make it 2-1. Woolhouse made it 3-1 and the contest was over when Spiksley made it 4-1 and even though Tom Little reduced the arrears it was the side from Sheffield that progressed to the next round. Or had they? Derby protested that Allan had broken FA rules by playing in a summer six-a-side match in Scotland. With no evidence the claim was worthless but, just in case, Arthur Dickinson had prepared his own appeal based on the fact that Derby had played a charity match in Grantham in October 1892 without seeking the FA's approval.

The FA were totally fed up with this farcical state of affairs. They thus changed the rules. In future all clubs competing in the FA Cup had to send in a full list of players two weeks prior to each match and any appeals had to be made seven days prior to kick-off.

Wednesday overcame Burnley next in the FA Cup courtesy of a goal scored by Fred Spiksley. Burnley's robust style of football meant they were known as the 'Burnley Butchers.' From one corner the Clarets centre half Tom Nicol ignored the ball and, with the referee's attention elsewhere, planted his knee into Spiksley's ribs. The injured player needed smelling salts to be revived before being carried off and strapped up with swathes of tape and bandage. The pain in his side was excruciating and a wiser man would have ignored captain Tom Brandon's half-time pleas to return to the field. When he did return, he was virtually a passenger and his opponents ignored him. Burnley pressed strongly for a winner but with Brandon in great form, Wednesday refused to concede.

One boisterous fan wouldn't leave Fred alone. The man was a milkman but swore like a trooper. He taunted Fred with cries about how he wasn't going to score. With minutes remaining the ball was mistakenly kicked his way and ignoring the pain the unmarked Wednesday player rushed forward and shot before Tom McLintock could reach him. The ball swerved past Jack Hillman for the winning goal. The Wednesday hero recalled years later three men had won the game: "Tom Brandon, myself and the milkman."

Fred endured severe pain over the following weeks and was grateful to his co-tenant in Talbot Street, Thomas McCabe, who regularly turned him over so he could lie comfortably in his bed. Although it was not initially diagnosed Nicol had broken two of Fred's ribs. It was a minor miracle that he had played on with such a serious injury, let alone score the winning goal.

A badly-injured Fred missed his side's following two League games. However, he did play against Everton in the FA Cup. Writing in 1907, Fred claimed that Wednesday had persuaded him to play and in return the club issued a public denial. His presence, and it was no more than that, had little effect as Everton won 3-0.

On 11 March 1893, Wednesday lost 1-0 at home to Wolves. Two days later Fred debuted for England against Wales. The following Saturday a poor Wednesday side were beaten 3-0 at West Bromwich Albion and fell to eleventh in the table. This was just one place outside the bottom three. A 2-2 draw with Derby helped provide some relief but with Fred Spiksley away with England over Easter, Wednesday lost 4-0 at Burnley and 1-0 at home to Stoke.

A New Hero Rises

With just one match remaining the new boys knew that defeat at home to Notts County would see their opponents leapfrog them in the table. This would put Wednesday into the bottom three, thus forcing them to play in a test match series against one of the top three sides in Division Two, with the winners playing in Division One in 1893–94 and the losers playing in Division Two.

The final League game was a repeat of the first. It was played on Easter Monday and Wednesday were buoyed by the return of Fred Spiksley, fresh from his triumph against the Scots just two days earlier. The England international was greeted with a two-minute standing ovation when he ran out before kick-off. Wednesday had abandoned their traditional blue and white shirts in order to avoid a colour clash with the Magpies' black and white stripes. This was in line with the rules then in place that required the home team to change shirts, usually to white, as Wednesday had done.

The game started frantically but after four minutes Jimmy Oswald scored for County. The scorer was then booked for two rough challenges on Allan in the Sheffield goal. There were no yellow or red cards at this time and spectators could only tell if a player had been booked when they witnessed the referee take out his note book and record the offender's name. Often it was very difficult to tell who had been booked. Just before the interval the away centre half Jack Hendry, a robust character, was also booked. Then on 41 minutes, Harry Brandon rolled the ball to his cousin Tom and his shot levelled the scores when it beat England 'keeper George Toone. Just 5ft 7in tall, Toone relied on his great agility to confound attackers but it was to no avail on this occasion.

After the interval the pace failed to slacken. Brady headed home but it was disallowed for offside and with 75 minutes gone the score remained 1-1. County were then denied when Allan made three great saves before Harry Brandon hit one of his trademark long ground shots that put his side ahead. The lead lasted just 30 seconds as County captain Jack Oswald, a boilermaker by trade, hit a low fast shot into the Wednesday net. County's hopes were dashed within a minute, Harry Brandon hitting home a free kick from twelve yards to ensure that Wednesday had survived by finishing in tenth place.

County finished in twelfth, while below them were Accrington and Newton Heath. When Sheffield United, who finished second in Division Two, beat Accrington 1-0 in the test match series it proved to be the defeated club's last ever match. Heavy debts meant that on occasions they had been unable to raise a team. The club tendered their resignation to the League and soon afterwards went out of business. Fred Spiksley had been fortunate when he opted not to sign for the East Lancs side in 1891.

After a fine start, Wednesday had faded. Good crowds, though, meant that the money invested in Olive Grove was being quickly repaid and there had been some great games to watch. In the League, Wednesday had scored 55 goals and conceded 65. Equal top scorers with thirteen were Fred Spiksley and Rowan, who, with 28 games, had played two more than his colleague. The outside left had, however, outscored the Scot in the FA Cup to end up as top scorer for the season. In addition to his success at club level, Fred Spiksley had also played brilliantly for England.

Yet he was supposed to be dead!

During the winter of his first season in Sheffield, Fred had contracted a terrible choking cough. He found himself waking up in pain and when it failed to clear in the spring he approached Arthur Dickinson who took him to the doctor. The medic paid particular attention to his chest and lungs and after the examination he asked to speak to Dickinson alone. When he emerged Dickinson handed the player a prescription before dashing away.

Thereafter Dickinson always appeared busy whenever Fred sought to speak to him and when the player then asked Harry Pearson and Arthur Nixon about a contract for the 1892/93 season the responses he received were evasive. A confused Fred Spiksley started looking elsewhere for a contract and when Alf Shelton, his friend at Notts County, heard about his predicament he arranged for him to see Mr Brown, the Notts County secretary. Shelton, an England international, was County through and through and in the summer of 1892 he turned down an offer to join newly-promoted Liverpool who were willing to pay him £5 a week, a considerable sum in those days. Sadly, he lost his life in an industrial accident at Cammell Laird in Nottingham in 1925.

When Dickinson found out what Fred was up to he was presented with a major dilemma as the doctor's diagnosis was that the examined patient had galloping consumption with a life expectancy of just twelve months! Should he tell Fred Spiksley he had tuberculosis? After much soul-searching he decided to keep quiet and he then gambled by offering the seriously sick player a twelve-month contract.

One year on and despite his serious rib injury, Fred Spiksley looked in great condition and so Dickinson was confused. He took the player to see Sheffield's top consultant, Mr Pye-Smith to obtain a comprehensive medical condition. At the end of the examination the patient was asked to wait outside. Ten minutes later a delighted Arthur Dickinson danced out of the doctor's consulting room to tell Fred the good news and let him know why he had not been able to look him in the eye the previous year when the pair had visited the doctor together.

Fred's lungs were now as clear as a bell, with no trace of consumption or chest weakness. According to Pye-Smith, Fred Spiksley was not dying although he was suffering from exhaustion and overwork. The remedy was plenty of fresh air and relaxation.

"Well, well, well; and here you are, an England international, and you're supposed to be dead!" cried Arthur Dickinson.

On hearing the news the Wednesday directors were equally jubilant. Determined to retain one of their star players, they offered Fred Spiksley a three-year contract, the first ever awarded in football. The increased terms were £4 a week for all 52 weeks and it was further agreed that the player could again enjoy the benefits of clean Lincolnshire air by living in Gainsborough during the week and playing for Wednesday at weekends. The only proviso was that Fred would pay his own travel costs.

Of course, by living in Gainsborough it gave the player an opportunity to frequent the race tracks he so enjoyed but it also meant Fred would be away from the serious pollution for which Sheffield was well known; indeed, an anonymous visitor in 1768 commented: "The town is exceedingly dirty and ill-paved. What makes it more disagreeable is the excessive smoke from the great multitude of forges with which the town is crowded." Many of Sheffield's better-off residents later migrated towards the west of the city as the prevailing wind blows from that direction.

CHAPTER 8

A BLUE CAP
England debut and a special day at Richmond

SINCE 1884 ENGLAND had in each season contested matches against Ireland, Scotland and Wales for the Home International Football Championship. Ireland, where organised football only got off the ground in the late 1870s and the Football Association was not formed until 18 November 1880, and Wales didn't have the depth of quality enjoyed by England and Scotland and, consequently, what every English footballer desired was the blue cap awarded for matches against Scotland.

While playing for Wednesday in the Football Alliance, Fred Spiksley had been chosen as England's first reserve for the 1892 international against Wales but had not been called upon to play. The England side were chosen by an FA Council sub-committee of seven drawn from every region of the country where the organisation were represented. Throughout the season the seven attended matches to determine which players should be considered for selection.

Flying over an Olive Grove

Before the championship started a trial match would be staged between the North and South with the teams being composed of amateur and professional players. Following this game all seven selectors would dine together before retiring to select sides for the Wales and Ireland games. These matches were often played on the same day and it was tradition up until 1895 to select one England side consisting of all amateur players to play either Wales or Ireland, and a second consisting of ten professional players and one amateur, who would captain the side, in the other game. Not surprisingly, the team for the big game against Scotland was then strongly influenced by the performances against Wales and Ireland.

With Wednesday having made the leap into Division One in 1892–93, the England selectors were aware of Fred's good form against better opposition, his healthy goals total and his ability to create numerous goal-scoring opportunities for his teammates.

When the teams were chosen for the Ireland and Wales games (played on 25 February and 13 March respectively), the former consisted largely of players with Corinthian connections. Gilbert Oswald Smith from Oxford University made his debut in the match. G O was to play twenty times for his country, sixteen as captain, and was considered by many to be the best player of the late nineteenth century. He scored once against Ireland as England won 6-1.

For the game against Wales, the England team selected were a fully professional one and were as follows

John Sutcliffe (Bolton Wanderers), Tom Clare (Stoke), Bob Holmes (Preston) (captain), John Reynolds (West Bromwich Albion), Charles Perry (West Bromwich Albion), Jimmy Turner (Bolton Wanderers), Billy Bassett (West Bromwich Albion), John Goodall (Derby County), John Southworth (Blackburn Rovers), Edgar Chadwick (Everton), Alf Milward (Everton)

A Blue Cap

Today, club versus country remains a contentious subject but back in 1893 there was never any argument, England came first! There was, therefore, a historic moment when a club refused to release players to represent England. Everton were facing an FA Cup semi-final replay against Preston three days after the international match. England captain Bob Holmes was a Preston player and his club were happy to release him but Everton were concerned that if Chadwick or Milward was injured playing for their country then their Cup chances would be jeopardised. In the event, the selectors refused to make a fuss and elevated Stoke's Joe Schofield and Wednesday's Fred Spiksley to the starting line-up. This especially delighted followers of Schofield as the match was to be played at the Victoria Ground, Stoke.

Spiksley became the first Gainsborough man to play for England. He was followed by Alf Spouncer, one cap in 1900, and Arthur Brown who played twice, scoring once, between 1904 and 1906. All three started at Gainsborough Trinity.

A third change was forced on the selectors on the morning of the game when star forward John Southworth was forced to withdraw with a troublesome leg injury. John Whitehead of Accrington was summoned by telegram to play at inside right with John Goodall moved to centre forward. Spiksley's selection for England elevated him to playing alongside the finest players in England – such as Goodall and Bassett who had established themselves with the greatest sides of the 1880s and early 1890s.

Bassett charged down the wing like a whippet. He was clever on the ball, possessed a powerful right-foot shot and served his club for a grand total of fifty-one years: thirteen as a player (1886–99), six as a coach (1899–1905), three as a director (1905–08) twenty-nine as chairman (1908 until his death in West Bromwich in 1937). He scored 77 goals in 311 first class matches, played in the 1888 and 1892 FA

Cup-winning sides and in the losing side of 1895; he made sixteen appearances for England.

Wales lined up in the usual 2-3-5 formation as follows:-

James Trainer (Preston), Dai Jones (Chirk and Bolton Wanderers), Charles Parry (Llansilin), Joseph Davies I (Druids and Wolves), Edwin Hugh Williams (Flint and Crewe), Edward Morris (Chirk), Edward Jones (Middlesbrough), James Vaughan (Chirk), John Butler (Druids), Benjamin Lewis (Wrexham and Chirk), Robert Roberts IV (Crewe)

The England professionals in the team received an appearance fee of £1 for home matches. Players stayed overnight before the game at a hotel near to the ground and shared a room with a teammate. Lunch consisted of roast mutton with dry toast. After this, one small cigarette was allowed! The players and officials were then taken to the ground where the trainer took charge. After the game the players would return to the hotel before completing their expenses forms and having their heads measured for their England caps. They then returned home.

The FA liked to move England matches around the country so that as many supporters as possible could see the national side. The game was the second time that Stoke had been chosen to host an international match, the first being four years earlier when England beat Wales 4-1. England had won eleven out of the fourteen matches between the countries with two Welsh victories.

The people of Stoke had done their city proud and a 12,000 capacity crowd cheered the sides' emergence from the dressing rooms. With no wind there was no advantage to be gained when Bob Holmes won the toss. Butler kicked off seven minutes after the advertised time of 3.30pm.

Fred Spiksley had his first touch of the ball at 3.41pm and he did not hang around as he darted past the Welsh right back Dai Jones before sending a perfect cross into the path of Billy Bassett. To everyone's amazement,

Bassett spurned the chance. A minute later Spiksley and Schofield combined from a free kick and when the former pushed the ball across to John Goodall it was surely going to be 1-0. However, the Derby man inexplicably blazed wide.

Wales responded on fifteen minutes and Sutcliffe needed to make a fine save from Butler. A Goodall scorcher then sizzled just by and with the England forwards now combining superbly the Welsh side were unable to hang on. On thirty minutes, the England outside left picked up the ball and dribbled with pace past the Welsh defenders before hitting the ball round Trainer to make it 1-0. It was a fine individual goal combining speed, skill and composure. The England side now fed the scorer who did not disappoint as he notched his second with a blistering left-foot shot and England went in at half-time leading 2-0.

Wales were not going to go down without a fight, though, and Sutcliffe was forced to make three fine saves. Nevertheless, the game as a contest was over when, from a Spiksley through ball, Bassett banged home England's third. The two then combined superbly to set up Goodall for the fourth goal.

Goodall made fourteen appearances for his country and scored twelve times, including two marvellous efforts when England beat Scotland 4-1 in April 1892. This might not have pleased his Scottish father! Goodall combined great speed and clever footwork with a willingness to shoot from distance and his accuracy in front of goal made him one of the best marksmen the game of has ever seen. Goodall had finished as top scorer for Preston in the inaugural Football League season after which he quit the League and FA Cup winners, moving to Derby County and accepting the tenancy of a local pub.

England extended their lead when Bassett found Reynolds and as the final whistle loomed Schofield was unfortunate when Trainer made a diving save with his right hand. When the ball ran loose it was Fred Spiksley who was first to it and drove it home to make it 6-0 and complete his hat-trick.

Years later, Fred was to say of his England debut that it seemed he could do no wrong and he was playing as if in a dream. Everything he touched turned to gold and the Welsh defenders just could not contain him. If it had not been for Trainer the result would have been more comprehensive. Trainer was capped twenty times but fell on hard times when he retired and any football team who visited London, where he was experiencing the seamy side of life, used to expect him as a caller in search of some cash.

For many years the record of England's final goal against Wales has been incorrect. The reason for this is that *The Times* newspaper credited the sixth goal to Schofield. Several other papers, all of whom must have relied on a single source, reported that Spiksley and Schofield had broken through to score England's sixth goal. Schofield was seen as the latter player and this served to back up the *Times* match report.

Fred Spiksley laid claim to scoring a hat-trick on his England debut several times in writing, including his biographical pieces in 1907 and 1920. When a larger number of newspaper reports are examined it is clear that the Fred has been hard done by, with the vast majority of reports crediting him with scoring a hat-trick, including those listed below. Indeed, modern day statisticians and historians agree with the authors of this book that Spiksley did indeed score the hat-trick and records should be amended to recognise this, including the England Online database, which is the most authoritative voice on statistics for the England international team.

Manchester Courier, Lancashire General Advertiser and *York Herald*, 14 March 1893: "Trainer saved a grand attempt from Schofield, but Spiksley caught the leather on the rebound and scored an easy goal."

A Blue Cap

Wrexham Advertiser, 18 March 1893: "Trainer managed to save, but Spiksley quickly clinched matters by adding the sixth point."

Lincolnshire Echo, 27 March 1893: "Fred scored three against Wales and had a hand in a fourth."

For clubs of the 1890s the ultimate accolade was to win the FA Cup, but this was very much seen as a team effort. So for an individual player the biggest recognition was to be selected to play against Scotland, effectively meaning that you were considered the best in the country in your position. At the time, players received a red cap when selected to play against Wales, white against Ireland and blue against Scotland.

In the early hours of Sunday 26 March 1893 an anxious Fred Spiksley was lying awake fretting over whether he had been selected for the following Saturday's game in London between England and Scotland. The England selectors had convened after the previous day's FA Cup final between Everton and Wolves to select the England XI.

The signs were mixed, the Wednesday man had notched a hat-trick against Wales but had not been selected for the final trial match at Derby on 22 March. The selectors were expected to select eight professionals including Sheffield United's Ernest Needham. In the event a good FA Cup final display by amateur George Kinsey for Wolves saw him preferred to Needham.

In his autobiography, Fred Spiksley recalls overhearing a paperboy outside his Talbot Street window drumming up custom. He was up like a shot when he heard "Read all about it – Spiksley picked for England." He was down the stairs, out the door and running barefoot into the street to grab a paper. It was true, at aged 23 he was going to earn his first blue cap in six days' time. Neighbours poured into the street to congratulate the player as a lump came to his throat.

The selected team were as follows:-

Lewis Hewitt Gay, (Old Brightonians), Alban Hugh Harrison (Old Westminsters), Bob Holmes (Preston), John Reynolds (Aston Villa), John Holt (Everton), George Kinsey (Wolves), Billy Bassett (West Bromwich Albion), Robert Cunliffe Gosling (Old Etonians) John Goodall (Derby), Edgar Chadwick (Everton), Spiksley.

With the Scottish FA refusing to select Scots who played their football in England, their team were all home-based and also amateur as professionalism had yet to be accepted in Scotland.

Scotland:- John Lindsay (Renton), Walter Arnott, Bob Smellie (both Queen's Park), David Mitchell (Rangers), James Kelly (Celtic) (captain), William Maley (Celtic), William Sellar, Tom Waddell, James Hamilton I (all Queen's Park), Alex McMahon and Campbell (both Celtic).

The sixty-strong Scottish FA party that travelled to London did so in two groups. To relieve the boredom a storytelling competition was organised and Wattie Arnott won hands down with a selection of stories that would have made a publisher a fortune. With rumours that Nottingham football scouts were intending to shadow their star players – and make them offers they couldn't refuse to play permanently in England – the SFA officials kept a keen eye on the squad. As they travelled from Euston by wagonette to their hotel the advance party witnessed a spectacular blazing fire on Ludgate Hill close to St Paul's Cathedral.

Fred Spiksley came south on the afternoon of Thursday 30 March and met with the England team at the Third Avenue Hotel ahead of the game at the Richmond Athletic Ground. He was naturally excited. At the same time, knowing that he would miss two League games over Easter, he was also concerned about what might happen to Wednesday, struggling close to the bottom of Division One.

A Blue Cap

Like the Scots, he saw the flickering flames that lit up the cathedral dome.

By Friday morning only eight of the England side had arrived – Goodall, Gosling and Harrison were missing – for a light training session at Richmond. The temperature was the hottest on record for this time of year. Having donned dark grey suits the journey was naturally uncomfortable for the players. The exception was Leslie Gay, the England 'keeper, who by wearing white flannel slacks, a short-sleeved white linen shirt with an open collar, topped off with a fancy straw boater, was not only cool under the collar but well ahead in the fashion stakes. David Beckham would have been proud.

Richmond Athletic Ground was a hive of activity as workmen struggled to get it ready for the big match. A temporary stand was being constructed and a grand marquee being erected. The previous evening a message had been relayed from the Duke of Teck, Queen Victoria's cousin by marriage, saying that he would be attending the match with his family and friends. The Duke's butler was set to arrive at 2pm to approve the arrangements for his visit, including hamper deliveries from Fortnum and Mason. It would be the first time that royalty had attended an international football match.

The England players were informed they needed to finish training by 2.30pm so that the local fire brigade could water the bone-hard pitch. Fred was impressed with the playing surface. The ground was completely level and the turf was holding up well. Bob Holmes and Billy Bassett organised the training session that concentrated on high intensity cardio activity and a team exercise focusing on quick passing. A four-a-side game completed the team session before the players began working with colleagues from their section of the pitch. Full backs and half backs worked on throw-ins, goal and clearance kicks and long passing. Spiksley and Bassett practised meticulously together, hitting over crosses and corner kicks with the assistance of Edgar Chadwick and Leslie Gay.

Meanwhile, the Scots spent a leisurely day taking in the London sights with visits to Madame Tussaud's famous waxworks and Scotland Yard with an afternoon carriage to Hampton Court. Back at their hotel the England players did some light skipping exercises overlooking the River Thames after which games were played by all except Bassett. He was a practising Christian and it was Good Friday, so he read for the rest of the day. Football League founder, Aston Villa director William McGregor, was among the England party and he later reported how Kinsey, whom he described as "a rough diamond", looked round the hotel before saying, "Mac, if I brought my friends in here and told them I had dined here then what do you think they might say?" When the Villa man admitted he did not know, Kinsey told him "They would say I was a ******* liar."

Fred was up early on Easter Saturday and his newspaper brought bad news; Burnley 4 Wednesday 0. This may also have been the morning when Fred, who was still very much a junior international who had risen up from a working class Gainsborough terrace street, had the rest of the players laughing at him. Footballers are, of course, known for playing practical jokes on one another and they see it as part of team bonding.

It appears that on one of the mornings prior to the Scotland game in 1893 the team were driven though Hyde Park and when the Wednesday player saw gardeners bedding out young plants he asked what they were doing. One of his companions gave the rest a big wink before telling Fred that they really did take care of the flowers, so much so that they took in all of the geraniums every night and put them out fresh again the following morning. Fred was convinced and the rest of the players were delighted!

A Blue Cap

Following a light breakfast, the England team travelled to London Bridge station and on their arrival in Richmond pre-arranged carriages took them to the ground where they arrived at 11.00am. The sun was already beating down.

Half an hour later came bad news in the form of a telegram; John Goodall's slight knee strain had not recovered from injury and while the Derby man was on his way it was only in order to support the team. Charles Alcock was in a sweat. He was rescued by the coolest man from the previous day, Leslie Gay, who suggested the FA secretary should contact George Cotterill, his Old Brightonians colleague and England international. He was nowhere near as good as Goodall but he did live locally. Cotterill was also available and it just so happened he was on the phone, a service which at the time was controlled by the National Telephone Company until it was recognised that it was too important a communication system to be in private hands. Consequently, the Post Office was given control of all trunk lines in 1896. By 1900 there were 600,000 phones worldwide.

Cotterill had been capped for England in the international against Ireland. He was quickly summoned to appear.

The Scots greeted news of Goodall's absence enthusiastically as he had been the architect of their downfall in four out of five of the last internationals between the countries, scoring no fewer than five goals. He was the son of Scottish parents so the Scots could never accept Goodall was really English. They considered him a turncoat.

The Scottish side, chosen by seven selectors, were not without their critics in a nation that was now desperate to reassert its earlier supremacy over the Auld Enemy. Professionalism had seen England improve their playing standards and when Scotland were thrashed 5-0 in 1888 this first victory in nine years was achieved with seven professional players in the team. Since then England had won twice and drawn and lost once.

The Scots had triumphed 8-0 and 6-1 in their respective matches against Wales and Ireland in 1893. Two totally separate sides had been selected but the selectors chose the one that beat Ireland with the exception of the captain, John Adams of Hearts, replacing him with Queen's Park veteran,

Wattie Arnott. This was to be his tenth game against England and many Scots felt it was one game too many.

William Sellar had previously played six times against England and there were concerns that his record of just one victory would not be improved upon. James Hamilton was asked to lead the forward line but plenty of Scots were dismayed that Celtic's Jack Madden, Spiksley's former colleague at Gainsborough Trinity, had been overlooked, especially as he had scored four goals in the game against Wales. There was also the small matter that not one of Scotland's team had previously netted against their opponents! Scots consoled themselves with the fact that England's XI consisted of players from nine different clubs but in reality England had a nucleus of five experienced professionals in their ranks – Holmes, Reynolds, Holt, Bassett and Chadwick.

Goodall's absence was not the only concern faced by Alcock. Journalists who arrived were unimpressed by the facilities. Press accommodation consisted of an open-sided marquee on level ground several yards behind the perimeter rope. Telephone lines were not provided and there was no telegraph service.

The gates were not due to open until 1pm but with spectators starting to arrive at 10.00 the combination of the hot sun and the crush outside meant that at midday a decision was taken to open the gates and allow the crowd into the ground.

As more and more spectators arrived the demand for water grew and it became difficult to direct people into areas where they could see the match. Rather than send fans away disappointed, the ground authorities continued to allow people to enter and the area in front of the press accommodation was soon six rows deep, making it impossible for reporters to see the game. Some fans then began scaling trees to get a bird's eye view.

The ground capacity was 12,000 but up to 20,000 people were present, paying record receipts for an England international of £811.

The royal party and the Scotland team arrived just after 1pm (over two hours behind schedule) and found it difficult to gain entry. Two mounted policemen who cleared the crowd and escorted the carriage into the ground led the royal procession. It was unheard of in 1893 for royalty to extend their patronage to football so the attendance of the Duke and his wife Princess Mary Adelaide of Cambridge was seen as a sign of the growing importance of the game nationally. The Duchess was famous for her extravagant lifestyle and partying and was publicly known as 'Fat Mary' on account of her extremely wide girth. She was wearing a blue dress with matching hat and peacock feathers that delighted the Scottish supporters. FA president and Scot Lord Kinnaird and his predecessor, Major Sir Francis Marindin, who were intent on explaining the finer points of the game to the Duke and his guests, accompanied the Duke and Duchess.

Occupying the second carriage were the 24-year-old Princess Mary of Teck and the youngest of her three brothers, Prince Alexander. The princess wore a beautiful white dress and looked resplendent. She was better known as Princess May after the month of her birth. Sixteen months earlier she had been betrothed to Queen Victoria's grandson, Prince Albert, the Duke of Clarence who was second in line to the throne. However, tragedy struck six weeks later when Prince Albert caught pneumonia and died at Sandringham House in Norfolk. The appearance of royalty had encouraged the ladies to grace the grandstand seats and after halting at the royal enclosure, Charles Alcock offered his official greetings, the national anthem was played and the Union Jack and the Duke's standard were raised.

Both teams were presented to the royal party at 2.30pm, one hour before kick-off. Earlier the England team were all handed their white shirts complete with embroidered badge bearing the traditional three crowned lions worked in purple and red. After the game the players would return the shirts but would be allowed to retain the badge.

Princess May was fascinated by the size of Scotland captain Jimmy Kelly's boots and asked him about the prospects for the game. Generally regarded as someone who never enjoyed a fuss, the Scot was literally shaking in his boots but managed to predict a 2-1 victory for his country. Kelly confided in his fellow Scots that he now thought a lot more about his right hand after it had shaken hands with royalty.

Forty-five minutes before kick-off the teams, with England now captained by Cotterill rather than Goodall, had their photographs taken in a roped area behind the grandstand by Gunn and Stuart, a local firm of professional photographers. An injured Goodall was included in the photograph as was match referee Charles Clegg, who later called the two captains together in the pavilion for the toss that was won by the England skipper. Cotterill chose to defend the Thames River end of the ground, giving England the advantage of the sun behind them in the first period.

When their team emerged from the pavilion first, the Scottish supporters (who far outnumbered their English counterparts) burst into prolonged cheering when the skirl of the bagpipes broke out. The sight of millionaire Gosling performing his usual pre-match routine of making sure his limbs were relaxed by shaking himself down like a dog caused great hilarity among the crowd.

A Blue Cap

The bright sky and glorious sunshine were more suited to cricket than football. The game was set to be played on the maximum size pitch permitted under international rules – 130 yards long by 100 yards wide. With the field in immaculate condition the game was certain to be fast and there was no one quicker than the England outside left!

At precisely 3.30pm, Hamilton kicked the match off.

Great combination play on the England left saw Chadwick and Spiksley force Lindsay in the Scots goal to save in quick succession from Gosling and Chadwick. There were claims that the latter's shot had crossed the goal line but Charles Clegg waved away the protests. Hamilton then missed a good opportunity after Sandy McMahon and John Campbell combined.

The Scots fans urged the ball to be fed out to the celebrated Queen's Park right wing duo Tom Waddell and William Sellar. Johnny Holt, whom Fred described in his autobiography as only "a hop-o'-my-thumb five feet three inches", immediately set about scotching the tricks of the duo known as the 'Scottish spiders.' Intercepting the ball he knocked it back to Gay, who promptly picked it up and took five steps forward before hearing the referee's whistle. Picking up the ball from a back pass in 1893 was allowed but carrying it for more than two paces meant an indirect free kick for an offence committed just eight yards out. Fortunately, when Hamilton had the kick knocked to him he shot high over the crossbar.

On fifteen minutes, England took the lead when Chadwick drew Davie Mitchell before his pass found Spiksley, the England outside left then forcing Arnott to retreat before his perfectly weighted cross picked out Gosling who netted with a powerful header. The English fans' cheers were enthusiastic in the extreme. Lindsay did brilliantly to prevent the scorer doubling the advantage. Arnott's experience helped his fellow defenders retain a measure of control and the Scot then kept his side in the game by making a fine goal line clearance from a Bassett shot. The pace of the England forward line was simply too much for the Scots and but for some poor misses the match would have been over in the first half hour.

When England relaxed the Scots broke out of defence and stunned their opponents by equalising. McMahon and Campbell combined and when the ball was crossed into England's goalmouth, Gay was charged over by Sellar to allow Tom Waddell a free header to make it 1-1. Charging was allowed and Sellar had utilised the rules to Scotland's advantage. England were now on the back foot and Sellar hit a shot that smacked against the foot of the post. Hamilton shot narrowly wide and a Willie Maley shot dipped just over the bar as England held on to ensure the game remained level at the interval. The sides were cheered from the pitch and there was now the prospect of a really thrilling game in the second half.

Not everyone was in a good mood. Telegraphic arrangements had not been put in place and with insufficient telephones journalists couldn't send reports back to London or Glasgow during the game. The Scottish press were angry at being unable to send the half-time score to Ibrox.

In the first aid tent the St John Ambulance were doing a roaring "trade" as spectators collapsed from dehydration and sunstroke and were hauled away by overworked stretcher-bearers. Fortunately, Charles Alcock had arranged for water carts at the ground and the needy were soon back on their feet. However, no thought had been given to the provision of water for the press and they sweated pints in the 'press oven.'

When the game restarted, Scotland should have taken the lead but James Hamilton failed to shoot and when he tried to round Gay the 'keeper grabbed the ball. Jimmy Kelly was then unlucky with a dipping shot that ended on the top of the England net. On 55 minutes the away side struck their second after Sandy McMahon began a brilliant passing movement that was continued by Tom Waddell and finished with aplomb by William Sellar for his first goal in seven internationals against England. Scots fans danced deliriously including linesman Archibald Sliman, the SFA president.

Bassett was fuming. In 1889 he had scored both of England's first-half goals before Scotland struck three, including a last-minute effort, to win 3-2. Following the final whistle the winners had gloated so much that the West Brom winger, well known as a bad loser, vowed he would never again lose to what he considered were the arrogant Scots. He wasn't the only Englishman to get agitated at Scotland taking the lead in 1893. Sitting in the players' pavilion, Rupert Sandilands, a prominent England international, jumped up and after removing his jacket, collar and tie declared, "For heaven's sake get me some boots!"

England were dumfounded and Gay was forced to make several fine saves as the Scots sought to extend their lead. Holt, the experienced Holmes and the athletic Alban Harrison were, though, slowly developing an understanding and began to anticipate the Scottish forwards' intentions.

In midfield, John Reynolds, in later years known as "Baldy", started to rediscover his form. The Villa man, who at this stage of his career had started to show signs of his future baldness, was encouraged when he realised how heavily Willie Maley was breathing. Chadwick raised hopes of a comeback with a delightful crossfield ball to the unmarked Bassett, who left Maley struggling in his wake and as three defenders converged fed the ball through to Cotterill for a clear run on goal.

For the first time, Cotterill was able to show his athleticism and as Arnott and Kelly strained every sinew the England captain shrugged off their desperate tackles before sliding the ball beyond Lindsay to make it 2-2. For a brief second there was silence before an almighty roar

115

reverberated around Richmond Park. England had looked a beaten side, could they now win the game?

As the players regrouped for the kick-off, Fred Spiksley noticed a bare-footed young woman dressed in white emerge from the royal enclosure. She began running up and down the touchline and Fred recognised her as Princess Mary of Teck. She was clearly enjoying the game and, as Fred confided in his autobiography, he was, for one fleeting moment completely distracted by the sight of this beautiful princess and lost his concentration. In his defence, he probably wasn't the only one who had noticed her!

Driven on by Holmes, Holt, Reynolds, Chadwick and Bassett, England pressed. When Bassett collected the ball, Fred signalled with his left arm and in an instant the outside right sent over a brilliantly accurate 60-yard pass that Fred, leaving in his wake a struggling princess, met nine yards out. Instantly controlling the ball with his right and with Arnott, Smellie and Lindsay in front of him, the outside left hammered it with his left past all three to make it England 3 Scotland 2 on 78 minutes.

The execution was so brilliant that it looked like the whole task had been one single movement. The control of the ball, the changing of the feet, the speed of execution and the power of the shot were completed with such audacity and panache that all three defenders had no chance. None of them moved.

The Scots appealed vigorously for offside, but referee Charles Clegg, aware of Fred's lightning pace, had no doubt that it was a goal. After the game, the Scottish press continued to dispute England's third but, as Bassett pointed out, it was amazing that they had such a good view of the 'offside goal' when they complained throughout the match that they couldn't see. Bassett pointed out "Spiksley is the fastest man in football and has no need to wander offside as he can beat your boys in a foot race every time."

England were back in control and in Spiksley and Bassett they had players who were now unstoppable. On 80 minutes, Bassett hit another long ball out to the England left where Chadwick and Spiksley combined to send the latter towards goal with only Arnott to beat. An ageing Wattie knew he was out of his depth and at the risk of conceding a penalty he tried to hack down his opponent, who leaped over his flailing boot and then beat Smellie before making it 4-2. Arnott appealed that he had fouled the England man and argued it should be a penalty. It was a desperate appeal that the referee simply ignored.

With Scottish heads dropping, Bassett left Maley trailing yards behind and delivered a crossfield pass which was picked up by Cotterill. Running in at pace, Cotterill linked with Spiksley to beat the last line of the Scottish defence. Spiksley took aim from distance and Lindsay could only parry his shot out to Cotterill. Cotterill again set up Spiksley who from fifteen yards out volleyed home with his left foot to make it 5-2 on 84 minutes.

It was as spectacular a goal as you are likely to see and it completed Fred Spiksley's hat-trick, the first ever by an English player against Scotland.

The England winger also noticed Princess May waving a white handkerchief in appreciation of his achievement. The princess married Prince George of Wales in 1893 and became Queen Mary when her husband became King in 1910.

"And didn't the Duchess of Teck enjoy the game!" – William McGregor in 1902, quoted in *Sunderland Daily Echo* and *Shipping Gazette*.

Throughout the game the English had been upstaged by the Scottish singing that had been led by Mr Hay of Dumfries in the Scrimp Stand. The home crowd now called for the Scots to sing another song but this time there was no encore. At Ibrox Park the half time score was only just going up and was met with general satisfaction among

Glasgow football fans. When the result did finally arrive in the city many hours later there were many who thought it was an April Fools joke.

Home fans made a guard of honour for their heroes and there was great cheering and clapping. "Three cheers for Fred" was the shout and the crowd responded heartily. As the England player was lowered to the ground he noticed that McMahon had tears streaming down his face. The Scots captain had constantly urged those under his direction to keep the ball away from England's left wing during the game but that had proved impossible.

Lord Kinnaird was content to award each England player his blue cap as the police cordoned off the area to hold back the spectators keen to get a view of royalty and the players.

Fred was bombarded by a horde of Scottish reporters once he left the sanctuary of the pavilion. Much of the questioning was about the third England goal and whether he was offside.

The scorer explained how he had met the ball with three players in front of him and that as they were off balance he shot the ball through. "I suggest you speak to Mr Clegg. All I know is that I did my best for England and it is beyond all doubt that the Scottish team was licked by superior play."

The game was won and lost by the speed of the England wingmen and the stamina shown by their professional players in the heat. In contrast the Scottish backs and half backs had nothing left in their legs in the final quarter of the match with goals conceded in the 78, 80 and 84 minutes. England had run their opponents off their feet and for many years afterwards the shrewdest football experts proclaimed that the Richmond international was the fastest ever played.

England's victory gave them the Home International Championship title for 1893 with three victories and seventeen goals for, three against.

A Blue Cap

Fred Spiksley had scored a hat-trick in each of his first two internationals, becoming the first of only three players to do so. He was followed by Steve Bloomer in 1896 and Vivian Woodward in 1908. In recognition of him becoming the first England player to score a hat-trick against Scotland the FA presented him with a gold fob watch chain, detailed with a small metal plate that bore an inscription that credited the hat-trick. (Sadly a family burglary means there is no knowledge today of this chain's whereabouts but its existence was reported in the centenary issue of the *Gainsborough News* in May 1955.)

Only two other players have scored hat-tricks against Scotland – Dennis Wilshaw of Wolves in 1955 and Jimmy Greaves, then of Chelsea, in 1961. By scoring three times in six minutes, Fred Spiksley also became the scorer of England's fastest hat-trick, a feat beaten by Middlesbrough's George Camsell, (three in five minutes) in 1929, and Spurs' Willie Hall (three in four minutes) in 1938.

According to the official record books, Fred Spiksley scored two goals against Scotland in 1893. With one exception – which credited the goal to Holt – the contemporary match reports awarded England's fifth goal to Reynolds, who more than 120 years later is still credited with it.

We are not certain why this should be the case but we know that throughout the game the journalists complained that they could not see the action clearly. By the time the final goal was scored the game was impossible to see, particularly as it was scored some 80 yards away from where the press tent was positioned.

The following is a small selection by journalists on this issue.

"It was hardly possible to follow the game with any accuracy owing to the crowd".
Dundee Courier.

"The arrangements proved wretchedly inadequate, and the reporters saw even less of the game than at Fallowfield for the FA Cup Final last week".
Derby Daily Telegraph
(Note – for more on Fallowfield in 1893 see chapter 9)
"The reporters had to thank the FA for their inability to see the game properly.....Some hundreds of people were placed in front of and on a level with the press seats, the arrangements being a disgrace to the Association, and an insult to the press".
Aberdeen Journal.

Doubts about who did score England's last goal in 1893 began to emerge when high profile characters engaged in writing their own memoirs later in life. Firstly, Fred's exploits featured in two lengthy series of articles newspaper articles that he wrote. These appeared in 1907, when all of the England team that featured in 1893 were alive, and 1920. In both accounts he recalls how he scored three times against Scotland.

Sir Frederick Wall was the FA secretary from 1895 to 1934. He was present at the match against Scotland in 1893. In 1934, Wall's book, *Fifty Years in Football*, was published and it contains considerable coverage of the game and in it he states that Spiksley scored three.

Like Wall, J A H Catton had no special friendship with Spiksley. Catton wrote under the pen name of 'Tityrus,' and was a popular sports journalist who after starting out as an apprentice journalist to the *Preston Herald* in 1875 later became editor of *Athletic News*.

As stated by Paul Brown in his book *The Victorian Football Miscellany*, "Catton was famous for his impartiality."

In his book *Wickets and Goals*, published in 1926, Catton credits Spiksley with the last three goals, scored in the space of ten second-half minutes. He also describes the kind of player that Spiksley was.

There are also other eye witness accounts that include J A Brierley, who was a highly-respected sports journalist who worked for the *Lancashire Evening Post* from late 1898 through to the early 1940s.

There are also numerous newspaper articles, some of which were written on the centenary of Spiksley's birth in 1970, in which it is stated that Fred Spiksley scored three. These include one in the *Sunday Express* of 19 March 1933, which is headed "When Queen Mary ran up and down a football pitch" and describes what it contends was the "greatest international match ever".

There do not appear to be any articles that were written following the game in 1893 in which Reynolds or any eye witness states he scored against Scotland. As stated earlier, Reynolds became famously nicknamed 'Baldy' and during our research it was suggested that it was this that made it possible for journalists at the game to be sure that he did, in fact, score the last goal. However, the England team photograph that is included within this book shows that Reynolds was not bald by 1893.

Unfortunately, there is no-one at the FA we can turn to for an official review on the information that we have collected which can be viewed online at:– www.spiksley.com

Such was the level of the defeat that the Scottish FA called an emergency evening meeting to discuss how to respond, with many of those present pushing the case for the Scottish League to fully embrace professionalism. Consequently, in May 1893, the SFA agreed that Scottish clubs could pay players. Three years later it was agreed that Scottish players playing in England could play for their country and on 25 March 1896 five were chosen in the Scotland side who beat England 2-1 at Celtic Park.

Meanwhile the England party visited the Palace Theatre in Cambridge Circus to enjoy an evening of popular music hall entertainment.

Many were back in bed early, the pace of the game having taken its toll. Those who did manage to stay up enjoyed a few drinks in Reynolds's room where, according to McGregor, the Villa player showed the other players how to charge the brandies and sodas they were enjoying to the FA. McGregor commented later how such future bills became so large that the FA had eventually to concede and allow the players an allowance for expenses above the match fee.

On the Sunday morning, the Wednesday man was disappointed to hear that his club had been beaten in the penultimate game of the season and would now need to win their final match the following day to avoid the test match series. Thinking about that game, Fred joined his England colleagues on a pleasure trip to Kew Gardens before taking the train home for a do-or-die match in Sheffield that saw Wednesday beat Notts County 3-2 to ensure First Division survival.

CHAPTER 9

FALLING SHORT
Wednesday's FA Cup exploits
1894 & 1895

WEDNESDAY STRENGTHENED THEIR squad for the second season of League football. Inside forward Jock Smith had won a League championship medal with Sunderland in 1892 before moving to Liverpool. Jim Jamieson joined from Everton and proved an outstanding left half with great heading ability and a never-say-die attitude. Centre forward John Miller had been part of a fine Dumbarton side who won the Scottish League title in 1891–92. He arrived after a season with non-league Liverpool. He began stylishly but his form faded as the season progressed.

Jack Earp arrived, initially as an amateur, in late September 1893. He had previously played for the great amateur side Corinthians and his hometown club, Nottingham Forest. As one of the outstanding full backs of his generation he became a firm Olive Grove favourite as he slotted in at right back following Tom Brandon's departure. Totally reliant on his right foot, Earp was very fast, highly competitive and a leader of men. He was soon made captain of the team.

This was despite the fact that he usually kept himself to himself and, because he was an amateur, changed alone at the Arundel Hotel before a hansome cab (a two-wheeled horse-drawn vehicle) at the club's expense took him to the ground.

Earp forged a fine partnership with Ambrose 'Mick' Langley, whom Fred Spiksley had played alongside for Horncastle Town in 1883. After representing Grimsby, Langley, then playing for Middlesbrough Ironopolis, was spotted by Everton. The player signed to play for the Toffees. However, soon afterwards a letter arrived from Merseyside saying he was being granted a free transfer as, having watched him again, Everton believed a knee injury had left him too slow for their side.

This injury would trouble Langley throughout his career. But it helped him choose Wednesday over Aston Villa in 1893, with the former content to sign him without the necessity of a medical whereas the Birmingham club were insisting on one before confirming their contract offer. Langley's strength coupled with his tactical knowhow, tackling, heading ability and long clearance kicks made him the perfect defender. Wednesday's calculated gamble paid off handsomely. Langley finally left Sheffield to sign for Hull City as player-manager in 1905.

In addition to the new signings, the 1893–94 season was to see regular reserve winger Johnny Webster make his Football League debut against Newton Heath and go on to play his best football.

Wednesday began the season impressively; recovering from a 2-1 half-time deficit to draw with champions Sunderland after Miller netted his second goal. Wolves had lost their opening game at Nottingham Forest 7-1 but recovered to beat Wednesday 3-1 at home and then the losers were heavily beaten at Blackburn Rovers 5-1. These defeats marked the end of the Wednesday players taking their food to away games and the club began providing them with a round of sandwiches and a bottle of ginger beer for the train journey.

A further uplift in catering arrived in 1896 when Wednesday won the FA Cup and the players were served with cold ham and chicken. After Fred and Langley had left, Wednesday began paying the railway company to serve the players with hot lunches. Langley complained the club had deliberately waited until he had departed to start this practice!

If the catering in 1893 had improved for Wednesday's players what had not was the kit provision. Each player had to clean his shirt and knickers. Fred Spiksley was lucky as his mother always did his, although he always insisted he did the ironing. In addition they had to buy their own boots, stockings and shin guards. It explains why in the Olive Grove era the Wednesday players wore multi-coloured stockings.

Wednesday's poor start to the season continued with a home defeat by Newton Heath, a draw at Sunderland and a 4-2 loss at West Bromwich Albion, where Spiksley opened his scoring account for the League's bottom-placed club.

Fortunately Wednesday's form picked up over the following weeks with victory at home to Blackburn Rovers and a 4-0 thrashing of Derby County in which Brady netted a hat-trick. There was also a first Football League derby match against Sheffield United, promoted at the end of the previous season, that ended 1-1. Spiksley scored the Wednesday equaliser in front of a highly enthusiastic crowd of 27,000 packed inside Bramall Lane. The attendance was even more remarkable considering local miners were in the sixteenth week of a national strike over a living wage.

The game was so rough that the referee Mr Fitzroy Norris halted proceedings before half-time and spoke to the teams. With the injured Davis unable to play after the interval the away side struggled but would have won the game if Fred, escaping the clutches of a tight-marking Rab

Flying over an Olive Grove

'Gypsy' Howell, had not snatched at a late chance when left with only Hewlett to beat. During Fred's career, Howell was arguably his most difficult opponent and United's outstanding record against their near neighbours in the late Victorian era – they lost just once between 1893 and 1900 – can partly be credited to this.

Fred said of Howell: "He followed me like a shadow and stuck closer to me than a brother. The crowd would shout 'Keep yer 'ands out of 'is pocket, Rab' at which he would just grin and move closer to me. If I ever looked like I might outwit him the bounder would grab either my shirt or my shorts and pull me back. If he could not reach me he would scythe me down."

United had started their first season in League One in great form and on 13 November they beat their near neighbours 2-1 at Olive Grove.

There was no Christmas cheer for the Wednesday fans who travelled to Goodison Park. The game started well as on five minutes "Spiksley went down in one of his speedy runs and eluding Parry and also beating Williams, scored easily." (*The Liverpool Mercury*)

The lead lasted just seconds as Southworth, signed from Blackburn Rovers in the summer, equalised and then put his side ahead soon afterwards. The striker notched his third before the interval at which point Everton led 4-1. His fourth was a goal of sheer brilliance as he ran rings round the Wednesday defence before he netted. The home side then ran away with the game to win 8-1, condemning Wednesday to what was, at the time, their record League defeat. After drawing at Bolton on Christmas Day, Wednesday dropped into the test match zone with a Boxing Day home defeat by Burnley.

Wednesday faced league leaders Aston Villa on 6 January 1894 and they raced into a two-goal lead after Fred Spiksley netted from a return pass from Johnny Webster and then scored with a bullet header. These efforts took

126

the outside left's goals for the season to ten, almost 30 per cent of Wednesday's total of 36. Jack Reynolds reduced the arrears before England international Dennis Hodgetts equalised with a close-range finish as the game ended 2-2.

Concerned that they were going to finish in the bottom three, the Wednesday club president John Holmes convened a special meeting to discuss the precarious situation. The outcome was that the players were offered £50 to share if they could win five out of their last six games to ensure they finished outside the test match zone.

The following game was at Clayton against bottom-placed Newton Heath on a very heavy pitch against opponents not afraid to employ some rough house tactics, especially against the Wednesday outside left who in the circumstances did well to avoid serious injury. It was Earp, though, who was man of the match for the away side who won 2-1 with Woolhouse netting twice. With it having rained during the week the Wednesday players were also able to enjoy a bath after the game as Newton Heath were reliant for a water supply on collecting water that ran off the pavilion roof into butts.

Two days later, in a game that had been abandoned at 2-0 on 58 minutes in December, Wednesday beat Darwen 5-0 at Olive Grove. The 1893-94 season witnessed three Wednesday matches abandoned with the Stoke home game called off due to heavy snow on 18 November when Wednesday were leading 3-1 and the match at Darwen abandoned due to mud with the home side leading 1-0 after fifteen minutes. Darwen won the subsequent match 2-1.

The two recent victories meant Wednesday entered the 1893-94 FA Cup in fine heart and for Fred Spiksley there was the chance to return to Royal Arsenal whose side now contained two of his great friends – Charlie Booth and Arthur Elliott.

A long, tiring journey to Plumstead was made by the players and 200 Wednesday fans whose arrival at the

Manor Ground was greeted with great cheers by the 12,000 home fans. Early in the game, as Arsenal pressed, Fred Spiksley prevented a goal when he inadvertently fell on the ball just inches from the goal: he was kicked black and blue as the home attackers attempted to wrestle the ball into the goal. Amazingly the ball squirted wide and when the Wednesday winger emerged from the floor he was covered in mud from head to foot. It was almost impossible to recognise him but soon afterwards he opened the scoring when full back Joe Powell, misjudged a cross and he nipped in to net. Sharpshooter Archie Elliott equalised for the home side but the tie was settled when Spiksley showed pace and poise to put his team into the next round. The Wednesday scorer was again cheered as he left the field at Plumstead.

Before the next cup-tie against Stoke, Wednesday beat fellow strugglers Preston North End 3-0 at Olive Grove with Spiksley, Earp and Brandon all scoring from free kicks, Brandon's a bullet from the halfway line. All the goals came in the second half as in the first a nervous Fred, mocked by Jimmy Ross as he shaped to shoot, had flashed a penalty several feet over the crossbar and was berated by the Preston man afterwards. During the interval Mr Holmes visited the home dressing room and it was agreed that Fred would not take a penalty again for Wednesday. He did in fact take two, scoring once and also missing a vital last-minute effort against Blackburn in 1899.

Wednesday maintained their good form by beating Stoke 1-0 in the Cup. Woolhouse put his side ahead before Spiksley curled a corner kick up and over all the defenders and England 'keeper Bill Rowley and into the far corner of the net. It was a remarkable effort but not one that counted as until 1927 all corner kicks were indirect.

The draw pitched Wednesday at home to League leaders Aston Villa, who were hoping to emulate Preston's feat of 1888-89 by becoming the second club to win League and

Gainsborough Trinity in 1887.
Back Row: Sharman, Vamplew, Fergus, Brown, Jubb, Howlett, Curtiss.
Front Row: Smith, Chambers, Madden, Spiksley, Robinson.

Reverend George Hodgkinson. Founder of Trinity Recreationalists in 1873.

John Madden in Gainsborough Trinity strip: a major influence over a young Fred Spiksley.

The Crown and Anchor public house on Bridge Street, Gainsborough. Fred Spiksley's home from the age of eight until he left to play for Sheffield Wednesday.

Charlie Booth. Spiksley's coaching partner and sprint trainer. Booth would become Arsenal's first club captain in the Football League.

Workers leaving Marshall's Works in Gainsborough circa 1900.

Aerial photograph of Gainsborough from the 1960s, which illustrates how Marshall's Works dominated the small Lincolnshire town. The Northolme ground is pictured towards the top of the image.

Gainsborough Trinity pictured in 1889 on the Northolme. Spiksley stands in full length knickerbocker trousers on the far right of the team.

A Baines card depicting The Wednesday's Teddy Brayshaw who broke Fred Spiksley's leg on his 19th birthday. Baines cards were first produced in 1887 and were an early indicator of the commercial potential of football.

Gainsborough Trinity favourites; Top: Charlie Jubb, Middle: Billy Brown and Bottom: George Vamplew.

A frozen River Trent at Gainsborough in the 1890's, where Fred Spiksley would take part in speed skating competitions.

The Wednesday Football Club, pictured during Fred Spiksley's first season with the club in 1891–92. Back Row: T. Brandon, Smith (Wearing a cap to indicate he was the keeper), Darroch. Middle Row: H. Brandon, Mumford, Thompson, Cawley, Spiksley. Front Row: Gemmell, Betts, Richardson.

All players, with the exception of the player taking the penalty kick and the opponents' goalkeeper, shall be outside the penalty area. The opponents' goalkeeper shall not advance beyond his goal-line.

A rare cigarette card, produced during Wednesday's time at Olive Grove.

Wednesday v. West Bromwich Albion

Played at Olive Grove Ground, January 2nd, 1893.

Sheffield		Wednesday
Right Wing		Left Wing
	Goal:	
	W. Allan	
	Backs:	
T. Brandon		J. Brown or Mumford
	Half-Backs	
H. Brandon	W. Betts	B. Chalmers
	Forwards:	
Davies	R. N. Brown	Brady Spiksley
	A. Rowan	

SCORE

CORNERS	GOALS	CORNERS	GOALS

Referee—Mr. F. T. Norris

Forwards

Geddes	Pearson		McLeod	Bassett
		Fellows		
		Half-Backs:		
Groves		G. Perry	T. Perry	
		Backs:		
McCulloch			Horton	
		Goal:		
		Reader		

Left Wing		Right Wing
West Bromwich		Albion

An 1893 match card containing the famous left wing combination of Brady and Spiksley. Both were on the score sheet as Wednesday won this match 6-0, in front of a crowd of 15,500. Olive Grove match cards were sold for 1d (1/2p) by Billy Whitham, a great character from the days before Hillsborough days.

CRAWSHAW BEATS ALSOPP WITH A BEAUTY.

MR. WEST SENDS F. J. FORMAN BACK FOR THE BA

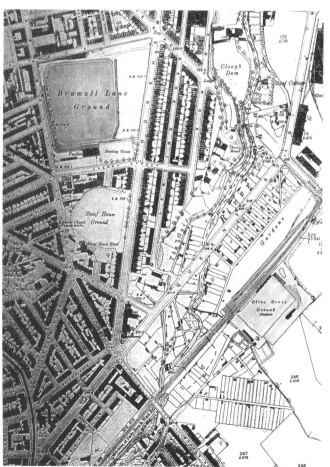

Above: An illustration of the northern aspect of the Olive Grove ground which shows how close trains would pass the ground. The drawing shows Tommy Crawshaw opening the scoring in a 3-0 victory over Nottingham Forest in 1895.

Left: A map from the early 1890s showing the location of Olive Grove football ground and its close proximity to Sheffield United's Bramall Lane and the Sheaf House Ground, which was another prominent location where football matches took place in Sheffield.

Olive Grove. Taken from distance, the grandstand is painted with the name Sheffield Wednesday, even though the club were actually 'The Wednesday'. The stand at the Sheffield end of the ground is visible just above the railway wagons in the centre of the image.

A funeral card made by the supporters of Sheffield United in the 1890s to celebrate a victory over The Wednesday, such as the 5-0 victory at Olive Grove 26 October 1891.

Tom Cawley, one of the men who forced The Wednesday Football Club to turn professional in 1887. It is possible that Wednesday would not have survived without his actions.

"SHEFFIELD WEDNESDAY" FOOTBALL CLUB,

14, COMMERCIAL STREET,...... 18

Ground:—OLIVE GROVE.   Dressing Room:—"EARL OF ARUNDEL AND SURREY," Queen's Road.

DEAR SIR,

You are selected to play at.. *Worksop*

versus ...... *Worksop Town* .

on...... *Saturday* ......Train leaves.. *Victoria*

Station at...... *1.5* ......Kick-off......

Have got your photo If unable to play please reply by return.

Thanks for your card There was no H. E. PEARSON, HON. SEC.
match. Was it Attercliffe or Carbrook C.? ~~H. E. PEARSON~~

A Wednesday team selection card. This is how players were informed of their selection in the Olive Grove era. Fred Spiksley was not happy when he did not receive one for his expected debut against Sunderland Albion in 1891.

Two goalkeepers who played in Lincolnshire. Jack Robinson (left) was to play for Lincoln City early on in a career which gained him the title; Prince of Goalkeepers. Famous for being the first to make diving saves, he was the best goalkeeper of the era by some distance. Charlie Howlett, (right) the spectacle wearing Gainsborough Trinity livewire who later went on to play for Sheffield United.

Fred Spiksley is pictured in 1894 in a Jasper Redfern magic lantern slide wearing his England strip and Blue Cap, which was awarded for playing in the Scotland international that year.

*An illustration of one of Spiksley's three goals against Scotland
at Richmond on 1 April 1893*

*The England side that defeated Scotland 5-2 at Richmond in 1893.
Back Row: Gosling, Holt, Kinsey, Holmes. Middle Row: Bassett, Reynolds, Cotterill
(captain), Gay ('keeper), Harrison. Front Row: Spiksley, Chadwick.*

Top left: Fred Spiksley c.1894

Top right: Princess Mary of Teck, who so admired Fred Spiksley during the 1893 Scotland international that she ran up and down the touchline waving her handkerchief. She became Queen Mary in 1910.

Left: Thomas Crawshaw of England and The Wednesday. Arguably the finest centre-half in the World during the 1890s. He is the only player have won the FA Cup twice for Sheffield Wednesday and captained them during the 1907 final. He was fast and superb at heading the ball.

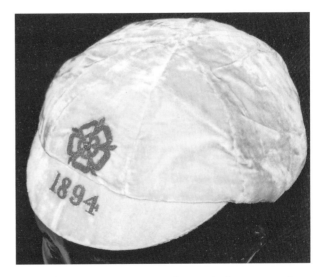

Above Left: Gilbert Oswald Smith, the famous amateur centre forward who went on to captain England 13 times. Above Right: Spiksley's England cap from the 1894 Ireland international, played on Cliftonville's Solitude Ground.

The Scottish crowd celebrate one of Scotland's two goals against England in 1894. This illustration also documents the huge masts used during experimental floodlit fixtures at Celtic Park, which along with the electric cabling became known as 'Madden's Rigging'; a nod to John Madden's career in the shipbuilding industry.

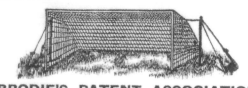

49 BLOOMER. DERBY COUNTY.

Above left: A newspaper advert for John Alexander Brodie's goal nets, which he invented in 1889 but were not in use for the Ireland vs England match of 1894, resulting in great controversy. Goal nets are still not a compulsory element of the game.

Right: Steve Bloomer, England and Derby County goal machine and good friend of Fred Spiksley. Bloomer scored 28 goals for England in 23 appearances.

The England side that rescued a draw against Scotland in 1894.
Standing: Ernest Needham, Fred Spiksley, Gilbert Smith. Seated: Thomas Clare, John Reynolds, William Bassett, John Goodall (captain), John Holt, Fred Pelly, Leslie Gay ('keeper). Front: Edgar Chadwick.

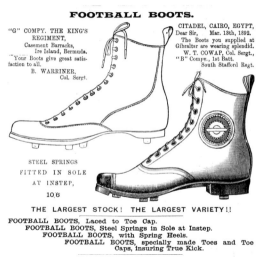

Above right: Close up of Fred Spiksley's boots. Despite the restrictions that these boots created, Fred Spiksley was a master of ball control and had no equal at bending and curving the ball into the opposition's goalmouth, famously always using the outside of either foot. bove left: Newspaper advert for the style of boot worn by Spiksley and his contemporaries.

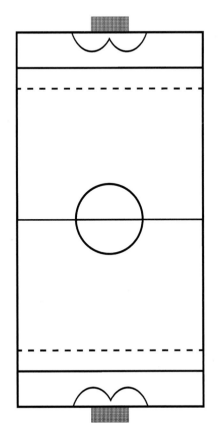

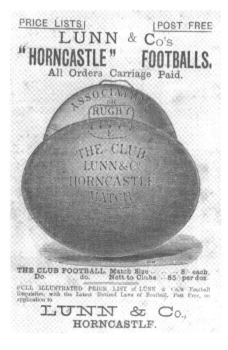

Left: Football pitch markings from the 1891-1902. These included a 12 yard and a 15 yard line, as well as the distinctive double semi-circle goal area. Penalties could be conceded anywhere within the 12 yard area.
Above: Advert for Horncastle footballs; the ball Fred Spiksley's father gave him as a present.

THE ENGLISH CUP.

REPLAYED SEMI-FINAL TIE.

BOLTON WANDERERS BADLY BEATEN.

A GLORIOUS VICTORY FOR SHEFFIELD.

WILL WEDNESDAY WIN THE CUP?

PATON STICKS TO SPIKSLEY LIKE A BROTHER.

BRASH PASSES TO SPIKSLEY WHO SCORES
WEDNESDAY'S THIRD GOAL.

Spiksley seals victory against Bolton Wanderers in the 1896 FA Cup replay at Nottingham Forest's Town Ground.

Kick-off at the 1896 FA Cup final at the Crystal Palace in front of a record crowd of 48,836.

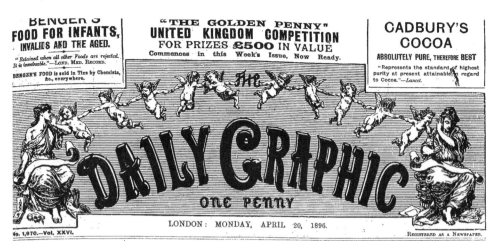

The DAILY GRAPHIC
ONE PENNY

No. 1,970.—Vol. XXVI.

LONDON: MONDAY, APRIL 20, 1896.

REGISTERED AS A NEWSPAPER.

The Weather.

"FAIR, DRY." (See page 3.)

THE MATABELE RISING.

GENERAL CARRINGTON ORDERED TO THE CAPE.

FIGHTING AT BULUWAYO.

ALARMING TACTICS OF THE ENEMY.

REBELS CLOSING ROUND THE TOWN.

PREPARATIONS FOR A DESPERATE RESISTANCE.

MEAT RUNNING SHORT.

(THROUGH REUTER'S AGENCY.)
GIBRALTAR, Saturday.—Major-General Sir Frederick Carrington, commanding the infantry brigade here, has received telegraphic instructions to proceed immediately to the Cape.

Captain Vyvyan, brigade major, and Lieutenant Ferguson, aide-de-camp to Sir Frederick, have also been ordered to accompany him as staff-officer and aide-de-camp respectively.

With reference to the above telegram, Reuter's Agency learns on good authority that Sir Frederick Carrington, who has great experience in South African warfare, will command the forces in Matabeleland.

(REUTER'S SPECIAL SERVICE.)
CAPE TOWN, Saturday. — Official despatches of yesterday's date from Buluwayo state that telegraphic communication has been established with Figtree Fort at the northern end of the Mangwe Pass.

The rebels continue to increase in numbers, and are passing in closer proximity round the town. On the north and east they form a semi-circle about three

(Continued on page 3.)

1. First goal to Sheffield.   2. A free kick.   3. A double header.   4. A scrum mage.   5. Throwing the ball in.

THE FINAL FOR THE ENGLISH CUP: SATURDAY'S FOOTBALL MATCH AT THE CRYSTAL PALACE. (See Page 5.)

257

Cup in the same season. One thousand Villa fans travelled to Sheffield and were buoyed by their team having beaten Sunderland away in the previous round, a result that confirmed Villa's status as England's top club. The away side were favourites to progress but Wednesday fans were optimistic and there was a tremendous atmosphere among the 22,100 crowd inside Olive Grove.

Woolhouse opened the scoring and celebrating home fans sent hats, caps, scarves, and handkerchiefs high into the air. The game then settled down with the Villa half back line of Jack Reynolds, James Cowan, known as the 'Prince of half backs', and Bill Groves dominating possession.

In return, the Wednesday side fed the ball to Fred Spiksley and after two dashing runs and near misses, John Devey, the Villa captain, detailed both John Baird and Reynolds to mark him. With seconds of the first period remaining Bob Chatt made it 1-1.

Playing with the breeze, Villa were dominant and on 73 minutes Chatt drove his side ahead after which the Villa faithful sang out, "We've won to-dye – we've won to-dye." A Birmingham journalist in the press box predicted 3-1. Arthur Dickinson must have been feeling sick at the sight of Chatt scoring two goals against Wednesday at Olive Grove, for he had secured the signature of the promising Middlesbrough Ironopolis forward in a double deal alongside Ambrose Langley in the summer of 1893. However, this triggered an unusual chain of events which resulted in Chatt becoming a Villa player for the following season. It was best summed up in the *Athletic News* on 10 April 1893;

"Although the Wednesday club were perfectly within their rights under the rules of the Football Association in signing Chatt, of Ironopolis, they did not deem it advisable to fight against the decision of the emergency committee of the League, which declared Chatt Aston Villa's player, and so they transferred him to the big Birmingham club.

Wednesday were fined £25 by the League, but the Villa have paid this fee and I don't suppose that the Wednesday folks are more than a £5 note out of pocket by the whole transaction – but they didn't get Chatt, and they do say that Chatt is disappointed."

The whole event seemed quite bizarre, but appears to show how the heavyweights of Villa used their powers of influence to get their man, with the founder of the Football League, William McGregor, being Aston Villa's club president.

In the 1894 FA Cup-tie Chatt would go on to miss horribly with only seven minutes to go, leaving Wednesday still in the game. However, there was less than 120 seconds remaining as Spiksley collected the ball. The Wednesday fans stirred, remembered Fred's last minute winner against Derby County in 1893, crossed their fingers and looked on transfixed.

With most journalists having sent off their telegrams advertising the final score to the 'sports specials', the winger tricked his way round his two markers before leaving Cowan and Groves in his wake. A great roar went up as Villa's players realised they were now under serious threat.

As Bill Dunning, Villa's six foot two inches tall 'keeper, advanced the Wednesday forward sent the ball with just the right amount of pace round him and into the back of the net. It was 2-2 and absolute pandemonium among the relieved home fans, including those who halted their trek home by rushing back inside the ground to watch the 30 minutes of extra time that followed.

Amid an intense atmosphere the game remained at 2-2 on 115 minutes when Spiksley did it again. In an almost exact repeat of his first goal, he beat his markers and defenders before this time pushing the ball into the path of the unmarked Woolhouse who, with every watching Wednesday fan's heart beating strongly, drove home his second goal of the match for the winner.

Technically, Villa still had a chance of an equaliser but Langley was taking no chances and on the restart he promptly kicked the ball into the nearby allotments. When another ball was put into play he belted it on to the railway line. He kicked the next one even further and in an era when referees did not add on time for interruptions the away side had no time to force an equaliser.

Fred Spiksley had hauled his side back from the dead. And unlike in 1893, when his goal against Derby County had afterwards been wiped from the record books, this time there was no preventing Wednesday going through to the next round.

The Villa game thus became known for years afterwards as 'Spiksley's match'. It was recalled as such when the *Sheffield Evening Telegraph* ran an article on 6 March 1914 on the history of Wednesday-Villa games and Fred's exploits reinforced his growing reputation as both a big match player and winner. An excited crowd hung around for a long time after the final whistle so unexpected was Wednesday's success.

Before the semi-final, Wednesday boosted their League chances when a Davis goal was sufficient to beat Nottingham Forest 1-0. Being a working day, the crowd inside Olive Grove was just 3,500. One victory from the final two League matches would ensure Wednesday would achieve the 'great escape'.

On 10 March 1894, thousands of Wednesday fans packed out Midland Line Station (MLS) excursion trains to Fallowfield Station in Manchester. Trains to Manchester were among the first to run from Sheffield with the first ever departing from Bridgehouses on 14 July 1845, although the Woodhead Tunnel number 1 was not opened until December 1845. At three miles it was one of the longest in the world at this time. Woodhead 2 was completed in 1853 and Woodhead 3 exactly a century later. The tunnels are now defunct.

Flying over an Olive Grove

The suburban village of Fallowfield was besieged as supporters tramped down the cobbled streets to what was now one of the country's finest football grounds.

Eleven months earlier the Manchester Athletic Ground in Fallowfield had staged the 1893 FA Cup final between Wolves and Everton. There were 45,000 spectators in the ground and thankfully thousands were refused entry since the crush inside was horrendous. It was a miracle no-one was killed amid the ensuing chaos especially as there were insufficient policemen and marshals on duty to deal with any disaster. There were lots of injured people and a considerable amount of fighting but no fatalities. Following the game, J J Bentley, the Football League president, personally oversaw much-needed ground improvements.

The Wednesday players and officials arrived at the ground in two horse-drawn decorated wagonettes. On the way, a black cat had run in front of the leading pair of horses. Was this a good luck sign?

Blaring trumpets announced the teams' arrival. The Bolton XI were clearly bigger and stronger and, kicking with the sun behind them, employed both full backs, John Somerville and Dai Jones, to hit high balls that their bulky, heavier forwards could chase down.

Wednesday hung on. Then on twenty minutes Harry Brandon took possession, advanced and hit a lovely ball beyond the Bolton backs. As 'keeper Willie Sutcliffe moved to collect, Fred Spiksley beat him to the ball and headed into the empty net. Sutcliffe hated losing and the keeper constantly challenged referees' decisions. He rushed over to referee Mr Armitt and vociferously argued that his England colleague was offside.

Fred Spiksley knew there had been five defenders between him and the goal when ball had been released by Brandon. "It was one of the best goals of my life. The ball travelled diagonally over 20 yards and running at top speed I met the ball perfectly with my forehead and headed it like a bullet into the back of the net." Throughout his career Fred used his pace and anticipation to judge a cross to score many goals with his head but this time his effort was disallowed for offside without the referee even consulting his linesman. Further salt was rubbed into Fred's wounds when two minutes later a second effort from him was also disallowed for offside.

Bolton then took the lead through a dubious hand ball decision against Jamieson. When Bob Tannahill knocked the free kick to Handel Bentley the Bolton player's miskick confused Allan in the Wednesday goal to put his side ahead. Towards the interval a scything tackle on Fred Spiksley by Alex Paton prevented a possible equaliser.

Bolton's luck appeared to be in when the second half started. In the first half Wednesday had faced a strong wind and the sun but now the wind dropped and the sun went in. The Lancashire side were then gifted a second goal after Allan's attempt to fist away Bentley's shot resulted in the ball rebounding from the crossbar and entering the net off the back of the 'keeper's head.

Bolton 2-0 up, were taking no chances as Archie Hughes committed an ugly foul on Fred Spiksley. The worst was to come when Jimmy Cassidy committed a flying rugby tackle on Langley and escaped censure. Then Spiksley created a great scoring opportunity but was wrongly penalised for offside. Jones, Paton and Somerville all hauled him down over the next few minutes before Paton dragged over Woolhouse amid strong penalty claims.

Finally, Wednesday got their reward when Woolhouse brilliantly netted following a speculative long ball from Earp. The search was now on for an equaliser. Brady's ball sent Spiksley through but he was felled from behind by a dangerous two-footed Somerville challenge that was so bad that for the only time in the game Mr Armitt rebuked a Bolton player. When the final whistle sounded, Bolton had won 2-1 and advanced to play Second Division Notts

County in the final where they were outplayed and lost 4-1.

Wednesday left the field devastated and convinced they had been robbed. Writing years later, Fred Spiksley was quite forthright in saying he blamed the referee for Wednesday's misfortune as he had no doubt both of his first-half efforts were goals. He was convinced that Mr Armitt had his back turned when the ball from Brandon was hit towards him and the referee was wrongly persuaded by Willie Sutcliffe to disallow his effort, as he was well onside.

Having suffered FA Cup disappointment, Wednesday held their nerve in the following League game when a first-half goal by Fred Spiksley helped overcome Burnley 1-0 at home. It meant that when the season ended Wednesday had finished in twelfth place in the League that was won by Aston Villa with Preston, Darwen and Newton Heath in the bottom three test match zone. The great escape had been achieved and the Wednesday players were rewarded with a £50 bonus between them. There was disappointment, however, when a 40-yard shot by Jack Drummond, described by Fred as the hardest he saw during his career, meant Sheffield United beat Wednesday in the Wharncliffe Cup final.

In the League and FA Cup, Wednesday played 34 matches during the 1893-94 season. They netted 56 goals and conceded 62. With thirteen League goals and three in the Cup, Fred Spiksley, who missed just one match, was the club's top scorer with Miller second with eight.

Wednesday's most important addition for the 1894/95 season was a local lad who began playing for local teams, the most prominent being the Attercliffe Reds After a brief period with Heywood Central in the Manchester League he became a professional at Olive Grove. Tom Crawshaw was a player of such great ability that it seemed certain he would play for his country in double quick time, and so it proved. Tom was a Wednesday star from the start and was to perform with distinction for fourteen seasons during which time he collected two FA Cup and Division One winner's medals as well as captaining his side to the Second Division title. Crawshaw's arrival meant no first-team place for Betts and the centre half retired at the season's end. Crawshaw was rated by Fred Spiksley as the best centre half and finest header of a ball ever. According to Langley, only the Notts County centre-back Walter Bull was anywhere near as good as Crawshaw in the air.

Wednesday also signed three Scots in the summer of 1894. Winger Archie Brash was speedy and tricky and subsequently played a major role in helping Wednesday win the 1896 FA Cup. Inside forward Bob 'Rabbie' Ferrier arrived from Dumbarton and quickly formed an effective right side attacking partnership with Brash. Ferrier was clever with the ball, could shoot powerfully and worked tirelessly. He later became a fine full back. His son and grandson, both also called Bob, enjoyed successful sports careers with the former making a record 626 Motherwell appearances and the latter being a noted sportswriter.

All four new signings featured in the opening game of the season at Everton which was lost 3-1. The game's first goal was scored by one of Spiksley's England colleagues from the 1893 Richmond international, Edgar Chadwick, one of the greatest players of his generation and a master strategist and dribbler. He played seven times for England.

Wednesday then beat Preston 3-1 and Blackburn Rovers 4-1 at home. A couple of 2-1 victories, away to Derby County and at home to Bolton Wanderers, when Spiksley opened his season's account, put Wednesday in third place. Three defeats in four, including a 3-2 home loss against Sheffield United, stilled any hopes of a title challenge before five victories and just one defeat in eight established Wednesday in a comfortable League position.

On New Year's Day 1895, Wednesday, with Crawshaw and Spiksley in 'fine form' (*Birmingham Daily Post*) beat

Everton 3-0 on a frosty pitch. Four days later, Liverpool were beaten 5-0 at home with Fred Spiksley scoring two to take his goals total to a rather meagre five for the season.

Wednesday remained fifth but a single point from three away games saw them drop one place in the run-up to the FA Cup-tie with holders Notts County at Olive Grove. A crowd of 12,000 assembled for the big game.

The FA Cup was the invention of Charles Alcock when on 20 July 1871 he proposed in his role as FA secretary "a competition for the prize of a silver challenge cup and the prestige of becoming the best football team in England".

Sitting in a small, oak-panelled room in the offices of the *Sportsman* newspaper just off Ludgate Hill in London, Alcock's fellow FA committee members realised the brilliance and simplicity of the proposal, which Alcock had taken from the annual football tournament at Harrow Public School where he had been a pupil. The knockout element would add extra excitement to matches and the prize would give clubs an incentive to join the FA and play in the competition. It would ensure the Association's position as the game's guardian. The proposal was voted upon, passed and recorded in the FA minute book. The first national football tournament, the best known in the world for many years afterwards, was born.

Silversmiths Martin Hall designed a silver cup to be presented to the annual winners. It was heavily embossed, eighteen inches high with a capacity of four pints and mounted on an ebony plinth. Two handles curved from its sides and on the top was the figure of a footballer. The engraving on the cup's body read: "The Football Association Challenge Cup." It may have been a humble trophy costing just £20 but it was to become a national treasure known throughout the nation as 'The Little Tin Idol' but generally referred to everywhere as the 'English Cup'.

The original concept was that, after the inaugural season, the holders would not be required to play until the final. Each year there would be a knockout tournament to decide who challenged the holders for the cup – hence the title 'Challenge Cup'. This happened in the second season when Wanderers retained the trophy but the challenge element was then dropped. All subsequent competitions which use the word "challenge" in the title do not realise they have got it wrong!

The first game in the tournament, which attracted fifteen clubs in its first season, took place on 11 November 1871 and saw Barnes beat the Civil Service, who only managed to raise eight players, 2-0. Wanderers won the 1872 FA Cup.

The first northern side to take the trophy were Blackburn Olympic in 1883. Then as professionalism seeped into the game, Blackburn Rovers completed a hat-trick of successes. In 1889, Preston North End won the trophy without conceding a goal, beating Wolves 3-0 in the final.

In 1894, Notts County had become the first side from Division Two to win the FA Cup. The Lacemen, so called because of Nottingham's association with the hosiery trade, had in their side Jimmy Logan, whose hat-trick was only the second ever achieved in a final.

The County side against Wednesday were essentially the same from the previous season. They did, though, include debutant Wattie Arnott, the legendary Queen's Park full back that Fred Spiksley had destroyed two years earlier when England beat Scotland 5-2. Facing his nemesis in the 1895 English Cup was going to be another step towards the completion of Arnott's career. Wednesday were five up before County replied with a late penalty from Elijah Allsop, who thus maintained his record of never having missed a spot-kick. County's hold on the cup ended after just one game. The *Sheffield Telegraph* reported: "Watty Arnott is not the man he was." He made one more County appearance.

Two days later, Fred Spiksley participated in the Trent River Ice Race in Gainsborough. It was so cold that the Trent had frozen over with ice that was eleven inches thick. Hundreds of skaters took the chance to demonstrate their skills – or lack of them! Former Trinity captain Billy Brown enlisted the support of local tradesmen to organise an ice race and Charles Caldicott advertised the event in his newspaper.

The winner of the one-mile race would receive a gold medal, the runner-up a silver medal and third a smaller silver medal. Eighteen entrants were cheered all the way by a 2,500 crowd. Fred Spiksley won his heat and was joined in the final by another former Trinity stalwart in Abe Watkin. The race favourite was M S Blundell who, by winning comfortably, made it a bad day for bookmaker William Spiksley. In a fierce three-way race for second, his brother, Fred, overtook Mr Robinson but could not manage to overcome Watkin and thus finished in third place. After the presentation of the prizes there were great celebrations including one, no doubt, at the Crown and Anchor pub in Bridge Street. The landlord was no longer Fred's dad, however. He had returned to work for Marshall's Yard as a boilermaker when Fred had joined Wednesday.

The reward for Wednesday's success against Notts County was a home tie with Middlesbrough, then an amateur team in the Northern League. With Sheffield United having drawn a much more attractive home tie with West Bromwich Albion, it was agreed that Wednesday's game would be brought forward an hour to 2.30pm. Unfortunately, Middlesbrough were so outplayed that many in the small crowd of 4,000 left at half-time to rush down to Bramall Lane and watch a more competitive match. Imagine that happening now, but in the 1890s and for many years afterwards it was not unusual for fans in any city or region with two clubs to watch one team one weekend and the other the next.

The Wednesday game ended in a 6-1 success for the League side with Spiksley scoring twice, one with a header. Davis did even better as he scored three times.

Consolation for Boro came later in the season when they won the Amateur Cup for a second time, beating Old Carthusians (now known as Corinthian-Casuals) 2-1 in the final.

The quarter-final against Everton was certain to be much tougher for Wednesday. In 1895, Everton were reputed to be the world's wealthiest club and they were certainly the best-supported averaging 17,420 at home in the League in 1894-95. Wednesday were the third best supported with 9,625 with Sheffield United in seventh place with an average of 7,510.

Until the 1980s, FA Cup-ties tended to attract more spectators than League games and this was certainly the case on 2 March 1895 when 28,000 – nearly three times as many for the League game on New Year's Day – squeezed inside Olive Grove to see Wednesday take a 25th-minute lead through Everton old boy Brady, who slipped home a Spiksley pass. The home side were then reduced to ten men as Davis had to leave the pitch following a rough challenge by Dickie Boyle.

Some great defensive work by Earp, Crawshaw, Langley and Brandon kept Everton away from Allan's goal but the home side then suffered a further blow when Ferrier was lamed with a dead-leg, the injured player being moved out to the right wing. Amazingly, with just seconds remaining of the half the ball somehow made its way to Ferrier at the far post and he tapped it home to double the home side's advantage.

At the start of the second half Wednesday's goal was under siege. Chadwick should have scored before Brady, Brash and Spiksley dropped back to inside the Wednesday half. Spiksley showed great pace on one occasion to take him through the Everton defence but was over confident and with just Tom Cain to beat fired horribly wide.

As the game ticked away from them, Everton pushed the Wednesday defence further and further back but could not manage to fashion a serious scoring opportunity. With minutes remaining, Brash became the third home player to sustain an injury but Everton still could not beat Allan and the game ended 2-0 to Wednesday. It had been a magnificent backs-to-the-wall effort and success convinced Wednesday fans that this was finally going to be the year when their side would win the FA Cup.

Standing in the way of a second ever final were West Bromwich Albion, the Cup winners of 1888 and 1892, who had defeated Small Heath, Sheffield United and Wolverhampton Wanderers on their way to the semi-final. Their side contained the irrepressible Billy Bassett and in Joe Reader they possessed one of best 'keepers of his generation and one who as a player, coach and steward served the club for a total of 65 years. He played once for England.

The semi-final took place on Derby's Racecourse Ground where the football field was just a small part of a large plain of grassland between the River Derwent and Derby town. The racecourse and cricket ground were in close proximity. After paying entry the 18,000 spectators crossed the circular racecourse and cricket enclosures to reach the heavily-grassed football pitch.

Ferrier's place was taken by Woolhouse. After the referee, Lieutenant Simpson, started the game there was an early attempt by Brady that Reader skilfully saved. However, on twenty minutes Harry Brandon dallied and when Roddie McLeod perfectly controlled the ball and sent it to Tom Hutchinson, the West Brom player escaped an ill-prepared Crawshaw to score a magnificent opening goal.

There was a second blow to Wednesday when it became apparent that Davis was suffering from a recurrence of his stomach injury from the Everton tie. All his passes had gone astray. To compound Wednesday's problems an elbow from

Billy Richards laid out Crawshaw. Play was held up for five minutes, after which the Wednesday defender played the rest of the game wearing a great swathe of bandages as blood continued to pour from the wound. It was an incident similar to that many years later when centre half Terry Butcher sustained a similar injury playing for his country.

Richards added to Crawshaw's problem by laying him out a second time with his elbow but the Wednesday man was swiftly revived with a sniff of sal volatile (smelling salts) and refused to leave the field. Today it would have been Richards who would have done so as he would have been sent off. The referee did not even speak to him.

Bassett had been very quiet but he was a player who was always looking for an opportunity to give him an edge over his opponents. Langley had done well to keep the winger away from the goal and with 35 minutes gone the pair raced for a ball bouncing towards the corner flag and well within the twelve yard penalty area that in 1895 ran right across the pitch. Bassett reached the ball first, trod on it and fell over writhing on the ground as though he had been shot as Langley flew over the top of him.

The *Sheffield Telegraph* was at odds with many spectators as it felt the incident merited a penalty. But that didn't prevent the paper also heavily criticising Bassett who, when the referee awarded the penalty, immediately rose from the ground and began dancing a jig. "From being lame, Bassett recovered instantaneously."

Billy Williams, a non-stop dynamo at full back, doubled the lead and at the interval the score remained 2-0. The injustice ripped the heart out of the Wednesday side and their 8,000 followers who had hoped to see a famous victory. There was no chance of that but the losing side fought to the end as Crawshaw and then Petrie smacked shots against the crossbar.

Albion responded with a horrendous tackle on Spiksley by an unidentified opponent, which meant that the

Wednesday player virtually disappeared from the game. With Crawshaw and then Earp suffering injuries the game was to be dominated by Albion who would have won more comfortably but for poor misses by Bassett.

It meant Wednesday had lost in consecutive semi-finals and had proven a catastrophic disaster considering the pre-match expectations.

Albion faced local rivals Aston Villa at the Crystal Palace, the third time the sides had met in the final and the scores were level with one victory each. Victory went to Villa thanks to a goal in the first minute, the quickest ever in a Cup Final at the time.

A disappointed Wednesday returned to League football and a week later faced leaders Sunderland who were too good for them and won 2-1. Sunderland went on to win Division One for the third time in five seasons.

The Wednesday season came to a much less glorious end as, with only one win and one draw from their last half-dozen games, they finished in eighth place. Since beating Liverpool 5-0 in January, Wednesday had played eleven League matches and drawn twice and won just once – 3-2 at home to West Bromwich Albion.

The season ended with a 6-0 hammering at WBA, a result that meant the losing side conceded more League goals than they scored – 55 to 50. Of the half century scored, Fred Spiksley notched just seven and was outscored by Davis who got one more. Both men scored three in the Cup.

West Brom had needed to win the game by six goals if they were to avoid the test match series and afterwards it was generally felt that the defeated side had not tried too hard. This was a charge Fred Spiksley disputed when interviewed in 1907, claiming the winning side were "very fit...and I never witnessed a better right wing combination exhibited by Billy Bassett, Roddy McLeod and Tom Perry that day at Stoney Lane."

CHAPTER 10

NO NETS
The Home International series
1894

WALES BEAT IRELAND 4-1 in the opening game of the
1894 Home International Championship. England opened
their campaign against the Irish in Belfast on Cliftonville's
Solitude Ground on 3 March 1894. A team of professionals
were selected to cross the Irish Sea. They included debutants
Josiah Reader, Jimmy Crabtree and Henry Chippendale
while Jimmy Whitehead and John Devey were playing in
only their second international. Four of England's finest
– Bassett, Goodall, Southworth and Chadwick – were
left out to make way for the new men. The impeccable
credentials of Ernest Needham, by now the finest left half
in England, were also overlooked. Dennis Hodgetts was
also selected when his finest days were behind him and
with Spiksley playing at outside left the Villa man was
played out of position at centre forward. Sports journalists
called the team selection a "hotchpotch". The decision to
field a weakened team devalued an England cap and was
disrespectful to their opponents.

The sea voyage on Thursday 1 March 1894 was Fred
Spiksley's first and he later made a firm resolution that it
would be his last after the England players embarked from
Fleetwood with R P Gregson from Blackburn Rovers in
charge of the party.

Flying over an Olive Grove

Not long after the players had enjoyed a fine meal, the boat began to play some strange tricks as it rose and fell to such an extent that it soon had the passengers heading for their cabins. It quickly became impossible to stand up and every hatch on the boat was battened down as all of the England players, except Johnny Holt, became seasick. When Fred Spiksley attempted to stretch his legs he was sent flying down the corridor and had to crawl back on his hands and knees to the safety of his bed.

The ship proved her seaworthiness and by dawn the England party had arrived in Belfast. With the ship's stewards sauntering along as though nothing untoward had happened the players were urged to make haste to the dining saloon where breakfast was to be served. Jimmy Crabtree was missing and even after a thorough search of the boat could not be found. The Burnley man had been given up as lost when a hollow groan was heard coming from under one of the tables in the dining room. Only when it was repeated did the search restart and Crabtree was found safe but certainly not well, curled up in a state of semi-consciousness.

He had stayed clinging to the dining table leg after losing his way to his berth. A cup of coffee and news that the ship had docked soon had the 'dead man' back on his feet.

The England side had just over 24 hours to recover from their traumatic experience. The result that followed demonstrated they did not do so properly. Afterwards, following Gregson's report on proceedings, travel plans to Ireland included the need to use the shortest route, which was Stranraer to Larne, and allow two additional days to acclimatise and train at Cliftonville in Belfast.

England: Josiah Reader (West Bromwich Albion), Bob Howarth, Bob Holmes (both Preston), John Reynolds (Aston Villa), John Holt (Everton), Jimmy Crabtree (Burnley), Henry Chippendale, James Whitehead (both Blackburn Rovers), Hodgetts, John Devey (both Aston Villa), Spiksley.

Ireland: Tom Scott, Robert K Stewart, Sam Torrans (capt), Samuel Johnston II, Robert George Milne, John Burnett, Bill Dalton, George Gaffikin, Olphie Stanfield, James H Barron, William K Gibson.

The England captain for the match was Jack Reynolds, who had previously scored against his country while playing for Ireland! He is the only man to score both for and against his country. The son of an illiterate mother and a labourer father, Reynolds worked as a weaver before enlisting in the East Lancashire Regiment and being posted to Ireland in 1887. While there he played regularly for the regimental football team against local sides, who in turn invited him to guest for them. He did, however, miss a few matches as he was in hospital on three occasions for some form of venereal disease, probably gonorrhoea.

The Distillery club bought Jack out of the Army on Boxing Day 1889. This was a risky move as professionalism remained illegal in Ireland. When Distillery cut their illegal payments, the Blackburn-born player transferred his allegiance to Ulster FC in Belfast. In February 1890, Reynolds made his debut for Ireland against Wales in Wrexham. He was now William and the *Ulster Football and Cycling News* reported he had been born in Ireland and attended school as a child in Portglenone and Ballymena. He had then emigrated to Lancashire.

In Jack's (or William's) second game he netted Ireland's only goal as they were beaten 9-1 by England. Reynolds made five appearances for his adopted country before finally deciding he was really English and signing for West Bromwich, where he collected an FA Cup winner's medal in 1892. Immediately afterwards he joined Aston Villa for £50 and with them he won two more FA Cup winner's medals and three League championships. He later won the Scottish League with Celtic. Highly competitive, Reynolds had some remarkable ball skills and at times his footwork was brilliant.

The Irish crowd were disappointed at the appearance of an under-strength England XI. The selectors were clearly using the game as a trial for the match against Scotland. Despite the insult, England were given a rousing reception when they entered the arena. With Fred Spiksley pulling the strings, England started well with Jimmy Crabtree settling in confidently on his debut.

Fred was disappointed when his tenth-minute effort was overruled for offside as he knew that when the ball had been played he had started his run from behind the Irish backs. Five minutes later Bob Holmes, the England captain, limped out of the game for good and as the away side reorganised Reynolds dropped to centre half with Holt going to left full back.

This gave James H Barron and William K Gibson, who at just aged sixteen was making his International debut before his home crowd, some space and time but it was England who should have scored when Whitehead, who had done little in his first England game, missed horribly after Fred created a simple chance.

On 42 minutes England did take the lead when following two fine Reader saves a long punt upfield by Crabtree was pounced upon by Devey to put his side ahead at the break. Only just, though, as within seconds of the goal George Gaffikin smashed the ball home only for the effort to be disallowed for an earlier foul. It was a harsh decision.

On the restart, England were put under pressure from Ireland but in truth Reader in his long goalkeeping trousers was rarely threatened. On 55 minutes, England made it 2-0 when Spiksley set off on one of his trademark runs to score a goal that, according to many contemporary match reports, must have borne a striking resemblance to Ryan Giggs's famous goal at Villa Park for Manchester United against Arsenal in the 1999 FA Cup semi-final replay. This was how the *Athletic News* described it:

"A second goal came through a brilliant individual effort on the part of Spiksley, who, receiving (the ball) from Hodgetts, raced past Stewart, got almost to the line, and with a slight touch by the side of his foot sent the ball just under the bar."

It was, by all accounts, a truly remarkable goal and the Irish were stunned and might have fallen further behind only for Devey, set up by Spiksley, to miss when clean through. A grateful Scott cleared long and with Crabtree and Holt upfield, William Dalton centred and as Howarth and Reader froze, Distillery's Olphie Stanfield, who played thirty times for his country between 1887 and 1897, nipped in to reduce his side's arrears to just a single goal. There was great jubilation and excitement only for it to be stilled when Spiksley broke beyond the home defence soon afterwards. However, the Wednesday man could only hit a tame shot.

On 87 minutes the final goal was scored when Gibson, who made thirteen appearances for his country as a whole and was remembered forty years later by Sir Frederick Wall as one of the three finest players ever to appear in an Irish XI, poked a bouncing ball home to level the score and cause further excitement among the home fans. The England players objected to the decision to award the goal, arguing the shot had gone wide. In the absence of goal nets the rights and wrongs of what had happened were left to the referee and he decided Gibson's effort had gone between the posts.

A brilliant game thus ended 2-2 following which the 'was it or wasn't it' debate raged and after all the players were consulted and enquiries made of spectators behind the goal it was admitted that the ball had gone wide. Had not Ireland lost a goal in 1892 when an effort that flashed through the posts against Scotland was not awarded allowing Scotland to win the game 3-2? For the Irish the 'goal' against England simply levelled things up! It meant that for the first time in thirteen meetings Ireland had scored more than a single goal against England and also the first time they had avoided defeat.

The England match against Wales took place on the Racecourse Ground, Wrexham on 12 March 1894. The all-amateur away side won easily, 5-1, thanks to John Veitch (3), Cunliffe Gosling and an own goal against a John Bowdler consolation effort. On 24 March, Scotland beat Wales 5-1 at Cardiff Arms Park. In Belfast one week later, Scotland scored twice, one an own goal, to overturn a single goal deficit and thus overcome a spirited Ireland side who could so easily have won. Football at times is a strange sport. Ireland had really lost to England and on another day would have beaten Scotland. Now the Scots needed only a draw against England to become Home International champions for 1894.

On Thursday 15 March, Fred Spiksley played for the Whites in the England trial match against the Stripes at Leyton. He was then selected to face Scotland at Celtic Park on 7 April. With concerns over the fitness of one or two players the England selectors chose to take thirteen to Glasgow and in the event one of the standby players, Gilbert Oswald Smith, took the place of the injured Jack Southworth. As was pointed out by many Scottish papers, this was a big blow to England as Southworth was in top form with Everton in 1893–94. A career-ending injury the following season meant he had played his final international.

Ever since the SFA had awarded them the match the Celtic executive had gone to great lengths to ensure their ground was perfect for the game. Over £750 was spent, much of it on returfing the pitch. A column in the *Glasgow Evening News* under the pseudonym of 'The Scottish referee' was highly critical of what he called questionable tactics by the SFA for producing a pitch with a rich lush covering of long grass that would slow the pace along the ground and thus neutralise England's speed, especially out on the wings. The Scottish Referee also criticised those in the press who had suggested that Sandy McMahon was no longer the "master of ball control" and lacked confidence.

On Friday afternoon the England professional players, including debutant Ernest Needham, met up at Preston and took the train to Glasgow where they were booked into the Central Station Hotel. They later attended the theatre where they received generous applause from the audience and a formal welcome from the SFA president. The players were back in bed by the time the three amateur players, Gay, Pelly and Smith, checked into the hotel.

At breakfast time there was a small crowd outside all eager to catch a glimpse of a player. There was a general buzz right across the city and after a light lunch the England side changed into their familiar white shirts with navy blue shorts and stockings.

At 2.30pm the horse drawn carriages arrived at the hotel and as the England party embarked the crowd outside expressed their condolences and genuine sorrow at their impending defeat!

England: Gay, Tom Clare (Stoke), Fred Pelly (Old Foresters), John Reynolds, John Holt, Ernest Needham, Billy Bassett, John Goodall (captain), Gilbert Oswald Smith, Edgar Chadwick, Spiksley

Scotland: David Haddow, Donald Sillars, Dan Doyle (captain), Isaac Begbie, Andrew McCreadie, David Mitchell, William Gulliland, James Blessington, Alex McMahon, John McPherson, William Lambie

The Scotland side included four debutants in 'keeper David Haddow, Andrew McCreadie, James Blessington and William Lambie. At right back the selectors had chosen Donald Sillars, a soldier, footballer and gentleman. He was an amateur with Queen's Park and his selection was a surprise. The fastest sprinter in the Scotland team, his job was to stop Fred Spiksley. The *Glasgow Evening News* called him the 'Demon'. It was his fourth cap. Up front for

Scotland, Alexander 'Sandy' McMahon had told the local press how he was going to show Johnny Holt 'the double shuffle' on the new turf.

The English had more international experience with their players having 50 caps between them against 21 for Scotland. Also, only McPherson had scored against England whereas four of England's players had scored against Scotland and England had not lost on Scottish soil since 1884.

Nevertheless, Scotland fans were convinced their side would win and they were intent on employing their greatest weapon – themselves – to ensure that was the case. Overwhelming home support, it was argued, would carry the day and it was also pointed out that the England side were one of the smallest ever with only Goodall of the forwards taller than 5ft 7in while none of the half backs exceeded that height.

The ground still had electric light posts round the pitch. These had been employed in a failed experiment designed to make night time football possible. The posts became affectionately known as 'Madden's rigging', a reference to Celtic centre-forward John Madden having worked as a riveter in a Glasgow shipyard. A magnificent illustration, which is reproduced in this book, of one of the Scotland goal's being lustily celebrated, clearly shows these electric light posts, which were also mentioned in contemporary match reports of the game.

The number of Scottish fans keen to see the game also proved a headache. Despite careful planning by Celtic and the SFA the arrangements were inadequate for the quickly-growing enthusiasm and popularity of football which had led to unprecedented numbers descending upon Celtic Park. There were not enough police officers on duty outside the ground, too few gatemen to take the entrance money and no stewards inside the ground to prevent the enclosures becoming overcrowded.

No Nets

Once the gates were opened the crowd surged forward and, as people struggled to pay for entry, the pushing intensified. Fearing a catastrophe, the main gate was opened to allow greater access and spectators rushed into already overcrowded enclosures. The palisade fence in front collapsed under the crush and spectators fought for their lives as hundreds spilled on to the cinder track encircling the pitch. Many people were injured before the police and St John Ambulance arrived to restore order and ensure treatment for those hurt in the melee. With an official attendance of 45,107 a new world record had been achieved. The truth was that more than 50,000 had entered the ground and it was a miracle that no-one had been killed, especially as two brothers were badly injured when a barrier collapsed on top of them.

With the kick-off delayed there was a subdued atmosphere. The mood brightened considerably when Pipe Major Wallace marched his massed band of pipes and drums on to the field accompanied by referee John Reid and his two linesmen, N L Jackson for England and A Sliman for Scotland.

The sides were met with a great cheer as excitement mounted. Scotland, in blue, won the toss and started well as Gulliland, in a sign of things to come, left Pelly for dead before forcing Gay to save. England responded. First Reynolds hit the crossbar and then, from the rebound, Needham hit the base of the post.

Within minutes of the game starting, it was clear that the pitch was a problem. Divots could be seen lying on the surface as Scotland took the lead on seven minutes. Gulliland stormed past Pelly and with Blessington and McMahon acting as decoys he found an unmarked Lambie who netted.

With the noise in the stadium almost deafening England responded and Doyle did well to clear after McMahon misdirected a Spiksley corner towards his own net. The

England outside left then used his searing pace to go past Sillars. Haddow saved his shot but before he had time to recover his bearings John Goodall kicked the ball out of his fingers and coolly netted before turning and walking calmly back to the halfway line.

It was 1-1 after just twelve minutes. The away side, though, were restricted by Southworth's absence as a nervous Smith knew nothing of combination play and was on a different wavelength from his fellow forwards. Smith was a brilliant dribbler and had a great shot on him but passing, link-up play, distribution and finding space were, as an amateur player, alien to him. Apart from the trial match at Leyton he had never played alongside professional footballers before.

The other outfield amateur player in the England side, Fred Pelly, was also out of his depth. His selection was bizarre as the week before the trial match he had undergone a serious eye operation that saw him lose the sight in his left eye. He wore an eye patch and to make matters worse he was accidentally elbowed in his good eye after fifteen minutes of the game at Celtic Park and left virtually blinded for the remaining 75 minutes. Pelly was from then on known as "the only blind man to have played football for England". Pelly's lack of eyesight left Clare and Needham sharing the full back duties and the pair combined successfully to dispossess the Scotland forwards.

With Chadwick out of sorts, Fred Spiksley was starved of the ball. He had few opportunities to shine, especially after the first goal when Sillars suddenly realised that all the pre-match warnings about the England winger's speed were true. From then on the Scotland full back was taking no chances as he tugged his opponent's shirt, tapped his ankles and tripped him when he got the chance. With the referee content to let things pass, Sillars floored Spiksley and then gently smiled as he helped the injured man up off the ground.

On 30 minutes, Goodall stepped round the Scottish defence and with the goal at his mercy tripped on the turf. He kicked out in disgust and the game settled into a pattern as the play flowed from one end to the other before, just before the interval, Gay was forced to save four tremendously powerful shots. When the half-time whistle sounded the England players surrounded their 'keeper and patted him on the back and shook his hand.

With England kicking with the wind, Spiksley and Chadwick created a great opportunity for Smith but Doyle outsprinted him to clear. Then Bassett had his close-range shot saved by Haddow as England piled forward and were only denied by a Doyle goal line clearance from a Spiksley shot.

With Holt dominating McMahon, Doyle switched the Scotland centre half out to the left and put McPherson in the middle. The move paid off on 74 minutes when Davie Mitchell beat Clare and crossed. With Pelly unable to spot the danger, Gay dashed out to intercept but was beaten to the ball by McPherson who sent it into the net as the stadium erupted in ecstasy. England were stung and were mighty fortunate when almost immediately after his goal the Scotland scorer missed from a good position.

How would England react? Pelly could not see, Smith was out of his depth and Chadwick was clearly out of sorts.

The Scottish players and fans were growing in confidence and already looking forward to the final whistle. Holt could hardly hear himself as he urged his colleagues to double their efforts. Goodall and Spiksley were determined not to be beaten and they combined brilliantly only for the former to flash his shot just over the bar. Dan Doyle pushed and prodded his team to get forward and finish off the game but in Holt, England had a man mountain and the Scots were reduced to long-range efforts.

There were 85 minutes on the clock when England were able to push forward to find Bassett, who had been remarkably quiet until then. The winger jinked past Mitchell before slowing down as Doyle approached and then surprising his opponent by back-heeling the ball to Reynolds, the England pair thus employing a trick they had perfected during their time together at West Brom.

Reynolds advanced from 25 yards, looked up briefly and, using the strong breeze, hit a powerful shot that sped just under the crossbar and into the top corner of the net. It was a sensational goal, one of the best from the 1890s, and left Celtic Park in a silence that was only broken by the cheers of the England players and small knot of officials.

Neither side were able to snatch a winner in the remaining time; Scotland, in particular, were content since they would finish with five points compared with their opponents' four. England were grateful they had emerged with honour after being forced to overcome a number of problems – such as Southworth's injury, Pelly's eye operation, an inexperienced Smith's unfamiliarity with team play and the fact that Chadwick should not have played. There was also the case that England and Scotland, would have finished joint top if there had been nets for the match with Ireland! Goal average was not in those days taken into account in the competition and if two countries finished top on the same points the trophy was shared.

In 1895 the England selectors chose not to select Fred Spiksley for any of England's three Home International matches. In the first, a side consisting of professional players beat Ireland 9-0 with Stoke's Joe Schofield playing his third and last international at outside left. A week later a team of amateur players drew 1-1 with Wales where Sandilands played at outside left.

England then beat Scotland with a team containing two amateur players, one of whom, Gosling, captained the side. Stephen Smith had been in fine form for Aston Villa during the 1894–95 season, notching eighteen goals in 31

League and FA Cup matches. He marked what proved to be his only game for England by scoring the third from outside left in a 3-0 victory that earned his country top spot in the table.

In 1896, England's first match was away to Ireland on 7 March. The previous season's results had made it clear that England performed better with professional players in their side. Fred Spiksley had been in fine form in January and February 1896 and had played especially well in Wednesday's 2-1 success at Sunderland in the FA Cup. Fred was selected to play his fifth international for his country. He was one of seven professionals in the side.

England: George Raikes (captain) (Oxford University), Lewis Lodge (Corinthians), William Oakley (Oxford University), Jimmy Crabtree (Aston Villa), Tom Crawshaw (Wednesday), George Kinsey (Derby County), Bassett, Steve Bloomer (Derby County), G O Smith (Oxford University), Edgar Chadwick (Everton), Spiksley

Ireland: Tom Scott, John Ponsonby, Samuel Torrans, James Fitzpatrick (capt), Robert Milne, Hugh Gordon Gideon Baird, Edwin Turner, Olphert Stanfield, Jim Kelly, John Peden.

The England party left Stranraer on 5 March 1896 and embarked on a ferry crossing that left many of them seasick. There were huge sighs of relief when they arrived in Larne and were soon settled in the nearby Olderfleet Hotel. Billy Bassett had been particularly badly affected by the trip and, after only twenty minutes of the international, he told his teammates not to pass to him.

On the day of the game, transport arrived at 11.15am to take the England party to the 15,000-capacity Solitude Ground in Cliftonville, Belfast. Although good weather was forecast the skies opened half an hour before kick-off and the ground conditions quickly became treacherous. The match referee Mr James Robertson was an army man from Dumfries and had caught a ship on the Friday night from

Stranraer. The ship, however, was blown off course and he was in a bad way when it docked, although thankfully he had gathered himself sufficiently to referee the game.

Ireland, wearing their St Patrick's blue-coloured shirts (Ireland wore blue until 1914), started very well and Ollie Stanfield should have put them ahead. In goal for England, George Raikes was extremely nervous and his handling throughout the game was poor.

When England pressed, Spiksley set up Bassett but the Baggie missed an easy chance. The England outside left was being fed a lot of balls from his half backs but it was from a Bassett cross that Smith hit a first-time low shot that flashed beyond Scott to give England the lead on 40 minutes. Steve Bloomer then slipped on the soggy surface in the goalmouth and the interval arrived with the away side leading 1-0.

With the wind behind them, England had more of the play in the second half and after Spiksley tricked his way round John Ponsonby he delivered a perfect centre for Bloomer to make it 2-0. The Wednesday man had again delivered on the international stage. With Gideon Baird and Edward Turner overpowered by Lodge and Oakley, England's Oxbridge heavyweights, it was difficult for Ireland to conjure a goal and a game ruined by the conditions ended in victory for England by two goals to nil before a 12,000-strong crowd.

England's second international match in 1896 took place on Monday 16 March at Cardiff Arms Park. Sandilands took Fred Spiksley's place at outside left and Goodall replaced Chadwick. England won 9-1 and Bloomer created a record by becoming the first player to score five times for England in an international.

Sandilands failed to score and he was missing for the England trial match at Leyton on Wednesday 25 March 1896. Four days earlier, Fred Spiksley had rescued Wednesday by crafting an undeserved equaliser against Bolton in the FA

Cup semi-final that, after finishing 1-1, would be replayed three days after the trial game. It was a sign of Fred's patriotism that he was willing to make a 290-mile round trip to play but knowing his record and ability it was surely unnecessary for the selectors to make him do so.

Representing the Players, Fred was in direct competition for a place in the England team against Scotland with amateur Cuthbert J Burnup of Cambridge University who was at outside left for the Gentlemen. The professional side suffered a blow before kick-off when Bloomer was forced to withdraw due to an injury sustained in the previous weekend's FA Cup semi-final between Derby County and Wolves. The Rams player had scored six of England's eleven goals in 1896 and it was simply unthinkable that he might not be fit to face Scotland. Pat Finnerham, the Manchester City inside forward, was Bloomer's replacement.

A 10,000 crowd turned out to watch some of the finest footballers in England. The Gentleman, easily recognisable by their greater height, muscular strength and plain rude health, scored after just five minutes when MH Stanborough's shot took a wicked deflection off Jimmy Crabtree and left Willie Sutcliffe stranded. The professionals, much quicker and more skilful than their opponents, then took control of proceedings and Goodall was unlucky to be ruled offside following a superb pass from Spiksley. In the meantime, George Raikes was again visibly nervous and appeared unable to catch the ball. At half time the Gentleman still led but it was more by good luck than design. Five minutes after the restart the Players equalised when Lodge and Oakley collided leaving Finnerhan to run clear and score.

On 65 minutes, Raikes spilled a Bassett shot and Goodall put his side ahead. The Gentleman rallied and using their great strength and physique they laid siege to their opponents' goal, forcing Sutcliffe to make several impressive saves. However, the Bolton goalkeeper was helpless when with fifteen minutes remaining Cotterill equalised from one of a series of well-placed corners from Arthur Henfrey. With no further goals the game ended 2-2.

Fred Spiksley had not played particularly impressively but neither had his opposite number Burnup, who had never previously played football for his country and was generally regarded as a cricketer.

On Saturday 28 March 1896, Fred Spiksley was in inspired form as he was the man of the match as Wednesday beat Bolton 3-1 in the replayed FA Cup semi-final in which he also scored. Having previously scored seven goals in five England internationals he was surely a 'cert' to play against Scotland. 'Pa' Jackson, the head of England selectors committee, had other ideas and on Monday 30 March he used his power over the other selectors to gift Cuthbert 'Pinky' Burnup with what proved to be his only cap. In goal, Raikes, a clergyman, was selected and there were also places for amateur players Lodge, Oakley and Smith.

Respected journalist JAH Catton claimed he had heard Jackson on one occasion attempt to get someone to play for the Corinthians by saying, "Come and play for me and I will get you your international cap."

When left half Ernest Needham was forced to withdraw at the last minute with a bacterial infection a sixth amateur, Arthur Henfrey, was selected to replace him even though he was right-footed. So little influence did Henfrey have on the match that the Scottish papers later suggested he might have been a ghost.

Over the previous seven years no England side to face Scotland had contained so many amateur players as the generally accepted rule was that when professionals formed the majority of the team then England won. To reduce even further England's effectiveness, Bassett had been selected even though he was suffering from flu. Scotland had abandoned their previous policy of not selecting English-based Scots and their side included Sunderland's Ted

Doig in goal, Tom Brandon from Blackburn Rovers, James Cowan of Aston Villa, John Bell of Everton and Tommy Hyslop of Stoke.

Many of the England side had no idea of what was to face them as they walked out at Celtic Park on Saturday 4 April 1896 without Fred Spiksley, playing that day for his club against Small Heath.

A gate of 51,345 fanatical Scotsmen helped curdle the Sassenach blood and Raikes gifted the home side the opening goal by dropping the ball to allow William Lambie to follow up his original shot to net. Jimmy Cowan doubled the lead on 40 minutes and the Scots left the field two up but wondering how they hadn't scored at least four.

In the second half England did provide tougher opposition and Goodall created a chance that saw Bassett reduce the arrears. In the end, though, Scotland had beaten their arch rivals for the first time in seven years and the highest ever attendance at a football match at the time celebrated wildly as a sorry England side left the pitch with their heads bowed. The result meant that Scotland won the 1896 Home International championships. In truth, 'Pa' Jackson had gifted them top spot. Two weeks later one of the England professionals who was left out of the Scotland game, Fred Spiksley, arguably then the greatest footballer in the world, scored two of the finest goals ever seen in the FA Cup to give his side a famous victory in the final.

CHAPTER 11

ALL THE WAY TO THE PALACE
Spiksley guides Wednesday to their second FA Cup final

THE MAJOR DEVELOPMENT in the summer of 1895 was the signing of twenty-year-old Lawrie Bell from Third Lanark. This solved Wednesday's goal-scoring problem with the additional bonus of allowing Harry Davis to return to his preferred inside forward position. Bell was an excellent dribbler with a powerful and accurate shot; he linked up well with his wide men and was a clever passer. He was to have an outstanding first season.

In the season's opener, Bell played against the side that had also tried to sign him and he opened the scoring at Everton in a game that ended 2-2 in front of a 14,000 crowd.

Three days later, on Tuesday 5 September, Fred Spiksley took part in another big match that was attended by just five people when he married Ellen Robinson in Sheffield. The marriage ceremony was conducted by J Chas Barber the resident registrar at the Sheffield Register Office and was witnessed by Mr J Bennett and Henry Canham, neither of whom appears to have had any previous connection with the bride and groom or their families. It seems that they were approached in the street and asked to witness the ceremony.

On the marriage certificate the groom is listed as 25 years old, living at 19 Talbot Street, Sheffield and working as a printer with the *Sheffield Telegraph*. Only the age was correct, as Fred Spiksley had quit his job with the paper when he moved back to Gainsborough in the summer of 1893. It seems possible that Thomas McCabe, whom Fred had lodged with between 1891 and 1893, had put the couple up for a few days before the wedding.

Ellen had lived with her mother, Jane Robinson, in an extended family that included three brothers and four sisters, all younger than her. Ellen told the registrar she was 21 years of age but this was a lie as she was three years younger. It was said that her father had died two years previously and was therefore unable to give his eldest daughter away.

Why the secret marriage? Probably because Ellen was four months pregnant so there was an urgent need to marry without fuss or publicity. Attitudes to sex before marriage were changing – especially among the young – but having a child out of wedlock was still heavily frowned upon in late Victorian times. If the news had got out then Fred Spiksley would have been in the middle of a scandal. It meant that no one from Gainsborough or Fred's team mates attended the wedding, which went smoothly. Sadly, that was not the case with the pregnancy as baby Frederick Walter Spiksley died within a few days of his arrival in January 1896.

Wednesday's opening home League game in 1895–96 was against Sheffield United, and another effort from Bell, a header from a Spiksley cross, was enough to win the day. This was the only time Wednesday beat United in the League or FA Cup in the nineteenth century.

The ever increasing market of readers for football journalism meant that the *Sheffield Independent* launched a

Saturday evening paper, *Football World*, on the night of the derby match. It failed to last long because the owners of the *Sheffield Evening Star* took legal action. They cited the agreement made in 1888 when they purchased the paper from the *Independent*. This stated that the latter would not launch an evening paper for the next twenty years.

Consecutive defeats at Wolves and Derby were a disappointment but Wednesday played much better back at Olive Grove and another double by their outside left saw West Brom beaten 5-3. This was followed by home victories against Wolves and Sunderland. When Wednesday then won at West Brom they rose to fourth in the table. A 6-1 hammering at Bury showed there was still work to be done.

Fred Spiksley was on the score sheet at Blackburn Rovers, netting after a glorious run and shot. Leading 1-0 at half-time, the away side collapsed to lose 2-1 with Spiksley missing three gilt-edged chances. In the next game, at home to Burnley, the England winger provided the talking point when he performed one of the back-heel manoeuvres for which he became famous. It put the ball directly into the path of Brady who scored the only goal of the game.

Defeats against Stoke and Derby meant Wednesday entered the New Year back in eighth place. If a trophy was to be won it would have to be the FA Cup. Wednesday faced Southampton Saint Mary's away in the first round. Saints were one of the top Southern League teams. While inferior to the Football League the standard of the Southern League was still good enough to mean the Yorkshire side would need to play well to progress. The Saints had recruited five Stoke players, had already won four preliminary games to reach the first round proper and had yet to lose a home League game during the season. The Wednesday party left for the South Coast at 11.48am on Friday and arrived eight hours later before walking a few yards to their accommodation at the Davis Railway Hotel. The following morning the players took a leisurely stroll along the dockside before inspecting the Antelope Ground pitch that was found to be in reasonable condition with a slight slope towards one of the goals.

The Cup-tie gave Hampshire football fans a chance to see one of England's top clubs and the game was the talk of the town in the week leading up to it, with some Saints fans being so confused that they turned up on the Wednesday to watch it! The Antelope Ground witnessed a record crowd of 12,000 including some who had climbed on top of the corrugated iron stands to seek a better view. Shortly after the players went on the pitch there was a loud bang as one of the stands gave way under the weight. Miraculously, no-one was hurt and the game started shortly afterwards when Lieutenant Simpson sounded his whistle.

The away side were swiftly into their stride as the Southampton defence struggled to protect Jack Cox, their young 'keeper, He had leapt from third to first choice due to injuries and military commitment ruling out 'keepers one and two, Tom Cain and Matt Reilly. Unsurprisingly, he looked nervous and was fortunate when Davis failed to net from close in. However, despite enjoying virtually total possession, Wednesday were struggling to create decent scoring opportunities. They were grateful when Jimmy Massey made two fine saves. He had kept his place in the side after replacing an injured Bill Allan in goal for the previous League game. Massey, signed from Doncaster Rovers in 1893, would remain in goal for the next four and a half seasons. He was to play brilliantly, especially in the latter stages, in the 1896 FA Cup final. Throughout his career Massey was particularly noted for his bravery.

Without the injured Langley, the Wednesday team selection had not been well thought out with right half back Harry Brandon switched to left back and Bob Petrie, a natural left footer, playing at right half. Earp and Brandon were still trying to work out a joint understanding when Watty Keay, the home inside left, darted between the full backs and scored a goal that on another day might have raised the roof. The home crowd were ecstatic but within 120 seconds their side were behind.

From the restart the ball went out to Fred Spiksley and he curled it inside to Brady who shot powerfully past Cox to equalise. When the ball was next in Wednesday's possession the young 'keeper made two smart reflex saves but as the ball ran free, Spiksley controlled it. As the outside left feinted to shoot the Saints defenders rushed forward only to find the Wednesday winger had rolled the ball into the path of Brady, who from almost the same spot as his first goal, knocked it home to stun the home fans. Wednesday netted again shortly afterwards but the referee disallowed it for offside as he couldn't believe that Fred Spiksley had started his run from an onside position. At the interval the away side led 2-1 and they doubled their lead in the second half through a Davis diving header.

Southampton St Mary's, who dropped St Mary's from their title in 1897, got back into the game when Jack Farrell netted following a corner. The game became highly competitive. Massey made a number of good saves and Earp, Crawshaw and Brandon combined to prevent an equalising goal and ensure their side deservedly progressed to the next round. As a bonus a share of the £250 gate money was safely in Arthur Dickinson's pocket.

There is no doubt that Wednesday should have come away from Southampton with a win, but the Hampshire club were a side making considerable progress as history would prove. The following season Southampton won the Southern League for the first time and would win the title for three consecutive seasons. A further three titles followed in 1901, 1903 and 1904. In the FA Cup Southampton were unluckily knocked out in an 1898 semi-final replay against eventual winners Nottingham Forest, a second-half blizzard blowing into the Southampton goalkeeper's eyes meaning that he never saw the ball beat him for Forest's two goals. In 1900 and 1902 Southampton reached the FA Cup final, losing to first Bury and then Sheffield United. Wednesday could look back on this fixture as a job well done.

Wednesday were handed a home tie in the second round. The opponents were the reigning League champions Sunderland and the match attracted a then record crowd for a Wednesday home game of 22,000 who paid £729 to watch the action.

Sunderland had won Division One on three occasions but had never won the FA Cup. Standing in the Wearsiders' way were a side that had turned Olive Grove into a fortress in the FA Cup. So Fred Spiksley was nettled when he bumped into Will Chatterton, the Derbyshire and England cricketer, and was asked who he felt would win the 1896 FA Cup. With League leaders Aston Villa out, Chatterton's choices were Derby, Sunderland or Everton.

Fred challenged the cricketer. "Are we out already?" He was told Wednesday would be when Sunderland beat them and when he argued he was asked to place a bet at odds of 10-1. He paid his £1 and it was only time that Fred Spiksley bet on football.

After losing a gruelling Birmingham Senior Cup match with Aston Villa 4-3, the build-up for Wednesday's players was a recipe of light exercise, fresh air and relaxation. Sunderland meanwhile had spent a week of strenuous training.

The teams ran out to a tremendous roar and the game started frantically before Wednesday began dragging the Sunderland defence out of position and shots rained in on Ned Doig's goal. From a half-cleared corner, the normally reliable Robert McNeil, the Sunderland right back, was too slow in closing down Spiksley and, taking advantage, the Wednesday man chipped the ball to the back post where Bell headed the first goal. With Doig performing heroics, this looked like being the home side's only reward in a first half they had dominated. However, on 44 minutes Bell made another scintillating break. As the Sunderland defenders were sucked towards him he fed the ball beyond them to Spiksley "who with a really brilliant run and shot put on the second goal for the home side amidst enthusiastic cheering" (*Sheffield Telegraph*, 17/02/1896).

Sunderland had been outplayed in the first half and understood that they needed to keep much better possession of the ball. The Wednesday players had to work hard to close down the away side. In doing so the effects of the hard game against Aston Villa began to take their toll.

Sunderland reduced the arrears when Jimmy Millar's quick throw-in to Johnny Hannah put several Wednesday players out of position. Hannah drew Massey out of goal and squared the ball to Millar who pushed it into the empty net on sixty minutes.

Sunderland were now right back in the tie and their chances increased considerably when a high tackle by Hugh Wilson on Spiksley left the winger out of the game. It was now the turn of Earp and his lieutenants, Crawshaw and Langley, together with the support of Brandon and Jamieson, to defend for their lives. They did so with great resolution and when the final whistle sounded the home side were in the final eight of the FA Cup. The cheers of the home fans could be heard right across Sheffield.

After beating Sunderland, Wednesday faced Everton in a home League game with the sides knowing they would meet again later in the FA Cup. The Toffees entertained hopes of a League and Cup double and were locked in a three-way battle with Aston Villa and Derby County for the title. The Merseysiders were unbeaten since 12 October 1895.

"A preliminary canter for the Cup Tie" was the headline in the *Sheffield Independent* after Wednesday beat Everton more easily than the 3-1 scoreline would suggest. The home goals came from Bell, Davis and Spiksley. Everton's unbeaten run of sixteen League and Cup games was over.

The Wednesday players spent the week leading up to the FA Cup-tie in Matlock. They stayed at the Chesterfield House Hydro, 600 feet above the meandering River Derwent looking north over the ravine to High Tor and Matlock Bath two miles away. A ten o'clock curfew was put in place. Each morning after a cold shower and breakfast there was a long walk followed by lunch, massage treatment, an hour of intensive football practice and drills before a 60-minute game in which no tackling, tripping or charging was allowed in order to avoid injuries. There followed relaxation in the steam baths and a light tea.

The party arrived back in Sheffield on the Friday afternoon. The main concern was a rash of injuries to five senior players – Langley, Bell, Brady, Davis and Spiksley, with the last of them suffering from a liver infection and the least likely to play.

Inevitably news leaked out that the Wednesday line-up might be a weak one. In 1896, there was no match-day programme and so, in the days before decent Tannoy systems, never mind giant screens, noticeboards or the internet, anyone who wanted to know the side prior to kick-off bought a match card, costing a penny, from the legendary cricket and football scoreboard printer, Billy Whitham.

However, the card for the Everton match was inconclusive. Langley was out and was replaced by Harry Brandon. Bell, Brady and Davis were fit and there was a surprise with the recall of Brash at outside right. That left the left wing position to be filled and the match card revealed it would be occupied by either Anthony Richards, a youngster with eight previous appearances, or Fred Spiksley. Everton were also struggling to field their first team and in the end Tom McInnes, Smart Arridge and the irrepressible Johnny Holt were missing.

Rain had fallen steadily all night and two hours before kick-off the heavens opened. With no paved pathway to

Olive Grove the footpaths were quickly turned into mud that in turn found itself on to the ground embankments and enclosures thus adding to the fans' discomfort. Unsurprisingly, the size of the crowd was much reduced to just 12,000. This was an era when catching a cold could be potentially fatal and, with no such thing as sick pay, taking time off from work was a luxury very few working class people could afford.

The teams ran on to the pitch to a muted welcome until the outside left was spotted and a huge cheer went up as though the home side had already won the game. They hadn't as yet but the tie was to be very one-sided and after fifteen minutes Spiksley met the ball in the air and his header found Brash who netted. Bell doubled the advantage before half-time after Jack Hillman spilled the ball.

At the interval both teams changed into clean shirts. This was necessary as the mud had completely covered the players' jerseys so that it was difficult to tell who was on whose side! When play did resume a long-range shot from Petrie crashed against the cross bar before Brash set off on a solo run that ended with him making it 3-0. With the Everton players' confidence now in ruins the home side stepped up the pace and when Spiksley collected the ball 70 yards from the Everton goal he ran unchallenged before finding Bell who made it 4-0. Wednesday were through to the FA Cup last four for the third consecutive season.

Their opponents were their conquerors of two years earlier, Bolton Wanderers. In the other semi-final the bookies' favourites and Will Chatterton's last surviving tip, Derby County, were up against Wolves.

Bolton had progressed against Wednesday in 1894 thanks to foul play and poor refereeing and there was therefore disappointment when it was announced that the referee from that day, Mr Armitt from Leek, would take charge of the 1896 semi-final involving the same sides.

Wanderers were going well in the League and were unbeaten in 1896 having played nine competitive matches. They had beaten Crewe, Blackpool and Bury to reach the semi-final.

The teams were equally matched and a tight game was predicted at Goodison Park, scene of Bolton's defeat by Notts County in the 1894 FA Cup final. On the morning of Saturday 21 March the Sheffield Midland Station was awash with Wednesday fans wearing their blue and white favours. Finally, the promised 'football specials' arrived and fans crammed on to them to make the journey to Liverpool Lime Street Station. The Wednesday players and staff arrived at Lime Street at 1pm and were greeted with three cheers by 300 Wednesday fans.

After a light lunch at the Alexandra Hotel the Wednesday party were taken by horse-drawn carriages to Goodison. They departed ten minutes after Bolton, who were staying in the same hotel. When the teams reached the ground they saw fans queuing up and down the streets of terraced housing waiting to get into the ground. It was immediately obvious that Sheffield fans outnumbered those from Bolton. This was confirmed when the teams came out with the Bolton cheers totally overwhelmed by the enthusiasm of the Wednesday followers.

Having won the toss the Bolton captain Jimmy 'Surefoot' Somerville chose to defend the Park End goal with the sun behind them, possibly recalling that Wednesday 'keeper Bill Allan had fumbled the ball over his goal-line with the sun in his eyes in 1894. With Langley suffering a twisted knee, Harry Brandon was again asked to play out of position at left back. Bolton also had an experienced full back missing in Dai Jones with E Hamilton replacing the Welsh international.

The game's first goal arrived on five minutes when Cassidy hit a shot over the Wednesday full backs and, blinded by the sun, a nervous Massey missed the flight of the ball and parried it to Tannahill who scored from close range. Somerville's decision had paid immediate dividends.

Their confidence high, Wanderers sought to double their advantage. Paton, who at the 1894 FA Cup final had, like many other Bolton players, taken to the field swathed in bandages – a gamble that backfired badly – fired home from a free kick. However, the Bolton fans' joy was stilled because no-one had touched the indirect effort. Jack Wright then went close as his shot smacked the crossbar.

Having hardly left their own half Wednesday almost equalised when Brash sent over a cross that Spiksley reached just before Somerville. The Wednesday winger improvised by knocking the ball off the Bolton man's shin pads which sent it beyond a surprised Sutcliffe. He reacted by diving backwards to push the ball behind for a corner. It was a magnificent save.

Much less pleasant was a deliberate hack on the Wednesday outside left by Jim McGeachan, the Bolton centre half. Wednesday appeals for a penalty were overlooked as Mr Armitt inexplicably decided to award an indirect free kick on the twelve-yard line and failed to speak to the offender. The game was now, however, all Wednesday and Sutcliffe, who had played brilliantly in the 1894 FA Cup final, showed his international class to ensure Bolton stayed ahead. He was eventually beaten twice, Hamilton first clearing a Spiksley shot from the line and then also blocking a Crawshaw header with a remarkable overhead scissors kick.

When the sides returned from their half-time break the sun had dipped and so did the quality of the football. The equaliser all Wednesday fans craved should have been scored by Davis but, clean through, he curled his effort wide.

There was then a terrible challenge from behind by McGeachan on Petrie that went unpunished. But with 70 minutes on the clock the deserved equaliser finally arrived after Spiksley's swerving cross had Bolton 'keeper Sutcliffe coming out to collect before he realised the ball was moving away from him. It was too late and an unmarked Brash rushed in and volleyed home as everything handy – hats, caps, flowers, favours – was flung upwards by the delighted Wednesday fans.

With Bolton dead on their feet and Wednesday down to nine fit men because Petrie was limping and Jamieson was suffering from an injury sustained in an earlier League game the tie failed to sparkle after that and was set for a replay. Then, in the last minute, Archie Fairbairn tricked his way past Brandon and raced in on goal. The Bolton man's nerves failed him at the last minute and his shot hit Massey's shins. When the ball spun free the 'keeper was forced to make a good save from the follow-up shot from 'Sparrow' Brown. So the tie ended 1-1 before a thoroughly entertained crowd of 37,000.

The replay was at the Town Ground, Nottingham Forest's home on Arkwright Street. In the 1890s working class men seldom travelled to away matches because of work commitments and the expense involved. Cup semi-finals were the exception and 12,000 Wednesday fans made the short trip and only worried about how to pay the rent and feed the family on the way home. On their arrival in Nottingham, fans set out to enjoy Nottingham Castle, the Caves, England's oldest inn, Ye Olde Trip to Jerusalem, Trent Bridge and the embankment.

Bolton fans were outnumbered 3 to 1 in the 16,000 crowd that also contained some locals who were rooting for the Sheffield side. Vail, who had replaced Cassidy, and Langley were to dust each other's jackets pretty well over the following 90 minutes.

Despite a heavy breeze and a difficult pitch Wednesday took the lead after two minutes when Crawshaw hit a twelve-yard free kick beyond Sutcliffe. The goal was compensation for another poor decision by Mr Armitt as the free kick was awarded for a hand ball so close to the Bolton goal that it should have been a penalty.

Bolton equalised on twenty minutes when Brown headed past Massey before Vail was booked for a terrible tackle on Langley that left the Wednesday man crippled for the remainder of the game. At the interval the Wednesday fans had the terrible feeling that with the wind behind them Bolton would again eliminate their side from the FA Cup.

With Petrie performing well to cover for the injured Langley, Wednesday were still in the tie. When Bolton conceded another dangerous free kick, Petrie took it splendidly and found Davis whose diving header restored the Yorkshire side's lead.

With Vail performing like a bull in a china shop, Bolton were beaten and in the final minute Wednesday confirmed their place in the 1896 FA Cup final when from a Brash cross, Fred Spiksley used his instep to fizz the ball over Sutcliffe and under the bar. "You would have to attend a great many games of football before you could see a better and more well-fashioned goal," wrote Langley in 1925.

When the referee sounded the final whistle the pain in Langley's massively swollen knee was agonising and with his mind in torment he was carried from the field by Earp and Petrie in a state of delirium. That evening thousands of Sheffielders went into Nottingham and celebrated wildly. It had been a famous occasion.

CHAPTER 12

1896 HERO
Wednesday win the FA Cup
for the first time

TO THE SURPRISE of the football world, Wolves overcame Derby County 2-1 in their 1896 FA Cup semi-final with goals from Joe Tonks and Billy Malpass. Tonks had earlier in the season replaced David Wykes in the first team after the latter died from typhoid fever.

It was the third time in eight seasons that the Black Country side had made it through to the final, losing 3-0 to Preston in 1889 and winning 1-0 against Everton in 1893. In addition to beating Derby in 1896, Wolves had also beaten Notts County, Liverpool and Stoke. Unlike Wolves, Wednesday were hoping to capture the FA Cup for the first time. The trophy itself was a new one as the original had been stolen.

A team of amateurs called the Wanderers were first to win the original trophy in 1872. When they also became the first to win the competition three years in succession between 1876–78 they gave up their right to keep the trophy on the understanding that any side equalling their feat would also return it to the FA. When Blackburn Rovers were successful three years running between 1884–86 they were awarded a commemorative shield.

After Aston Villa beat West Bromwich Albion 1-0 in the 1895 final they displayed the cup in the window of a football outfitters called William Shillcock. It was stolen on 11 September 1895 and never recovered. This was despite a £10 reward for its return.

Villa were fined, a new trophy was made and nothing was heard about the original for over sixty years until in 1958 when 82-year-old Harry Burge, a criminal who spent more than 46 years behind bars, claimed to have been among those responsible. However, his claim to have gained access to the shop through the back door was at odds with evidence that the thieves had entered through the roof.

Seventeen years later 68-year-old Edwin Tranter told the *Birmingham Evening Mail* his grandfather Joseph Piecewright was involved before another twenty years passed before evidence surfaced which author Mike Collett said was "as reliably substantiated as possible came to light."

Mrs Violet Stait, now aged 80, had married Jack Stait in 1935, the son of John 'Stosher' Stait. She claimed her husband had told her that his dad "pinched that cup out of Shillcock's window" and following further extensive investigation by the Aston Villa club magazine *Claret and Blue,* and later the BBC, it was agreed that Stait had been one of four unemployed men who had broken into the shop through the roof before walking out the front door with the trophy. Little good it did them financially as the four were double-crossed by their receiver who only gave them ten shillings (50 pence) to share. Melted down, the cup disappeared forever.

Sheffield Wednesday played three League games before the Cup Final. They won two and lost one with Fred Spiksley scoring in the 3-0 defeat of Small Heath, his tenth goal of the League campaign. Wednesday finished seventh.

Wolves, meanwhile, had faced a battle to finish out of the test match zone and they won two and lost two before a 5-0 last-day defeat of Bolton Wanderers saw them leapfrog Small Heath and avoid playing in the test match series.

In a surprise move the Wednesday directors decided to depart from tradition by preparing the team for the big game at home. Headquarters were established at the Earl of Arundel and Surrey Hotel and training took place each morning at Olive Grove with the ground open to anyone interested in seeing their heroes close up.

Once training finished the players changed and then walked to catch a train from Heeley station to Dore and Totley where on arrival there was a stiff four-mile uphill walk to Peacock Inn on the heights of Owler Bar. A substantial meal of steak and onions left everyone full enough for the four-mile hike back to catch the train.

The Wednesday party departed for London at 2.30pm on Friday 17 April 1896 with the train stopping momentarily at Nottingham's Midland Station to collect Fred Spiksley and Jack Earp and complete the playing contingent of thirteen. Who, though, were going to be the unlucky two not to make the final eleven?

After arriving at St Pancras Station at 6.10pm the party journeyed across the capital to reach the Queen's Hotel, the name of which had been a closely-guarded secret with everyone under strict instructions not to divulge it.

Following their evening meal, Arthur Dickinson gathered all the players together and told them that the side would be announced in the morning. All week long the papers had been full of reports that if the Crystal Palace pitch was firm and dry then Langley would play at left back. If the pitch conditions were heavy, however, Dr Jim Jamieson would play at half back with Harry Brandon moving to full back and Langley dropping out of the side.

Fred Spiksley and Ambrose Langley, whom everyone knew better as Mick, shared a twin-bedded room at the

Queen's Hotel on the night before the big game. Fred had been left bemused by the press reports believing that Mick had proved he was capable of playing well whatever the pitch conditions.

Writing for the *Thompson Weekly News* in 1920, Fred Spiksley said: "It was my considered opinion that for a game of this importance and stature, the team chosen should have been announced well in advance to allow the eleven players selected sufficient time to prepare mentally for the game ... I shared with Mick Langley, and neither of us had more than two hours' sleep. I was anxious for him. I kept getting out of bed, going over to the bay window and looking out to see what was happening with the weather ... this state of affairs continued throughout the night. Other players were restless, not least Jim Jamieson, who had played in every Cup-tie that season and yet faced the possibility of missing the final if it didn't rain heavily!'"

After breakfast on the Saturday morning the players gathered in the hotel library at 10.30 to find out their fates. Coach Bill Johnson had visited Crystal Palace and had returned with his pitch report.

The team selection up front proved to be something of a surprise but the Wednesday selectors were aware that their opponents were composed of some big strong players. Brash and Ferrier had performed brilliantly in both League and Cup but both were small in stature and so it was thought best to beef up the right flank by using Brady in support of Brash. Davis was switched to inside left to partner Spiksley on the left wing, with Bell at centre forward. In defence Langley was selected with Jamieson missing out.

The composition of the Wednesday side was therefore:-

Massey, Earp (captain), Langley, Brandon. Crawshaw, Petrie, Brash, Brady, Bell, Davis, Spiksley

It was six years since Wednesday had last played in the Cup Final and no-one from the 1890 match represented the club in 1896. The 1890 side had included nine local lads. It was a sign of how quickly football had changed following the development of professionalism that in 1896 only Crawshaw was from the Sheffield area.

Wednesday were the bookies, favourites to win the 1896 Cup Final but the 1893 winners Wolves were not without their backers.

As one of the original twelve members of the Football League, Wolves had appointed tobacconist John Addenbrooke as secretary/manager in August 1885 and he did the job until June 1922. He was an exceptionally fine administrator and office worker as well as possessing the ability to spot good footballers and recruit fine scouts. Under Addenbrooke, Wolves had some great players.

The Wolves side was as follows:-

Billy Tennant, Dickie Baugh, Tommy Dunne, Hillary Griffiths, Billy Malpass, William Owen, Jack Tonks, Charlie Henderson, Billy Beats, Harry Wood (captain), David Black.

Included in the eleven were a number of local lads: Tennant, the only amateur in the side, Baugh, who had played in Wolves' first League match in 1888, Griffiths, Owen, Tonks, Wood and Malpass. Baugh, Wood and Malpass had played in the 1893 final while Baugh and Wood had also played in the 1889 final against Preston North End.

The thirty-year-old amateur goalkeeper, Tennant, had quickly established himself as a fans' favourite after England international Billy Crispin Rose was injured.

Baugh was a Wolves man through and through and played from 1886 to 1896. He was a genuinely fine player with a tremendous appetite for hard work topped off with the ability to head the ball powerfully to safety. Son, Richard junior, played for Wolves after World War One. Tommy Dunne was a Scot who made 102 Wolves first team appearances. He was a no-nonsense defender, a strong tackler and a good header of the ball.

Right half Hillary Griffiths was one of three brothers who played for Wolves. He made 201 first team appearances, scoring once. He and Fred Spiksley had frequently tangled in earlier games. Centre half Billy Malpass had played superbly in the 1893 FA Cup final and during his Molineux career from 1891 to 1899 he made 155 League and FA Cup appearances, scoring nine times including goals against Notts County, Stoke and Derby County in the 1896 FA Cup run. Billy Owen completed the half back line. He was the tallest wolf in the pack at 6ft. In the 1895–96 season he played in every single League and FA Cup match. He did the same in 1896–97 and 1897–98.

Jack Tonks was a dashing outside right and fine crosser of the ball. His goals had helped his side overcome Stoke and Derby in the quarter and semi-final stages. Scotsman Charlie Henderson was Tonks's right flank partner in the 1895–96 season, his only one with Wolves, during which he scored eleven goals in 36 League and Cup appearances before signing for Sheffield United.

Billy Beats was signed a year after he scored three times for Port Vale when they beat Wolves in the 1894 Staffordshire Cup final. He made 218 League and FA Cup appearances for Wolves in which his ability to run at defenders was supplemented by fine ball skills, a delicate touch and a powerful shot. He spent seven seasons at Wolves during which he scored 73 goals; he also represented England on two occasions.

Harry Wood signed for Wolves in 1885 and went on to make 289 Football League and FA Cup appearances in which he scored 126 goals. He was the scorer of Wolves' first League hat-trick, against Derby County, in 1888 when, with thirteen goals, he topped the season's scoring charts for his club. He repeated that feat in 1890–91, when he was equal with Sam Thomson, 1892–93, 1894–95, 1895–96 and 1897–98, when he was equal with Beats and Bill Smith. Wood played football with great skill and enthusiasm and he won three England caps. He later signed for Southampton where he became a big favourite at the Dell, scoring 65 goals in

180 games. He played in the 1900 and 1902 FA Cup finals where he completed a hat-trick of defeats and also won four Southern League championship medals between 1899 and 1904. Like many footballers, on retirement he took over the running of a pub, the Milton Arms near Fratton Park, Portsmouth.

David Black was a coalminer's son who, after playing internationally for Scotland in 1889, moved south to play professional football at Grimsby and Middlesbrough before signing for Wolves for the start of the 1893–94 season. His tricky skills on the Wolves left helped him score seventeen goals for his club in 84 appearances.

In 1896 you could not visit the Crystal Palace without quickly realising it was "The Home of the English Cup Final" and the "Finest in the Kingdom". For starters there was an unequalled opportunity for sightseeing. The Crystal Palace was a gigantic glass building constructed in Hyde Park to house the 1851 Great Exhibition that was a showcase for Britain's industrial and economic might. Among the items displayed was the Sheffield-manufactured Norfolk Knife of Joseph Rodgers and Sons. This was a spring knife of 75 blades, which demonstrated that the skills of Sheffield craftsmen were unsurpassed.

In the summer of 1851, six million visitors attended what was the first ever international industrial fair. The building was then dismantled and re-erected in an enlarged form at Sydenham in South London, its location a 200-acre park, being renamed the Crystal Palace. Ornamental gardens, terraces and fountains were added, as were two massive fountains. These were switched on for the first time on 18 June 1856 by Queen Victoria and Prince Albert, the prince having co-organised the Great Exhibition with Henry Cole.

A massive blaze in 1936 burnt down the palace. The ruins still remain in the park along with a couple of statues, a few flights of stairs and some dinosaur sculptures that were built in the 1840s.

Flying over an Olive Grove

In 1895 the FA were desperate to bring the English Cup final back to London after the two previous finals had taken place in Lancashire. Kennington Oval was clearly too small to host the big game and so the FA approached the Crystal Palace company to see if they could assist. J A H Catton was one of the FA council members who was placed on the sub-committee to confer with the Crystal Palace. He claimed "There was nowhere else to go, or so suitable, as the arena was not used by any club, was absolutely neutral, and was so situated that a massed multitude on the lawn and the rising ground behind could obtain a view of the game".

It was agreed to create a new football field within the grounds and a vast area of the parkland that previously formed the south basin of the water fountain was turned into a massive arena extending to 25 acres of ground. The playing field was laid out in an elipse shape with a cycle track installed.

The goal posts were sited at the north and south ends of the ground and around the playing field was a railed area called simply "The Ring". Landscaped banking was introduced to form a natural amphitheatre that could accommodate tens of thousands of football fans in relative comfort with most having a reasonable view of the pitch.

At the north end there was an entrance and a standing area with the banking behind that extending round the goal to the east side. The banking then rose rapidly upwards to the tree line directly in front of a strong retaining fence. On the other side of this fence was a switchback railway fairground attraction.

There is a magnificent photograph, featured in this book, taken as the game kicked off in 1896. It shows the west side, where John Aird and Sons built a pavilion and where 'honoured guests' sat comfortably under cover and were guaranteed a great view when the captain of the winning side received the FA Cup directly in front of them.

There were 6,000 additional seats in blocks of 3,000 in two multi-span stands on either side of the pavilion, which contained provision for 100 members of the press to watch the action in comfort.

On 20 April 1895, Aston Villa beat WBA to become the first winners of the FA Cup at the Crystal Palace, when 42,560 fans watched the action. With football becoming more popular a larger crowd was expected for the 1896 final. This proved to be the case with the official attendance recorded at 48,836. The large crowd was keen for a good game.

Although the occasion in 1896 was nothing like as big as today's major football matches in terms of its coverage there had been plenty in the newspapers in the days leading up to it, including photographs and cartoon drawings of the players. The *Sports* newspaper, which was advertised on the final's match card, gave away photographs of both the Wednesday and Wolves teams.

On the day itself photographs of action on the pitch were taken. Never previously published, some of these are reproduced in this book.

Excursion trains from Sheffield to Kings Cross and St Pancras railway stations started leaving at 6.00am on 18 April 1896. Thousands of blue and white-dressed Wednesday fans streamed south where they poured out of the stations and hopped on to open-topped horse-drawn omnibuses travelling into central London.

Sheffield blue merged with Wolves black and gold as all along the River Thames the big game was the main topic of conversation. A feature of the journey across London was the music of partisan Wednesday fans, singing songs in honour of their side. At Sydenham Hill and Crystal Palace railway stations the fans disembarked and after a short walk the multitude of Wednesday fans arrived at the gates.

It was barely noon as the black and gold and blue and white favours poured into the ground. There were four

Flying over an Olive Grove

hours to kick-off, plenty of time to picnic and sightseeing opportunities to enjoy. Best not miss the kick-off, though, as the previous season had seen the quickest goal ever scored in an FA Cup final. It was timed at 30 seconds and is credited to Aston Villa's Bob Chatt although many Villa fans, and a certain Steve Bloomer, behind the goal where it was scored, were adamant that their captain John Devey had got the final touch.

By two o'clock on Cup Final day 1896 a massive number of fans were populating the ground and by 3 o'clock the people holding reserved seat tickets were busy taking their places while right up to kick-off the crowd continued to swell with fans from both sides.

Wednesday and Wolves walked out a good fifteen minutes before kick-off and while familiarising themselves with the conditions the players also warmed up with exercises and stretches to get themselves loose. The Wednesday XI were all fit, their splendid conditioning undertaken by coach Bill Johnson and his faithful ally John McReynolds to whom the players owed a great debt of gratitude.

At kick-off the weather was fine and warm without even the slightest breeze. Just before the advertised starting time the referee, Lieutenant Simpson, summoned the two captains to the centre spot. The toss was won by Wolves captain Harry Wood who elected to defend the southern 'Railway End'. In truth the conditions meant there was no real advantage in winning the toss.

With the referee allowing the teams a few minutes to settle into their formations, Fred Spiksley glanced across at his 'old friend' Hillary Griffiths and saw he was taking up a position a couple of feet across the whitewash. The Wednesday outside left immediately knew his opponent would have a dodge or two up his sleeve and if he was to make an impression then he needed to be at his best from the start. Fred knew what to expect from Griffiths. Little trips and kicks at ankles and knees were routine for

182

Division One and especially at Molineux, which even then had a reputation for being a difficult place to play as the crowd was so partisan. However, Fred was feeling fit and more than ready to perform on what was the biggest stage in football in 1896. He also had a point to prove as he had been inexplicably left out of the England side that faced Scotland exactly two weeks before.

Fred scores what seems likely to be the quickest goal ever in an FA Cup final. (The information which follows is taken from extensive research that can be found at:- www. spiksley.com)

"Sheffield scored in the first few seconds."
  The Times – 20 April 1896
"Less than 20 seconds had passed"
  Manchester Guardian – 20 April 1896

At 4pm Lawrie Bell started the game by passing to Brady who pushed the ball forward to Spiksley on the Wednesday left with the winger moving the ball back infield to Crawshaw who under pressure by the advancing Wolverhampton half backs misplaced his pass to send the ball out of play on the Wednesday right around 35 yards out from the Wolves goal. In what proved to be Wolves' only touch of the ball before it entered the net a hasty throw sees Crawshaw regain possession before sending the ball forward on the Wednesday right to Brash who beat his marker before reaching the goal line and crossing to Davis who laid the ball off for Spiksley to beat Tennant from around 25-30 yards out to make it 1-0.

Sadly, the exact time of Fred Spiksley's goal cannot be officially confirmed. No-one thought to ask the referee afterwards if he had noted it in his notebook and there was no reason for him to do so as it was not common practice in 1896. According to the former FA historian David Barber the FA do not have the referee's notebook and they have no idea if it still exists. All this has allowed Louis Saha to become known as the quickest scorer of an FA Cup final goal when his effort for Everton against Chelsea in 2009 was recorded at 25 seconds.

However there is more than ample evidence that the honour of the quickest FA Cup final goal is Fred Spiksley's.

The *Monday Sportsman* reported the goal as follows:- "Few will forget the dash with which the Wednesday went off, and the lightning goal credited to Spiksley inside the first minute of the game had a great deal to do with their ultimate victory."

The same day's *Manchester Guardian* is more specific:- "Less than 20 seconds had passed, when Wednesday scored the first point of the game. Archie Brash on the outside right passed the ball into the path of Fred Spiksley who scored with a powerful shot that Tennant in the Wolves goal was unable to reach."

"In about a quarter of a minute Spiksley registered the first goal."

Morning Post (London) of 20 April:
"Sheffield scored in the first few seconds."

The Times – 20 April:

The following newspapers reported that the goal had come within 30 seconds: *Sheffield Daily Telegraph, Nottinghamshire Guardian.*

The following newspapers all reported that the goal had come in less than a minute: *Leicester Chronicle, Pall Mall Gazette, Northern Echo, Derby Telegraph, London Standard, Reynolds' News, Glasgow Herald, Wrexham Advertiser, Liverpool Mercury, Sportsman, Lincolnshire Chronicle, Buckinghamshire Advertiser, Lloyd's Weekly, Dundee Courier.*

As the Wednesday fans celebrated, a shell-shocked Wanderers side restarted the match. Harry Davis, though, dispossessed Charlie Henderson and drove forward to hit a shot that was deflected for a corner. This was taken by Fred

Spiksley and only just scrambled away by a panic-stricken Wolves defence desperate to avoid going two down.

There were four minutes on the clock when Wolves made their first advance into Wednesday territory but Langley cleared to great South Yorkshire cheers. On eight minutes the side a goal down had their first real chance for a shot at goal when a free kick was awarded against Langley. Jack Tonks floated the ball into the Wednesday six-yard box and when it bounced up kindly, David Black, with his back to the goal hooked it over his head and towards the Wednesday net. The hush in the crowd was ended when at the very last moment the ball seemed to dip into the goal Wolves had equalised thanks to a touch of skill and good fortune. Massey, playing against his home town club, could only look on in anguish as the black and gold ranks roared their approval as it was now 1-1.

Four minutes later a determined Petrie hit a fine shot that fizzed just over before Spiksley beat Griffiths and bore down on Tennant's goal; his shot was only just wide drawing oohs and aahs around the ground. Wednesday, though, were determined to restore their lead. They did so on eighteen minutes with what Fred Spiksley agreed at the end of his long career was the best goal he ever scored.

The initial movements were almost identical to those of the opening goal with the ball being crossed into the centre from the right wing. Lawrie Bell then helped it on into Spiksley's path 35 yards out from Billy Tennant's goal. This was five yards further out than from where the Wednesday outside left had shot in the first minute but those five yards were to prove crucial as he drove the ball with great power. This time though he put spin on the ball and the initial groan from the crowd meant most believed he had badly miscued his shot. Then when the spin took hold the ball swung violently and at just three feet off the ground smacked against the far right hand goalpost before entering the Wolves net.

So powerful was the strike that when the ball hit the back of the net it rebounded back on to the field. This left Tennant totally confused. It meant that after he kicked it away he missed Billy Beats restarting the game as the shocked crowd tried to work out exactly what they had just witnessed.

Tennant kept his side in the match on 25 minutes when he denied Brady with a fine stop but as the game settled down neither side could exert any serious pressure with Wolves happy to concede a number of free kicks in their desire to prevent the quicker Wednesday forwards grabbing a third. The side a goal up then adopted a neat passing style that forced Wanderers on to the defensive. Yet with few real chances thereafter the interval arrived with Sheffield Wednesday still leading 2-1.

The Black Country side were again pushed back in the opening minutes of the second half as twice Brady and Brash combined with Dunne and Baugh being forced to make last-ditch tackles to prevent a Wednesday third. Spiksley, who on more than one occasion had confused his opponents by performing his back heel trick, was then upended from behind by Griffiths but fortunately he was not injured.

On 57 minutes there were great cheers among the Wolves fans when Tommy Dunne drove a free kick beyond Massey but these were soon stilled when it was realised that no one had touched the ball. Griffiths then flattened Spiksley again before Langley made a great tackle to deny Tonks a shooting chance.

Pushing forward, Wednesday had a great opportunity to double their lead but Bell failed to direct his header from a Crawshaw free kick beyond Tennant from just yards out. The Wolves 'keeper then performed heroics when Spiksley put Davis through and the Wednesday player was denied by Tennant's outstretched fingers. Exactly half the second half had elapsed and it was then that Wolves stepped up their efforts and for the first time in the match became the better side.

Massey was forced to rush out to deny Beats as the Wolves man dashed forward. The Wednesday 'keeper then made a fine save from a Black hot shot that brought cheers from the increasingly anxious Wednesday fans. From a corner Massey punched clear amid half a dozen Wolves players all trying to clatter him. Wednesday were dropping ever deeper and from a second corner there was the remarkable sight of Fred Spiksley making one of the only half a dozen clearances he made during his entire career.

In desperation, Earp, the Wednesday captain, then asked Crawshaw to drop back and, as a foretaste of the general system of defence that was later perfected by Herbert Chapman at Arsenal in the 1920s and 1930s, perform the role of a stopper centre half.

With just ten minutes remaining, the Wolves captain Harry Wood could see that Wednesday were wilting and he urged his defenders to hit the ball high into their opponents' box. The aerial bombardment did create the anticipated panic but in the event Wolves might have done better to keep playing the way they had been as the Wednesday defenders were exhausted and virtually unable to move. Hitting in long balls allowed them to stay where they were and when the ball was cleared the Wednesday forwards could hold it up and run down the clock, which is exactly what Spiksley did when he used all his trickery to prevent Wolves gaining possession.

However, Wolves were not about to lie down and on 89 minutes the goal they craved was only denied by another great Massey save before the Wednesday defenders began to literally throw themselves in front of further Wolves attempts on their goal. The game finally came to an end when the ball was cleared into midfield with the referee's whistle bringing jubilation among the Wednesday players, officials and fans.

Wednesday had won the FA Cup.

Bell then made a successful determined grab for the match ball and later declared that it would be taken to his home town of Dumbarton, where it would remain for eternity. The current whereabouts of the ball is unknown.

While Fred Spiksley was having his hand 'shook-off', as reported in the *Athletic News*, a bizarre story was unfolding in the centre of the Crystal Palace football pitch. One player couldn't understand what all the fuss was about. As the players were walking off the pitch, Billy Tennant innocently enquired of Mick Langley when the date for the replay was.

"Replay, old chap, there won't be any replay, we have won the English Cup by the odd goal in three".

Tennant was adamant. "Get away, there were only two goals scored today."

"Why, man alive, where on earth were you when we scored our second goal?" enquired Langley.

Years later, Fred Spiksley wrote about this in his autobiography stating:

"I was lucky to score the third and winning goal, hitting the ball with such force and spin that when it hit the back of the net the ball catapulted back into the field of play with Billy Tennant still wondering where the ball had vanished. Eventually he turned round to see the ball lying on the ground in front of him. Believing the ball was still in play Tennant leathered it down the ground, blissfully unaware that Lieutenant Simpson had already awarded the goal to Wednesday. In his moments of searching to see where the ball had gone Billy contrived to turn his back away from the action and in consequence he missed seeing both the ball being returned to the centre spot and Billy Beats taking the kick-off."

At least Tennant was given a medal. Wednesday's unlucky reserve, Bob Ferrier, came running over from the bench, where he had been watching the game, and congratulated all the players and after shaking their hands he finished up by tearfully saying; "You know I should have so liked to have had a medal." Fred later acknowledged that nobody who played in the final could possibly have understood the true feelings of a fellow player such as Ferrier and Jim Jamieson who had been left out in the cold. The sheer thrill of winning the FA Cup and collecting a winner's medal in this era is perhaps best illustrated by Roy Massey, grandson of the Wednesday 'keeper. Interviewed for this book, he recalled "My grandfather always wore his medal on his waistcoat."

Roy played as a forward for Rotherham United, Leyton Orient and Colchester United before undertaking coaching roles at Colchester, Arsenal and Norwich and in 2016 was working as a scout for Everton. He has had 50 years in football and is very proud of his grandfather, who lived to the ripe old age of 91.

"I would visit him every Sunday and sit in the armchair in front of the living room fire listening to his tales. I recall he told me in his first game for Wednesday he had gone to catch the ball and was knocked over the line with it in his hands by the centre forward. A goal was awarded but the next time in a similar situation he tipped the ball over the bar and then crouched down and flipped the forward over him and into the post where he suffered a broken arm."

"'Keepers are a breed apart and to be a good one you have to be mentally tough but from reading about him he was also very brave, handled the ball well, had good reflexes and was physically strong. In terms of training I understand he did a lot of shot-stopping with the players shooting at him. He was clearly a good player but he made apparent to me that Crawshaw and Spiksley were the best players in the team that won the FA Cup. He really admired both those players."

"He told me there was, like in most dressing rooms,

great comradeship between the players and of how they were treated by Sheffielders like kings when they returned with the FA Cup in 1896. He said it was a close game and he was proud he had made a couple of good saves late on to keep Wednesday in the lead. At home games he said that Wednesday often attracted big crowds who were rarely abusive like can be the case today and who would be very happy if Wednesday won. When he finally finished playing football until he retired he largely worked in the coal mines around Mexborough."

At the same time that the Wednesday first team had been playing in the Cup Final the second team had been at home against Barnsley St Peter's. Four thousand Wednesday fans shouted with joy when a telegram arrived on fifteen minutes with news their side led 1-0 and there was further pleasure when the half-time score arrived. At the end of the reserve game spectators assembled in one vast crowd in the main stand and when the tinkle of a telephone bell was heard they could hardly hold their breath.

At first there was silent hush, ears straining for news and then there was a cry – "WE'VE WON THE CUP!"

Two hundred miles south, Lord Kinnaird, the FA president, surrounded by a surging crowd of excited spectators, presented the cup to Wednesday captain Jack Earp and he lifted the trophy high above his head with pride. No one could really hear what Kinnaird said such was the tremendous cheers but he was understood to have said how delighted he was with the match and spirit in which it was played. After a few words from Earp, Sir Howard Vincent MP proposed a vote of thanks for the president, seconded by Sir Alfred Hickman, the Wolverhampton MP and Wolves president. He expressed the belief that the better team had won the day.

Lord Kinnaird then presented the gold medals to all twenty-two players who played in the final. These were memorable moments for the players before Jack Earp was able to lift up the new FA Cup again and bring deafening cheers from the Wednesday supporters.

When the presentations were over, the players washed and changed before joining the Wednesday officials for the short walk back to the Queen's Hotel and a high tea. A remaining hardcore of Wednesday fans had waited outside the ground and when they saw the players they cheered them to the echo. Arriving back at the hotel, the FA Cup was placed proudly in the centre of the tea table. Gleaming in the sunlight it looked magical and quite took the breath away.

John Holmes, the Wednesday chairman, stood up to say a few words.

"Gentlemen I have been hunting this Cup for the past twenty years, and whilst Mr. Dickinson has been the huntsman, and his clever hard-working team, the hounds, there has also been a tremendous number of members in the hunt who joined the chase with a will, and yet experienced continual disappointment year after year, but they still kept their courage, and in doing so were in at the kill at the Crystal Palace at Sydenham this afternoon. In closing this part of my notes I must refer to a great man connected with our great game. I refer of course to Mr Arthur Dickinson, our financial club secretary, and I congratulate him upon the success that has at last crowned his work".

Arthur Dickinson rose to his feet and replied; "Yes, I'm glad we've won it at last, as I can now bow out in a blaze of glory." This was clearly said tongue in cheek as Dickinson continued serving Wednesday for many years.

After finishing their tea the Wednesday party collected their belongings and relocated to the Temperance Hotel, Euston Road, close to St Pancras Station, where they were booked in for two nights. The accommodation was not so good and, to the disappointment of the players, there was no champagne and oysters. The Wednesday committee were all a bit old-fashioned and whereas they had been meticulous in planning for the English Cup final none had really given a thought about what to do if their players actually won. This lack of foresight also extended to what to do when they arrived back in Sheffield. It was common knowledge it would be at the Sheffield Midland Station at 5.28pm on Monday afternoon.

When the Wednesday players and officials caught the train home from St Pancras they could not have anticipated the massive welcome they would receive in Sheffield. Other football fans also wanted to catch a glimpse of the trophy and from Derby onwards the numbers grew gradually with the Wednesday players holding it up to carriage windows for people to see.

Jack Earp had purchased thirteen blue and white silk ties for the Wednesday players who had travelled south and when Mick Langley suddenly noticed there were no blue and white ribbons adorning the FA Cup he removed his from round his neck and tied it to one of the cup handles.

When the doubled-headed locomotives finally steamed into Sheffield they were met by Fred Spiksley, who had journeyed home independently. Travelling separately to games and living and training in Gainsborough all helped to make Fred a bit of an outsider. There was absolute chaos as the arrival platform was swamped with thousands of fans all desperate to see the winning players and the FA Cup. Inspector Bestwick's Brass Band started belting out See the Conquering Heroes but they had hardly got started when the crush of the crowd separated the bandsmen from the conductor.

The conquering heroes were forced to retreat to the safety of their saloon carriage and it was a further twenty minutes before the band could form up again and the players could board a coach and horses waiting to take them on a parade around Sheffield.

All the streets were absolutely packed and it took an age for the coach to make progress as the crowds spilled out on to the road as they sought to catch a glimpse of the FA Cup, which for most of the time was held aloft by the player who had scored the Wednesday goals at the Crystal Palace.

The sheer numbers of people made it impossible to travel up Commercial Street and, to the disappointment of the players and the crowd, the coach pulled sharply to the right and went straight to the Royal Hotel where Councillor George Senior and Mr Arthur Nixon had arranged a dinner for the honoured guests. The band by this time had long since disintegrated.

Later that evening the players visited the Empire Theatre where another enthusiastic reception awaited them, especially when the FA Cup was displayed. Having re-formed, the band managed to play a few tunes.

Four nights later an official dinner was held at the Masonic Hotel. By this time, the scorer of Wednesday's two goals in the final had received a cheque for £11. This was sent to him by Will Chatterton whose confidence that Wednesday would not win the 1896 FA Cup had proved to be misplaced. This concluded Fred's football betting career, but, sadly, not his addiction to gambling.

Fred also received, like all the rest of the Wednesday players and directors, a special jug from Wednesday board member, the Earl of Wharncliffe, who was so delighted at winning the FA Cup that he commissioned a number of jugs from Staffordshire Pottery.

CHAPTER 13

NUMBER ONE FOOTBALLER IN THE WORLD
Fred Spiksley's benefit year

AT THE END of the 1895–96 season Fred Spiksley was the most talked about footballer in the game. Aged twenty-six, Spiksley had completed five seasons with The Wednesday Football Club and had risen from a speedy young winger with promise to become the most feared outside left in Great Britain. In fact, he was the only surviving member of the side from Wednesday's days in the Football Alliance and since joining the club that year Spiksley had scored 52 league goals (including those scored in the Football Alliance) and fifteen FA Cup goals. A further 32 goals in regional cup competitions and club games meant Fred Spiksley had notched 99 first team goals in just five seasons and all from playing out on the wing. Spiksley had demonstrated, in the Burnley FA Cup tie, how just his presence on the pitch alone was enough to encourage his ten team mates to play better and believe that no game was lost. The FA Cup ties against Derby and Aston Villa, where Fred turned what seemed like certain defeats into famous victories, were already documented as legendary games

194

that would go on to live long in the memory of those who witnessed them.

In Spiksley, Wednesday had a player who had performed at the highest level of the game. Not only this, but he had destroyed the Scots in 1893. If this had not made Spiksley the most talked-about player in football, his two stunning strikes in the final of the FA Cup certainly did. In 1896 no player in the world was as famous as Fred Spiksley, as proved by an illustration which featured in the national newspaper *Sports* which placed Spiksley's name right next to that of cricketer W G Grace and can be seen reproduced in this book.

The Olive Grove Flyer at this time in his career was a respected foe feared by opposing teams. Many backs could only adopt rough tactics to try to contain him and when he did get away he was rarely caught as he raced away with the ball seemingly stuck to the outside of his foot. Spiksley was full of tricks that we are familiar with today, dinking his shoulder, feinting one way and then another before invariably putting in defence-splitting passes and crosses.

This really was Spiksley at the peak of his career and full of confidence. Although no-one would suggest that he was on top form for every match, there is no doubt that when the big game came along Spiksley was a man who invariably rose to the occasion and proved to be the difference, as was the case in 1893 and 1896.

Wednesday were obviously keen to retain him and Fred was happy to sign a rolling one-year contract on the same terms as before. Although today it's hard to believe that Wednesday offered their star player only a one-year contract these were different times and this was not unusual. Both parties were happy with the terms as Fred knew that Wednesday had no intention of losing him and the club were at the pinnacle of football success as FA Cup holders and were confident that their squad would push on and maybe challenge for the League title, a competition that they had not quite mastered yet.

An added sweetener for Spiksley was offered when the Wednesday committee agreed to a benefit match as thanks for his six years' service. Fred was delighted and his pleasure doubled when the famous amateur club, Corinthians, based at Queens Club in London, agreed to provide the opposition in the game on 30 December 1896.

The only new signing for the 1896–97 season was former reserve Bill Regan, back after a season with non-league Fairfield. It meant the Wednesday committee were content largely to rely on the thirteen players who had travelled south for the 1896 FA Cup final.

The action began with 2-1 defeats, at home against promoted Liverpool and away to Everton. Following a 3-1 victory at home to West Bromwich Albion, the Cup holders "with the exception of Spiksley and Brady" (Charles Francis) fell to pieces in the second half at Blackburn and despite kicking with the wind and rain behind them in the second half conceded three goals to lose 4-0. There was gloom all round when, next game, Stoke led 3-1 at half-time at Olive Grove but a brilliant second-half performance saw Wednesday win 4-3. Fred Spiksley scored his first goal of the season and also scored as Wednesday completed the double over West Brom, winning 2-0 away.

Seven days later, a series of remarkable League results began against Sunderland when the home game ended 0-0. In December the same score line was recorded in Sunderland and after that Sunderland won the next five League encounters between the sides without Wednesday scoring a goal. This failure to score in seven consecutive League matches against one club is a Wednesday record, although not one worth celebrating.

Much better was the home game that saw Everton beaten 4-1 as Wednesday rose to sixth place. Fred Spiksley then scored twice as, backed by hundreds of away supporters, Wednesday drew 2-2 at Nottingham Forest. His first equalised a Frank Forman goal and it was a real beauty.

Following a fine passing move involving Brash and Bell, the ball was passed to Brady who let it run into the path of the Wednesday wide man who showed great coolness and judgement to lift it over the head of 'keeper Dan Allsop and into the net.

A double-header against runaway League leaders Aston Villa saw Wednesday heavily beaten 3-1 at home and 4-0 away. With the home game tied at 1-1 Villa side scored twice through Johnny Campbell and Charlie Athersmith.

Campbell was a wonderfully gifted clever inside or centre forward. He was brave, aggressive when required, possessed plenty of tricks and above all had an instinctive knack of scoring goals. He had exceptional balance, close control and dribbling skills. Campbell was part of a brilliant Villa forward five in 1896–97 that also consisted of John Devey, Wheldon, Athersmith and Stephen Smith. Only Campbell of the five failed to net when Wednesday were beaten the following week. Villa were to end the League season on 48 points, eleven in front of second-placed Sheffield United.

On 28 November 1896, Fred Spiksley netted as Derby County were beaten 2-0 at Olive Grove before three consecutive draws left Wednesday in mid-table prior to the Boxing Day fixture away to Sheffield United that was lost 2-0. Two days later, Wednesday's best performance of the season saw Blackburn Rovers hammered 6-0 with Ferrier scoring three. Just 5,000 spectators watched the game, which was at least better than the attendance of just 1,000 against Wolves on 12 December. Blackburn's next away game was again in Sheffield and this time they lost 7-0 to United.

With Germany and the USA beginning to pull ahead to become the world's leading super powers, the British economy was struggling. The result was fewer jobs and lower pay, while all the time political tensions with Germany, over colonial rule, bubbled under the surface.

Between 1876 and 1900 the area of Africa under European rule rose from 10 to 90 per cent.

Fred's testimonial match against Corinthians was on 30 December. The game fitted in with the amateur club's traditional Christmas tour and they agreed they would field their strongest possible team including England internationals G O Smith, Charles Wreford-Brown, John Gettins, Vaughan Lodge and Bill Oakley.

Sorting out the financial arrangements for the match wasn't easy. In truth, the amateur designation was a sham. The expenses demanded by the Corinthians were always hefty and in this case were double the wages of Wednesday's professionals, who were all donating their match fee. In late Victorian times it was said that the Corinthians were like the Prince of Wales because they bargained for the whole of the gate money before agreeing to turn up. These young amateur gentlemen, steeped in wealth and privilege, could tour the country indulging in their favourite pastime, assisted by having their considerable expenses covered by less wealthy opponents.

In the event, a good gate, a cracking game and a well-supported subscription list combined to make Fred Spiksley's benefit an unqualified success. £291 was raised including £30 from his former club, Gainsborough Trinity, and there were donations from players at Sheffield United.

It helped that the rain stayed away to allow 8,000 fans to pay a well-deserved compliment to Wednesday's Olive Grove Flyer.

Wednesday: Massey, Earp, Langley, Petrie, Crawshaw, Jamieson, Brash, Ferrier, Davis, Brady, Spiksley

Corinthians: William Campbell, Lewis Vaughan, Bill Oakley, Bernard Middleditch, Charles Wreford-Brown, Arthur George Topham, M H Stanborough, Gilbert Oswald Smith, J H Gettins, C L Alexander, Cuthbert 'Pinky' Burnup.

Fred Spiksley had the honour of leading his team out and he was greeted by a rousing reception that continued when Charles Wreford-Brown led out the visitors.

Facing the wind, Wednesday struggled. Massey dealt with three shots before Burnup missed a glorious chance. With the away side dominating it was no surprise when they took the lead with Burnup atoning for his earlier miss. The lead was doubled when the referee Mr J Fox overruled strong offside appeals and John Gettins raced clear from fifty yards out before beating Massey. Wednesday's concerted efforts to get back into the match were thwarted by Campbell in the Corinthians goal.

On changing ends Wednesday had the benefit of the breeze behind them but it was the Corinthians who scored the next goal when G O Smith's low fast shot made it 3-0. On Fred Spiksley's big day the Corinthians were determined to show that the amateur game was superior to the professional one. Earlier in the season the Corinthians had beaten Wednesday 2-0 at the Queens Club in the annual match between the FA Cup winners and Corinthians. In 1903–04, the Corinthians hammered the FA Cup holders, Bury, 10-3 and the following season beat Manchester United 11-3, the Manchester club's heaviest ever defeat.

However, fears of a thrashing were quickly ended when Davis headed the ball on to Fred Spiksley who in turn headed it to his partner Brady who nodded the ball beyond Campbell. The left wing partnership between the two players was now almost telepathic and according to Fred "they were my happiest football days in every respect." Despite the brilliant understanding between the pair they only once spoke to each other on a football pitch when following a poor pass Alec Brady remarked "That was a bad 'un, Fred" and the reply was "It wasn't a good 'un, Alec."

Although it is not clear why the two players did not speak to each otheron the pitch, the reason could lie in Alec Brady's brief association with Gainsborough Trinity in the 1888–89 season. Spiksley had threatened to walk out on the club if Trinity continued to play their 'Scottish Professors' who had starved the local player of the ball. No doubt Fred may have been quite frosty with Alec upon his arrival at Olive Grove, which could have led to little verbal communication in their opening matches. Whatever the reason, this odd stand-off was to continue as Wednesday needed to keep them on the left wing as together the pair were irresistible and must go down as one of the club's greatest ever pairings.

It is certain that Spiksley must have warmed to his Scottish compatriot, as he knew that when Brady was on his inside he was much more effective in creating and scoring goals. Ultimately this must have been much more fun.

Encouraged by reducing the deficit, Wednesday pressed and an under-pressure Oakley, in attempting to clear Petrie's effort, diverted the ball past his own 'keeper.

With the Wednesday fans cheering vociferously there was disappointment when Brash had an effort disallowed for offside but on 70 minutes a well-directed long pass from Brady was thumped past Campbell by Brash to make it 3-3. The atmosphere was now electric as the sides traded blows in their efforts to fashion a winner. When clever play by Davis ended with a powerful shot and the rebound from Campbell was knocked home by Brady the cheers of the crowd seemed set to herald a famous victory for the FA Cup holders.

The Corinthians, though, were not going to go down easily and Smith netted only for it to be disallowed for offside. Massey pulled off a great save from Alexander before Brash failed to wrap up victory when he missed from close in. With the light fading, Gettins sent in a powerful shot that Massey failed to spot until it was too late and moments later a highly competitive game ended 4-4.

Wednesday began 1897 by beating Preston North End 1-0 with Fred Spiksley scoring the goal. There was major disappointment when any hopes of retaining the FA Cup were snuffed out when Nottingham Forest won 1-0 with an Arthur Capes goal before a best-of-the-season Olive Grove crowd of 16,639. The trophy would eventually pass to Aston Villa who won it for the second time in three seasons, beating Everton 3-2 in a thrilling final in which the lead changed hands twice in the first half. By winning the trophy, Aston Villa became only the second side to record the League and FA Cup 'double' first achieved by Preston in 1888–89.

After being beaten by Forest, Wednesday had nine League matches to play and they won three, drew four and lost two. One of the victories was on the final day of the season when Bury were beaten 2-0 before another sparse crowd of 1,000.

The game might have marked the final football match for Fred Spiksley. During it, one very deliberate attempt to put him out of action almost cost him his life when an unidentified opponent made a back for him that was intended to ensure he would come down to earth on his head rather than his feet. As he hurtled towards the turf the fear that he might come down on his neck had the Wednesday winger frantically trying to break his fall with his flailing arms. The England international failed to prevent the heavy fall but amid total silence he was able to rise slowly to his feet and stagger through the remainder of the game. When he later visited the doctor he was told that if the fall had happened to a heavier man then a broken spine was the most likely outcome. The injured player later said: "Only two things saved me from paralysis, a miracle and my light weight."

Beating Bury meant Wednesday finished in a respectable sixth place, the club's highest since entering the Football League. In previous seasons, Wednesday had never conceded fewer than 53 goals but in 1896–97 the goals against column was just 37, the second best in the table with Sheffield United conceding one fewer. At the same time, Wednesday's goals total of 42 was their lowest ever with only one player – Fred Spiksley on ten – reaching double figures. After the previous season's excitement the Wednesday fans had been left disappointed.

On the 28 April 1897 Spiksley's benefit season was capped off with a formal dinner and presentation at the King's Arms Hotel in Sheffield. Speaking at the dinner, Wednesday Club president, Mr John Holmes had this to say about Spiksley;

"In England, Scotland and Ireland Spiksley's fame has been sustained for many years, and he has not done playing yet. Wherever he has played, and wherever he is known, he is always respected, and has conducted himself in a proper manner both as a football player and as a man. As far as The Wednesday club is concerned he has been for some years a faithful servant and his benefit was well deserved."

At the end of his speech a cheque for £291 12s 1d (£291.61) was handed over to Spiksley who in reply thanked the Wednesday club and all involved in organising his benefit. He drew special attention to his friends in Gainsborough, whom he referred to as being "chiefly from the working class". They had collectively contributed a sum of £30 to his benefit cheque. As far as the Gainsborough Trinity club and their officials were concerned he had received practically nothing. He rounded off the evening by saying he had always done his best for Wednesday, not only for his money, but because he took an interest in the club. On the field he had always been a trier. At that Fred sat down amid cheers, whereupon his health was drunk with 'musical honours'.

A few short weeks after the presentation, Sheffield Town Hall was officially opened on 21 May 1897. It had been constructed over a seven-year period from 1890 onwards. On the roof of the building was a Vulcan with its hand in the air. Wednesday fans quickly began referring to it as 'Fred' as it appeared to show him appealing for a foul.

During the 1897 close season, which saw the adoption of the existing regulations on the dimensions of the field of play, Wednesday signed right-winger William Dryburgh from Cowdenbeath and his form during the 1897–98 season was considered good enough for Brash to depart when it finished. Albert Kaye had been spotted playing for non-League Eckington and the new Wednesday centre forward was to play impressively and ended up with ten goals in 27 League and Cup matches. Wednesday finished in their highest ever League position, fifth, but this feat was overshadowed by Sheffield United, who roared to the League title.

Wednesday began badly and lost four of their first five matches with the only success coming at home to Liverpool. In the sixth match, Wednesday beat champions Aston Villa 3-0 with Spiksley scoring twice. In a 3-1 defeat of Notts County, he again scored twice and he was also on the score sheet as Bolton were beaten 3-0 at Burnden Park after which the victors lay in fourth place in the table on eight points, five fewer than top-placed Sheffield United.

The two great rivals faced each other in the ninth League game. It was at Olive Grove and having lost just once in the eight previous meetings, Sheffield United were confident. The away followers in the 24,000-plus crowd breathed a sigh of relief when Billy Foulke, who joined United at the start of the 1894–95 season, made a great early save from Fred Spiksley. Foulke was 12st 5lb when he signed for United from Blackwell and steadily grew to over 25st by the time his career ended at Bradford City in 1907.

Fred and Bill were to become close friends as both shared a great love of horse racing. Fred, like many others, appreciated Bill's wry sense of humour and later recalled going to visit Ernest Needham at Bramall Lane. When he arrived he asked Bill if he had seen his colleague and was told, "Yes, he was here just a few minutes ago." Then as he looked into the depths of fog he continued: "Why, there he is crossing the ground to the cricket pavilion." When Fred looked across and could only see a vague shadow in the mist he challenged the United keeper laughingly saying, "Come off it Bill, you can't kid me that you can identify a shadow in this thick fog."

"Okay then," said Foulke, "I bet you a quid it's Needham. Can't you tell it's Ernest, why, just look at the long strides he's takin' to save on 'is shoe leather."

The United followers were elated when their side took a fourth-minute lead. The goal came when John Cunningham cut into the centre before laying the ball off to Walter Bennett, a fine marksman whose confidence and incisive play earned him the nickname 'Cocky'. He fired his shot beyond Massey. Bennett was to play twice for England during his career but was killed in a colliery accident in 1908.

With right half Rab Howell again sticking close to Fred Spiksley, the Wednesday wide man was left with little room to manoeuvre and the away side might have doubled their lead before half-time but Bennett's shot clipped the top of the bar before going over. An injury to Almond meant the United centre forward had missed much of the first-half action and although he returned for the second he was unable to make any serious contribution to the game. There was a further blow to the visitors when Bennett was injured on the restart and thereafter struggled.

Wednesday now dominated and would have equalised except for a poor miss by Fred Spiksley. United were then stunned when Fred Priest was injured and not surprisingly the home side controlled possession. Such was Wednesday's determination to equalise that Foulke was even bundled over the line only for the 'goal' to be disallowed. It took two Wednesday forwards to achieve the feat. United followers, who worshipped their giant 'keeper, regularly sang "Who ate all the pies?" in his honour. United in general were a weighty side during what was the most successful period in their history. Between 1897 and 1902 they captured the League title and twice won the FA Cup while also finishing runners-up twice in the League and once in the FA Cup.

Plenty of chances were made but all were missed and remarkably it was United who went closest when a shot hit the bar and dropped to the injured Priest who fired an easy chance wide. The winners retained top spot in a game that had been a typical no-holds-barred local derby in which quality had been lacking.

Off the pitch, the conduct of the fans was starting to become a problem. What had been friendly rivalry between supporters was making way for unruly behaviour. 'Looker On' in the *Sheffield Telegraph* reported that "scores of really good sportsmen are heartily glad" when the derby matches are over due to "the bad blood too often engendered and the unhealthy, almost ferocious, excitement manifested by the crowd." There was press criticism of the verbal abuse directed by fans of both clubs towards the match referee, Mr Brodie.

By the time of the return match at Bramall Lane on 27 December both Sheffield teams were in the top three with Wednesday having taken twelve points from eight games. Fred Spiksley had scored seven goals in these games including netting on Christmas Day when Stoke lost 4-0 at Olive Grove.

However the outside left failed to complete the game as he was sent off. The referee was Lincoln's Mr. West, well known to Fred from his Gainsborough days as being so biased that when he acted as the Lincoln City linesman he was reported by teams in the Midland Counties League for intimidation. Fred was not happy to discover that Mr. West had been elevated to referee status and feared he might use his new powers to get his own back on those who had objected to him acting as Lincoln City's 'twelfth man'.

Flying over an Olive Grove

Olive Grove was rock hard from the frost. This made the ball unusually bouncy and difficult to control. Stoke right back John Robertson, who later captained Liverpool to the League title, was a dashing, daring and slightly reckless opponent who seemed to make no allowance for the treacherous underfoot conditions when he tackled for the ball. From a high kick the ball bounced to a tremendous height and when Fred used his shoulder and ball skills to manoeuvre away from his marker it was a masterful move not appreciated by Mr West who blew for a free kick. When Fred politely enquired why he had been penalised the referee ignored him.

When the Wednesday winger then complained about the decision Mr West simply pushed him over on to the icy ground, causing him to fall on his bottom much to the amusement of the crowd. West then told the player to retreat down the pitch but when he positioned himself back the six yards required under the rules then in place this failed to satisfy the referee who told him to retreat further. Fred stood his ground and informed the referee that he was abiding by the rules. The player was intent on defending the free kick at which point Mr West said that for deliberately ignoring his instructions he was dismissing him. Fred initially refused to leave the field but eventually gave way for what was the first and only sending-off in his football career.

Fred's dismissal meant he appeared before the FA's disciplinary committee on 5 January 1897. He was exonerated of any blame and was neither fined nor suspended and his unblemished record and good name in football remained intact. That record was not to be sustained over the following two seasons as in 1898–99 he was involved in a heated argument with the referee at the end of the home game with Everton on 4 March 1899. Afterwards he was forced by the FA to apologise and Wednesday were warned about the conduct of their players. Fred was fortunate as earlier in the same season he had been involved in another confrontation with the referee at the end of the FA Cup-tie at home to Stoke on 28 January 1899. The match ended 2-2 and although an injured Fred wasn't even playing in the game he had been left angry at what he felt were two unfair challenges on Massey in goal, both of which resulted in Stoke goals. The second in particular was disputed by the home players. Fred limped into the dressing room after the final whistle and berated the referee and even told him to make a detailed study of the laws of the game. Luckily for Fred, the referee took no notice and Fred reflected, "He did not even report the matter to the FA as I had expected him to do. Had he done so, I have no doubt that I should have been suspended for a lengthy period."

With both teams entertaining title aspirations there was massive interest in Sheffield in the lead-up to the return game with United on Boxing Day. The Bramall Lane gates were opened at 12.45pm and the then largest ever attendance of 37,389 – paying £916 at the turnstiles – packed the ground for a game where both sides were at full strength. Pre-match entertainment saw the band play Auld Lang Syne and Lead Kindly Light, the entire crowd singing along to create a great atmosphere.

The rain had left the pitch greasy and with the wind behind them the away side almost scored in the first minute as Alec Brady fizzed a shot across the face of Foulke's goal. A long shot from Harry Thickett was only just scrambled away by Massey but it was Wednesday who created most of the scoring opportunities. The away side had strong penalty appeals when Spiksley was upended from behind by Thickett and although it seemed a bad foul referee Aaron Scragg waved play on.

It was a Wednesday player who opened the scoring when, after Massey was forced to save from Bennett, the unfortunate Earp sliced the ball into his own net on 25 minutes. The Wednesday captain later blamed the band for playing Lead Kindly Light on a gloomy day!

With the away side continuing to push forward the game was finely balanced at the interval. In the second half it continued to be an exciting affair. On the Wednesday left, Brady and Spiksley continued to probe and when the latter curled over a cross to Brash, the right winger was clean through with only Foulke to beat. The United 'keeper's presence put off Brash who fired wide to the groans of the Wednesday supporters.

The home side were determined to keep Spiksley quiet and Rab Howell was detailed to help Thickett but the England international managed to escape both before finding Kaye whose shot was blocked by Bob Cain. Unfortunately for the home side, the ball rebounded into the path of the Wednesday outside left who smashed it beyond Foulke to level the scores.

The game was all-action from then on with half chances for both teams before Brash yet again created a one-on-one situation with Foulke, but, as previously, the 'keeper won the contest. Consequently the game ended 1-1.

This left the top of the table as follows;

Villa	19 games – 24 points
United	16 – 23
West Brom	17 – 21
Wednesday	18 – 21
Wolves	18 – 21

It was generally agreed that the game had been the best so far between the two top Sheffield sides and the *Sheffield Independent* paid tribute the following day: "Yesterday there was little scrambling and less roughness. Both sides played out their hardest and their best. Lovers of good football, who attend such matches, will have thoroughly enjoyed themselves. Wednesday showed that they understood the kind of football that was required for the occasion by passing and crossing the ball into the danger area in front of the goal, whilst United combined beautifully whilst being dogged and steady in defence, proving that they were back to their top form."

Despite their performances, both teams lost their following matches with Sheffield United going down 2-1 at home to Liverpool and Wednesday beaten 6-3 at home by Nottingham Forest on New Year's Day. However, whereas United went on to win their following match – and the subsequent six – Wednesday then lost away to Everton and by the time they ran out in the return fixture with Forest they had dropped out of the title race.

The Forest game brought another defeat, the only goal coming after a misunderstanding between Massey and Langley. Afterwards the normally easy-going Wednesday chairman John Holmes was so upset that he knocked on the dressing room door, pulled it open and took a couple of steps inside. When he gained the players attention he told them, "Gentlemen, there's two men in this team who want their backsides kicking." Without saying another word he turned on his heels and left a very quiet dressing room. Time seemed to stand still before a voice piped up, "All right, Jimmy and Ambrose, prepare yourselves for your arse-kicking."

Defeat meant the match at Sunderland in the FA Cup first round had assumed even greater importance.

After winning the League title three times in four seasons, Sunderland had struggled in the previous two seasons. Manager Tom Watson had departed to Liverpool and prolific striker Johnny Campbell to Newcastle United. Sunderland had played well over Christmas and January and had won all six of their League games to rise to second place in the table, the position in which they would finish the season.

Sunderland were playing their final season at Newcastle Road. Work was under way at nearby Roker

Park, which would become Sunderland's home for the next 99 years.

Having beaten Wednesday twice earlier in the season the home fans were in a confident mood and a 17,893 crowd turned out for the big occasion. In the week leading up to the game the main topic of debate among Wednesday fans was the bad injury to Harry Brandon against Derby County. This was the match in which, with regular penalty taker Mick Langley missing through injury, Fred Spiksley scored from the penalty spot for the only time in his Wednesday career in a 3-1 success. Brandon had been replaced in the subsequent League game with Forest by Thomas Stevenson. The newcomer's workmanlike performance in his second first-team appearance made him a contender to play in the cup-tie.

The day after losing to Forest a party of Wednesday players and officials journeyed by train to Saltburn by the Sea and settled into the magnificent Zetland Hotel. Built by the Stockton and Darlington Railway Company, the first public railway to use steam locomotives, the hotel even had its own railway platform. The hotel had one hundred rooms and had been built on a lavish scale to attract wealthy customers. It contained a telescope room where guests could look out to sea and watch the fishing boats while there was also a reading room, library and billiard room.

Wednesday needed a good Cup run to boost their finances and so John Holmes was determined to give his team the best chance of creating an upset. He set out to provide the players with a happy and relaxed atmosphere away from the public glare of Sheffield. Saltburn was literally a breath of fresh air with miles of beautiful golden sand and a shelved beach stretching for miles up the North Yorkshire coast. A cold breeze brought colour to the footballers' cheeks in a week when the aim was to build up a great team spirit with an emphasis on hard physical training.

John Holmes asked the party to pay attention after they had eaten their dinner on the Sunday evening. As the room went quiet he pulled out a rope and held it up.

"You see this rope, gentlemen? Well if you don't win the FA Cup-tie with Sunderland, then I, John Holmes, the man you see before you, will be no more, for he will have hung himself with this very rope!"

From then on, Holmes kept regularly brandishing his 'hanging rope' and telling the players, "Remember, lads, my life is in your hands." It was all meant in fun but his curious method of motivating the team caused quite a few eyebrows to be raised, especially among the hotel staff.

The following morning, after a light breakfast, the trainers and officials took advantage of the firm wet sand – perfect for passing the ball – to put the players through their fitness regime and skills training that ended with a serious but sometimes light-hearted seven-a-side match.

On the Monday afternoon a number of players wrapped themselves up against the elements and, after taking advantage of the Saltburn Tramway that took passengers from the cliff tops to the beach, took a relaxing stroll along the sand to soak up the ozone. A crowd had gathered to see the launch of The Mary Batcher lifeboat that was named after its Leeds benefactor. Captain Thomas Holmes, an inspector from the National Lifeboat Institution, performed the official ceremony following which the boat was launched into the sea amid great cheers. When the boat gave every satisfaction in its subsequent two-hour trial run, everyone departed after a highly entertaining afternoon.

Training was going so well that by the Wednesday evening everyone was feeling quietly confident of success. After dinner the Wednesday selection committee privately convened to discuss team selection and tactics. As a senior player, Langley was generally allowed to attend such meetings without having any say in the selection process. Club chairman John Holmes headed the committee which also included Arthur Dickinson, trainer Bill Johnson, first team captain Jack Earp, who was absent on this occasion as it was agreed he could do his training near home, and Fred Spiksley, the senior professional, who had become a committee member during the 1896–97 season.

Dickinson began by sharing his thoughts on why Wednesday had twice lost earlier in the season to Sunderland. Why no goals had been scored was the crux of the discussion. Speaking on Earp's behalf, Dickinson said that Albert Kaye had missed the first defeat against Sunderland but had now scored seven times in seventeen games. This included a goal against Preston when the first time the opposition had touched the ball was to pick it out of the back of the net. On the left, the Brady and Spiksley partnership had notched eighteen goals.

In comparison, on the right, Brash had not scored and at inside right Ferrier had hit only two. Both men were small and had suffered some deliberate and targeted charging by heavy defenders so that their play had become ineffectual.

It was agreed to beef up the right wing and A J, as Dickinson was known, argued to general consensus that Brash should not play. However, Ferrier should stay in the side. Noticing Fred Spiksley's look of dissent, A J asked about his thoughts. Fred was a great fan of Harry Davis and he believed that his current fine form for the reserves should not be overlooked. Davis had been Fred's left wing partner when the FA Cup was won in 1896 and Fred felt that Davis's subsequent willingness to act as cover for other players who were injured had cost him his first-team place when everyone was fit. Fred sought to address what he felt was a gross injustice to his friend and argued that Davis should play at inside right. When Bill Johnson agreed it was decided that Davis would be recalled to the side after just one first-team appearance since September.

The committee now turned their attention to Brash's replacement and John Holmes immediately proposed

Dryburgh as the best candidate. The forward had been in fine scoring form for the reserves and on his return to the first team, Dryburgh had also scored against Nottingham Forest and Derby. There was no disagreement that Dryburgh should play and Wednesday would turn out at Sunderland with a new right flank partnership of Dryburgh and Davis. Brash and Ferrier would be left out.

Fred Spiksley felt, however, that Ferrier should play. The other selectors found this amusing, saying, "Nay, Fred, it's against the rules to play twelve men." Chuckling away, it was Langley who asked for Fred to be listened to.

He explained that Wednesday would need three good half backs at Sunderland and he was convinced that Ferrier would be better at right half than Stevenson. But hadn't the latter done well at Forest? The speaker agreed but felt the cup-tie would be a much tougher encounter and Sunderland could be expected to take advantage of any weaknesses.

But hadn't Ferrier never previously played right half and wasn't he too small for such a position?

Fred argued that Everton's Johnny Holt was the same size as Ferrier and as the meeting became heated he stood up to plead his case by stating, "Gentlemen, Bob Ferrier has played in 90 competitive games for the club, including five English Cup-ties, four of which we won. He is experienced, tenacious, skilful and committed. Most important of all he knows what it's like to play in a 'blood and guts' cup-tie and he knows both the taste of victory, and the bitterness of defeat."

The committee conceded and that was how Fred Spiksley finalised Wednesday's team to face Sunderland in 1898. The decision to move Ferrier would prove not only an inspired choice for the cup-tie but one that stood the test of the time as Ferrier went on to become a quite brilliant right half.

Sunderland had undergone their own special training at Gosforth for a match that was keenly anticipated and demonstrated why the decision to move to Roker Park was the correct one as by 1.45pm, one hour before kick-off, Newcastle Road was full to capacity with the gates locked. Hundreds of spectators that had been turned away were determined to see the game. At each end of the ground people climbed on each other's shoulders and scrambled up 20ft high walls before reaching down and assisting their helpers to gain entry and then leaping into the packed crowd. It was a miracle nobody was killed.

With Earp having joined up with the Wednesday party, the players were lined up ready to run out when Bill Johnson roared, "Go on my little beauties – you can win." The away side was cheered on to the pitch by their supporters, many wearing blue and white favours. The home fans were in great voice and after cheering for their own favourites a number began to abuse Langley, who had previously played extremely vigorously when the sides had met.

Sunderland attacked with the wind at their backs and from the off the away side were pegged back. Massey rushed out to prevent Hugh Wilson scoring and then made two brilliant diving saves. Meanwhile Langley had managed to further anger the Sunderland crowd with some robust tackling. One supporter threw his breakfast can at the Wednesday full back and when it hit a policeman he, displaying not the slightest degree of surprise, simply pocketed it. No doubt it would come in handy for his lunch.

High balls into the Wednesday goalmouth was Sunderland's preferred option but all they did was prove that Crawshaw was the greatest header of a football in the English game with Langley not far behind. Corner after corner was headed clear and when Sunderland did get the ball and Wilson ran clear, Crawshaw timed his tackle perfectly to come away with the ball.

The Wednesday goal was finally breached when Boyle's 30-yard free kick beat Massey, but the 'keeper knew it had not touched anyone, so there was no alarm and the game restarted with a goal kick.

When Wednesday did get forward an overhead bicycle kick by Davis was brilliantly saved by Doig amid huge cheers. Dryburgh was then denied by a last-ditch Peter Boyle tackle as Wednesday began to dominate possession and Doig did well to save a Kaye effort. With the interval only minutes away Langley prevented Hugh Morgan getting his shot away and this prompted another bout of jeering, booing, hissing and missile-throwing at the Wednesday man. Langley ignored the abuse as he left the pitch at half-time.

With the wind in their favour the visitors were confident they could now go on to success although in the first ten minutes of the second half it was Sunderland who threatened. When Spiksley did get away he was hauled over. Minutes later a terrible Philip Bach challenge on the Wednesday player left him writhing in agony convinced the kick he had received to his arm had left it broken. There was a two-minute delay while the doctor examined the severely bruised arm after which the England international continued despite his obvious discomfort. Minutes later he hit a great shot that Doig tipped over.

When Sunderland pushed forward Massey saved at the expense of a kick to his head but after he recovered the play was virtually from then on all up the other end of the ground. Spiksley had a shot cleared off the line and Kaye rifled a shot over the crossbar.

Doig fisted away a shot from Dryburgh as the game entered the final ten minutes at which point, true to tradition, the Sunderland flag on the flagpole was lowered as a signal to players and fans that time was running out. On 82 minutes the goal that the away side deserved arrived when Brady and Spiksley combined to send Kaye clear. The Sunderland defenders chasing him down but the Wednesday centre forward held them off before dinking the ball over Doig. As the ball nestled in the net the Wednesday fans let out an explosion of noise while, in stark comparison, the Sunderland fans and players stood disbelieving in stunned silence. Sunderland were beaten and the better team had won.

Many in the crowd were unhappy with the result and were looking for someone to blame. Their target was Langley and when the game ended a number of home fans were threatening to spill on to the pitch and get their hands on the Wednesday man. Fortunately there were sufficient policemen on hand to protect the Wednesday players by escorting them to the safety of the dressing room.

In view of the hostility towards Langley, the Sunderland executive thought it wise if the crowd didn't see him again after the match. Unruly elements had gathered around the main entrance shouting "Where is he – the bastard." Langley left by the back door with a police escort. Sunderland hired a hansom cab to take him to the hotel where they had hired a private room and laid on food, drink and refreshments for the Wednesday party. The rest of the Wednesday players left Newcastle Road an hour late and after running the gauntlet of the Sunderland mob they were taken by a circuitous route through Sunderland as they shook off any remaining pursuers. On arrival at the private dining room they found Langley sitting quietly in front of a roaring log fire sipping tea and consuming buttered toasted muffins.

Fred Spiksley was keen to get moving south as he wanted to catch the train at Retford that would get him back to Gainsborough around 10pm. Nellie was on her own with a new young baby, Frederick Hayward Spiksley, otherwise known as Fred junior. When the train did leave Sunderland it was too slow to allow Fred to catch the London Express from Newcastle. When he finally reached Retford it was after midnight and too late to find overnight accommodation.

It was twelve miles by road to home and with no fire in the station waiting room, Fred decided to walk and calculated he could shave a mile and a half off the journey by walking along the railway track. Having played in a hard physical game the Wednesday player was not in great shape but set off at his best pace and in dense fog he whistled to keep up his spirits.

Arriving at Clarborough Bridge, where the railway line crossed the turnpike, he hesitated before deciding it was unwise to leave the railway track for the road in such foggy conditions. Sticking to his guns he pressed on but when he reached Clarborough Tunnel he quickly realised that his plan to climb Clarborough Hill and then rejoin the track on the far side of the tunnel was impossible. The hill was simply too steep to clamber up.

The Wednesday man did not want to walk through a tunnel that hardly seemed wide enough for two trains to pass but on the other hand he did not want to retrace his steps. Plucking up the courage he plunged into the pitch dark tunnel and by keeping his left hand on the tunnel wall he made slow progress. He discovered recesses were built at intervals into the tunnel walls and this knowledge ultimately saved his life.

Suddenly he heard a great roar as he realised a train had entered the tunnel. He had only seconds to decide what to do when another roar indicated a second train had entered the tunnel on the opposite track. Fred froze like a rabbit caught in the headlights. In a flash of inspiration he remembered the recesses and he threw himself blindly to the far side of the track and miraculously he landed in one of them and proceeded to press his backside as close as he could against the wall.

Seconds later the first train whistled by and the frightened man's ears were blasted by the fierce noise. This was the Lincoln Express. The second train was a mineral one bound for Grimsby with two double-headed engines

217

pulling it at around eight miles an hour. Fred saw one of the stokers shovelling coal into the fire box. Evidently one of the train drivers had spotted him and he yelled out but Fred could neither hear nor understand. Once both trains had passed, Fred threw caution to the wind and raced as fast as he could through the rest of the tunnel. He was delayed when he ran into a spoil heap at the side of the track and fell head over heels. After removing the grit from his teeth he scrambled to safety as quickly as possible.

Fred's tribulations were not yet over. Before the railway track reached Gainsborough it crossed the River Trent on a wooden trestle 150 yards in length and high above the river. The trestle bridge beams were three feet apart and if Fred missed one of them then it was a sheer drop into the fast swirling river. Doing the best to steady his nerves and keeping his eyes wide open, Fred Spiksley negotiated the bridge safely, after which a reaction quickly set in and he began shaking uncontrollably with sweat pouring down his face and neck.

After managing the final half mile walk home the Wednesday player stumbled through the front door before lighting the gas and looking at his grimy face. He only had cold water to wash with and it took five bowls before he could recognise himself in the mirror. When he finally stumbled into bed he had nightmares about his experience.

Wednesday's defeat of Sunderland raised hopes of another FA Cup run. These were ended in the following round when West Bromwich Albion beat Wednesday 1-0. The away side had plenty of chances to win the game but were undone by a neat piece of gamesmanship by Bassett.

The Baggies had kicked the ball out of play and, as it hit one of the boundary boards that surrounded the pitch, it rebounded on to the field. Langley threw it to Jamieson for him to take the throw-in. For some inexplicable reason, Mr Hulme, the linesman stepped in to award the throw to Albion and when a disappointed Jamieson let the ball go it was thrown to Bassett by Langley. Immediately, Bassett began shouting that the ball had been thrown at him, at which point the linesman, without consulting the referee, John Lewis, ran on to the field and placed the ball down for a free kick, possibly for handball.

When this was taken the ball was crossed into the Wednesday goal where the only goal of the game was scrambled home by Flewitt. Lewis was one of the finest referees in the game at the time and he later told Langley that he had no idea why the linesman had waved for a free kick. The referee had been many yards away and he later admitted he had made a mistake in not intervening. Bassett was a sly old fox with any amount of cunning tricks. He had taken his team through to the third round but they then lost 3-2 at home to the eventual winners, Nottingham Forest.

Wednesday's defeat in the FA Cup left just seven League games to play. Away to Derby County, Fred Spiksley scored his fifteenth league goal of the season as Wednesday won 2-1. At Stoke he scored his sixteenth although this time Wednesday lost 2-1.

On 9 April, a day after Sheffield United had beaten Bolton Wanderers to clinch the League title, Fred Spiksley scored his seventeenth League goal of the season in a 3-0 defeat of West Bromwich Albion at home. It meant he finished in second place behind Villa's Fred Wheldon at the top of the Division One scoring charts. This was a remarkable feat for an outside left in an era where the focal point of a side's attack was always the centre forward.

The victory put Wednesday third in the table but heavy away defeats at Liverpool (4-0) and Wolves (5-0) saw them drop down to fifth. Two victories would have left Wednesday in second place behind Sheffield United but nevertheless it was still Wednesday's highest ever League placing and raised the prospect of a stronger challenge in the following campaign.

United's success meant it was the first time the Football League championship had come to Sheffield. Under captain Ernest Needham's direction the champions had introduced a new style of football with long swinging passes from the centre forward out to the wings, wide passing between the half backs, all backed up by tremendous dash and strength. Fred Spiksley was a great admirer of Needham as a player, captain and tactician.

"I give him the honour of being the greatest player association football has ever seen," said Fred in 1907. Needham had played particularly brilliantly on the day that his side had clinched the title. Switched to inside-right, he scored a sensational goal to win the game at Bolton.

CHAPTER 14

BEST OF THE BEST
Spiksley gives a man-of-the-match performance in England's greatest pre-1900 forward line

FRED SPIKSLEY'S ABSENCE when England played in Glasgow against Scotland in April 1896 had contributed to his country being easily defeated. The Wednesday man was also left out of all three international games in 1897. In these, England first beat Ireland 6-0, with the Liverpool outside left Tom Bradshaw failing to net in what proved to be his only appearance for his country. Wales were then vanquished 4-0 at Bramall Lane in a game where Foulke played his only international match and where the Everton outside left Alf Milward, playing internationally for the first time in six seasons, scored twice. Against Scotland, Milward was selected but it was the Scots who triumphed 2-1 with goals from Tom Hyslop and James Millar against an early opener by Steve Bloomer. Milward missed three good chances during the game. The match was played at the Crystal Palace where a year previously Fred Spiksley had scored twice for his club in the FA Cup final success against Wolves.

By 1898 professionalism had prevailed to the extent that professionals could be selected for both the Wales and Ireland matches. For the first time players like Fred Spiksley had the opportunity to earn a maximum of three England caps a year. The FA probably saw this move as necessary as England were definitely a more competitive outfit when the side contained a majority of professionals. With players like Billy Meredith, the Welsh promised to be a stronger side so the selectors would have been focusing more than ever on securing England's dominance.

Fred Spiksley's form in the early part of the 1897–98 season had seen him score fourteen goals in 23 League and Cup matches. It placed the Wednesday winger in second place in the scoring charts. Nevertheless, when the England side were selected to face Ireland he was left out in favour of West Brom's Ben Garfield. England struggled in Belfast and only a fine display by 'keeper Jack Robinson enabled them to squeeze home 3-2. In the following match, against Wales in Wrexham, Fred Spiksley was restored to the England team at outside left. The game was played just six days before the Scotland game and the selectors chose a strong team.

England: John Robinson, William Oakley, Billy Williams, Ernest Needham, Tom Perry, Tom Booth, Charlie Athersmith, John Goodall, G O Smith, Fred Wheldon, Spiksley

Wales: James Trainer, Charles Parry, Smart Arridge, John Taylor, Caesar Jenkyns (captain), John Leonard Jones, Billy Meredith, Thomas Bartley, Maddox Morgan-Owen, Alfred E Watkins, Edwin James

Directly inside Fred was the man he was competing with to finish as top scorer in Division One, Fred Wheldon. Nicknamed 'Diamond', Wheldon ended the League campaign with 23 goals, six more than his England colleague. Wheldon had scored three times against Ireland in 1897 but had failed to net in Belfast in 1898.

With the selectors telling the England side that they should treat the match against Wales as a final trial for the Scotland game, the away side started quickly on a sodden pitch. After a series of early misses they took the lead on nine minutes when, from a Spiksley free kick, Wheldon hooked the ball towards goal where Trainer made a valiant effort to keep it out, only for it to creep over the line and send visitors from the neighbouring English counties jumping for joy.

The game from then on was a tight struggle but came to life when Robinson was penalised for running with the ball. From the resulting free kick the 'keeper was beaten but the home fans' celebrations were swiftly stilled when the referee overruled the effort as it was from an indirect free kick. England thus held a narrow lead at half-time.

Although the away side were forced to defend deeply by a dashing Billy Meredith, then of Manchester City, they played much better in the second half and really should have extended their lead before the Welsh winger drilled a shot beyond Robinson. Welsh celebrations were once again cut short when the referee ruled that Maddox Morgan-Owen, the Corinthians centre forward, had held down Robinson. The Welsh players and spectators believed there had been an injustice.

There was further Welsh disappointment when Spiksley joined forces with Wheldon and after a series of passes the former's cross was superbly hit home by Wheldon to make it Wales 0 England 2. The England left wing partnership had won the game and the away side completed the scoring when Charlie Athersmith, who had previously hardly made a run down the right wing, crossed for Smith to score with a header.

The performance and result was deemed so satisfactory that by the time the England party had reached Chester the selectors had chosen the team to play Scotland. Steve Bloomer came back in for Goodall, Frank Forman of Nottingham Forest was selected to replace Tommy Booth and, to the surprise of many, the amateur Charles Wreford-Brown replaced Tom Perry at centre half and was also made captain.

With Sheffield United locked in a battle with Sunderland for the League title, Ernest Needham had written to the England selectors asking to be excused from playing against Scotland. When this request was refused, Fred went over to Bramall Lane to discuss travelling with him to Scotland.

Fred bumped into Bill Foulke and, before he could ask him where Needham was, they were interrupted by a keen, enthusiastic footballer from Sheffield United's reserve side.

"Please, Mr Foulke, I wonder if I might ask you a question?" enquired the nervous youngster.

"Fire away, lad".

"Well, sir, I was wondering why I am always played in United's second team."

"Are yer sure yer want t' kna th' answer lad?"

"Yes, sir, I'm sure".

"Well, if tha really wants t' kna it's because we 'aven't got a third team t' play you in."

England arrived in Glasgow for a game that all of Scotland was talking about. The England team and Goodall, the travelling reserve, trained on

Celtic Park on the Friday lunchtime before taking a guided tour round Glasgow and returning for high tea at the Central Station Hotel.

An enterprising bicycle merchant had offered a brand new bicycle to the player who opened the scoring the following day. When the England players gathered after tea it was agreed that should they be fortunate to score first then the bicycle should be sold and the proceeds shared among the professional players with Oakley, Smith and Wreford-Brown waiving their share of the proceeds in order to avoid breaching their amateur status. Fred Spiksley then stood up and offered to buy the bicycle if England won it and pay the professionals their shares.

Charles Wreford-Brown had previously played in just three internationals and had been selected out of the blue to captain England in his fourth. Unlike many other amateur players who played for England he had few airs and graces and his energy and enthusiasm knew no bounds. He was a born optimist and he stood up to deliver a great speech in which he admitted he would be the proudest man alive if England gave the Scots a good hiding the following afternoon. Every player left the room determined not to let the England captain down.

The Scottish fans, though, were convinced that England had no chance and may as well have stayed at home. Yet the home side had been weakened by the withdrawals of Sunderland's Ned Doig and Hughie Wilson. The Wearsiders were going head to head with Sheffield United for the title and the sides clashed on Thursday 2 April at Bramall Lane where a Sunderland side containing the two Scots had lost to a home side missing Needham. Needham was to be back to play for his club side in the next game when he scored the only goal as Bolton were beaten and Sheffield United thus became Division One champions for the only time in their history.

Celtic Park had been upgraded since the last time Spiksley had played there for England in 1894. It now had no fewer than 35 turnstiles in operation and they were worked overtime so that the action was watched by 62,000 fans, who paid £3,229 in total. However, many young boys were excluded from attending due to the decision by the SFA not to offer reduced prices for youngsters.

The size of the crowd, slightly more than what the Emirates Stadium in North London holds today, was the biggest that Fred played in front of during his long career. It was a sign of how football had grown in importance as the year when Fred had signed his first professional contract with Gainsborough in 1887 the crowd for the England–Scotland game at Leamington Street, Blackburn was 12,000.

The first time that Fred had played at Celtic Park against Scotland it was a miracle that no one had been killed as the facilities were not adequate to deal with a large crowd. Not so in 1898 and the scene was a remarkable one as the match passed off without the least disturbance.

Before kick-off Scottish pipers and half a dozen men with kettledrums entertained the packed crowd. The noise was almost deafening when the heavens opened and umbrellas went up. They had been taken down by the time a brass band began a selection of Scottish tunes that are always guaranteed to set the blood racing. The swirl of the Argyll and Sutherland Highlanders' pipes ended the pre-match entertainment as England strode out on to the pitch. Fred Spiksley was certain his side would win as he felt it was the greatest England team he had ever had the privilege to play in. The huge roar that followed when the Scots then came out meant not everyone agreed with him!

Despite the earlier rain, the pitch was in good condition although there was also a strong breeze blowing down the ground. England lost the toss but from the kick-off they made great headway into the Scottish defence. It was a sign of things to come over the following ninety minutes.

Scotland: Ken Anderson, John Drummond, Dan Doyle, Neil Gibson, James Cowan (captain), John T Robinson, John Bell, John Campbell, William S Maxwell, James Millar, Alex Smith

England: John Robinson, Billy Williams, William Oakley, Charles Wreford-Brown (captain), Ernest Needham, Frank Forman, Charlie Athersmith, Steve Bloomer, Gilbert Oswald Smith, Fred Wheldon, Spiksley

The Scots were chasing shadows and on three minutes England's left wing partnership of Wheldon and Spiksley ripped apart the home defence with a series of pass and moves that left the latter in front of the goal with only John Drummond and Kenny Anderson to beat. As he was about to shoot his teammate shouted "Mine!" Taken unawares, Fred had the ball whipped from under his feet as Wheldon put England ahead.

How could he complain? But what was the England captain handing to the goalscorer?

It turned out to be a gold sovereign and the Wednesday man couldn't help thinking that Wheldon had known before the game of Wreford-Brown's intention to reward any scorer with that valuable item. The incident still rankled enough with him that he wrote about it in his autobiography more than twenty years later. Wheldon gave the coin to the referee and asked him to look after it until the end of the game.

With their team a goal down, the Scottish crowd were silenced. Try as they might, Scotland saw their attempts to make space for a shot confounded by an England half back line in fine form. Ernest Needham was constantly collecting the ball and finding Wheldon and Spiksley out wide and Drummond simply couldn't cope with the Football League's most prolific goalscorers playing together. Their understanding was becoming almost telepathic. It soon nearly became 2-0 when Smith shot narrowly wide after ghosting away from Cowan, the hero of Scotland's victories in the previous two matches against England.

A second England goal was not long in coming, however. Smith slipped through a pass for Bloomer to put his side 2-0 ahead. The Scots appealed energetically for offside but Mr Thomas Robertson, the Stirling-born referee, was certain the goal was a good one.

At half-time the Scottish forward line was rearranged with Campbell moving to centre, Maxwell to inside left and Miller to inside right. When Miller netted on 50 minutes it seemed that the switches had worked but, in truth, the goal owed more to England's over-confidence and Wreford-Brown was not averse to letting his colleagues know how disgusted he was with their attitude.

The goal was not going to stop England winning the game but it remains historic because a photograph of it would appear to be the oldest ever of a goal scored in an international match. Featured in this book, it's the first time it's been published. Robinson can be clearly seen as the shot from Miller speeds past him with the Scottish forwards celebrating.

A third England goal was not long in coming, though, as Fred Spiksleyleft the Scots' dependable right-half Neil Gibson in his wake, hurtled past Drummond and then delivered a great pass into Bloomer's path. The Derby man hit a shot that rocketed home off the underside of the crossbar. Bloomer was rewarded with a second gold sovereign from his captain. The Derby man's shorts were not as big as his captain's and he asked the referee to keep his money until the end of proceedings. Robinson replied, "If you keep this up, Steve, I will have to go for my handbag!"

In the event, neither Bloomer nor England scored again but the game was already over with 35 minutes to go. Scotland never threatened the away goal and left the field well beaten. Fred later purchased the bicycle at the bargain price of £10 and moaned about the loss of 'his' sovereign, taken from him just as he was about to shoot for the first goal.

When, many years later, he finally wrote about the 1898 game at Celtic Park he said:

"To put it kindly, the Scots were completely and utterly outplayed from start to finish that day. England won by 3 goals to 1, humbling the Scots in front of their own fanatical supporters. In my opinion the amount of possession we had, the territorial supremacy that we maintained throughout the game, the number of shots at goal and on target, and the meagre scraps of possession that Scotland had to feed off; England were a good five goals better than our opponent on the day. It was a comprehensive dismantling of the Scottish team, the England fans were on top of the world, and I was a proud man that evening."

According to Needham, this match "produced the finest football I ever saw an English eleven play during my career ... and, if I am permitted to say so, I played one of my best games that day. I attribute this to the fact that I was so used to Fred Spiksley's methods, having combined with him in many internationals and inter-association matches."

Needham was full of praise for the Scotland 'keeper Kenny Anderson for keeping the scoreline respectable.

The newspapers were fulsome in their praise of the England side with many singling out the England left partnership. "Special words of praise are due to Wheldon and Spiksley," said the special correspondent in *the Umpire*, for the role they had played in the Scots' defeat. At the same time there was little doubt that a special role had been played by Wreford-Brown who was everywhere and never failed to encourage and support those under his direction. For many years the 1898 England forward line was considered the finest of all time and it was generally agreed across the press that the man of the match was the little fellow from Lincolnshire on the left flank.

Fred Spiksley travelled back to Sheffield a proud man. He had come back into the England side after a two-year gap and they had won both matches. Success in the game in Glasgow prevented the Scots from winning for the third year in a row and ensured England recaptured top spot in the Home International Championship.

The Wednesday winger had played seven times for England and had been successful in five games with draws in the other two. He had scored seven times, including hat tricks in his first two internationals, and had also made a number of goals for his England colleagues. His partnership with Wheldon against Scotland in 1898 had been brilliant.

Fred could not have known it but he had played his final international. The following season he and Wednesday both struggled. In 1900 Needham wrote that "Spiksley had been a certainty for selection in all the 1899 Home Internationals, but was unlucky to miss out through injury." This was the first of a long string of persistent injuries that would dog Spiksley's career until he eventually bowed out of top flight football in 1904. Spiksley had achieved almost every single honour in the game, the only missing medal of value to him was a First Division winner's. Wednesday had never really been able to muster a challenge for this and, in truth, had peaked in 1896. A serious rebuilding job was needed before they could harbour hopes of helping Fred complete his collection. Time was already starting to run out for a 28-year-old Fred Spiksley.

Spiksley was not forgotten by those who regularly watched England over many years, however. In 1926 a book of his personal reminiscences by J A H Catton was published and in it he named his all-time best England XI. It was as follows:

E Taylor, R Crompton, H Burgess, J Crabtree, W Wedlock, E Needham, W Bassett, S Bloomer, Tinsley Lindley, J Goodall, F Spiksley

Catton claimed "Spiksley was a natural footballer who had the advantage of playing at Gainsborough and Sheffield with some Scotsmen who had the characteristic quality of their race – ball control.

"Thus a youngster who could use either foot with equal facility had the advantage of developing his gift to the top of his bent. Whenever I saw him he played well, but never better than at Richmond, for he scored the last three goals in about ten minutes".

Catton was adamant that the disputed goal Fred Spiksley scored against Scotland at Richmond was onside as "the moment the ball left Bassett's boot Spiksley was off in a flash. He would trap the ball with his right and crash it into the net with his left. This seemed like one movement because he was so rapid ... Spiksley had sleight of foot. He did most of his dribbling with the outside of his right foot ... I do not like making sweeping statements, but I have never seen so thoroughly competent an outside left as Spiksley, who relied not on weight, or even on speed alone, but upon his craft and power over the ball."

CHAPTER 15

END OF AN ERA
The sad end to Wednesday's years at Olive Grove

FOLLOWING THEIR ENTRY to Division One, Wednesday struggled in their first two seasons before progressing, in subsequent years to finish in eighth, seventh, sixth and fifth respectively. Winning the title seemed unlikely in 1898–99 but there was surely no fear of relegation, which following the abandonment of the test match series, was the fate of the bottom two clubs in a division now containing eighteen sides.

The new season brought bad news. The Olive Grove lease had expired. Renewal was expected to be a formality. Out of the blue, however, new landlords, gave notice to quit at the end of the season. Wednesday were unaware the land had been sold by the Duke of Norfolk to the MLS Railway Company, who were planning to expand. Wednesday faced an uncertain future and the committee would need to devote a lot of time to finding a new place to play.

Spirits were further dampened after an opening day 4-0 thrashing by Liverpool. Nevertheless there was a healthy crowd of 11,000 inside Olive Grove for the first home game. Goals from Dryburgh and debutant Bill Hemmingfield ensured that Nottingham Forest were beaten 2-1; then after drawing 0-0 at Bolton Wanderers the same two players scored in another 2-1 home victory – over Preston. Hemmingfield had arrived from Mexborough. He had a decent first season, making 22 first team appearances and finishing as Wednesday's top scorer with eight goals

Wednesday rose to second in the table when goals from Spiksley, Brady and Hemmingfield saw Derby beaten 3-1 at Olive Grove. This was to be the season's highlight.

After defeat at West Bromwich, Wednesday drew 1-1 at home to Sheffield United in a Monday afternoon game with Hemmingfield again netting. Action photographs were taken during the game by Jasper Redfern. Some that have rarely been seen before feature in this book including one in which Fred can be seen in front of the packed main stand at Olive Grove as the ball is cleared by a United defender.

Redfern was a Sheffield optician who by 1898 was also taking photographs. He specialised in local films of interest including football and cricket. He appears to have toured Africa in 1900 before moving into the moving picture business. He later engaged in research into X-rays and the treatment of cancer, from which he eventually died, through exposure to ionising radiation. Redfern was a particularly keen photographer of Spiksley and Foulke.

Harry Ruddlesdin played his sixth Wednesday first team game in the derby. Barnsley-born 'Ruddy' arrived from village side Birdwell in the summer. He was considered a left winger, but regular training revealed he was more of a left half. Over the next five seasons, Ruddlesdin was to be the man behind Fred Spiksley and he formed a brilliant defensive trio with Ferrier and Crawshaw.

Dryburgh notched his third goal of the season when Blackburn Rovers played at Olive Grove. With Brady injured, the Wednesday committee experimented by selecting club captain Jack Earp up front. The gamble looked like it might pay off when, from a Spiksley cross, Dryburgh headed home. Thereafter it was the away side that dominated. It was no surprise when Ben Hulse scored an equalising goal before the interval.

On the resumption, Fred Spiksley took the game to Rovers but was denied by James Carter. With Earp struggling he reverted to right half with Ferrier pushed up to support Dryburgh. On 60 minutes, John Moreland gave the away side the lead with a fine finish.

The home side were then denied a clear penalty when referee John Adams was so far behind play that he failed to recognise that the foul by Booth on Spiksley was inside the area. The resulting free kick came to nothing before Carter made another fine save from a Spiksley shot.

Wednesday finally gained their reward when in the last minute former Wednesday man Tom Brandon came from behind and chopped over Spiksley, an action that gave Adams no problems in awarding a penalty.

The Wednesday outside left dusted himself down to take the spot kick but as the crowd held their breath he flashed the ball a yard wide of the goal, following which the final whistle sounded. A disappointed Fred Spiksley was adamant that the penalty was the last he would take.

The following home games saw Wednesday beat Bury 3-2 and then Wolves 3-0, with the latter proving a personal triumph for Albert Kaye as he scored all the goals. They proved to be his last for Wednesday. After failing to notch in his next eleven games Kaye departed for Kent non-league side Chatham.

Defeats at Everton and Stoke were followed by a home loss to Notts County. At Stoke, Brady played his final game for Wednesday as an injury kept him out for the remainder of the season at the end of which he returned home to play for Clydebank. John 'Jocky' Wright was signed for £200 from Bolton Wanderers to play inside Fred Spiksley. Wright was a skilful player but nowhere near as good as Brady and the Wednesday left was the poorer for the enforced change.

Wright debuted in what proved to be the longest League match ever. Aston Villa were again in contention for top spot when they arrived at Olive Grove on 26 November 1898. The game had been earmarked by the Wednesday committee as decision day on the new ground's location. One suggestion had been to play at Bramall Lane with the Sheaf House Ground employed for both Sheffield clubs' reserve team matches. However, when negotiations over Sheaf House stalled the project was abandoned.

A huge effort had gone into finding suitable locations. Four were selected with the merits of each extensively discussed in the local press. Two were in Carbrook and two in Owlerton and Wednesday fans were asked to vote at the Aston Villa game for their preferred choice.

Around 10,000 voted and after a number of spoilt votes were deducted the results were:

Carbrook 4,767
Owlerton 4,115
Neutral 124
Sheaf House 16

The way was now open to begin negotiations with Carbrook Cricket Club who owned the land on which Wednesday hoped to make their new home. These discussions were to founder and it was not until early April 1899 that John Holmes could report that a plot of land at Owlerton could be purchased by the club.

In the meantime there was the small matter of the Villa match. With Wednesday's office personnel occupied with the ballot, everyone missed a telegram to the Earl of Arundel and Surrey Hotel from match referee Aaron Scragg saying he had missed his connecting train to Sheffield. A new referee was going to be required for at least part of the game. With panic setting in the advertised 2.30pm kick-off time passed before it was discovered that

Fred Bye, an experienced local referee, was present and would take charge.

It was 2.45pm when the match started in gloomy conditions. Heavy ground made passing difficult. Crawshaw's opening goal on twenty minutes was cancelled out within a minute by Frank Bedingfield, making his only appearance for Villa.

Dryburgh restored the lead before the interval at which point Scragg arrived to take charge. Hemmingfield scored with a diving header to make it 3-1 but with the light deteriorating by then the players, already caked in mud, could hardly recognise one another. Birmingham press man Argus Jud had bet a Sheffield reporter a cigar and cognac that the match would not finish and it proved a winning wager. On 79 minutes and 30 seconds, Scragg, under pressure from Villa captain John Devey over the conditions, blew his whistle and abandoned the match at 3-1.

An almighty row now ensued with Wednesday arguing that Villa should concede the points. Villa contended that the home side should have arranged an earlier kick-off time as it was known that November days were short. The whole game, they argued, should be replayed.

Scragg notified the Football League that he had abandoned the game because of bad light. Following an inquest the Football League management committee decided that Aston Villa must return to Olive Grove and play the remaining ten and a half minutes. To Wednesday's annoyance they were instructed to pay the away side's expenses for their trip north. Stuck in a battle with Liverpool for the title, Villa continued to argue that the whole game should be replayed.

The restricted 'game' was set for 13 March 1899. The 'loss' of two points meant that when Wednesday were thrashed 5-0 at Burnley on 3 December they fell to fifteenth in the table. This was the seventh away game and Wednesday had failed to net in any of them. There was relief all round, therefore, when goals from Wright and Spiksley ensured a 2-2 draw at Newcastle.

However a 2-1 Boxing Day defeat at Bramall Lane saw Wednesday drop into bottom place.

They stayed there when Liverpool won 3-0 at Olive Grove on New Year's Eve. A 0-0 draw at Bury followed by a 1-1 draw at Nottingham Forest and then a 1-0 home win over relegation rivals Bolton Wanderers did, however, lift Wednesday out of the relegation zone.

Wednesday made the short trip to Derby on 21 January with an unbeaten record in 1899. It was not to last as what followed was a 9-0 hammering. The result was at the time Wednesday's heaviest defeat in the club's professional era and much of the blame for the shambles was due to the sprint training the players were forced to endure in the days before the game. There was a heavier defeat for Wednesday in 1912 when Aston Villa beat them 10-0.

With the FA Cup only weeks away and with Wednesday struggling in the League the club decided to organise a special training week at the Jackson House health spa and clinic in Matlock Bath. A J Dickinson had given strict instructions to the coaches who accompanied the team to improve the players' fitness and skill levels while also building team confidence. Wednesday enthusiast Mr Ernest Bowling was given charge of the training party.

Alas, continual rain made it a depressing week. After three days of indoor work the players, ordered to bed at 10pm, were restless but training outside was impossible as the ground was waterlogged. The week was proving a disaster and in his desperation to improve things, Bowling fastened on to using an old 'clinker path' for sprint training. The surface had not been rolled for many years and when Fred saw it he used his status as a senior player and selector to assert his contractual rights to be allowed to train on his own. He feared ending up with a sprained ankle or worse still with ligament damage. However, he could do nothing to prevent Bowling insisting the other players use the treacherous surface.

After a lengthy walk, Fred returned to Jackson House to be told he must join the other players. Rather than standing his ground he relented. Over the next couple of days the Wednesday squad did their best to avoid getting injured.

Fred knew the England selectors would be at the Baseball Ground and would be watching his performance with interest. He was therefore left heartbroken when, after six minutes, he was carried off on a stretcher with a snapped right hamstring. There was no chance of returning to the field and he subsequently missed the next four games.

Soon after Fred's removal from the field, Wednesday's ranks fell to nine fit men when Ferrier pulled up lame. Later the Wednesday side became just eight fit men when Earp began limping and although he remained on the pitch he could hardly move. Taking full advantage, Steve Bloomer blasted home three goals in the opening twenty minutes.

Four down at the interval, Wednesday did well to avoid a double-figure hammering. Steve Bloomer was simply irrepressible and used the space left by his injury-ravaged opponents to drill home six goals, his best being his fifth when he combined with Billy MacDonald before blasting home. He also forced Massey into making a series of fine saves. Bloomer was certain to play for England after this performance. Yet, earlier in the season, he had been suspended for insubordination and dropped to the reserves in a dispute over wages. Derby's greatest footballer was never truly appreciated by the East Midlands club and it was surprising he stayed so loyal for so long. Especially as other more successful clubs such as Aston Villa and Sheffield United wanted him to sign for them. Bloomer's six helped him score 30 League and FA Cup goals in 1898–99 with Derby again earning a place in the FA Cup final where they lost 4-1 to Sheffield United.

Speaking after the Wednesday game, Bloomer said: "It was one of those days when I could do nothing wrong, if I had shot with my eyes closed I would still have scored."

According to Fred it was "the most miserable day in my footballing life ... but as I sat on the sidelines I was amazed to see such brilliant shooting ... had it not been for good goalkeeping I hate to think what the final score might have been." Bloomer and Spiksley never played together for England again and Fred had little doubt that it was because of the clinker path. Back in Sheffield, Wednesday were pleased by news that neither Earp's nor Ferrier's injury was as serious as first thought but to Fred's dismay he was sent back to Matlock for specialist treatment.

Wednesday's poor form continued when they were beaten 1-0 by Sunderland at Olive Grove. A return attempt by Fred Spiksley failed when, wearing an elasticated stocking on his left leg, he played on the right wing and hardly featured. He missed the 0-0 draw away to Wolves, where Langley became separated from his teammates after the game and was kicked and punched by home fans angered by his severe treatment of some of their players.

There then followed a third consecutive home defeat for Wednesday as Everton won 2-1. The game marked the debut of forward Jack Pryce who had been signed from Glossop North End. It was hoped he would do better than Kaye but, despite playing for the remainder of the season, he failed to net in eight games. Photographs of this game at Olive Grove feature in this book, but it is a game which Fred Spiksley would have wished to forget. The realities of being trapped in a relegation fight were starting to envelop the Wednesday players, and both Earp and Spiksley were showing signs of frustration during the match, which on the final whistle ended with a heated confrontation between the two Wednesday men and the match referee, Mr Price of Nottingham. An emergency League disciplinary meeting followed; Earp was cleared, but Spiksley was found guilty and made to apologise to the referee.

Then came a 1-0 defeat at Notts County, where Crawshaw missed a penalty after Ernie Watts had scooped away Fred Spiksley's shot that appeared to have crossed the goal-line. To add to the misery the County goal scored by Fletcher seemed well offside. Following this defeat, Villa returned to play the final few minutes of the game that had kicked off on 26 November.

It had been agreed that after the resumed game was finished it would be followed by a testimonial match for Harry Davis, the long-serving Brummie. Around 3,000 Sheffield fans turned out to support Davis and watch the longest Football League game ever to be completed.

Villa's slim chances evaporated when Spiksley fastened on to a desperate clearance and used his electrifying pace to dash clear. Advancing towards goal he squared the ball for Richards, who had not played in the original fixture. He netted to make it 4-1 at the final whistle. It meant two valuable home points had been earned from a fixture in which everyone who played some part in either game is counted in the record books as making one appearance. That includes Bedingfield, who was replaced by Billy Garraty in March.

The sides met again in the League twelve days later and Villa won 3-1 with the Wednesday consolation coming from Spiksley. The defeated side left the field with just four games to play and lying in seventeenth place. One angry Wednesday fan decided to take his revenge on the players. A letter arrived at Olive Grove addressed to 'The Blind Eleven' and once opened it was seen to contain a copy of the team photograph at the start of the season. The sender had carefully drawn a pair of spectacles around the eyes of each player and then pricked out their eyes. Underneath he had written in bold black capitals 'THE BLIND XI!'

Generally, the Wednesday players accepted the supporters' attempts at black humour but this time it left them very upset and offended. The letter did little for team morale.

Wednesday were beaten 3-1 at home by Stoke and looked doomed but a 1-0 victory over Burnley at home raised hopes of avoiding the drop.

However, these were dashed thanks to a defeat against Preston, which meant that Wednesday were as good as relegated when they faced Newcastle United on 15 April in the final game at Olive Grove. For the many who had enjoyed watching Wednesday play there it was a very sad occasion not made easier by fears that the new ground would require loyal supporters to make quite a trek out into the countryside. The spirits of home fans were dealt an additional blow when the away side won 3-1. Wednesday ended in bottom place with just 24 points from 34 games. Only 32 goals had been scored. This was just seven more than Brady and Spiksley on the Wednesday left had scored between them the previous season. Brady's loss was crucial in Wednesday's unsuccessful relegation battle.

Wednesday were the lowest scorers in the League, which ended with Villa as champions while Sheffield United won the FA Cup. Bramall Lane was easier to get to and Wednesday fans feared that the more successful United side might now become much more popular than their own with the Sheffield public.

CHAPTER 16

THE OWLERTON GAMBLE
Wednesday bounce back after risky move away from heartland

FRED HAD NO wish to play in the Second Division but the Wednesday directors persuaded him to back the club in their time of trouble and focus on winning promotion. Rejoining Fred was Archie Brash, his confidence restored after a successful season at Crewe Alexandra. Dryburgh left for Millwall Athletic. Centre forward Harry Millar cost £100 when he was signed from Bury. The transfers meant that of those forwards who started in the Wednesday first team on the previous season's opening day only Fred Spiksley remained. Dryburgh, Davis, Kaye and Brady had been replaced by Brash, Pryce, Millar and Wright.

The left wing partnership between Brady and Spiksley, one of the strongest in the country, had finally ended.

Changes off the pitch mirrored those on it. Paul Firth replaced Johnson as trainer with the latter moving to Tottenham to help train them to FA Cup glory. Pre-season training was conducted at the Sheaf House Ground and the Niagara Grounds at Wadsley Bridge hosted three public practice matches as Wednesday's new ground in

Owlerton was not yet completed. The fact that it was to be ready for the opening League fixture against neighbours Chesterfield on 2 September 1899 was largely due to Arthur Dickinson's efforts.

With finance needed to buy land and construct a stadium, and with only £250 capital, the Wednesday committee was dissolved and 'The Wednesday Football Club Limited' was formed in June 1899. On its share prospectus it was stated it had "been formed for the purpose of providing another suitable ground whereon to continue the old Club. After considerable difficulty, the Company have fortunately been able to acquire a most suitable piece of land on the Penistone Road, near the High Bridge, Owlerton, containing 10 acres, for £5,000.

"There will be good approaches to the ground from the Penistone Road, and also from Leppings Lane. The Corporation Tramcars will run within 1 minute's walk from the ground, and the present Railway Station at Wadsley Bridge is about 5 minutes' walk from the ground."

The share issue raised £7,000 with George Senior, Charles and William Clegg, Alfred and John Holmes, Colonel Robert Hughes and Dickinson all subscribing. Senior, a self-made man who owned Ponds Forge, became chairman.

A £500 deposit was paid to wealthy local silversmith Wilf Dixon, the owner of the land, which was on the north bank of the River Don at High Bridge, Owlerton.

Following the purchase, uncovered terracing was constructed at each end of the ground, using deposited rubbish, the brick stand from Olive Grove with a capacity of 2,000 was transported to the new venue and another new stand, capacity 3,000, was erected in record time. The dressing rooms for both sides were good with full bathing facilities. There was a pleasant refreshment room, a separate ladies' tea room and a bicycle room. A small fence ran round the pitch perimeter.

Flying over an Olive Grove

Eager to impress the media Arthur Dickinson had collected J A Brierley of the *Lancashire Evening Post* from Sheffield's Midland Station and had driven the popular sports writer to the new enclosure so that he could have a personal tour of the new facilities. Brierley clearly liked what he saw and later wrote:

"Looking round, I was most impressed with the excellence of the dressing accommodation for teams and officials. Each team has a big, airy, well-lit dressing room and a splendidly-fitted bathroom, in which the players can get a slipper bath, followed by shower, needle, or wave bath, while in the home apartments there is such a rare luxury as a big plunge, in which it is quite possible to have a swim. This can be heated and hereby hangs a great advantage for when the players come off, perhaps after a perspiring struggle in a heavy storm, they can all at once jump into this bath, and so appreciably minimise the risk of contracting a chill, as players frequently do in waiting their turn for a bath. Under the same stand – a stand, by the by, built on the lines of that on the Nottingham Forest ground, and, if anything, a slight improvement on the latter, which a committee of inspection visited ere the building at Sheffield began – are all sorts of apartments, including, of course, refreshment bars."

"Owlerton will in future challenge Bramall Lane very strongly for such welcome plums as cup semi-finals, internationals and inter-league matches, while in due course it will be almost equal to accommodating such great gates as the Association have been getting at the final in recent years. Having such an excellent pitch, the Wednesday authorities determined to make the appointments and accommodation thoroughly worthy of the club and city. They have succeeded admirably."

Season tickets costing ten shillings and sixpence (52.5p) were available with match day prices of 1 shilling (5p) for seating and six pence for standing; boy's tickets were half price. Would the Wednesday fans turn up though? First, unlike at Sheffield United, the fare on offer was Second Division football. Secondly, Owlerton was several miles beyond the city boundary, poorly served by public transport. Would fans consider a long walk to the ground, especially in winter? Despite the uncertainty, Sir William Clegg delivered a rousing speech to the players in which he urged maximum effort and promised each of them a 10s (50p) bonus for every point won at home and a pound for each one won away, the bonus being paid in one sum at the season's end.

The Wednesday team for the club's first ever match in Division Two, against Chesterfield, was: Massey, Earp, Langley, Ferrier, Crawshaw, Ruddlesdin, Brash, Pryce, Millar, Wright, Spiksley.

Before the game, both sides had their photograph taken in the goalmouth at the Leppings Lane end of the ground by Jasper Redfern. The famous Sheffield optician also used this game as an experiment in recording moving image, using his stereoscopic camera, which took a series of photographs that then could be used to create short animations of the action. It was a technique that he had been experimenting with from around 1898 and his first trials at recording a football match took place a few months prior to Wednesday's first match at Owlerton, when Redfern took his camera to the FA Cup final to record Sheffield United defeating Derby County 4-1.

More than 12,000 people were in the ground, testament to the loyalty of the Wednesday fans. The Lord Mayor of Sheffield, Alderman William Clegg, a Wednesday director, started the match at 3pm.

The first goal at the new stadium was scored by the Chesterfield captain Herbert Munday. The experienced Fred Geary, a member of Everton's title winning side in 1890–91, saw his shot come back off the post and Munday netted to the utter joy of hundreds of away fans.

Less pleased were the home fans and some began questioning the Wednesday players' desire. This scepticism, however, was unfounded as Fred Spiksley became the first Wednesday player to score at the new home when he ran past the Chesterfield defence and levelled. Ferrier put the home side ahead and in the second half two Spiksley crosses were knocked home by debutant Millar before Brash made it 5-1.

The following weekend had the potential to be a special occasion for Gainsborough-born Fred Spiksley when he returned to play on the Northolme Sports Field where he had first established his reputation as a player. Gainsborough Trinity had finished as Midland League runners-up in 1895–96. Their subsequent Football League entry application saw them finish above existing League sides Port Vale and Crewe Alexandra in a ballot and thus break into Division Two in 1896–97. Following a highly creditable seventh place finish, Trinity had finished in the bottom half of the table in the following two seasons.

There were 4,000 spectators packing out the small ground, generating almost £100 receipts. The teams walked out together before Scott, the Trinity captain, lost the toss and found his side had to attack with both the sun and breeze in their faces.

With Earp having badly injured himself against Chesterfield, there was an opportunity for Bill Layton to establish himself as the regular Wednesday right back while Arthur Dickinson selected Langley as captain. Earp was to play just four more games and left to become Stockport County coach at the season's end. He didn't stay there long, however, as he soon joined Lord Baden Powell's First Battalion and served in the Boer War.

Despite Trinity's best efforts, Wednesday won the match 2-1 with goals from Millar and Wright. Fred Spiksley, however, did not enjoy the match as he had a goal wrongly disallowed for offside and was the victim of some very heavy challenges from Pycock and Hall that were greeted with delight by some onlookers. He was also upset at being booed by sections of the crowd. The hostility was picked up by the *Gainsborough News* journalist who hoped that the fans who had acted so ungraciously to a former Trinity favourite might feel ashamed of themselves. As an experienced professional, though, Spiksley should not have allowed the abuse to get under his skin.

Wednesday won their third game of the new season the following weekend when, before another 12,000 crowd, they beat Bolton Wanderers 2-1 with goals from Spiksley and Millar. The latter was a real comic off the field and his tricks included turning up at the Empire Theatre, Sheffield and conducting the orchestra until being chased out by the theatre manager. Langley believed Millar might have done better as a footballer by taking the game more seriously.

The game against Bolton had its own comic moment when just before the interval a Sheffield dog turned up to assist his fellow townsmen. When a free kick was awarded to the home side he joined the attackers and when the second goal was forced home he seemed delighted. He did not join in the handshaking. Thereafter youngsters attempted to secure him and the dog was finally removed from the pitch when Massey darted after and caught him before pitching him into the crowd. The game, which had by now been temporarily suspended, was resumed.

Wednesday played impressively at Lincoln City where a 2-1 victory was secured by goals from Wright and Spiksley. The latter's success was in contrast to when he had played as a young man against Lincoln City. Then the home captain Jack Duckworth had regularly dished out good hidings to the frail winger on the sloping pitch on the John O'Gaunt's Ground. Duckworth was long since gone and City now played on the level playing field at Sincil Bank.

On 2 December 1899, Fred Spiksley became the first player to score a hat trick at Owlerton when, along with two from Pryce and one from Wright, Wednesday beat Luton Town 6-0. Edwin Daw in the away goal prevented a massacre and had no chance as Fred netted the Wednesday second, hit home the third from a free kick and finished off the scoring with a glorious shot.

On Christmas Day, Wednesday drew 2-2 at New Brighton Tower. Man of the match was the home centre forward who startled those brilliant headers of the ball, Langley and Crawshaw, by coming from nowhere to powerfully head home a corner kick. Both men looked at each other in bemusement. No-one was laughing at the final whistle, though, and after the game Crawshaw, Langley and Spiksley were as one in wanting Wednesday to sign Sam Raybould. Knowing that the player had previously made many appearances in non-League football, the Wednesday directors believed he was too old and they failed to check that he was born in January 1875. Weeks later, Raybould was signed by New Brighton's near neighbours Liverpool for just £250. He became a big hit and in 1902–03 he finished as top scorer in Division One with 31 goals. He helped Liverpool to two top-flight titles – in 1900–01 and 1905–06.

Only two days before the start of a new century, Wednesday lost a Second Division game for the first time. Despite enjoying the backing of a good number of the 4,000 Saltergate crowd, Wednesday were beaten by near neighbours Chesterfield. On New Year's Day, there was a return to winning ways when Grimsby Town were beaten 2-1 at Owlerton with Wright notching his eleventh goal of the season, taking him one in front of Spiksley and four ahead of Millar.

Millar drew level with Wright when he netted four times as Gainsborough Trinity were beaten 5-1 five days later.

The following game pitched first against second when Wednesday travelled to Bolton Wanderers. Following their defeat at Owlerton, Wanderers had embarked on a sixteen-match unbeaten run and were in the middle of a run of six straight victories which included 5-1, 5-0, 6-1 and 7-1 successes. The biggest home gate of Wanderers' season, 12,235, witnessed a fine game in which a single goal by Bob Jack gave the home side both points.

The losing side were forced to play 80 minutes with just ten players when Spiksley sustained an injury that virtually ended his season. He made a few failed comebacks but would be sidelined for a year. He had been looking forward to the game with Bolton. His right hamstring had completely healed and he was confident that his decision to remain with Wednesday was going to prove the right one, as promotion was very much on the table. This meant that he could look forward to a healthy bonus from Mr Clegg at the end of the season.

The moment that ruined Fred's season came after the referee had whistled for offside. As he was the nearest to the ball the Wednesday winger went to retrieve it. He had just put his foot behind the ball when the Bolton right half Jack Fitchett gave it an almighty kick. Fitchett later claimed he had not heard the whistle and was going for the ball but the impact of his kick against his opponent's foot sent a shock wave up the leg to his knee and hamstring. Fred was carried from the pitch.

Fred was unavailable for the 5-0 home defeat of Lough-borough Town, but he was able to return for the FA Cup first round home tie against Bolton Wanderers that was won by Wednesday courtesy of a Jack Wright goal.

The following weekend, Wednesday included in their forward line a £200 signing from Barnsley, Harry 'Joe Pluck' Davis. He went on to become an automatic first team choice at Owlerton for many years. His nickname came from his courageous, never-say die attitude and he was to become a full England international in 1903 when he was capped three times. He formed an effective partnership with Harry Chapman and became assistant trainer at Wednesday in 1907. Davis served in the Army in the First World War.

Missing Spiksley, Wednesday lost 1-0 in a very rough game at Newton Heath. A clearly rankled home side sought to take revenge on Mick Langley for his challenge during the fixture at Owlerton earlier in the season which had left his opponent with a fractured wrist. Newspapers reported the game was stopped on more than 50 occasions for foul play and there was a near riot when Langley sought revenge for the punishment he endured by dumping one of the home forwards over the touchline and into the crowd.

Thankfully, there was the FA Cup to look forward to. It could not have generated greater excitement in Sheffield as United, the cup holders and Division One leaders, had drawn Wednesday at home. It was the first time the sides had met in the competition and a crowd of 32,381 packed out Bramall Lane.

Fred Spiksley was persuaded by the Wednesday directors to play even though he was by no means fully fit. With Langley believing the players would welcome a motivational pre-match speech he shocked Fred by asking him to make it. The words proved a real rallying cry as the Wednesday team stormed on to the pitch. Asked by his skipper to explain where the "bullshit" had come from, the outside left admitted he had no idea, but it sounded good at the time.

In the event the only real winner was the weather. The pitch was not playable as it was frozen. Snow continued to fall and when it turned into a blizzard the referee Mr Lewis took the players off and then waited unsuccessfully for fifteen minutes to see if there was a change in conditions before abandoning the game after 53 minutes.

The decision was certainly less favourable to the away side, who had proved the superior outfit and should have led at half-time only for their unfit outside left to miss two great chances. On 52 minutes, Fred had found Brash with a great ball and his shot was cleared off the line. Wednesday fans complained bitterly that the referee had robbed their side of success.

The Owlerton Gamble

The rearranged match before a 23,000 crowd at Bramall Lane took place on Saturday 17 February 1900. It had been planned to hold the game on the fifteenth and the groundsmen had worked hard to make the pitch playable only for another blizzard to force another postponement. Two days later a thaw had reduced the ground to a muddy one. Referee John Lewis pronounced it as "fit for play."

The home side were boosted by the return from injury of Fred Priest, scorer of United's winning goal in the semi-final match against Liverpool the previous season and who also netted one of the United goals in the 4-1 defeat of Derby County in the final.

Despite being the top flight side, United were largely outplayed by their Second Division opponents in the first twenty minutes. The Cup holders responded by trying to kick Wednesday off the park but United were fortunate when a Spiksley 'goal' was harshly overruled for offside. In the twentieth minute, Wednesday finally retaliated when Langley and Ruddlesdin sandwiched Cocky Bennett, who had been putting himself about quite a bit. The result was a warning to the two offenders. Whenever the Wednesday and United sides contained Langley and Bennett the crowd witnessed a rough duel between two men who off the field were close friends. Bennett's mother promised to fell Langley if she saw him in her home town of Mexborough. Like all the Wednesday players, Langley rated the United players and was adamant that Foulke was the greatest 'keeper ever while Needham was "head and shoulders above any other half back in the country."

The opening goal arrived in the 25th minute when Spiksley and Wright combined before the former produced a weighted cross beyond Foulke and into the path of Brash who sent the Wednesday players and fans jumping for joy by netting. Thereafter the game continued at a fast pace but it was the Division Two side that led at half time.

On the restart United resorted to a series of very rough challenges. Harry Thickett hacked Fred Spiksley down from behind. It was an offence that would be a straight red today but carried no punishment in 1900. The injured player had his knee strapped up.

Massey was then badly hurt in a crude challenge and the serious injuries to two of the Wednesday players were compounded by knocks to Millar, Brash and Crawshaw. Still suffering from what happened to him in the first half, Bennett had to go off during the middle period of the second half but his absence was temporary. On Bennett's return, Jack Almond pounced to make it 1-1 and afterwards it was something of a miracle that the away side held on to obtain a creditable draw.

The replay two days later attracted a record attendance for the new ground of 23,000. Massey, Millar and Spiksley were all ruled out of the match. Bill Mallinson came in for his third game in goal, youngster George Lee was selected at centre forward for the last of six first-team appearances and Jack Topham, a prolific scorer in the reserves, replaced Fred Spiksley.

United named a full strength side. Their tactics had paid off but only because of weak refereeing. Mr Lewis must have realised that he had performed badly at Bramall Lane. Prior to kick-off he entered the Owlerton dressing rooms and warned all the players about their behaviour and told them he would be severe on dangerous play.

There was a poor opening period to the game, and Jasper Redfern was again present with his stereoscopic camera to film it. While, sadly, no footage has survived there is a stereoscopic image still in existence which belongs to the Sheffield City Library collection.

There were many free kicks awarded. Brash then caught a stray Jack Russell dog and brought the largest cheer so far. On 38 minutes Lee sustained a serious fracture to his right leg courtesy of a careless Thickett challenge that despite the tricky conditions should have led to the United man's dismissal. The incident virtually ended Lee's professional football career. He was released at the end of the season and thereafter struggled financially and died five years later at aged 29.

At half-time, ten-man Wednesday reshuffled, putting Layton at centre forward and leaving just the one full back, Langley. The intent was to use the three-man offside rule then in place to catch the away forwards offside but within two minutes Almond beat the trap and when he was brought down from behind by Langley, Needham scored from the spot. Eight minutes later Langley brought down Bennett with a rough challenge before a great Foulke save kept his side a goal ahead.

Immediately afterwards, John Lewis dismissed Pryce for what he deemed was an over-the-ball challenge on Hedley. The United player had gone down heavily for what was little more than two players running into each other. Hedley left the field but returned within minutes as eleven-man United sought to finish off their nine-man opponents. With only minutes remaining Bennett and Langley collided out wide and although the Wednesday captain made only glancing contact he was dismissed, the referee ignoring Needham's plea that the collision had been an accidental one. The Wednesday fans were outraged at the referee's performance and told him so in direct language.

Down to eight men, the home side finally yielded when Beers scored a fine goal as United progressed to face Bury. The Shakers were to beat them and later win the FA Cup by beating Southampton 4-0 in the final.

Langley was forced to appear before the FA disciplinary committee. Despite JJ Bentley, a prominent Football League official, travelling down to support him and telling everyone Langley had not made one bad foul in all three matches, he received a one-month suspension when the linesman insisted the player's challenge on Bennett demanded a sending-off.

With Fred still injured, Topham retained his place in the starting line-up for the following four matches which saw Wednesday win three and lose just once. This was enough to put them top of the table.

Fred returned to the side as Wednesday beat Woolwich Arsenal 3-1 at home. He thus earned a further £1 bonus. He wasn't fully fit, though, and his final appearance of the season was at Grimsby Town. A then record Blundell Park attendance of 8,000 was delighted when with seven minutes remaining the home side led 1-0. Throwing caution to the wind, Langley went up front and it was later reported by Grimsby fans that he had run amok. Certainly, John McAvoy was badly injured following one of his challenges and soon afterwards Crawshaw equalised. Then, with just two minutes left, the Wednesday captain scored the winning goal.

When the final whistle sounded, William Bellamy, a Grimsby Town director who was also a Football League management committee member, stormed on to the pitch and demanded that Langley be dismissed for persistent foul play. When the player told Bellamy to mind his own business the latter didn't speak to him for many years.

The victory put Wednesday within touching distance of an immediate return to Division One. This was confirmed the following day when Burslem Port Vale were beaten 4-0 at Owlerton before a crowd of 5,000 on Easter Saturday. Three points were then gained from a 1-0 victory at home to Lincoln City and a 1-1 draw at Walsall.

Middlesbrough were beaten 3-0 in the final game. Victory established a club record as it meant that Wednesday had won every home League match during the season. The club had returned to the top flight by finishing in top spot to capture the Division Two Victory Shield with Bolton second.

Fred thus added another medal to his collection. Now all he needed was a Division One winner's medal. He was in no rush to celebrate even though there was also the additional financial reward of £26 earned from the nine home victories, seven away victories and three draws in the 21 League games he had played.

Thickett's challenge had put his recovery back substantially. He had twice attempted a comeback. Now he was ordered by Dr Lockwood to take a complete rest to allow for the natural healing of the ligaments. He could do daily leg exercises for an hour and go for some light walks but it was going to be a while before he could play again. Fred was now in his thirties and must have feared for his future as a professional footballer especially as many playing careers were cut short in the Victorian era.

When it became clear that Fred Spiksley was going to be incapacitated for many months the Wednesday committee agreed to renew his contract for the 1900–01 season but only on the condition that it would be immediately terminated if he broke down again and was unable to play. Four years after winning Wednesday the FA Cup and the club were not even guaranteeing him a full season's contract!

Fred's absence left Wednesday needing to find a replacement for him in the summer of 1900. John 'Jock' Napier Malloch cost £50 from Dundee. The Scot would use his superb ball control over the following seven seasons at Owlerton.

Another Scot, Andrew 'Andra' Wilson also came south to sign from relegated Clyde at £200 record fee. He received a £10 signing-on fee. Those who questioned the wisdom of spending so heavily would prove to be mistaken as Wilson went on to become Wednesday's all-time top scorer and appearance maker. It would take the Ayrshire teenager a little while to get going, Wilson stating later that after his first game he thought "it was no game for me as the speed simply staggered me. English football is played at breakneck speed ... making it less clever than in Scotland where the crowds do not tell a player to get rid of the ball quickly." However, he soon blossomed into one of the greatest players of his generation with his professional attitude, allied to a thunderous shot, making him a dangerous opponent.

Wilson, who actually preferred playing at left back, went straight into the first team with Millar. Trouble lay ahead for the latter, however, and he was later suspended without pay in October 1900 for missing training, relegated to making just four appearances during the season, at the end of which he moved to QPR.

The campaign got under way with Wright notching Wednesday's goals in a 2-2 draw with Manchester City at the antiquated Hyde Road and a 1-0 victory over Bolton at Owlerton. In the third game, FA Cup holders Bury enjoyed a 2-0 success at Gigg Lane with goals from Jasper McLuckie and Jack Plant, both of whom scored against Southampton in the 1900 FA Cup final.

Andrew Wilson scored his first two goals as Wednesday beat Notts County 4-1 before the promoted side picked up just a point from the following four games. Relegation fears were calmed with successive 3-2 home victories against Aston Villa and Liverpool and over Christmas and the New Year there were victories at home against Derby County, Wolves and Manchester City. On 1 January 1901, Wednesday lay tenth out of eighteen teams.

On 27 October 1900, Fred Spiksley had played well in a 3-0 success for the Wednesday reserves at home to Montrose Works in a Sheffield Association League match. It was reported in the *Sheffield Independent* that "his appearance in the first team may be expected shortly."

He was selected at outside right for the following fixture at home to Aston Villa with Malloch retaining his place at outside left. Wednesday managed to win the game and match reports praised Fred for his efforts but, despite Dr

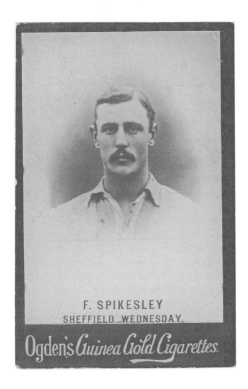

F. SPIKESLEY
SHEFFIELD WEDNESDAY.

Ogden's *Guinea Gold* Cigarettes.

The opening goal scored by Fred Spiksley in the 1896 FA Cup final against Wolves. It is arguably the fastest goal ever scored in an FA Cup final.

Spiksley's name continued to be misspelt by the newspapers throughout his life, as it is here on an Ogden Guinea Gold Cigarette card, possibly the most attractive set of cards produced during the Victorian era.

The FA Cup that was first presented in 1896 and was used until 1910.

Fred Spiksley's FA Cup winners medal.

The first of a set of four photographs of the 1896 FA Cup Final. These are the earliest known close-up action photographs of FA Cup Final in history.

The photograph of the 1896 FA Cup Final at the Crystal Palace, where the football ground was sited in a 200-acre parkland, shows the famous switchback roller coaster that was turned off so that part of the enormous crowd could stand on the tracks to obtain one of the best views in the ground.

Spiksley shows his athleticism during the FA Cup Final with this mid-air challenge. Spiksley's performance in the game made him probably the bets known footballer in the world in 1896 and certainly the greatest.

Spiksley demonstrates his trademark combination of pace and ball control as he takes on the Wolves defence during the second half of the 1896 FA Cup Final.

AT THE ASYLUM.

KEEPER.—" Oh, yes, this one is perfectly harmless; but he fancies he's W. G. Grace, Fred Spiksley, Corfield, Morny Cannon, Lord Dunraven, all in one; so we rig him up like that to keep him quiet!"

In the above cartoon, published a few months after his winning goal in the 1896 FA Cup Final, Fred Spiksley is placed alongside that of cricket's greatest of his era, W.G.Grace.

A marvellous drawing of Fred Spiksley's 1896 FA Cup Final winning goal.

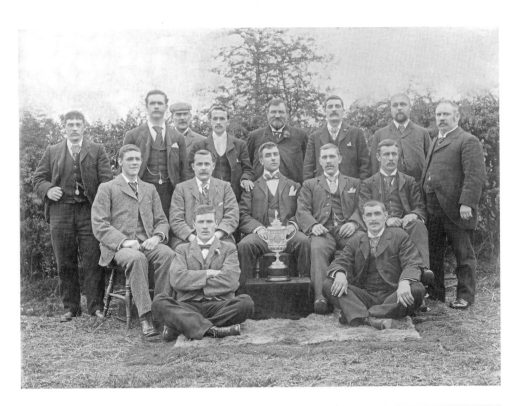

Above: The Wednesday team with the FA Cup.
Back Row: H. Brandon, Langley, Johnson (Trainer), Brash, Holmes (President), Jamieson, Dickinson (Hon. Secretary), Nixon (Director). Middle Row: Bell, Brady, Earp, Davis, Spiksley. Front Row: Crawshaw, Petrie.

Right: Inside the Clarborough Tunnel. Could this be the recess that saved Fred Spiksley's life on 29 January 1898? After an away victory at Sunderland in the FA Cup Fred missed his last train home and decided the quickest way to Gainsborough was along the railway tracks. He was only saved from being killed by two passing trains because he jumped into a recess.

These action shots show Wednesday fighting to remain in Division One of the Football League. Here they are playing Everton at Olive Grove on 4 March 1899.

By the time this game took place Wednesday had already begun searching for a new home and Olive Grove was starting to become a little run down.

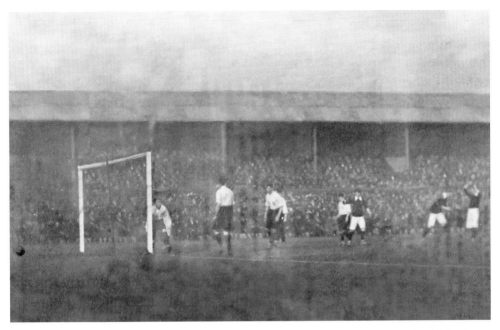

James Millar scores Scotland's only goal past Jack Robinson in the England goal during the 1898 international at Celtic Park. This is the earliest known photograph showing an international goal being scored.

The England team that faced Scotland in 1898. For several decades the forward line from this team was considered the greatest of all time. Back Row: Athersmith, Forman, Oakley, Robinson. Front Row: Bloomer, Williams, Smith, Brown, Needham, Wheldon, Spiksley.

A packed Olive Grove witness the last ever Steel City derby to be played on Olive Grove on 3 October 1898.

SHEFFIELD WEDNESDAY V. ASTON VILLA.

"WHEN FELL THE SHADES OF EVEN"

A quirky illustration depicting the night closing in on Wednesday's infamous match against Aston Villa on 26 November 1898. The match was completed on 13 March 1899.

Fred Spiksley is pictured in front of the Olive Grove grandstand on the strip of grass where he earned the nickname 'The Olive Grove Flyer'.

This image from the Sheffield end of Olive Grove shows how similar goal nets in the 1890's were to those in use today. Goal nets became an established part of football from 1891 onwards and yet they are not compulsory.

The first match at Owlerton (or Hillsborough as it later became known). The Wednesday side lined up at the Leppings Lane End of their new home in 1899. From left: Ferrier, Earp, Pryce, Brash, Massey, Crawshaw, Spiksley, Wright, Millar, Langley, Ruddlesdin.

The Glasgow and Sheffield Association teams pictured together for their Inter Association match in 1899. Sheffield - where shirts only. Back row: Langley, Massey. Middle row: Hall, Layton, Field. Front row: Haigh, Davis, Hutton, Needham, Spiksley, Crawshaw.

Wednesday take to the field at Owlerton, which later became known as Hillsborough.

Above: Fred Spiksley's Football League Championship winner's medal.

Left: Fred Spiksley's bandaged knee is clearly visible in this photograph taken just before the 1902-03 football season started.

The Wednesday Football Club photographed wit their five trophy haul in 1903. Trophies pictured from left to right: Plymouth Bowl, Sheffield Challenge Cup, Football League, Midland League and Wharncliffe Charity Cup.
Back row: Eyre, Ryalls, Hemmingfield, Beech, Stewart, Bartlett, Thackeray, Morallee, P. Crawshaw, W Ruddlesdin. Middle row: J. Davis (Asst tainer), Marrison, H Ruddlesdin, Ferrier, Layton, Langley, Lyall, T. Crawshaw, Stubbs, Burton, Crawley, Firth (trainer).
Front row: V.S Simpson, H Davis, Chapman, Wilson, Malloch, Spiksley, G Simpson

Left: Andrew Wilson - Sheffield Wednesday's all time top goalscorer.
Right: Fred Spiksley in 1903 - Sheffield Wednesday's third highest goalscorer across all first team futures with 170 goals, which included 100 in the Football League.

Above: Harry Weldon – who played the lead role of Stiffy the Goalkeeper in Fred Karno's Football Match.

Left: Charlie Chaplin, pictured shortly after touring with Fred Spiksley.

BLACKBURN.

PALACE.   "Football Match."

Harry Weldon, Will Poluski, jun., Chas. Chaplin, Bob Lewis, Jimmy Fletch, James Monrow, R. J. Hamer, Bert Royston, Frank Hayter, jun., Fred Newham, Fred Onzella, C. Turner, J. Thuro, Harry Fergusson, Harry Douglas, Jock Roberts, J. Jackson, L. Calvert, Jack Melville, H. Reeves, Clifford Walton, Fred Spikesley, F. Gamble, J. Fitchett, W. Wragg, F. Arkeeden, Elsa Beresford, Irene Wood, Lucy Walden.

Manager, FRANK CALLAGHER.

Stage-Manager, T. ELLIS BUXTON.

Fred Spiksley takes to the stage at Blackburn's Palace Theatre alongside a young Chas (Charlie) Chaplin. Fred was an original cast member of Fred Karno's Football Match, eventually touring with it on three separate occasions between 1906 and 1908.

Coach Fred Spiksley (far left, back row) stands with his Swedish international team on the less than smart Rasunda Stadium pitch in 1911.

Above: A newspaper clipping from the 1960's highlights the impact that Fred Spiksley had on the development of Swedish football.

Above: A press photograph of Spiksley in 1920.

Wearing a hat, Spiksley is next to the trophy in this photograph of an unidentified Mexican team in the 1920s.

Fred Spiksley, always in a hat, was the coach of 1FC Nuremberg in 1914. When war started he was imprisoned, later managing to escape.

Left: Nuremberg supporters enjoying their victory over Munich 1860 in the semi-final of the German championship in 1927.

A German newspaper reports Nuremeberg's famous 4-2 victory over Burnley.

Below: Filmed at Craven Cottage, Spiksley utilised slow motion technology and audio descriptions in a ground-breaking film aimed at teaching boys how to develop their skills. Several of the drills he pioneered in the 1920s are still used in some form today.

Wharton Hood declaring to the media that Spiksley was as "sound as ever", he was clearly not ready for regular action and he would not return to the side until 19 January 1901 against Notts County. Back at outside left, he was impressive but County 'keeper Harry Pennington played better than anyone else to ensure his side won 2-0.

At Owlerton four weeks later, Fred continued his rehabilitation as Wednesday drew 1-1 with Blackburn Rovers with the home goal being scored by debutant inside left Harry Chapman. He was to make another 298 first team appearances and became a big favourite with Wednesday fans for his tireless enthusiasm, solid tackling, acute tactical brain and his great versatility.

Chapman netted again in his second match as Wednesday beat Stoke 4-0 at home, the season's biggest victory.

The following weekend saw Fred Spiksley score his first goal of the new century, a header, but his side, weakened by Crawshaw's absence on England duty, lost 2-1 at Aston Villa. Two weekends later, the scorer nipped in front of Bill Perkins to head home at Anfield in a game that ended 1-1. New signing William Gosling, who cost Wednesday £100 from Jarrow, made a decent debut in that game yet was destined to make only five appearances before being released in the summer of 1902 after being convicted of being drunk and disorderly.

Playing against Everton at Owlerton, Fred was again on the score sheet with his head in a game that was played in gale and, at times, hurricane-force winds. Crawshaw was again absent on international duty. With Chapman netting twice the home side won 3-1.

Wednesday thus rose to eighth place but the following match they conceded three goals for the first time in the season, losing 3-2 at relegation-bound Preston. Fred Spiksley had driven his side ahead late in the game before the home side netted twice in the final few minutes. It was a futile gesture of defiance by North End as they had only one more game to play. They lost it at home to West Bromwich Albion who accompanied them into the Second Division.

The Preston game almost had dramatic repercussions for Langley who was angered by constant abuse from a passionate farmer standing behind the goal. Finally, when taking a goal kick, Langley, thrust his left arm back into the farmer's face. A broken nose and two black eyes resulted in the Wednesday man being summonsed to appear at Preston Police Court but Langley and his solicitor Mr Dronfield were able to persuade the injured party to meet them along with his solicitor Bob Holmes, the former Preston and England full back. The matter was settled out of court for the sum of £9 after which Langley advised the younger players to keep a cool head. Years later, the Preston chairman, Tom Houghton told Langley that he had, in fact, done the club a good turn as the farmer, previously well-known for his abuse of Preston's opponents, never offended again.

On 13 April 1901, Wednesday played host to title challengers Sunderland in their penultimate home game of the season. The Sunderland side's success was based on a solid defence who conceded just 26 goals in 34 League games.

Up against right back Andrew McCombie, Fred Spiksley had the beating of his opponent and from his cross, Chapman set up Wilson for what proved to be the only goal of a wind-affected match. Sunderland's defeat allowed Liverpool to win their first Division One title.

Wednesday ended the season by winning 1-0 against a Sheffield United side that two days earlier had lost 3-1 against Southern League side Tottenham Hotspur in the replay of the FA Cup final after the first match had ended 2-2.

Wednesday thus finished in eighth place with new man Wilson having netted thirteen times. This was three more than Wright. Fred Spiksley's shortened season saw him score four times in thirteen League matches. The Wednesday winger had turned 31 in January 1901 but, having played well on his return, was rewarded with a new contract for the following season. This allowed him to pluck up the courage and successfully ask for a 10s (50p) a week increase to cover his travelling expenses from Gainsborough. This took his wages up to £3 10s (£3.50). Unlike in 1899–1900 there was, however, no end-of-season bonus.

This new deal would have been a great relief to Fred Spiksley as he had come through what was probably his most frustrating time as a professional footballer. At the turn of the century football had already become a sport where there was little room for sentiment and with hundreds of young men aspiring to become footballers there were plenty willing to fill the boots of a player who was past his prime. Malloch had proved a more than capable deputy for Spiksley and Fred would have been worried that Wednesday might stick by their recent signing and look to a future without him.

Spiksley's difficulties didn't end there, as off the field his gambling addiction was starting to catch up with him.

Around the start of the 1901–02 season, Spiksley became embroiled in a regrettable episode that resulted in him being publicly cross-examined in court. Fred's usual support when he was in financial difficulties was his brother William. However, William was going through a difficult time of his own and his marriage had broken down. William had been found guilty of assaulting his wife and was forced to serve a one-month prison sentence.

Fred turned to a Gainsborough money lender, named as Mrs Bell. She was well known and Spiksley was aware that banking a cheque from her would draw suspicions from his bank. Trying to be discrete, Spiksley gained help from a friend called Joseph Nash. Nash said that Spiksley was "in such desperate measures that he was prepared to help him all he could." A cheque was made out to Nash for

£10 and Mrs Bell was handed security from Spiksley in the form of pawnbroker tickets for his English Cup winner's medal and other medals. Nash was right, Spiksley must have been at rock bottom at this point to consider using his Cup winner's medal as surety.

Mrs Bell was happy for the transaction to proceed, as she considered Nash to be someone who would 'joggle' Spiksley along into paying off his debts. However, it appears that at some point Nash double-crossed Fred by pocketing some of the repayments for himself. It turned out that Nash himself had a string of debts, and was in fact more financially stricken than Spiksley.

The result was that Spiksley ended up taking Nash to Sheffield County Court to try to recoup his losses. The court found in favour of Spiksley but it was not long before Nash was in front of the bankruptcy court and Spiksley had lost a friend and his money. In addition, Fred, who was still a famous top-flight footballer, had had to endure the embarrassment of his financial difficulties being widely reported across the local press.

It had also been a real kick in the teeth when a request from Nash's lawyer on 31 October 1901 to "have the pleasure in cross-examining him (Spiksley) again" was met by laughter in the courtroom. Following this, the judge chipped in: "Oh, he has been heckled enough lately." This was an obvious reference to Spiksley's lacklustre performances on the field for Wednesday. It was a low blow! Alas, it did not stop Spiksley continuing to search out other gambling opportunities.

The 1901–02 season began with a 3-1 home victory against newly-promoted Grimsby Town, who were backed by a following of several hundred spectators in a crowd of 17,500. With Massey injured, Frank Stubbs retained his place in goal. The giant 'keeper had been signed in the summer of 1900 from Loughborough Athletic, where he played just the single Second Division game, a 12-0 hammering by

Woolwich Arsenal. Stubbs's first season with Wednesday had proved a success after he replaced Massey and played the final fourteen games of the campaign, conceding just fifteen goals.

Fred Spiksley had spotted that Stubbs was a powerful runner and had hit upon a way of making money from this by entering him for the 100 yards professional sprint handicap at Sheffield's Niagara Sports Field. If he won Stubbs would collect the prize money but Fred intended to use his inside knowledge to bet on him winning.

He was confident that as long as no-one knew how fast the novice runner was then he would receive a handicap in the middle of the field and thus have a greater chance of success. Only two other players were aware of Spiksley's intention – Crawshaw and Langley. Stubbs agreed to keep his talents hidden but on arrival at the sports field it was apparent that the plan had failed spectacularly as Stubbs was 6 to 4 on to win. Joe Davis had taken on a second job as a bookie's runner and had informed his boss of what was going on. No money was waged at such short odds. This was a shame as Stubbs romped home and won £50 for himself!

When Wednesday played their second game of the season, at Notts County, they led 1-0 at the interval. Towards the end of the first period, Stubbs had gone down bravely to grab the ball at the feet of on-rushing forwards but had taken a kick to the head in the process. Wilson said later that Stubbs had asked what the score was as he left the field at half-time but as he was a great practical joker everyone thought he was just being funny.

However, the 'keeper was clearly concussed and conceded six goals in the second half and Wilson said: "Most of the goals were given to them by Stubbs, who saved the shots, and then turned the ball behind him." County won the game 6-1. Stubbs played only one more game for Wednesday. After winning the Midland Counties

League championship with the reserves, he rejoined Loughborough in the summer of 1903. He later became Mayor of Loughborough.

In February 1901, Wednesday spent £100 to sign Scottish-born 'keeper Jack Lyall from Jarrow. Replacing Stubbs, Lyall was beaten just once on his debut as Bolton Wanderers were crushed 5-1 at Owlerton. Lyall quickly established himself as the club's undoubted number one. He was eventually picked to play for England, only for it to be established that he had been born in Scotland before moving south as a youngster.

When on 12 October 1901, Wednesday beat champions Liverpool 2-1 at Anfield, it was their first away win in Division One since they beat West Bromwich Albion at Stoney Lane on 12 March 1898, 39 games previously. A goal down, the away side equalised with a Chapman header before Wilson followed up a Spiksley shot that was saved by Bill Perkins to net the winner. Any hopes of a title challenge were soon dispelled as Wednesday's form was indifferent although there was the pleasure of beating Sheffield United 1-0 with Foulke beaten when Wilson's shot glanced off Peter McIntyre and deceived the 'keeper. Fred Spiksley was out injured.

The following home game brought a 4-1 victory over Bury. The Lancashire side were late in arriving and were soon on the back foot following a thrilling Spiksley dribble that was rounded off with a goal. Then two fine crosses by the winger were netted by Dryburgh and Malloch respectively.

The Wednesday winger also scored at home to Stoke, who were beaten 3-1. Earlier, he was twice denied by eccentric amateur goalkeeper Leigh Roose. It was Roose who took great advantage of the law that allowed 'keepers to handle – but not carry – the ball anywhere in their own half. It eventually prompted a change in 1912, forbidding the handling of the ball outside the penalty area. Roose, like Billy Foulke, was notorious for being able to withstand some heavy barging by opponents as he bounced the ball towards the halfway line before launching it into the opposition danger area using either his hands or feet.

Roose, who also played for Aston Villa, Arsenal and Sunderland, was killed at the Battle of the Somme in 1916. His body was never recovered.

Fred's third goal of the season also came at home when Manchester City were beaten 2-1 on Boxing Day, his effort coming after he ran on to beat Francis Barrett amid great cheering. On 11 January he then netted in a 4-0 thrashing of Notts County that put Wednesday in sixth place. Three consecutive away defeats in the League and a 1-0 defeat before a 30,096 crowd at Sunderland in the FA Cup meant that any Wednesday fans who hoped to see their side collect some silverware in 1902 would be disappointed.

In early April, Wednesday faced the two sides that were competing for the League title and gained a creditable 1-1 draw at home to Everton before beating Sunderland 2-1 at Roker Park with goals from Chapman and amateur Vivian Simpson, a solicitor who played football purely for pleasure. Simpson ended up back in Sunderland in 1917 when he was invalided back from France during World War I and trained junior officers there. He later returned to the War Front and was killed by a sniper in the Belgium village of Outtersteene and where he is buried.

The performance against the Wearsiders demonstrated that on their day Wednesday could compete with the best but the season then ended in disappointment as, despite a Fred Spiksley goal, his fifth of the campaign, relegation-threatened Small Heath won 2-1 at Owlerton. This was especially disappointing in light of the fact that before the game an unknown team member had told Fred he had in his possession £55 to be divided between the Wednesday players if they won the match. It was believed that the money had come from someone connected to relegation strugglers Notts County. It later transpired that a further £55 had been on offer from a gentleman in Grimsby, another place where the local club were threatened with relegation

The final match of what had proven to be a disappointing season ended with a 2-2 draw at Derby County. Wednesday ended in ninth place in the table, ten points behind champions Sunderland and four points above relegated Small Heath.

Wednesday completed the 1901–02 season with a home match against FA Cup winners Sheffield United. This was played before a 4,747 crowd whose entrance fees went to the Ibrox Disaster Fund that was set up after 25 supporters had been killed when a newly-built stand at Ibrox Park collapsed during the Scotland-England game on 5 April 1902.

Another relief fund, this time in Gainsborough, was established in the summer of 1902. It was for the unfortunate William Spiksley, who in addition to his on-course turf accountancy and illicit under-the-counter bookmaking business owned three Gainsborough butcher's shops, two of which were run by his parents.

William had been woken around 1am on 3 June 1902 by the sound of screaming and the cracking of glass. Seeing the upper storey of the Hope Inn public house ablaze he rushed across to the White Hart Hotel where the local fire engine was housed and raised the alarm while also sending the stable boy to rouse the fire brigade commander. William then dashed to Market Street but recklessly used his hand to smash the glass casing around the fire hydrant. In doing so he severed the tendons of his right hand.

Ignoring the injury, William ploughed on into the blazing building where he heroically rescued the landlord and landlady and their two children, using water-soaked blankets over the latter's heads as he carried them downstairs to safety. In the meantime, the fire engine and hose-carts had been mobilised in record time enabling the saving of three nearby furniture warehouses.

Awoken by a messenger, Fred dashed to his brother's house in Gordon Street and accompanied him by carriage to the Lincoln County Hospital in Sewell Road where the badly-injured man was admitted and underwent surgery that would incapacitate him for some considerable time. A special relief fund was set up to provide for the hero although in the event only £7 15s 6d (£7.77) was raised.

This was only slightly less than Fred was to be paid each fortnight by Wednesday, the winger having ended the previous season with a run of a seven games without an injury. As he had shown some signs that he could still be of use, Wednesday were content to award the player a 10s (50p) a week wage rise to £4 a week for the 1902–03 season.

There was no doubt that this was a worrying time for Fred. His recent years at Owlerton had been frustrating and he had clearly not enjoyed playing in front of a home crowd that became increasingly impatient for the old hero to reproduce the form that made him a household name in the footballing world. Some of the crowd at Owlerton may never have seen him play at Olive Grove and may have been excused for asking what all the fuss was about. However, there would have been plenty of people inside the ground who would have put them right.

The player was keen to recover his international form and status. Shortly after the annual team photograph was taken he therefore gambled by deciding to throw away the bandages he had used for knee support over the previous two seasons. The bandages are clearly visible in the photograph.

CHAPTER 17

CHAMPIONS OF ENGLAND
Spiksley defies injury to win elusive medal

THROUGHOUT THE SUMMER of 1902 Fred maintained an intensive training programme that was aimed at strengthening his leg and thigh muscles in order to protect his right knee. The programme of swimming, running, sprinting and special weight-lift training was a lonely one but Fred knew that his time was running out and Wednesday would end his contract if he failed to do well on the pitch. He was as fit as he had ever been on his return to Sheffield at the start of the 1902–03 season. This saw the introduction of a radical change in pitch markings with a new rectangular six-yard box to replace the previous six yard semi circles – within which goal kicks were taken – and a new penalty area, 44 yards wide and eighteen yards, deep with a penalty spot exactly twelve yards from the centre of the goal. Two years later, 'keepers, who could previously advance up to six yards, were restricted to staying on their line until a penalty kick was taken. Later, 'keepers became required to wear a differently-coloured jersey from those worn by their teammates.

Despite his efforts to get back to full fitness, Fred received some abuse during the opening League match away to Sheffield United on Monday 1 September 1902. A friend told him afterwards that at 1-1, when the ball was passed out to him, a nearby spectator had shouted out "What's the point of passing to him? He's an old man." Fred had shown why he should have the ball as he then delivered a wicked curling cross that left Foulke stranded, allowing Wilson to head his side into the lead. Fred had earlier equalised with a low close-range shot that confirmed to the player he was coming back to his best. Some great runs down the wing helped boost his confidence even further.

Davis made it 3-1. Although they had to survive some near misses after Lipsham reduced the arrears the final result of United 2 Wednesday 3 was a fair reflection on a day when Harry Chapman faced his brother Herbert who was making his debut for the home side.

Herbert was to become more famous off the pitch than on it with highly successful managerial spells at Northampton Town, and later Huddersfield Town and Arsenal, transforming both the Terriers and Gunners into the best sides of their eras. Universally acknowledged as the finest football manager of his generation, Chapman was also instrumental in introducing new tactics and formations to the game. When asked in later life to name his finest football XI from the past, Chapman picked at outside left one of the opponents on his debut for Sheffield United – Fred Spiksley.

Wednesday maintained their highly impressive away form of four wins and a draw in five matches when they played at Bolton where the highlight of a poor first half was the ball bursting. Davis's blistering shot put his side ahead and then he headed back a Spiksley cross for Wilson to hit a rasping volley that ended the scoring. Davis and Wilson also scored in the first home fixture of the season as newly-promoted Middlesbrough were beaten 2-0 in a Yorkshire derby, which by attracting a 20,000 crowd showed that Wednesday had now established themselves in their new home.

A 3-0 defeat at Newcastle United ended Wednesday's unbeaten run but after drawing 1-1 at home to Wolves, Wednesday advanced to top spot by beating Notts County at Trent Bridge 3-0, a Friday match played on the day of the annual Nottingham Goose Fair. All the goals were scored by Fred Spiksley. The first came on 28 minutes when he sped past Tom Prescott and hit a powerful shot beyond Harry Pennington. On the interval Spiksley scored from close in and then in the 77th minute he and Malloch combined superbly before Spiksley, despite a tight angle, left Pennington with no chance as the ball flew into the net.

Following this success, Fred also netted the first goal "with a brilliant shot" the following day but Wednesday lost 4-2 at Liverpool, who having last played the previous Saturday were the fresher side. Two of the Liverpool goals, one a penalty, came from Sam Raybould who was the First Division's top scorer that season with 32 goals.

Sheffield United then took revenge for their earlier defeat when Fred Priest scored the only goal of the game at Owlerton after his penalty had been saved in the 50th minute. Both sides were forced to play without a key player as Crawshaw and Lipsham had been selected to represent the English League against the Irish League in Belfast.

The derby was as usual played at a frantic pace and in the first half Wednesday were the superior side but left the field handicapped after a late foul on Spiksley left him injured for the remainder of the game. Davis too was in considerable pain and he missed the first part of the second half while his fractured thumb was bandaged up. Towards the end of the game tremendous Wednesday efforts to equalise produced some great saves by Foulke.

Harry Chapman helped get his side back on track by scoring the only goal of the game at Grimsby and

Wednesday won their fifth away game of the season when they returned to Nottingham and beat Forest 4-1.

However, returning from a 2-1 defeat by Blackburn at Ewood Park on 15 November 1902 the Wednesday scorer, Mick Langley, said to Fred "There's no championship for us this year." Sunderland were favourites to retain their title but started the campaign disastrously and when Wednesday beat them 1-0 in late November it seemed their chance had gone. However, a strong run over Christmas and into January was to put the Roker Park club back into contention.

Fred Spiksley played well in the victory against Sunderland, with JH Catton, writing in *Athletic News:* "Spiksley was brisk, speedy and clever, and many years as he has played can yet hold his own with the best."

Wednesday enjoyed a good spell over the festive period. Before then they played superbly on 6 December 1902 to beat Everton 4-1 on a hard Owlerton pitch. Wilson cracked an early shot off the underside of the bar and into the net before Jimmy Settle equalised. Wilson then drove a fast low shot beyond 'keeper George Kitchen, who later signed for West Ham United and went on to score five penalties for the East London side. After Spiksley made it 3-1, Wilson prodded home his third goal after a dropping Spiksley corner led to a scrimmage in front of the goal.

Newly-promoted West Bromwich Albion had surprised everyone by challenging for top spot and it was a delighted Wednesday side who returned from Stoney Lane with both points in a thrilling 3-2 victory on 20 December 1902. With Lyall laid up in bed with flu, Stubbs was recalled in goal and he saw his half backs force the home side back before Chapman opened the scoring on ten minutes. In response, Albion worked energetically and with the wind at their backs pushed forward. Stubbs was forced to save smartly and the interval arrived with Wednesday still leading.

That lead lasted only another ten minutes but was restored following some brilliant wing play when Spiksley flashed past Daniel Nurse and Jackie Kifford, the home right half and full back respectively, before squaring the ball to Davis who beat Ike Webb. West Brom made sure there was to be no repeat performance as a minute later the Wednesday winger was taken down from behind and thereafter was unable to contribute anything worthwhile to events. However, Davis put the game out of the home side's reach by netting from a superb Ferrier pass.

Back in the West Midlands, Wednesday lost at Aston Villa on Boxing Day but this was then followed by victories against Notts County, Aston Villa and Bolton Wanderers in which nine goals were scored without conceding.

The return match against Aston Villa on New Year's Day attracted a large crowd, 28,000 witnessing a brilliant performance from Wednesday who won 4-0.

Against Bolton two days later, Davis scored all the goals in a 3-0 home win to become the third Wednesday player to score a hat-trick that season. On a soft pitch the bottom side in the League were easily beaten once Davis opened the scoring on 20 minutes, forcing home after Fred Thompson had saved from Spiksley. Before half-time Davis doubled the lead and completed the scoring on 70 minutes after fine play by Chapman and Ferrier. Wednesday rose to second place. Although Davis had clearly been the man-of-the-match there was praise for Fred Spiksley by J H Catton, who writing in the *Athletic News*, said, "Spiksley, the evergreen, showed the pace of youth and the art of experience. I wonder how much longer this little gentleman will delight the crowd with high-class football, for he never seems to get older."

Davis also scored in Wednesday's following two away matches but the side's inconsistency continued as the matches at Middlesbrough and Wolves were both lost 2-1. In between those two defeats, Wednesday, maintained their challenge with a 3-0 home win over Newcastle. Chapman netted twice before Spiksley rounded off the scoring.

Wednesday stayed in second and what undoubtedly helped the championship bid was that Wednesday were able to field virtually the same side throughout the season. This naturally encouraged a strong team spirit and work ethic in which the two full backs combined well together, the half back line played superbly and were supplemented up front by some great wing play by Davis and Spiksley, plus the steadily improving form of Wilson. The Scots centre was a big fan of the Wednesday outside left and especially admired him for his ability to cut inside and shoot, and for his desire and bravery, especially as many of his opponents would try to take him down.

Three players – Langley, Ruddlesdin and Wilson – played in all 34 League games in 1902–03 and four – Crawshaw, Ferrier, Malloch and Lyall – missed just one match each. Chapman missed just two games as did Spiksley. Remarkably, Spiksley survived the season injury free and was only missing due to an inter-league call-up and a bout of flu. The other two mainstays, Layton and Davis, missed five and eight games respectively. The highest number of appearances by any other player who featured in the season was just five by right back Fred Thackeray while eight players made a single appearance each.

At home to Liverpool, Wednesday won a hard battle 3-1 with Chapman scoring twice and Davis once. A 1-0 defeat in a replay at home to Blackburn Rovers in the FA Cup was a big disappointment for the 25,410 Owlerton crowd. Wednesday failed to score in either game against their great Lancashire rivals and they were to struggle in front of goal over the following weeks. The side were therefore grateful to Langley when he netted twice from the spot to earn a 1-1 draw at home to Grimsby and a 1-0 victory at Owlerton against Nottingham Forest.

Flying over an Olive Grove

The following match saw Fred Spiksley missing only his second League game of the season as Wednesday drew 0-0 at home to Blackburn Rovers. He was playing at Celtic Park for the Football League XI against the Scottish League XI. It was only the second time he had played in the game, his first being when the sides drew 1-1 at Goodison Park in 1894. Fred, who was joined at Celtic Park by his teammate Harry Davis, was keen to repeat his 1898 performance on the same ground when England had crushed Scotland in a full international. Coming more than a decade after he had made his international debut, Fred's appearance for the Football League was in this particular era of football a truly remarkable achievement.

Before a 40,000 crowd, the Football League were grateful to the impressive Wolves 'keeper Tom Baddeley for keeping them level at the interval before the away side moved up a gear. When Davis sent the ball across to his Wednesday colleague he left Drummond helpless to open the scoring. Raybould was set up by Spiksley for the second before Davis made it 3-0.

Fred had played brilliantly, with the reporter in the *Dundee Evening Post* stating "He is still a great player, fit for a place in any team." Consequently, the Wednesday man even harboured hopes that he might be called upon to represent his country when the full international with Scotland was held at Bramall Lane in April.

In the event the selectors called up seven of the successful Football League side to face Scotland. Davis was among them but not Fred, the left wing place going to Liverpool's Jack Cox. He was a reliable winger who had played in two previous international games. England decided not to play a local hero who was in fine form and who, importantly, liked nothing better than playing in a big game. Evidence of that was the fact that in nine matches for England and the Football League he never finished on the losing side. Without Fred, England were beaten 2-1 at Bramall Lane.

Champions of England

Fred returned to the Wednesday side at Sunderland, who had won nine and drawn two of their previous League games. A crowd of 22,000 was inside Roker Park for a real thriller which was decided when Wilson beat his Scottish compatriot Doig in the Sunderland goal with a magnificent twenty-yard shot early in the second half. The first had seen neither side able to exert any authority, with few chances created as the game became a fierce affair largely conducted in the middle of the pitch.

One behind, the home side pressed strongly but Crawshaw, Ruddlesdin and Ferrier at half back were in excellent form while in goal the ever-reliable Lyall was alert as always. The crowd were angered by referee Mr Armitt from Leek when he disallowed a goal for a challenge on Lyall that saw the 'keeper bundled into the net. The referee was booed, heckled, jeered and sworn at and even pelted with oranges; the game only continued after consultation between the referee and his linesmen. The win put Wednesday in top place.

Not that the Wednesday players initially had cause for wild celebrations because after the match had ended some of the home fans gathered outside the main stand on a road that was being repaired. Picking up stones, Sunderland supporters pelted the Wednesday team's wagonette as it departed Roker Park on its way to the railway station. It was something of a miracle that no-one was seriously injured as the players threw themselves on to the floor of the conveyance as rocks hammered off it. Those that missed smashed windows of nearby houses. The police, who also came under attack, helped take the referee out of the exit on the opposite side of the ground.

While the glaziers worked overtime the fans' actions forced the FA to order that Sunderland's next home match, against near neighbours Middlesbrough, should take place away from Roker Park. It was played at St James' Park

273

but that did not handicap the Wearsiders who won 2-1 to maintain their title challenge.

In the following game, Wednesday defeated Stoke 1-0 at home with debutant Tom Marrison scoring his only goal for the club in a game that was a stern struggle in the middle of the park. It was the fourth consecutive game in which Wednesday recorded a clean sheet.

The following Saturday, with England facing Scotland in Sheffield, Wednesday made the trip to face Everton and were a goal down at the interval after Jimmy Settle netted. Langley again proved his worth from the spot when he netted to level the scores before the away side appeared to enjoy a touch of fortune when a Bruce Rankin shot was fisted away on the line by a Wednesday defender without the referee noticing. It was a hard-earned point and meant Fred was now in with a chance of adding to his medal collection.

Everton would end the 1902–03 season at the centre of an investigation.

This saw the Blackburn Rovers secretary, Mr J Walmsley, suspended sine die from football management after he was found to have tried, without success, to arrange that his club beat the Toffees in their penultimate fixture. Rovers did win the fixture 3-0, but no action was taken against either side after it was decided Walmsley had acted on his own initiative. The start of the twentieth century saw a number of similar incidents including one involving Billy Meredith who unsuccessfully attempted to bribe Aston Villa captain Alex Leake in a title-deciding fixture in 1905.

Easter setbacks followed for Wednesday as they lost 4-0 and 1-0 respectively away to Bury and Derby County. Soon afterwards these two met in the 1903 FA Cup final, Bury cruising home 6-0.

An early injury to Davis at Derby, where the Wednesday side were missing flu victim Spiksley, proved to be too great a handicap. Lyall made a series of fine saves, but when he did well to parry Yorke's shot on 40 minutes he was left helpless as Billy Richards followed up.

The chances of winning a first title appeared to have disappeared but on the same day that Wednesday lost at Derby, Sunderland were defeated 2-0 away to already-relegated Bolton Wanderers. The Wearsiders then lost 5-2 at Nottingham Forest before defeating Middlesbrough in their penultimate match played on the day that Wednesday won their final League game of the season by beating West Bromwich Albion 3-1 at Owlerton.

Wilson made it 1-0 with a lovely rising shot on eight minutes only for Ted Smith to draw his side level before the home side were awarded a penalty. When Langley netted a huge roar rang out from the crowd who were delighted to see the home side go into the interval leading 2-1.

The second half was a thriller and Wilson was denied by Joe Lowe in the Albion goal. A Spiksley corner then hit the bar as Wednesday sought a crucial third.

Albion were not finished and when they broke quickly it was only through a superb Lyall save from Jim Stevenson in the final minutes that Wednesday stayed in front. It was described in the *Sheffield Telegraph* as "one of the grandest things of its kind on this ground". Then a flowing forward move ended with Spiksley scoring his side's third goal with a well-judged shot. Rapturously received by the crowd, it was the scorer's eighth goal of the season and just reward for a fine performance. Wilson's goal was his twelfth of the campaign but the top Wednesday scorer in the season was Davis with thirteen.

Fred did not know it but he had scored his final competitive goal for Wednesday. Like many times in the past it was a crucial effort. Speaking years later Ambrose Langley said, "Our last match of the season was against West Bromwich Albion at Hillsborough and we won by 3 – 1. It was an exciting match and all through the game the result was in doubt and it was one of our hardest

Flying over an Olive Grove

games of the season. But you could always count on Fred Spiksley to play a special game in the top matches when the circumstances dictated that Wednesday had to win with so much at stake. Fred Spiksley played brilliantly that day and I can still see his performance that remains vividly in my mind."

Wednesday's victory against West Brom meant Aston Villa's great rush up the table, which had seen them collect 24 from a possible 30 points, had been in vain. Wednesday had finished a point ahead of Villa but for them to collect the championship trophy they needed Newcastle to avoid defeat against Sunderland when the local rivals played each other the following Saturday at St James' Park. The Wearsiders had to win if they were to finish top as Wednesday had a superior goal average.

When Sunderland had faced Newcastle earlier in the season at Roker Park the game had finished 0-0. Sunderland, though, had won on all three previous occasions when they had played away to Newcastle. It was generally assumed in the press that Wednesday would miss out on the title because Newcastle would prefer their local rivals to win it! In 1925, Langley wrote: "Throughout the country in 1903 there was talk of a 'squared' match in that Newcastle was going to let Sunderland win."

The Wednesday board had agreed to undertake a West Country and South Wales tour at the completion of the League season and the team were playing Notts County in an exhibition match at the home of newly-created Plymouth Argyle when Newcastle met Sunderland. A special Plymouth Bowl was the beautiful trophy that was awarded to Wednesday after goals from Malloch and Ruddlesdin saw them win 2-0 before an appreciative crowd of 16,000.

Almost 400 miles north, the Tyne–Wear derby was tied at 0-0 at half-time before a crowd in excess of 26,500. Victory for Sunderland would give them their fifth title in twelve seasons but four minutes into the second half Robert McColl scored the home side's winner. McColl, who captained Scotland on the day of the Ibrox Disaster, scored thirteen goals in thirteen international appearances and later founded the RS McColl newsagents' chain. Defeat signalled the end of the most successful period in Sunderland's history.

When news of the result reached Owlerton during a Midland League match between Wednesday reserves and Worksop Town the enthusiasm among the crowd saw the game held up for several minutes.

Down in Devon, the news took a little longer to arrive. According to Andy Wilson, the party were "having tea at our hotel when someone dashed in and said that Newcastle had beaten Sunderland by a single goal. We thought that it was a joke at first, but soon telegrams of congratulations started coming in, and we found that we were League champions." In return, Wednesday quickly sent a telegram to Newcastle United thanking them for their efforts "and true sportsmanship" in defeating their local rivals.

Wednesday's hosts were equally delighted. In the evening, Football League president J J Bentley presented the Plymouth Bowl to captain Mick Langley at a local theatre; the Wednesday captain made a speech before the players returned to their hotel for a party.

Two days later, the League champions drew 2-2 at Bristol City before crossing the border to play against Aberaron, the Welsh Cup finalists. The English side were much too good for their hosts and, despite playing well within themselves, won 6-0 with Fred scoring two, possibly three. Either way they were to be the last goals he scored for Wednesday.

The touring party arrived back in Sheffield on 29 April 1903 at 4.30pm. Large numbers of people began gathering around the Midland Station hours before their arrival and Police Commander Scott was forced to guarantee a strong police presence in order to ensure the crowd's enthusiasm did not lead to any problems.

Emerging from the station the Wednesday contingent scrambled on to an Old Times coach and with the police band blasting out See the Conquering Hero Comes they headed up Commercial Street and High Street before alighting at the Carlton Restaurant for a slap-up meal. Enthusiastic crowds of workers lined the streets. They had been given special dispensation to leave work for a few minutes.

The restaurant gathering was presided over by Wednesday board member Mr Whitley Fearnehough who praised the title-winning team for their "fair play and thrilling brand of football." Mr A J Dickinson praised the players as being "a credit to the club" and added: I "am proud to take them anywhere." Fearnehough reported that although the Football League did not award medals to players of the title-winning team the Wednesday players would be getting commemorative medals presented to them by the club. Wednesday were also very much looking forward to flying the League champions flag at Owlerton throughout the 1903–04 season.

Following the meal, the players adjourned to the Empire Theatre to see the Fred Karno company perform 'The Dandy Thieves' starring Fred Kitchen. The Wednesday players were cheered to the rafters when they were taken on to the stage before being seated at the front to watch the sketch show.

On 24 August 1903 the club organised a more formal celebration banquet. With skipper Langley absent, Fred Spiksley made a short well-received speech on behalf of the players.

CHAPTER 18

THE BELL STARTS TO TOLL
Injury ends illustrious first class career

WHATEVER ELSE HAPPENED in his playing career, Fred, by capturing the League Championship had achieved every honour then going. These included Division One and Division Two titles, FA Cup success, playing and scoring for England. He had risen from being the local lad, playing for his local town, to become the finest outside left in the country. At his peak he was the most talked-about player in football and after many supporters and journalists alike had written him off he came back fighting, gaining a final representative honour and the prize he longed for. Fred scored exactly 100 League goals for Wednesday and fifteen in the FA Cup, making him Wednesday's leading goal scorer of all time, a record that would be beaten by his teammate Andrew Wilson in 1907. Spiksley had been the club's leading goal scorer a total of six times, accumulating enough goals to make him their seventh highest scorer of all time in League and Cup. Add his goals for Wednesday in the Football Alliance and it raises his total to a staggering 170, making him the club's third highest scorer across all first team fixtures, behind Andrew Wilson (233) and John Fantham (193).

Flying over an Olive Grove

At the start of the twentieth century, few footballers – especially those at the height of the game – played on or past the mid-point of their fourth decade. One player who did was Billy Meredith, who as a winger like Fred was never expected to chase back and whose responsibility was to concentrate on breaking down opposition defences. Fred had suffered a number of injuries in his career but there seemed every chance that, at 33 in 1903, he could go on playing for a good many seasons. Especially as he continued to enjoy training and stayed away from heavy drinking, which until relatively recently was a major curse for working class footballers such as Paul Gascoigne, whose ability with the ball can be compared to Fred Spiksley's.

Both Wednesday and Fred would have been encouraged enough to believe that he would have a few more seasons in him, especially after coming so close to another England cap only a couple of months earlier. Therefore Wednesday awarded their star outside left a new contract for the 1903–04 season. In early August he reported for fitness training and ball practice and played for the first team in a match against the reserves. The reserves' right back, marking Fred, was a 22-year-old local lad, Joe Ryalls, who had made the first of what proved to be two Wednesday appearances the previous season.

Receiving the ball, the Wednesday winger set off along the touchline when Ryalls attempted a tackle and somehow the players' legs became entangled. Fred's legs were crossed placing great strain on his knee joint and ligaments and so great was the downward pressure on Fred's knee that it caused a complete dislocation and severe ligament damage. When club physician Doctor Lockwood examined Fred's knee the prognosis was not good; if Fred was to have any chance of ever playing again he would need prolonged rest and recuperation. Fred's place at outside left went to Georgie Simpson, who had come from Jarrow. He played well and Wednesday started the season in fine form.

The Bell starts to Toll

Patience was never one of Fred's virtues and his early attempt at a comeback in the Wednesday reserves ended almost before it started. The doctors vetoed any further attempts for the foreseeable future. The Wednesday directors, though, were anxious to know when he would be returning as the club were paying him the maximum wage of £4 a week.

Fred was selected to play against Corinthians in a benefit game for Bill Layton on 29 December 1903. The winger lasted just five minutes; his knee was unequal to the strain.

Over the next few months the pain in Fred's knee eased and with inflammation and swelling reduced he could walk unaided. His right knee joint, though, was still unstable and playing football remained unlikely for the foreseeable future. His last competitive match for Sheffield Wednesday was for the reserves against Gainsborough Trinity reserves on the 26 September 1903 and he scored after four minutes in a 7-1 success. However, after playing impressively, he was forced to leave the field early in the second half "owing to the failure of his knee, which had given way on several occasions." (*Sheffield Telegraph*) It was also reported that as Spiksley left the field "he could not hide his frustration".

On 1 May 1904 he received a letter from Arthur J Dickinson informing him that the club he had represented since 1891 were terminating his contract. It was a bitter blow but there is rarely room in football for sentiment and it cannot have come as too great a surprise that the club had decided to let him go, especially as without him Wednesday had again won the Division One title, They finished three points clear of second-placed Manchester City with Simpson scoring six times in 25 League appearances. The title had been won because of the magnificent Wednesday defence who in 34 matches conceded just 28 League goals, of which a quarter were lost in just two games.

Flying over an Olive Grove

Fred left convinced that if it had not been for his unfortunate accident he would have continued playing for Wednesday well into his forties. His departure saddened his colleague Mick Langley who, commenting in 1925, said: "For what he did for Wednesday, the club ought to erect a monument in his honour. Fred could start at the halfway line, stop dead twice, and go on before he centred. Opponents were outmanoeuvred. They would run full tilt, Fred would stop, and before they had pulled up and recovered he would be off again. Spiksley used to play the ball with the outside of his foot, pushing it along, and when he centred he crossed the ball so it swerved, not inwards towards the goal, but outwards towards the advancing inside forward. He never placed corner kicks too near the goal. Defences had to come out. Fred Spiksley made Wednesday." According to Langley only Rab Howell could keep Spiksley in check by constantly holding on to his shirt and never moving a yard from him.

Fred's pressing need now was to find alternative employment and income. Sporting papers were advertising for professional footballers and when he wrote to several clubs he was buoyed to receive a number of replies indicating they'd be happy to employ him on the maximum wage.

It was then widely reported in the newspapers that he was returning to Gainsborough Trinity but this did not materialise.

He wrote to Wednesday requesting a free transfer and was informed that he needed to contact Tom Charnley, the Football League secretary. The return letter left him stunned as he was informed that Wednesday expected any new club to pay a transfer fee of £250 for him. It was common knowledge that his knee was suspect and so no club were ever going to take such a gamble if they were also expected to pay a fee. Wednesday had not only dismissed him but also stopped him from earning a living as a footballer. Such was the ruthlessness of football in Edwardian times.

Archie Goodall had informed his former colleague that he wanted to recruit him to play for Glossop North End, where Goodall was player/ manager. He told Fred that Wednesday would have to drop their £250 transfer fee. Wednesday were not for budging and so Fred decided to attend the Football League's AGM and put his case directly to the management committee. In the meantime, Fred was given a chance to earn some money by his brother William. He had many enterprises including an under-the-counter betting operation through one of his shops in Trinity Street in Gainsborough. Fred was in his element and for running the illegal trade he received a weekly wage.

Fred attended the Football League AGM at Manchester's Midland Hotel in June 1904, put his case for a free transfer and had it granted. Having overcome one obstacle another was quickly placed in his way when Goodall informed him that he must undergo a rigorous examination. If this proved successful the former Derby County player, brother of John Goodall, would approach Glossop's wealthy owner, Samuel Hill-Wood, about financing his contract.

Glossop had been elected to the Football League in 1898 and had immediately won promotion. This proved the height of their journey and immediate relegation was followed by a series of disappointing seasons culminating in seventeenth place, second bottom, in Division Two in 1903–04. The club survived re-election and Hill-Wood gave Goodall the job of rebuilding the side, starting with the sorting-out of a leaky defence followed by the recruiting of an experienced player with a cool head to galvanise a misfiring forward line. This was going to be difficult as in addition to not having a good side, Glossop lies in the High Peak district that is not the most hospitable place in the winter. Attracting good players was always going to be a problem. Praying for Fred Spiksley's knee to recover and then getting him fully fit was perhaps Goodall's best chance of reviving his new club.

So there was dismay all round when Fred failed his fitness test; his knee still required rest. Goodall was reluctant to throw in the towel just yet and he successfully persuaded his chairman to give Fred a contract on the basis that he would soon be fit and would move permanently to Glossop.

Fred thus became a Glossop player on Thursday 1 September 1904 and he made his debut in the first game of the season for his new club on 3 September 1904 at Anfield where Liverpool, First Division champions in 1902, were back in Division Two after being relegated two seasons later. The game saw Fred up against Ted Doig, whom Liverpool signed from Sunderland in the summer of 1904. The 'keeper was beaten twice as Glossop grabbed a point in a 2-2 draw. At right back in the Liverpool side was David Murray who later enlisted at the start of World War I for the Argyll and Sutherland Highlanders and was killed, aged just 32, in Loos, France, on 10 December 1915.

Glossop lined up as follows: Frank Davies, William Synott, Willie Orr, H Maginnis, John Boden, J Brown, Leon Gall, T Cairns, Archie Goodall, Eddie Murphy, Fred Spiksley.

Two-one up Glossop missed out on a point when Joe Hewitt scored in the final minute. In the combined Everton/Liverpool programme for the weekend of 10 September 1904 it was reported "Fred Spiksley is light of other days, and his usefulness is much diminished."

Fred was missing when Glossop drew 0-0 at home to Burslem Port Vale before a 4,000 crowd and was also absent in the following three games that were all lost as Glossop dropped to the foot of the table. Fred returned for the sixth game of the season on Saturday 8 October 1904 at Chesterfield.

Glossop: Davies, Orr, Synott, Phillips, Boden, Maginnis, Gall, Cairns, Brown, Murphy and Spiksley.

The Bell starts to Toll

The away side were one ahead when Spiksley scored an easy tap-in to double the score in a match that ended 2-1. Victory came at a cost, though, as the outside left had enjoyed no protection from the referee, had been badly kicked throughout the match and was forced to sit out the next game that Glossop won 3-1 against Bradford City.

The winger returned at Lincoln City where Goodall also played. Glossop were beaten 3-0 but there was enough in their display and Fred's performance to suggest they could comfortably survive come the end of the season. A week later, Glossop beat non-league Nantwich away in the FA Cup third qualifying round 2-1, with both goals made by the outside left.

Four games, two wins, one goal scored and two goals made. It was an impressive start but Fred was not happy as it was clear his pace had gone and he was going to have to rely on a more measured, relaxed approach. So when he received a letter from Samuel Hill-Wood stating he was suspended because he had failed to relocate permanently to Glossop, Fred was quite philosophical as he believed Glossop wanted rid of him because of his performances. He wrote back to the club requesting they forward him his final week's wages. By return post he was informed he was getting nothing as he was in breach of his contract and in consequence his registration documents were being retained. This effectively meant he could not play for another club.

Apart from his two years working in Sheffield, Fred had lived in Gainsborough for his whole life. His family were still there. He could also work for his brother's turf accountancy business during the week and then play football at the weekend. There were also opportunities to attend the Doncaster and Lincoln racecourses. In truth, Fred was never going to move permanently to Glossop but had hoped to do enough on the field to demonstrate that his services were worth retaining even without keeping his earlier commitment.

Flying over an Olive Grove

The *Glossop Chronicle* reported that he had been sacked and this led Fred to conclude it was his performances rather than his failure to move from Lincolnshire that had seen his contract terminated.

Nevertheless, it would now be difficult for him to keep playing football as Glossop had retained his registration papers. Fred thought of again applying to the Football League for a free transfer but soon put that to the back of his mind while he continued to work for his brother William. Fortuitously, early in 1905, Fred bumped into the respected Blackburn referee John Lewis who was also an influential member of the Football League management committee. When the conversation turned to the documents being retained by Glossop, Lewis promised to raise the matter at the next League meeting.

A few weeks later, Fred received confirmation that he had been granted a second free transfer. Despite this, Fred did play one more League game for Glossop, featuring at inside right when North End played at Grimsby, just forty miles from Gainsborough, on 25 March 1905. The home side won 3-0. According to the Glossop club historian Tom Sutcliffe it is possible that Fred's appearance at Cleethorpes was made "as an amateur". In return for their expenses, owner Samuel Hill-Wood was known for shipping players in to "do him a favour".

Glossop didn't do too badly in the 1904–05 season and went on to finish in twelfth place in Division Two and thus avoided the need to apply for re-election.

CHAPTER 19

LOBBYING AT ELLAND ROAD
Spiksley's role in the development of first class football in Leeds

FOLLOWING THE END of his Glossop contract, Fred Spiksley wanted to continue playing. He did not want to return to the newspaper trade and the money earned during his playing career wasn't sufficient to retire on. In August 1904 a new club had been formed – Leeds City. West Yorkshire had proved to have little interest in football with the general public much preferring Rugby League. There had been 30,000 spectators to watch Batley play Warrington in the Northern League Challenge Cup final in 1903. Rugby League's domination of professional spectator sport extended to a monopoly on the local playing fields, forcing football clubs into ground-sharing arrangements with Rugby League clubs who dictated terms and fixture lists. Disputes inevitably arose with football usually losing. Nevertheless, football remained popular among children and teenagers, especially as it was easier to play in the street.

Hunslet Athletic had been Leeds's premier football club but, after the West Yorkshire League (WYL) was disbanded in 1897, they had been forced to join the Sheffield and Hallamshire (S&H) League. They did well and also made good headway in the FA Amateur Cup. But when their ground lease was lost and they could not find a suitable alternative venue to satisfy the S&H, Hunslet disbanded. Club officials were present at a meeting at the Griffin Hotel at which everyone voted to set up a new premier football club in the largest English city without one.

Leeds City joined the FA, entered the FA Cup and negotiated with Bentley's Brewery to lease Elland Road football ground. A recruitment drive enlisted a group of players to play for the new club in the WYL and on 1 September 1904 a 2-2 draw was recorded in the first ever game, away to Morley. Two days later the first home match was played at Hunslet Rugby Club's Wellington Road ground with visitors Altofts winning 2-1.

On 13 October, Leeds City signed a lease for Elland Road and two days later they played their first game there against Hull City. In early November, club representatives signed a one-year lease at an annual rent of £75 with an option to buy the land for £4,500 in spring 1905.

Leeds City failed to set the world alight and league fixtures were treated with scant respect. Games were cancelled at the last minute. They were also knocked out of the local Hospitals Cup.

None of this mattered to the club's executive who were firmly set on joining the Football League. This appeared to be a pipe dream but the Football League hierarchy were desperate to extend their influence into West Riding following newly-formed Bradford City's successful election into the League for the 1903–04 season. Burnley director Charles Sutcliffe, a Rawtenstall lawyer, was the most powerful man on the Football League management committee and in 1903 his proposal to extend the League to accommodate twenty clubs in each division was agreed upon and was set to start two years later.

Before Leeds City could join the Football League they needed to demonstrate to other members that their application was good enough to justify election. With its new 'Scratching Shed' stand and accommodation for 5,000 spectators under a thirty-foot high wooden barrel roof, Elland Road was good enough to stage Football League matches and the new club also had the valuable option to buy the freehold. Additionally, wealthy wholesale clothier Mr Norris Hepworth had agreed to become the club's first chairman and principal benefactor.

However, the indifferent quality of the playing staff meant gates were poor and this in turn fed doubts about whether professional football could compete against rugby league.

Determined to demonstrate that there was an appetite for football the Leeds City executive began organising a series of high-profile exhibition games against seven top sides that were generously paid to play at Elland Road. Naturally, the games needed to be played on a Saturday but this created problems as most League clubs were already fully booked up. Leeds City thus invited those clubs who had been eliminated from the FA Cup and were without a League fixture on the dates for subsequent rounds.

West Bromwich Albion were the first side paid for their services in a game that was set for 4 February 1905. Further games against Sheffield United, Derby County, Preston, Leicester Fosse, Lincoln City and non-league Hull City were arranged.

What was now needed were good quality professional footballers. They were almost impossible to obtain in January and February as there were few available and no possibility of senior clubs releasing players during the season. With no scouting network, Leeds City could also not expect to identify young footballing talent in the amateur arena in time for the big games.

Only two players were available who might help – Fred Spiksley and Tommy Morren, formerly of Sheffield United and England. Tommy was just 5ft 5ins tall and weighed no more than 10 stones.

The day before Leeds City were due to play West Bromwich Albion Fred agreed to a 'pay as you play deal' of £3 a game and it is likely that Morren signed a similar agreement. To add to Fred's excitement his signing had been warmly greeted in the local press and his knee had healed beyond expectations. His confidence was high but when he discovered that, apart from himself and Morren, Leeds City had failed to strengthen the team, he was left despondent. With just two professionals it was going to be tough to compete against some of England's best sides.

The Leeds City committee were, however, delighted that Fred had accepted their offer and were keen to cash in on his popularity with players, coaches, committeemen, directors, referees, League and FA officials. He was, in many respects, the perfect ambassador for a club who were seeking to influence football's decision makers.

Norris Hepworth therefore asked Fred to greet visiting officials and dignitaries, introduce them to the Leeds City committee and generally highlight Elland Road's impressive facilities. Fred happily accepted the new role, for which, presumably, he was paid, particularly as it gave him the opportunity to meet and chat about old times with such notables as Billy Bassett and Steve Bloomer.

West Bromwich Albion were in Division Two when they faced Leeds City in early February before an excited crowd of 3,000 people who paid gate receipts of over £50. This easily covered the visitors' match fee. On a sticky pitch, the away side paid Leeds the compliment of fielding their first team.

With the wind behind them, the home side's enthusiasm initially helped them push back the League side. They should have been ahead after 30 minutes but after that Albion dominated. There was no score at the break but in the second half the home team fell apart and were slightly fortunate not to be more heavily beaten than 5-0. Afterwards, Morren left his new club by mutual consent.

Leeds City side: Chaffer, Bintcliffe, Burton, Storey, Hunt, Dixon, Morren, Howard G, Howard F, Nelson, Spiksley.

It was a very disappointed Fred Spiksley who met up with Billy Bassett, now an Albion director, and Harry Keys, the Baggies chairman. The West Midlands club had themselves been through some difficult financial times and had recently survived a banker's writ for moneys that were owed. The pair had set up a fundraising committee and done everything they could to put the club back on an even keel. Fred and Billy chatted about their England experiences before the former broached the question of Leeds City's application to join the Football League. Winks from Billy and Harry had Fred convinced there was at least one tick in the box.

On 18 February, Leeds City welcomed an under-strength Sheffield United side to Elland Road. The party did include two great personalities from the reserves in Bill 'Fatty' Foulke and William 'Cocky' Bennett as well as first team captain Ernest Needham, trainer George Waller, director Joseph Tomlinson and club secretary John Nicholson. All were strong characters whose views were respected by the Cutlers' board of directors who would decide whether to back Leeds City's application to join the Football League.

Another 3,000 crowd, possibly drawn by the chance to see Needham and Foulke, witnessed a match that was played in atrocious conditions and in which Hunt scored a last-minute equaliser for the home side in a 2-2 draw with G Howard scoring the other Leeds goal. Having been starved of the ball in the first game, Fred Spiksley had played the second at outside right in the hope of being more involved.

Hunt also scored in the next exhibition match against Leicester Fosse but the home side lost 5-1 before a crowd of around a thousand. Leeds City then lost their remaining four fixtures against Hull City (5-2), Lincoln City (3-1),

Derby County (2-0) and Preston (4-1). Fred Spiksley did not score in any of the matches but was one of only four players to play in all seven games, the others being Bintcliffe and the Howard brothers. The former Wednesday winger may have been disappointed at the standard of the side he had played in but he was pleased that his knee had not given way.

The exhibition games, attended by an average of 1,850 spectators each, meant Leeds City had a backlog of West Yorkshire League (WYL) fixtures to complete and they did this by employing reserve players in many of them. Nevertheless when the season ended the new club still had five outstanding fixtures and it was a small wonder they were not kicked out of the WYL in which they finished in eleventh place.

Fred played for Leeds in the WYL and he scored twice, one a penalty, when Beeston Hill Parish Church were beaten 5-1. He also scored in a 2-2 draw against Upper Armley Christ Church in April. It seems these may have been the only two league games he played for Leeds City.

Despite their lack of success the Leeds City committee remained enthusiastic about the future and on 5 June 1905, Leeds City AFC became a limited company with £10,000 capital put forward by the club's benefactors. In the meantime, Fred Spiksley departed after it was reported he had "helped convince club officials that entry into the Football League was not just a dream".

And so it proved as with 25 votes from the current clubs, Leeds City were elected to the newly-extended Second Division. The club then recruited the Chesterfield manager, Gilbert Gillies, as the boss. He put together a team strong enough to compete in the Football League including Harry Singleton, an outside left from QPR. Only one local player, Charles Morgan, was among the fourteen professionals recruited.

In their first ever League game in September 1905, against Bradford City at Valley Parade, a crowd of 15,000-

plus witnessed a 1-0 success for the home XI. In Leeds's first home League match a 6,800 crowd saw West Bromwich Albion collect both points in a 2-0 victory. On 23 September, Leeds beat Hull City 3-1 before an Elland Road crowd of 13,654 and there was a 22,000 crowd for the home derby with Bradford City in December 1905.

Come the end of the first season, Leeds City had averaged 9,000 spectators at home. Meanwhile the average gate for the Leeds rugby league club fell from 9,000 to 5,600. Football had replaced rugby league as the number one spectator sport in Leeds. Fred Spiksley had played a small part in making that happen and although Leeds City went out of business in October 1919 the subsequent rise of Leeds United has meant rugby league rarely matches football in terms of attendances.

CHAPTER 20

LONDON CALLING
Chelsea, Southern United and saving
Johnny Allgood's skin

IN EARLY APRIL 1905, Fred Spiksley successfully responded to an *Athletic News* advert for the post of secretary-manager with Southern United Athletic Company Limited.

The club had been set up the previous summer by six shareholder directors who were schoolmaster William Hooton, contractor John Diddle, publican William Smith, builder Richard Vidlar, Royal Navy Officer Patrick McGuire and timber merchant George Richmond.

Joining them on the board of directors was Baron William Edward Reiffenstein, the club's general secretary, and accountant William Thomas Moody, who lived at Honor Oak Park, London. The company address was listed at 6 Grocers Hall Court in the City of London, the baron's home.

The men believed that with half a million local residents in South East London there would be enough football fans to justify their endeavours as they set out to build for long-term success.

A successful application to the South Eastern Football League (SL) saw the new club placed in Division Two.

The search for a suitable home led to Brown's Athletic football ground in Nunhead. Negotiations with its owner, William Tipper of the local Railway Hotel, saw the new club agree to hire the ground for £3 for the initial games. There was then concluded a rental agreement of £70 from 1 October 1904 to 25 March 1905 with an option of a further two years' lease at a total of £170. The baron paid a £25 deposit.

'Brown's Field', which is still used today, had an interesting history. King Edward VII had regularly gone shooting there when he was Prince of Wales and it was reputed that W G Grace had frequently played cricket there in the 1890s. Most people reached the ground by walking up the hill from Nunhead Railway Station before turning into an alleyway that led to the backs of terraced housing in Ivydale Road and the ground entrance. Brown's Field was well drained and the football pitch was one of the largest in the country at 117 yards long and 75 yards wide.

The ground was well served by buses and was only a short walk from New Cross Gate station, which today is one of the stations that bring football fans to Millwall's ground. In 1904, however, Millwall (Athletic) then played their football north of the river on the Isle of Dogs.

With an increasing demand for space the number of suitable football grounds was diminishing and securing such a good enclosure was no mean feat. What was considerably less satisfactory was the failure to accrue sufficient funds to allow for the recruitment of a squad of players good enough to compete.

The nominal capital of the new company had been set at £1,000 divided into 4,000 shares at 5s (25p) each. Every director was expected to buy 250 shares and under this arrangement the club would have had £375 in the bank. John Diddle managed to buy 200 shares but the other five directors had more modest incomes and could only afford to purchase 122 between them.

Flying over an Olive Grove

On 6 September 1904 Southern United had just £80.50 in the bank. Set against this, Baron Von Reiffenstein had set up the company, dealt with the formation costs, opened a company bank account, paid the legal expenses, written the company prospectus and provided the company memorandum and articles of association that set out the rules and objectives of the company. He was owed £60 for this, plus £25 for the deposit on the field. There was also outstanding rent that was due on 1 October. In total the club's liabilities exceeded their assets by £67 10s (£67.50)

The directors set out on a charm offensive but failed to attract new investors. The baron even thought of floating the company on the stock exchange but it was far too soon to think that anyone would take this seriously and the plan was abandoned. However, by 1 October the efforts had helped sell £37 10s of season tickets at 7s 6d (37.5p) each to watch a side entirely composed of amateur players. Admission charges were set at 6d (2.5p) for men and 3d (1.5p) for women and children.

When the matches began the home match gate receipts proved to be around £42 and with all SL clubs retaining their home takings this meant Southern United had a weekly income of around £21. From this the club had to pay their expenses.

The future was not looking very rosy and on 1 December 1904 the man who had been the most enthusiastic supporter of the proposal to establish a major club in SE London quit. William Hooton was replaced by Alexander Stead, a Royal Naval officer. On 31 January 1905 Baron Von Reiffenstein resigned as general secretary and William Moody (who took it upon himself to find new investors for the club) took on his role. By 20 June 1905, Moody had achieved some success in recruiting new shareholders and it was reported that there were now 911 issued shares and £236 had been raised towards the 1905–06 season's running costs.

London Calling

The hope now was that Southern United would be able to recruit a professional playing staff and move up the table. The club may have finished bottom of the league in 1904–05 but only because an ineligible player had played in one match following which Southern were docked two points and fell down two places in the table.

Southern United had actually performed reasonably well, particularly as they had competed against professional teams, among them the reserve sides of Woolwich Arsenal and Tottenham Hotspur. Southern's problem had been stopping goals and they conceded 78, the division's highest figure.

Fred believed his new post would involve coaching and recruiting players as well as playing, an ideal opportunity to play out the remainder of his career, while developing the new skills required to subsequently earn a living out of football. His weekly wages were the maximum £4 then allowed in football and he also collected a £10 signing-on fee. On 2 June 1905, he left Gainsborough for his new role. He rented a semi-detached house not far from the Brockley Jack public house in Lewisham Borough.

Fred was in a good mood when he arrived at work the following day. He was just settling down at his desk when the former Sheffield United forward Jack Almond entered his room. The men had regularly clashed with each other in derby games in the past but were happy to see each other. Fred's mood darkened, though, when Almond told him he was Southern United's football coach.

Fred felt that being a coach would have allowed him to pass on his experience and understanding of the game to those under his direction. He had wrongly assumed that he would write a few letters and deal with transfer forms before leaving himself time to organise coaching for the players.

Almond's appointment was a big blow and the role of secretary-manager was essentially a desk-based job that even included taking weekly minutes at board meetings. Fred certainly had the skills to do the job. However, the Wednesday man had no wish to be at the beck and call of the directors.

He also loved the fresh air and an office job would prevent him following his racing passion on the courses throughout south-east England. Fred, though, had no alternative but to do his best as he had signed a contract for the new post. He was cheered by news that he was to be made team captain as in such a role he could expect to be consulted on players and transfer targets.

Over the summer, Fred was rushed off his feet as he sorted out the club's administration systems and, together with Moody and Almond, assembled a squad of professional footballers. They included former Bradford City 'keeper Fred Mearns who later played for Barnsley in the 1910 FA Cup final. James Whitehouse had been a member of the Aston Villa double-winning side in 1896–97 while centre half Micky Sullivan was a well-travelled professional fresh from a season at Brighton and Hove Albion. Centre forward Thomas McCairns had also played for Brighton in 1904–05.

Almond recruited Fulham's John Holmes and when West Kirby's John Wood did well in a trial match Fred Spiksley used his influence to get him a playing contract after which he took him under his wing.

In addition to their SL programme, Southern United joined the United League midweek competition where it was mandatory to play full-strength teams. The local press commented favourably on Southern's ambitions. To add to the growing excitement, the ground was much improved with a covered stand on the enclosed side erected for the first home game.

There was a shock, though, when only days before the season's start it was announced that Major John Sayers had been appointed as 'team trainer.' Almond quit in disgust.

All the hard work that had been put in appeared to have been wasted. Within half an hour of his arrival the Royal Military College man had destroyed the happy atmosphere that had been generated among players and staff. The players soon began complaining about Sayers's coaching methods and his dictatorial attitude towards them. Fred later commented on how he was glad to get away from Sayers when he left Southern United.

Southern began their SL fixtures with a 2-2 draw at Leyton where Fred Spiksley was given a great reception when he led his side out. The day was a great success for Wood who scored twice, the first of which was created for him by Spiksley. The former Wednesday player was on the score sheet in another 2-2 draw the following week in a friendly match at Loftus Road against Shepherd's Bush. He also scored as his side beat Reading reserves 2-0 in an away SL fixture.

Later Fred scored three goals as Southern United overcame a spirited fight by amateur side Nunhead in the FA Cup first qualifying round. The sight of 3,000 spectators at the home game to watch the 5-2 success was looked upon with delight by everyone associated with the infant club. There was further delight when the draw for the second qualifying round meant Chelsea would travel to Southern on 28 October 1905. The Stamford Bridge side had Bill Foulke in goal but he was ruled out through injury as was Fred Spiksley. Chelsea won 1-0 but the losers had the satisfaction of being the better side on the day. There was the added bonus that the match had attracted a crowd of over 7,000.

Chelsea had only been formed in early 1905 when Gus Mears announced he would spend £100,000 on transforming Stamford Bridge, which he bought in 1904, into one of Britain's finest football stadiums. Stamford Bridge had previously been used for many recreational activities, including circuses and the 1896 Amateur Athletics

Association (the three A's) championships where Arthur Wharton sensationally broke the 100 yards world record. A less pleasant occasion was when John Tickner held on to the trailing rope of a hot air balloon when a sudden gust of wind took it into the air. He had no chance of survival.

Mears's wealth and ambition meant that although they had yet to kick a ball, Chelsea were elected in the summer of 1905 to the newly-extended Football League. London now had three League clubs in Woolwich Arsenal, Clapton Orient and Chelsea. Slowly but surely the North's dominance was being challenged.

Chelsea then began seeking players for the start of their Second Division campaign in September 1905. Their first members' handbook proclaimed that all roads led to Stamford Bridge and with many local rail links and the steamboats that called at Chelsea pier, the new ground in the London borough of Fulham and Hammersmith was well served by transport. The ground was situated in a working class area but the wealthier parts of the adjoining boroughs of Chelsea and Kensington were within easy walking distance and this soon resulted in the new club attracting a number of showbiz personalities. A spirit of adventure and fun infected those who attended Chelsea's early games.

Finding players is always difficult and Mears offered a role to Fred Spiksley in his new set-up by asking him to seek out top young talent and persuade them to sign for Chelsea. Fred's role at Chelsea was to remain a secret. It would have initially been a conflict of interests, as Spiksley would have been seeking out players for Southern United at the same time. The secret was not revealed until Spiksley's *Thomson's Weekly* articles in 1920.

Initially, Mears accepted the England international's advice without demur. So when Scottish-born Tommy McDermott was wanted by Dundee the decision was taken to let him go as Fred Spiksley was convinced that his rival for the inside forward role, Jimmy Windridge, was, as it subsequently proved, a better player. However, he later found that Mears's other business interests made it difficult for Fred to get sufficient time to discuss with the Chelsea owner the merits of future stars.

In the summer of 1907, Fred wanted Chelsea to buy Harold Halse from Southend United at a fee of £200. When the Londoners failed to carry out the deal the player was sold to Manchester United where he achieved huge success in a fine side and later played for Aston Villa before finally ending up at Chelsea in 1913.

Earlier, Fred had mentioned two Crystal Palace stars – George Woodger and Charlie Wallace. Fred, who had regularly seen the pair play, had made enquiries and knew both players were available for a combined price of £100. Although the Chelsea board accepted his judgement, his advice was overlooked as it was considered unwise to spend money at a time when they were building the grandstands and improving the stadium. In addition to that, the first team were doing well.

A few months later, Chelsea came back and proposed buying the two Ws but by now the fee for each player had risen considerably. In May 1907, Aston Villa purchased Wallace for £500 and he had a great career there. He was still good enough to attract a fee of £1,000 when Oldham Athletic purchased him in 1921. Woodger joined Oldham Athletic and played for England in 1911.

Two weekends after the Chelsea cup-tie, Fred Spiksley scored twice as his side overturned a three-goal deficit to beat West Ham reserves 4-3 at Brown's Ground in an SL encounter. On Saturday 6 January 1906, Fred scored his side's goal in a 3-1 defeat away to Portsmouth. It proved his final piece of action for Southern United as he was then sacked from his post. Joining him out of work was trainer John Sayers, a move greeted with pleasure by the players.

Whatever reason the club officially presented for the two sackings it is not hard to read between the lines,

Flying over an Olive Grove

when you have the benefit of hindsight. Southern United were in fifth place in the SL but behind the scenes their finances were in disarray and the following Monday it was announced the club had folded, leaving the playing and ground staff without jobs and owing a substantial sum to a number of creditors. The Southern United directors had gambled in thinking big and without the resources to match their ambitions the whole affair had been a disaster. Instead of becoming a second Chelsea, Southern United were insolvent and out of business.

Fred Spiksley was now out of work but there was consolation in that he had played six months' football without his knee failing him. As a result, several managers were keen to offer him a playing role and in the days following his departure from Southern United he began to consider his options. A few weeks later he also contacted Derby County to recommend that following Steve Bloomer's surprise departure to Middlesbrough they should sign John Wood as his replacement. Wood did well for the Rams over the next fifteen months before signing for Manchester City. Fred would no doubt have expected to be paid for finding the East Midlanders a new player.

Organised football in Watford started around 1870, the year of Fred Spiksley's birth. In 1906 Watford's player-manager was John Goodall. With his team struggling 'Honest John' was intent on finding out if the rumours were true and his former England international colleague Fred Spiksley had lost his job at Southern United,

When he answered his front door, Fred Spiksley was delighted to see who was standing there. The pair had last met weeks earlier when Spiksley's fine performance for Southern United against Watford had helped his side win a United League match. This performance demonstrated to Goodall that the outside left remained capable of playing good football.

On establishing that the rumours of Spiksley being out of work were true Goodall, fearing relegation, offered him a contract at Watford. Fred was happy to sign what for what proved to be his last playing role.

Watford were out of the FA Cup and struggling in the League with thirteen points from twenty matches. The new signing would replace Kelly on Saturday 10 February 1906 against a Southampton side unbeaten in ten matches.

Getting Spiksley to play for Watford was welcomed by the *Watford Observer*: "John Goodall is to come out of retirement to play at inside left in partnership with the former international Fred Spiksley. What memories these two old internationals conjure up! There is still enough football in these men to make a clever and effective wing partnership."

Watford: Biggar, Aston, Lindsay, Main, McCartney, Richardson, Badenoch, Turner, Eames, Goodall and Spiksley.

Scotsman Billy Biggar in goal had a tremendous punch and kick but was prone to a rush of blood. Charlie Aston was well known for his swearing. This displeased the Watford directors because many of the club's followers were female. Charlie was reprimanded for his language. Matters didn't end there as his wife argued with a gatekeeper after she was caught trying to break ground rules by smuggling in her pet dog. Unpleasant words were exchanged and she was informed that any further histrionics would see her banned.

Local lad Joe Brooks was a former amateur cycling champion who would later fetch Watford's first ever three-figure sum when he moved to Sheffield United for £275. David McCarthy (or McCartney) was Watford's regular centre half and penalty taker. He later joined Chelsea. This would give an opportunity to George Fyfe, signed from Hibernian in the summer of 1905, and the solid centre half would give sterling service for five seasons. Jack Richardson usually played left half but, as a utility player, often filled a variety of positions.

Flying over an Olive Grove

George Badenoch, quick and skilful, was Watford's youngest first team player. Alas, he died in the First World War. Peter Turner was to finish the 1905–06 season as Watford's top scorer. Centre forward Wally Eames had initially played as an amateur before turning professional in 1903. He joined Spurs in May 1906. During the season Watford had recruited Jock Foster from Rotherham to replace Eames and the new man proved to be a prolific goalscorer. His performances led to a record transfer fee to Sunderland. Other Watford players in 1905–06 were William Roland Brown, a half back from Luton Town, and utility defender Billy Lindsay.

Goodall and Spiksley's inclusion created lots of interest. This meant that, despite suffering from flu-like symptoms, Fred felt obliged to play against Southampton when a wiser man would have stayed in bed.

A crowd of 7,250 was inside the Cassio Ground and home fans were to leave thrilled as Watford beat Southampton 4-1. Goodall quickly had his team passing the ball along the ground and keeping possession. Spiksley then put his side ahead with a powerful shot. The goal maintained his record of scoring for every club he had played for – Gainsborough Trinity, Sheffield Wednesday, Glossop North End, Leeds City, Southern United and, now, Watford.

The new signing continued to play impressively, sprinting with the ball at his feet and constantly sending over dangerous crosses. The away side were forced to try to kick the veteran out of the game. He might have scored a second only to be upended from behind as he tricked his way through to face the Saints 'keeper. Fred refused to take the resulting spot kick. It was dispatched by McCartney.

After such a marvellous display, the *Watford Observer* gleefully reported that Goodall and Spiksley had demonstrated how "the football of today is not in the same class as it was ten years ago. Here were two men long past their prime easily beating the younger generation. News of Spiksley's death has been greatly exaggerated."

Fred was delighted. "For the first in a long time I felt that warm inner glow of satisfaction in a job well done. Suddenly Watford felt like home." He noted that pre-match many wise heads predicted that Southampton's young side would dominate. Afterwards the discussions were whether a professional footballer was too old to play after reaching 40.

Watford faced Reading away the following weekend and lost 3-1. Fred Spiksley received heavy treatment from the Reading defenders.

Afterwards, he examined the big black and blue bruises down his thighs and legs and complained about having been more roughly treated in two games for Watford than at any time at Wednesday. No doubt his reputation brought about this rough treatment, from younger players, who had not made the top grade, out to prove they could out-muscle one of the game's most accomplished players.

On 24 February 1906 a snowstorm failed to prevent 3,600 fans watching Watford play Northampton Town at home. Latecomers missed a repeat of Fred's first against Southampton when he scored within a minute. Northampton then scored twice but Turner equalised just before the interval.

On the resumption, Spiksley nodded home from close range to make it 3-2. Eames made it 4-2 and, following a successful Northampton penalty, Spiksley completed his hat-trick in a 5-3 win. The game had been a fast, thrilling one and while Fred was clearly the man of the match, every player had played well. Watford's improving form continued as they beat Brighton 2-1 with goals from Eames and Turner.

Fred Spiksley and the Brighton right back Chris Buckley provided great opposition for each other and the pair shook each other's hands afterwards. Later Fred wrote to Derby County recommending they should sign the youngster. When he received a letter back agreeing, Fred departed to the south coast. There was disappointment when he discovered that Buckley had, after being granted a free transfer, bought a ticket to travel north and sign for Manchester United.

Buckley did, in fact, eventually sign for Aston Villa where he played for seven seasons and won the League title in 1909 before moving to Arsenal. Fred, desperate as always for money, had been hoping to get some commission from Derby if the deal had gone through.

Two consecutive 0-0 draws, away to West Ham and at home to Fulham, maintained Watford's climb up the table. The latter game was watched by 7,500 spectators among whom were some only interested in what other supporters had in their pockets. London pickpockets had noted how Watford's crowds had increased. Pick-pocketing was common across all London grounds and now many Watford fans were to experience having their watches and wallets stolen without them realising it.

Having been starved of the ball in the previous two games, Fred was left disappointed when this was also the case away to QPR. Watford lost 6-0. The following match, Fred created Watford's goal against Bristol Rovers as Turner scored in a 1-1 draw.

New Brompton then beat Watford 2-0 after which the *Watford Observer* reported that Fred Spiksley had played disappointingly with two of his corner kicks having gone straight out for goal kicks. The following match on Good Friday, the outside left was unlucky when two of his shots hit the Luton crossbar in a tense, keenly competitive derby match that ended 1-1.

Fred did get on the score sheet away to Portsmouth the following day but the away side lost 4-2. On Easter Monday, Watford played their final game of a difficult season. Fred Spiksley's arrival and the reappearance of John Goodall in the starting line-ups had helped bring about a revival.

But after three wins in his first four matches, Fred had not tasted victory in the following seven.

This rose to eight when Brighton won 1-0, after which the local newspapers were scathing in their criticism, describing it as a complete fiasco.

The result left Watford in fourteenth place in the final table with four sides below them. The decision to sign Fred Spiksley had paid off as in the games he played, Watford won three, drew four and lost five. Ten points from twelve matches was an improvement on the thirteen from the first twenty games. Nevertheless there was no new contract offer and Fred, realising the vast number of games he had played had taken its toll, bit the bullet and retired from playing professional football.

John Goodall remained in charge of Watford but, following an unsuccessful season in 1909–10, he was sacked. A notice in the *Athletic News* advertised the post. Fred Spiksley and Watford club captain Harry Kent were the two who applied and both were interviewed for the post. Watford took up a reference from the Wednesday club secretary, Arthur Dickinson.

Dickinson wrote, "I can say with confidence that you will not find yourselves a better judge of a professional football player. If you can get him to give up his on-course horseracing activities you will have secured an excellent football manager."

This reference did Fred no favours. The Watford directors challenged him at the interview about his racing passion and how it might interfere with his managerial responsibilities. Fred replied: "Well, gentlemen, I would very much like to take up this position. But what I do in my private life is no business of my employers. I am not prepared to forfeit my racing. If you wish me to do so, then, gentlemen, I shall have to say goodbye right now."

Harry Kent got the post but only after agreeing initially to submit his team selection to the Watford officials for approval. Fred certainly would not have tolerated this. Kent managed Watford for sixteen seasons and took them into the Football League after World War One.

On retiring as a professional footballer Fred Spiksley had achieved every major honour in the game. The small Lincolnshire lad had had his life transformed by the game of football. He was one of the earliest players to have been picked up from a working class, terraced house family, and able to make a living out of the game of football. No other player in the history of the game had scored the two winning goals in an FA Cup final, with one being arguably the fastest ever, and also scored hat-tricks for England on his debut and against Scotland. With approximately 350 goals to his name from outside left he was certainly the greatest player in his position from the 1890s and many that saw him play maintained he was the greatest outside left the game had ever seen.

We should not forget that Fred did not play for the glamorous clubs of the time and this makes his achievements even more remarkable. At his peak, Spiksley would have been first choice for any side in the country and should he have played for Aston Villa, West Bromwich Albion or Sunderland he would have captured more titles and medals. However, playing for Wednesday gave Spiksley the opportunity to develop legendary status, and although opportunities for top honours were severely limited, when they did come along he took them.

Fred Spiksley may well have been a vain man, but the statistics and eyewitness accounts certainly justify his ego.

CHAPTER 21

TREADING THE BOARDS WITH CHARLIE CHAPLIN
Touring the music halls with Fred Karno

FRED SPIKSLEY WAS now in desperate need of finding alternative employment. He had always been a major entertainer on the football pitch and so when he saw an advertisement for a footballer to perform on the stage he jumped at the chance. It would lead to him working for the inimitable circus and pantomime king Fred Karno and also to perform with Charlie Chaplin.

Fred Karno was born Frederick John Westcott in Exeter on 26 March 1866. His father's work as a cabinet-maker meant the family moved frequently before settling in Nottingham where Fred combined school with work in a lace factory, putting his two shillings (10p) weekly wage into the family purse. This upbringing stood him in good stead as it taught him the principles of tenacity, honesty and the value of money.

Despite his father arranging a plumber's apprenticeship, Fred absconded one day to watch an acrobatic troupe perform in the big top of a travelling circus. The spellbound youngster then ran away to join a travelling circus and his hard work and sheer dedication to become an accomplished acrobat would eventually pay off when he made his breakthrough on the flying trapeze. This meant he no longer had to undertake less glamorous roles such as handing out leaflets and banging a drum to encourage people to "roll up and see the greatest show on earth."

Like Fred Spiksley, Fred Westcott enjoyed horse racing. After watching the St Leger at Doncaster in 1886 he returned to Sheffield, where the Big Top Circus had been erected. After performing a spectacular routine of heart-stopping acrobatics alongside Bob Sewell and Ted Tysall as part of the 'Three Carnoes', Westcott was thrilled to discover that champion jockey Fred Archer was in the audience. Archer was a great circus-lover and after the performance had ended he was allowed to go behind the scenes and talk to the performers, including an overjoyed Westcott.

Already schooled in the world of hard knocks, Westcott loved the great outdoors, animals, clowns, grease paint, colour and magical atmosphere of the Big Top. But having found his feet, Westcott was intent on being a major star and he eventually turned solo in a circus act on the horizontal and double trapeze. This saw him combine being a ringmaster and clown while also working daily on twenty shows of sketches and slapstick comedy.

Following a highly successful season at the Scotia Music Hall, Glasgow, Fred, now calling himself Karno, toured with his acrobatic troupe on the continent, appearing in major circuses and shows in Cologne, Rotterdam, Amsterdam and Brussels. Back home Fred teamed up again with Sewell and Tysall in a series of performances across the South East where their slapstick knockabout routines raised the roof.

In 1894, the trio appeared for a week at Barnard's Music Hall, Portsmouth on a bill topped by boxer Jem Mace, whose sudden illness one evening led to Fred Karno and comedian Tom Leamore filling in with some improvised comedy based on Karno's old pantomime sketches 'Love in Tub.' This was so hilarious it went down a storm and within a few months Karno repeated it at the Gaiety Music Hall, Birmingham, following which the Karno Sketch Company was born.

The company soon started to become recognised and it was later said that: "Fred Karno was the finest exponent of pantomime in the country."

A brilliant acrobat, actor, director, manager, fixer and producer, Fred Karno was also a shrewd businessman with an eye for making money. Never seeking personal fame, he planned numerous laughable situations and possessed an almost unique ability to write slapstick comedy, which, with the help of scriptwriters, he turned into great success stories. Karno is universally accepted as the first person to perform the custard pie-in-the-face joke.

In the summer of 1906, Fred Spiksley was delighted when he saw a newspaper advertisement seeking professional footballers to take part in a new sketch show called 'The Football Match'.

Having retired from playing, Fred was desperate to find employment and confident that his flicks and tricks would be just what Fred Karno wanted. He grabbed his coat and set off to Vaughan Road in Camberwell to offer his services.

Karno was delighted to see Fred Spiksley and immediately agreed to hire him and empowered him to find two other recently-retired professional footballers for the show. Fred persuaded Aston Villa and England internationals Charlie Athersmith and Jimmy Crabtree to join him on the Fred Karno bandwagon at a handsome weekly salary of £7 10s (£7.50) each. Rehearsals started on 30 November 1906 and after these went well all three signed a six-month contract commencing on Christmas Eve.

While glad of the work, Fred had harboured hopes of a more prominent football role as, in November 1906, QPR had invited applications for the club's first ever 'football coach and manager.' Having narrowly avoided relegation from the Southern Division at the end of the previous season, the West Londoners wanted a top football man. He was to be charged with creating a team that fans would want to watch as the Great Western Railway Company had offered QPR the tenancy of a brand new Archibald Leitch-designed football stadium adjacent to Park Royal railway station.

Fred's application was thorough and seriously considered but the post was given to Jimmy Cowan, the former Aston Villa centre half who had played for QPR in 1902. He went on to lead his new team to the Southern League title in his first season in charge and did well before ill-health forced him to resign. Fred wondered if, in hindsight, he might have been wiser to have asked for less than £7 10s (£7.50) a week to do the job at QPR. Whatever the actual reason he lost out and was off on his travels with Fred Karno's company.

Recognising how popular football had become among the masses, Karno had collaborated with his lead comedian, Fred Kitchen, and opened his new show in Manchester's Palace Theatre on 27 December 1906.

A huge panoramic backcloth was commissioned for the show to stretch right round the stage. It featured a huge crowd of football spectators. The skill now was to bring this to life and this is where Karno's genius kicked in as he toured Manchester and recruited 100 extras – a mixture of adults, children and dwarfs – whom he placed precisely so that their faces merged with the faces painted on the canvas. It was almost impossible to distinguish reality from illusion. It was a technique replicated decades later by Alfred Hitchcock. Artificial hands and arms sewn into the cloth and the addition of two very powerful electric fans created a brilliant effect on stage for the twice-nightly show that also had a matinee four times a week.

The professional football players were introduced to the audience by the referee at the start. They ran out to tremendous applause when their names were announced. The footballers then displayed their ball juggling skills and tricks and the noise was deafening, especially for Fred Spiksley, who was back in his schoolboy days of showing off all his tricks to the audience.

The football match that was then played out thrilled the audience, so much so that at the Glasgow Coliseum performance on 4 March 1907 an occupant of a private box, Alexander Russell, became so excited he fell into the stalls 15ft below. He landed on William Forsyth, a clerk, who suffered a broken neck.

The Football Match was to be one of Fred Karno's most successful shows. There were three scenes – the training quarters, outside the football ground and the football match itself. The undoubted star of the show was Harry Weldon, a great friend of Billy Meredith, who was entrusted with the lead role of 'Stiffy' the 'keeper. Weldon's catchphrase was "S'no use!" and he had a curious and indefinable method of getting his audiences to laugh along with him. He also had a peculiar way of delivering his lines with a gurgle, followed by a unique whistle. Karno's casting of him as Stiffy was to bring Weldon his greatest success.

The Football Match told the story of a titanic struggle in a forthcoming cup-tie between the Midnight Wanderers and the Middleton Pie-Cans. It involved an attempt to bribe Stiffy and much of the realism and authenticity was supplied by the highly-skilled former professional footballers recruited for just that purpose. In addition to the dialogue the Stiffy Song was sung regularly throughout the show and the chorus in the first six months was as follows:

"But when Stiffy's between the sticks – when Stiffy's between the sticks, He can stop any kind of ball – a football or a brandy ball, And as Frederick Spiksley says when he starts to do his trick, What's the good of trying to score –

313

when Stiffy's between the sticks?" The chorus later changed with the times so that in 1910 Spiksley became Jack Fitchett of Manchester United and in 1912 it was Vivian Woodward of England and Chelsea.

After opening in Manchester the show broke all box office records as it moved across the country with the *Leicester Mercury* on 15 January 1907 stating: "Fred Karno has struck gold, much of this success is down to the remarkable drollery of Harry Weldon."

With the Fred Karno Company spending up to a week in a city, there was little to do during the daytime. So to fill in their time the performers decided to stage some charity football matches, giving the public the opportunity to witness an exhibition match full of ex-professionals. While performing at the Palace Theatre in Manchester in January 1907 the 'Fred Karno's Comedy Football Company' and 'Puss in Boots Pantomime Company' played on Manchester City's Hyde Road ground. Fred Spiksley, enjoying his second run in the sketch show, played at full back alongside Arthur Wharton and they helped guide the Karno side to a 6-2 victory.

The Manchester game raised little money for charity due to unfavourable weather conditions, with the *Manchester Courier* reporting:

"A hailstorm, accompanied by a veritable hurricane, prevailed at intervals in the second half. So terrible were the conditions that most teams would have left the arena, but the players stuck to their tasks, though Sam Mayo donned a heavy overcoat and thus endeavoured to prevent his blood from congealing."

Other charity matches would prove to be more successful as a spectacle and in raising money.

On 9 February 1907, a *Sheffield Independent* football reporter had bumped into Fred at the Division One match between Aston Villa and Sheffield Wednesday that the away side lost 8-1. The reporter noted: "Fred Spiksley was looking fit and well, and was well pleased with his lot as a member of the Fred Karno Company touring the country in a sketch called 'The Football Match.'"

Fred's contract with Fred Karno ended in May 1907. A month earlier the post of coach/football manager at Tottenham Hotspur had become available. After nine seasons in North London, John Cameron, who had led Spurs to FA Cup glory in 1901, had shocked the club by quitting his post. Fred had immediately applied for the job at White Hart Lane as did Sandy Tait, the current Spurs captain.

On Monday 15 April 1907, Fred played outside left at Tottenham for the Corinthians, whose side contained Tait, in a charity match for the Tottenham Drill Hall Fund. Fred had by chance bumped into Wreford Brown, his captain on the great day when England had beaten Scotland 3-1 in 1898. On hearing that Fred had retired from playing, Wreford Brown had surprisingly asked him if he might become involved in the game. "He described it as my swansong and I believe my appearance was the only time a professional footballer played for the famous amateur team," said Fred later.

Spurs won 2-1 but the defeated side's goal came from Spiksley. "A long dropping shot at the end of 25 minutes," reported the *Daily Mirror*. Only 1,000 were present. After what was his final game of organised football, Fred was taken round for a lap of honour by Wreford-Brown at the final whistle. He was given a standing ovation by a London crowd among whom might possibly have been some who had seen arguably his two finest performances, both in London, these being in 1893 for England against Scotland and for Wednesday against Wolves in 1896.

An extremely proud Fred thus departed White Hart Lane confident that with the Spurs fans on his side he was in with a chance of the post. In fact the post was unexpectedly given to a man who had not even applied for it – Fred Kirkham, a commercial traveller and experienced referee. As a football manager he was to prove unpopular all round and it was no surprise when he resigned on 27 July 1908.

In the summer of 1907 the FA opened up the possibility for professional footballers to apply to return to amateur status. Maybe the match at White Hart Lane gave Fred the idea and it was reported in the press that Fred and his stage partner Charlie Athersmith both applied with a wave of other players who were past their prime. While many players were successful in reverting to amateurism, both Athersmith and Spiksley were rejected. Fred's playing days were truly over and his only option was to take on coaching and managerial roles.

In 1908, Fred did reappear in a number of Karno shows – at the Newcastle Empire Palace on 2 March, Blackburn Palace on 9 March and Glasgow Palace on 30 March. This saw him performing alongside Charlie Chaplin on up to fifty occasions. After a successful short audition period in which he made his debut at the New Cross Empire on 10 February 1908, Chaplin was offered a permanent weekly contract at £3 10s (£3.50) on 21 February 1908. Charlie joined his older brother Sydney as a Karno employee.

Wearing a slouch hat and big cape, Charlie played the third lead sporting a small black moustache that in time would become one of his trademarks. He was said to have delivered his first lines in the Football Match: "Aha! Stiffy, my boy, a word in your ear!" However his presence, little antics and funny movements did not initially have Karno convinced that Chaplin was a star in the making.

When the tour finished on 25 May 1908, Karno subsequently sent Chaplin to accompany Sydney to theatres in Balham and Camden where he was allocated a minor role in the Mumming Birds sketch. In November 1908, Charlie Chaplin was back playing in the Football Match and by December the following year his standing had risen so much that he played the lead role of Stiffy at the Willesden Hippodrome on 13 December 1909. Chaplin was on his way to stardom as he was taken to America by Fred Karno in 1911. Performing in various sketch shows, starting with 'A Night in an English Music Hall' Chaplin's billing became increasingly prominent in the American papers until his name outgrew that of the Karno Company. While Chaplin's future was secure, Fred Spiksley's career was becoming an increasing concern.

CHAPTER 22

BANKRUPT
Gambling finally catches up with Fred Spiksley

FRED'S MONEY WORRIES intensified when on the 15 August 1908 he was forced to appear in the Sheffield Police Court on a charge of 'Loitering in the Streets for Gambling Purposes.' He was found guilty and fined £2. With little income this was a big blow.

Then on Monday 31 August 1908 he was again fined £2 after he was arrested at Lincoln City football ground two days previously where he had been seen by Police Constable Jewels to receive and pay out bets at the Lincoln bicycle sports event. Fred had claimed he had not taken any bets from any stranger but when his sports programme was handed to the Lincoln police court chairman, Alderman Harrison, it listed nearly 100 amounts from 1s to 2s 6d (5p to 12.5p). After the fine was levied Harrison remarked it was a great pity that English games should be vitiated by "the pernicious principle of betting." The case was reported in a number of newspapers.

Just over a month later, on 25 September 1908, the Midland Counties Football League appointed Fred Spiksley to their official referees' list as a replacement for Fred Bye who had recently resigned. Spiksley had earlier in the season been appointed as a linesman and his first two refereeing appointments were scheduled for October.

On Saturday 24 October Fred made his refereeing debut in a reserve game between Sheffield United and Leicester Fosse that ended 2-1. The following weekend he was in charge of the reserve match between Grimsby Town and his former club Leeds City that was won 3-0 by the away side. Four further reserve team fixtures followed over the following two months – Grimsby v Rotherham Town, Notts County v Barnsley, Notts County v Chesterfield and Sheffield United v Hull, which finished 7-1.

During this period, Fred's reminiscences were published in the *Sheffield Telegraph's* sports paper, the *Green 'Un*. This, and the refereeing, would have provided some badly-needed income but something more permanent was required.

Having completed his apprenticeship, the footballer did have a trade to fall back on but the number of compositors now required for the printing trade had fallen by half due to the invention of monotype in 1908. At the same time pay rates had risen from £1 to £2 a week. Yet it seems unlikely that Fred, despite clearly hurtling towards bankruptcy, would have gone back into compositing even if there had been plenty of jobs. He had become accustomed to a lifestyle that left him with plenty of free time for horseracing.

Fred's wages as a footballer had, of course, never been big enough to provide a nest egg for when he finished playing. A maximum of £4 a week was a good wage but nothing like the sort of money the top footballers of today get paid which, if managed properly, could ensure a very good standard of living after football.

With gates constantly increasing, it was not surprising that players at the major clubs wanted a better income in 1908. In December the previous year, the Association Football Players' Union (AFPU) was formed with Billy

Meredith at its head. The players wanted the maximum wage lifting and were also aware of how badly any injured footballers were treated by their clubs.

Fred Spiksley had been a vocal supporter of increasing players' wages in the years leading up to the formation of the AFPU. No doubt he would have always thought that his performances merited more money than other teammates on similar wages. After all, he was often the difference between winning and losing and he had scored about 350 goals across his career. In February 1906 it was reported in the *Dundee Courier* that Spiksley's suggestions were "sensible" and "most people would agree with him" when he stated that:

"The maximum wage of £4 a week is enough for 80–90% of the present day professionals. The other 10–20 per cent are worth more, and should receive remuneration according to their reputation. It should be possible for a player to earn a bonus on the year's play of £100 or £50, as the case might be, and one of the grounds for making such an award, or part thereof, would be the distinction earned in the matter of international caps."

As much as the *Dundee Courier* dismissed his suggestions as being a "novelty", many parallels can be drawn with how modern day footballers are rewarded with various performance-related bonuses.

The AFPU did manage to win a wage increase to £5 a week for the start of the 1910–11 season but the maximum wage was to remain in place for almost another half century. The retain and transfer system, that gave the clubs total control of who the players could play for, remained in place for just as long.

On 28 January 1909 a receiving order was made against Fred Spiksley in the Lincoln County Court. He was described as residing at 148 Moorgate, Retford. Fred himself had presented his own bankruptcy application and appeared in court on 5 March 1909. He was described by the Official Receiver as a printer/compositor and part-time journalist and his liabilities totalled £81 5s 2d (£81.26) with no assets available to his creditors.

The Official Receiver began the public examination process by enquiring about Fred's current occupations before it was revealed that he had been a professional footballer. Fred was asked how he had become a journalist and about his income and expenditure during his period as a footballer.

When asked about how he accumulated so much debt, Fred explained that it was a result of his final season with Sheffield Wednesday. Having won the League title in 1903, the footballer had expected the club to award him a second benefit match for his long, loyal service which stretched back to 1891. He had hoped to make around £300, more than enough to clear his debts, but a serious knee injury in a pre-season practice match had ended his top-class playing career and had denied him the chance of the benefit game.

He was asked about his house and its contents and informed the court that his wife, Ellen, held the tenancy and owned all the contents.

Fred claimed that at the time of his accident he had owed around £400 and although he had done his best to reduce this, he now had no income and did not know how he could pay his debts. When he was asked when he had stopped paying people, Fred did not reply.

He was then asked how he managed to live with no income and replied he was living on the charity of his mother, father, friends and family. He was asked if he had been reduced to begging. It was a question that nettled. "I do not beg and I have never begged in my life."

The Receiver attacked again asking Fred if he stood on street corners with his hat out?

Fred retaliated "No I don't."

"Do you solicit money from your friends?"

"No I don't."

He was asked about his wages as a footballer and stated that he earned £4 a week until he injured his knee. Asked if he had played football since the injury he replied that he had but his leg was not strong enough to withstand the rigours of professional football.

When the Receiver asked how much he was currently earning, Fred stated he was occasionally given not particularly lucrative assignments writing football articles for local and national newspapers, which provided him with £75 a year. He was also occasionally paid for scouting for professional football clubs when he was given a shopping list of a clubs' requirements and then had to travel right across the country searching out talent. There was a market for good professional footballers but unearthing a good 'keeper was no good if a client wanted a goalscorer. There was also competition from other scouts. Then it would come down to deviousness, persuasion and money to persuade the protégé to join a particular club. In 1909 professional football clubs might pay up to £1,000 for a really exceptional player. At which point, the Receiver intervened saying, "But they don't pay that amount of money to you though do they?"

"No," said Fred, "I wish they did!" at which point there was an outburst of laughter in the courtroom gallery and the public examination was adjourned. Fred was later declared bankrupt and it was not until 10 October 1916 that he was discharged, subject to five years' suspension, when appearing at Lincoln Bankruptcy Court It was reported "no dividend had been paid...(and) his assets (were) insufficient to pay the expenses of the bankruptcy."

Following his retirement as a professional footballer, Fred Spiksley's life had followed a series of ups and, more generally, downs. In 1911 a number of newspapers reported that he had been engaged as a coach to several distinguished English clubs but failed to shed much light on the subject. It is unlikely that Fred would have been appointed as a senior first team coach since his addiction to gambling meant he was notoriously unreliable. Club directors admired and respected his judgement as well as his coaching skills and ability to spot talented footballers but they would never offer him a top managerial post or permanent coaching position. They rightly judged he might disappear to a racecourse at any time. Better to employ the former wide man for short periods to address specific coaching, tactical and personnel problems.

Fred was left frustrated and in a need of a major challenge. Football was spreading across Europe. In 1908 Manchester United became the first English club to tour continental Europe with a summer trip to the Austro-Hungarian Empire that was followed shortly afterwards by the England team playing four matches in Austria, Hungary and Bohemia (as the Czech Republic was then called). In the autumn of 1908 the first men's football tournament was held at the London Olympics and third-placed Netherlands were coached by Fred's former England international colleague, Edgar Chadwick, who went on to manage the Dutch national team on 24 occasions, during which time the Dutch collected another bronze medal at the 1912 Olympics in Sweden.

In 1912, Stockholm was to set to be the venue for the Fifth Olympiad for which all competitors had to be amateur. Quite understandably the home nation wanted to do well in all sports. This was going to be difficult in the football as Sweden had been hammered 12-1 in 1908 by Great Britain, who went on to carry off the gold medal. No country needed a football coach more than Sweden.

Small local football competitions and matches had begun after 1894 and following the formation of local federations the Swedish FA was formed in 1904. In 1911 it was reported in the Swedish papers that the Lazarol factory owner Mr Anders Lindahl had agreed to provide funding to the Swedish FA for a top class football coach. The appointee would have an initial brief to prepare the Swedish national team for a high profile match against the German Federation on 18 June 1911. Thereafter he would remain throughout the summer with the specific aim of improving football in general and would provide specific help to, among others, clubs in the Middle Swedish League. (Mellansvenska series 1911). The Swedish FA approached the FA and Football League and received glowing references on Fred Spiksley's suitability from Frederick Wall, the FA secretary, top class referee John Lewis and Football League president John McKenna. The former Wednesday man was considered perfect for the post and it was just the breakthrough he was seeking.

On Thursday 18 May 1911, Fred Spiksley said goodbye to his wife Ellen and son Fred junior, now a thirteen-year-old teenager, and living at 141 Moorgate, Retford. He journeyed by train to Harwich and then boarded the Denmark ferryboat from Parkeston Quay. The overnight crossing on the Primula Steam Packet landed in Esbjerg at midnight.

After clearing customs, Fred had an eight-hour journey across Denmark before arriving in Copenhagen on Friday morning. After a hearty breakfast the English visitor took a stroll through the famous Tivoli Gardens before returning to the railway station and continuing his journey via Elsinore to join the Helsingor ferry to Sweden. It was a journey that his former club had made just a few days earlier on what was Wednesday's first overseas continental tour with games in Sweden and Denmark. Fred was hoping to meet up with some acquaintances when he docked in Gothenburg on the afternoon of Saturday 20 May 1911.

After booking himself into a hotel, Fred quickly obtained the information he required. Wednesday were staying in the Eggers Hotel but when he arrived there he discovered that the touring party had gone sightseeing for the day. The previous evening, everyone had watched FA Cup winners

Bradford City slip to a surprising 1-0 defeat by the Swedish national side.

Wednesday had been surprised to discover that their opening match was on a Sunday. Orgryte, winners of ten Swedish championships between 1896 and 1910, were coached by Chesterfield-born Charles Bunyan, who had played nine games in goal for Derby County but was best known for having conceded an English record 26 goals when playing in goal for Hyde United against Preston in the FA Cup. Not that this fiasco had dented Bunyan's self-confidence as he was something of a pompous individual who on his arrival in Sweden had had his own calling cards printed describing himself as 'Professeur de Fotboll'.

Wednesday proved much too good for Orgryte and, without breaking sweat, easily won 5-0. Despite Swedish enthusiasm for the game of football there was a decided lack of football knowledge on display and Fred was not impressed with the long ball game that the local team had adopted. If this was typical of Swedish football then he had a lot of hard work in front of him. At the end of the match, Fred was able to surprise the Wednesday officials and players and when it was discovered he was to remain in Gothenburg for a few days he was invited to act as one of the linesmen when Wednesday played an All Sweden XI in a match refereed by Charles Bunyan.

On Monday 22 May, Fred Spiksley joined up with the Wednesday party to visit a place where a magnificent view of the setting sun could be guaranteed. On the way, an open-air café with a piano was spotted where, according to Andrew Wilson: "Fred Spiksley, being a ripping pianist, began rattling away on the piano forte, while a number of girls very much amused at our doings began dancing. Fun and frolics became the order of the day, and when we spied some Swedish punch we thought we should like to sample it. Everyone in the party, other than Fred Spiksley, who were normally quite temperate fellows, drank fairly freely of this deliciously sweet beverage, thinking that it would have no more effect upon us than lemonade."

The result was that when everyone left the café and headed for the beach to experience the wonderful sunset they found an anxious Mr A J Dickinson who was not at all pleased that only Fred Spiksley was in a fit enough state to witness what had been the point of the outing. Wilson himself was reprimanded for not acting in a manner expected of a team captain.

The following day's game proved to be highly competitive with Wednesday marginally the better side, winning narrowly, 2-1. From his place on the touchline, Fred Spiksley was impressed with how well the Sweden XI had played but he had little doubt that the closeness of the result had much to do with the fact that the away players were suffering the effects of the previous 24 hours' drinking. The Swedish football fans themselves were delighted by the displays put on by Wednesday in their two games and they declared the Sheffield side the smartest team to visit their country. All the players and officials were presented with little silver medals before they departed for Denmark where they played a further three games.

After paying his hotel bill, Fred departed by rail with his sea chest from Gothenburg on Wednesday 24 May. He was met in Stockholm by Ruben Gelbord, a Swedish FA board member who owned a local sports shop. Fred was taken to his lodgings where he would spend the next four or five months.

Having arranged to collect Fred at 9.00am the following day, Gelbord allowed him to unpack and the Englishman was glad to know that his landlady spoke some English. Fred would have to rise early each morning for coaching and teaching football in two primary grass pitch locations – the Rasunda IP and Ostermalm Parks and Stadia. The former was inaugurated in the autumn of 1910 and only closed in 2012. It had been the home for 91 years for AIK, the 'General Sports Club', formed in 1891 with the football department launched in 1896.

Rasunda had cost 45,000 krona to construct, a huge sum in 1910. It had covered stands and seats for 1,300 spectators. Unfortunately, the swampy ground was not really suitable for growing grass and the stadium was considered to be too far away from the city by most people.

On his first day in his new job, Fred Spiksley was introduced to Swedish FA officials and players. He was then given a whistle-stop tour of the city and some tips on how to get safely around. On top of his coaching work Fred was expected to visit football clubs and centres in Sweden to watch matches and assess the abilities of the players. What was required was the building of a strong and skilful national side that could compete on equal terms with other nations. Fred needed to identify talented players who were passionate and enthusiastic about football and also willing to listen, work hard and constantly practise to improve their football skills.

Buoyed by a report in *Idrottsbladet*, the leading Swedish sports paper, that he was gentle, friendly and liked by the players who had met him, Fred enthusiastically watched numerous matches and players on his travels, setting up football clinics and organising coaching sessions.

Fred Spiksley's number one priority was to teach Sweden's top amateur footballers a different way of playing the game. As in all walks of life trying to introduce a completely different way of doing things is never going to be easy and it was therefore perfectly understandable that the players were apprehensive as they had never had a professional football coach before.

However, the new coach had a number of things going for him including his reputation and details of his exploits in the Football League, FA Cup and international matches. Fred's flair for languages also helped and he very quickly started to pick up Swedish, including a number of phrases that he employed to address his new players the first time they met. In return, the players immediately liked the new man in charge and considered him a warm, friendly gentleman.

Fred was to pull no punches in telling the players that he meant to change the style of football and that included fundamental ball skills. He also made no secret that there would be lots of hard work and he urged anyone not up to the challenge to leave. Furthermore, if players turned up so much as a minute late to training, they were sent home and therefore lost out on Fred's wisdom.

The new coach began by teaching players how to trap the ball and how to use the chest to cushion a ball in the air and bring it dead to a player's feet. He then turned to how to shield the ball from an opponent and keep possession, while at all times maintaining complete control of the ball with the outside of the boot. When the players had mastered the art of dribbling with the ball, Fred taught them how to kick a football and he coached them in the main ways to kick – the short crisp pass, the centre or cross-field ball, the corner kick and how to shoot.

He instilled in the Swedes the clear message that, after shooting, the most necessary skill was the ability to pass the ball to an unmarked teammate. This was achieved with the short crisp pass hit with pace to the intended recipient using the top of the foot known as the instep. Fred went to great lengths to explain that passing with the inside of either foot was misguided as the inside side muscles were much weaker than those on the outside. The difference was that when a player passed the ball with the inside of his foot it would slow down before reaching its target, thus allowing opponents the opportunity to intercept the ball.

Fred spent a lot of time helping the players to get the basics right. He taught them how to cross, taking great care to explain the importance of keeping one eye on the ball while looking out of the corner of the other eye to see where best to place the cross for the forwards. He would then make sure they planted their standing foot properly, before swinging their free leg through the ball using the instep for power and accuracy in the cross. He would spend hours rolling footballs into the path of players while constantly repeating, "One eye on the ball, look to your target, plant your foot, swing your leg through the ball."

Corners required a skill similar to the cross, but with one important difference – the need to kick a dead ball. In some respects it was easier to deliver as opponents could not charge until the ball was kicked. But taking a corner was a challenge. All eyes were on the kicker and it was easy to lose concentration and miskick the ball. A high percentage of Swedish players found it more difficult to kick a stationary ball. This was in line with Fred's experience when he played in the Football League and he had long since formed the view that a football team needed specialists for corner kicks, goal kicks, free kicks and penalties. Fred considered the problem to be as much a question of holding your nerve as of skill. Fred nominated his specialists and continued with his clinics while emphasising three words – practice, practice, and practice.

How to Shoot

Fred Spiksley believed that exceptional goalscorers were gifted and born with natural ability. It was possible, though, to become a good shot through practice and hard work. It was all a matter of intensive training. Fred handed down his guide to good goal scoring with the following tips:

Lesson 1 – Dribble with the ball from the halfway line, learn to shoot for goal while on the move before being closed down by opponents.

Lesson 2 – Shoot with power and direction by keeping your head overthe ball with your standing leg well planted.

Swing your free leg through the ball using the top of the foot.

Lesson 3 – For extra power in a long shot at goal. Flex the knee joint to accelerate the leg as it extends through the ball to generate increased power and thus get the best possible force behind the ball.

Lesson 4 – For accuracy keep your head over the ball and flex the ankle to steer and control the flight of the ball with confidence towards goal.

Lesson 5 – A shot at half speed that finds the corner of the net is better than a cannonball that flashes outside the goalpost.

Lesson 6 – Always be thinking, weigh up the goalkeeper and his strengths and weaknesses. Shoot to his weaker side. If he struggles to stop ground shots then shoot low. If he is nervous about dealing with high balls under the crossbar then try a heavy charge.

When Spiksley wrote about shooting skills in 1928 he drew particular attention to the best strikers of the day being 'endowed with the right kind of legs' saying that players such as "Steve Bloomer, Bob McColl and Dixie Dean have perfect legs for driving the ball, and a gift, doubtless unsuspected, of placing the unemployed leg in the right position to give proper effect to their drives. Those who saw Bloomer and McColl playing in the past, or have seen Dean today, will understand perfectly what I mean by 'shooting legs'. Without the right-shaped legs most players will find shooting a rather difficult art. Although there are, of course, exceptions to every rule."

Fred did believe that footballers were born and that only 10 per cent of a player's overall ability could be affected by training and the right kind of attitude. No doubt the shooting legs that genetics provided for Alan Shearer and Wayne Rooney would have impressed him.

Fred was a disciple of combination (pass and move)

football. He wanted short quick passing along the ground to unmarked colleagues in order to keep possession and outmanoeuvre opponents so as to create goal-scoring opportunities. As coach, one of his favourite exercises was to line up his forwards on the halfway line and get them to pass the ball along the line as they advanced together before one took a shot. Another was 'piggy in the middle' in which two players in the middle attempted to intercept an errant pass from players attempting to pass to one another. Several of the training drills that Spiksley believed would develop a player's skill can still be witnessed by top professional teams during training sessions and pre-match warm-ups. In terms of skill training, there is little doubt that he was way ahead of his time.

Fred had never worked harder in his life but he really enjoyed what he was doing and he could see that he was making a big difference especially as he quickly mastered Swedish and could use the language to pass on his instructions.

Most of the current Swedish side played for Orgryte and there were also Gothenburg-based players from IFK Gothenburg, FF Gothenburg and Kopings IS. From Stockholm there were players from AIK, Djurgardens, IFK, Gavle and Mariebergs.

The side selected for the big game against Germany at the Rasunda on 18 June 1911 were as follows:

Oskar Bengtsson (Orgryte); Knut Sandlund (Djurgardens), Jacob Levin (Orgryte); Ragnar Wicksell (Djurgardens), Gotrik Frykman (Djurgardens) captain, Sixten Oberg (Mariebergs); Herman Myhrberg (Orgryte), Gustaf Efkberg (Stockholm), Karl Gustafsson (Kopings), Josef Appelgren (Orgryte), Karl Ansen (AIK).

Germany: Moller (Kiel), Kipp (Stuttgart), Worpitsky (Victoria Berlin), Dumke (Victoria Berlin), Droz (Prussia Berlin), Hunder (Victoria Berlin), Burger (Munchen 1860), Ugi (Leipzig), Hempel ((Leipzig), Viggers (Victoria Hamburg)

Flying over an Olive Grove

Charles Buchwald from Copenhagen was appointed as match referee and Ruben Gelbord was Sweden's linesman for the game. The Swedish side were selected by a five-man committee consisting of Wilhelm Friberg, Anton Johansson (the 'General of Football'), John Ohlson, Hans Hallen and Edvin Sandborg. It is not known how much influence Fred Spiksley had in the team selection.

It contained in Gustafsson, Sweden's leading international goalscorer with nine goals in eight games. However, it was the outside left in the side, Karl Ansen, who was considered the best forward. He was 24 and had previously played eight international games. Bengtsson in goal was making his eighth appearance for his country while Sandlund, Oberg and Esbjerg were all making their first.

The game, which was the first international in Stockholm was played in warm sunshine in front of a crowd of 3,000. Having won the toss, Sweden chose to kick with the breeze behind them. The home side took the lead on 28 minutes when Gustafsson was sent clear courtesy of a brilliant ball from Myhrberg and he left Moller with no chance of saving his shot. One minute later and it was 2-0 when Gustafsson hit a great shot past the German 'keeper and this was the score at half-time.

Buoyed by their success, the home side played some excellent football on the restart but were guilty of missing four gilt-edged chances. This allowed the German team to take the initiative and the away side struck twice in quick succession to level the score. Things then went from bad to worse for Sweden when Bengtsson was beaten by a deflected shot and Germany led for the first time.

The home side were handed a lifeline on 68 minutes when Gustafsson was upended in the penalty area. Having already scored twice, the Swedish centre forward was the obvious man to take the spot kick. But to the crowd's surprise the captain of the home side, Gotrik Frykman, saw this as his responsibility and had agreed with Fred Spiksley beforehand that he would take any penalty kicks. Unfortunately for the Swedes, he missed but this did not stop the home side piling forward in search of a deserved equaliser.

However – and no doubt readers have heard this story many times since – in the final minute of the game, Germany broke forward to make it 4-2 with Charles Buchwald ignoring offside protests to allow the goal to stand. The Swedes had been the better team, had led for much of the game but Germany had won!

Fred was understandably upset by the result when on another day Sweden would have won comfortably. The Swedish coach also blamed himself for agreeing that Frykman should take the penalties. What had really counted against the losing side, though, was their lack of composure when shooting. Practice could help ensure that was less likely to be the case in the future and despite the result it was clear from their performance that Fred Spiksley's coaching had massively improved the quality of the Swedish side.

Over the following weeks, Fred had, according to Swedish FA reports, visited Vasteras and later Karlstad, which is 160 miles west of Stockholm. There he saw IFK Karlstad play short, fast passes to beat Karlskoga IF 9-0 with the latter reported as playing long balloon balls.

Fred also worked with the Stockholm AIK players as the *History of AIK*, published 2012, states in the section covering 1911: "Maybe the very first successful autumn of 1911 was due to the fact that the players in the summer got instructions from the English football coach Fred Spiksley who was moving round Sweden."

AIK won the Swedish championship, which was run as a knockout competition. They beat IFK Vasteras, IFK Eskilstuna, IFK Stockholm and then IFK Uppsala 3-2 in the final. There were 21 teams entered the tournament.

Fred appears to have left Sweden at the start of September as there is no mention of him being present at the international in Stockholm on 17 September that saw Norway crushed 4-1. Whether his contract had ended or he left early is unknown.

Fred's time in Sweden had been a very happy and rewarding one as he had transformed Swedish football by teaching the players how to play the combination game. He had instilled in the players a pride in their performances in working together for each other as a team.

He had also made many friends, including Ruben Gelbord and Torsten Husen, not forgetting his players and they were all sad to see him leave. Fred was disappointed at missing out on the chance of coaching Sweden at the Olympics but returned to Retford in a good mood.

The Olympics in Sweden took place in the summer of 1912 and in the football the home nation lost to the Netherlands 4-3 and Italy 1-0; there was to be no football glory for the hosts. Great Britain and Denmark eventually made it to the final and the former won 4-2 to take the gold medal.

Sweden's failure to make, at least, the semi-finals of the competition led to immediate recriminations with the departing Charles Bunyan heavily blamed for the failure to win a single game. Levin was left with egg on his face but survived calls for his resignation. The Swedish Football Federation were keen to recruit another English coach and so in 1913 the Swedish Olympic Association agreed to provide finance to employ one for the next two years. The Stockholm FA were determined to have Fred Spiksley and Levin was in no position to stop them. However, Fred had already obtained a new one-year post as coach to Munich 1860. If the Swedes wanted him they would either need to buy out his contract or wait. However, when Fred informed his prospective employers that he wanted a three-year contract up to the end of the planned 1916 Olympic Games the Swedish Olympic Association saw this as unrealistically expensive and it was decided to search for a new coach in a different direction. In the event, the First World War meant the Berlin Olympic Games were cancelled.

When the war ended in 1918, Fred resumed his correspondence with Torsten Husen, a sports journalist for the *Idrottsbladet* paper in Stockholm. The pair had become friends during the time that Fred had coached in Sweden. They regularly chatted together about all aspects of football and so when Husen decided to write a book on how to play good football he wanted Fred Spiksley's advice. The book was one of a planned series of five sports with football being the fourth one released. (Anyone wanting a copy of this book should get in touch).

CHAPTER 23

GERMANY 1914
A lucky escape from a German prison

BRITAIN WAS THE first nation to move from an agricultural to an industrial economy. From 1871 onwards Germany followed suit, accomplishing in thirty years what had taken Britain over a hundred.

By 1914, Germany was the major competitor to Britain and the US in world trade, banking, insurance and shipping. As it expanded, Germany was keen to transform itself into a global power. However, its late development meant it had missed out on the 'scramble for Africa' that between 1870 and 1914 had seen the percentage of the continent directly controlled by the European imperial powers rise from 10 to 90 per cent. This contributed to tensions between the imperial powers and led to a succession of crises. These finally imploded in August 1914, when a complex network of alliances drew the major European nations into military conflict.

Looking back over a century later it seems glaringly obvious that World War I was coming but that was not how events were viewed at the time. In the spring of 1914

Germany 1914

Burnley, Bradford City, Tottenham Hotspur and Celtic had no fears about touring Germany and all returned home safely.

On 28 June 1914, Franz Ferdinand, the heir to the Austrian throne, was assassinated by Serbian nationalists in the Bosnian capital, Sarajevo. This was a sensational event but few people predicted that the result would be war. Yet one month later Austria declared war on Serbia and by 4 August 1914, France, Germany, England and Russia were all at war.

Thousands of British subjects were left trapped on enemy territory including Fred Spiksley and his family. After completing his contract with the Stockholm Association Fred had been successful in seeking employment in Germany, although spells in Belgium, France and Switzerland may have preceded Fred becoming engaged as Munich 1860's head coach in 1912. The former England international was then headhunted for the same post by the ambitious 1FC Nuremberg (FCN), who had just built the brand new 'Zabo' stadium and were to go on to become the most famous club in German football history, with their record number of national championships only finally matched by Bayern Munich in 1986. Formed on 4 May 1900, the club started out playing rugby but after fourteen months switched to the round ball.

England and Germany had many ties in the late nineteenth century including the marriage of Queen Victoria to Duke Albert of Saxe-Coburg and Gotha. English schools for sons of the wealthy were common in major German cities. There were also many British merchants and businessmen in Germany. Football soon became popular and the first clubs formed beyond the classroom appeared in 1880.

In 1889 a team of English professional footballers that included Billy Bassett and Edgar Chadwick played on German soil and beat a combined Berlin XI on two occasions, by 13-2 and 10-2. Eleven years later the Deutscher Fussball Bund (DFB) was formed and in 1901 a combined Berlin side visited England to meet a handful of professional clubs and lost 5-1 to Southampton and 6-2 to Aston Villa.

The first national championship of Germany began in 1903. the same year that Spiksley secured the Football League title with Wednesday, and was won by VfB Leipzig. This marked the start of northern dominance in German football and although FC Freiburg – not to be confused with the current professional club – brought the championship south in 1907, this still failed to reverse northern supremacy. Walther Bensemann was determined to change this and in 1893 he had appointed a man named Coopers as captain and coach to FV Karlsruher as well as a priest named Archibald White as chairman of the newly-formed South German Football Union.

In 1908, Bayern Munich won the Southern Bavaria championship under the direction of a Mr Taylor. In 1910, FV Karlsruher lifted the national trophy with assistance from William Townley, the former Blackburn Rovers player famous for scoring a hat-trick in the 1890 FA Cup final against Wednesday. Townley then joined SpVgg Furth and, teaching the 'Scottish passing game', led the German side who defeated Newcastle United by two goals to one. Townley had just been appointed as coach to Bayern Munich when war broke out.

FCN had employed Felix Servas, an ex-Britannia player, and a man named Walker – his German amounted to "Beer good!" – as coaches before they recruited Fred Spiksley to the position.

1FC Nuremberg had developed a policy of inviting professional teams from England to compete against them in an attempt to learn and develop a style of play that would elevate them to the top of German football. Heavy defeats had been endured just prior to Spiksley's appointment, with a 5-1 defeat to QPR in 1912, followed

Germany 1914

by a 7-0 thrashing from Middlesbrough in 1913. Fred had impressed senior officials and the 1FCN players upon his arrival in Nuremberg, adopting the same approach that had gained him respect during his time in Sweden. His reputation was to grow further as the next English side to visit the Zabo were Tottenham Hotspur on 6 May 1914.

According to the official history of 1FC Nuremberg, the Tottenham players "met an almost unbeatable wall in our defence and found in that beautiful 'defence' was our goalkeeper Weschenfelder – our obstacle".

This draw with such a famous English club was widely considered as a 'kind of victory' for German football. Fred was doing well. He had published an article in the Athletic News. It was titled 'Leaguers Abroad' and parts of it read as follows;

'There is no doubt that Germany at the present time is receiving far more education in football than the German FA and the followers of the game thoroughly realise. Already this spring, Glasgow Celtic, Burnley, Bradford City and Tottenham Hotspur have made tours in various parts of the country, and the attendances and enthusiasm in connection with these games would compare favourably with what we see in England. The benefit derived from the visits of these English teams is far in advance of what could be accomplished in several months' work by a coach, as a collective display of good football is far preferable to an individual demonstration.

From the visits of these British clubs the Continental players receive examples in every art connected with the game – trapping, heading, dribbling, feinting, combination and the quick changing of positions – to say nothing of the strategy of the backs and half-backs. The superiority of the Danes over the other Continental teams was undoubtedly derived from the many English clubs that visited their country. The referees in the Sweden and German match at Stockholm in

339

1911, who was a Dane, was emphatic in his explanation to me that they owed much to the British professional teams for their success.

Bradford City and Tottenham have just concluded tours which, combined, entailed the carrying out of nineteen games. Nearly all of these games were played in South Germany and Switzerland, and both clubs have created a great impression by their gentlemanly and scientific displays. It was a great pleasure to me and many English people in Munchen to have the pleasure of seeing these clubs once again. Tottenham Hotspur's first game was against Hanover on 3 May, when before 8,000 people and after leading by three clear goals at half-time, they won by 6-3. Nurnberg were met on 6 May, and the result, 1-1 was received with great jubilation by the 6,000 visitors, a record crowd for the mid-week match in Nurnberg. The next two days were spent in Munchen, where everybody thoroughly enjoyed themselves.'

Fred's success was though to be abruptly cut short because a week after war was declared the *Gainsborough News* special war edition of 11 August 1914 reported: "No news has yet come to hand of Fred Spiksley who holds the position of head football coach of FC Nurnburg, who with his wife and son are presumably still in Germany."

Upon the outbreak of war, British subjects in Germany became classed as 'enemy aliens.' The Spiksleys had to report to the local police station and surrender their passports and travelling documents. They had their photographs and fingerprints taken and were told to report every three days. With British diplomatic representatives having left the country the US Embassy took over protection responsibilities for more than 4,000 British nationals.

German mobilisation was rapid and gigantic. War fever was everywhere and thousands of Nuremburg citizens took to the streets singing patriotic songs such as The Watch on the Rhine. A German told Fred: "If the Kaiser says we fight, then we fight." While the Englishman still had the freedom to roam around he soon discovered the railway station was out of bounds to all but the military.

Nevertheless, on 19 August, Fred, together with his wife, son and a young woman who was staying with them, were arrested as they alighted from a tramcar in Nuremberg city centre. The local public had taken to catching spies, real or, more generally, imaginary and the Spiksleys had been overheard speaking English. They were taken to the police station where after several hours in detention they were released when Fred produced an earlier police letter allowing the family to be at large.

However, four days later things changed for the worse. According to Fred: "On account of mythical statements in the German papers to the effect that a Bill had been passed by the English Parliament forbidding English firms to employ Germans and dissolving all partnerships with Germans, all foreigners in Germany between seventeen and 45 were at once arrested and thrown into prison as criminals."

Fred and Fred junior were placed in solitary confinement. The treatment they received was terrible and they were both bullied and beaten. The only sustenance they received over a period of four days was one piece of uneatable black bread and some water.

Overcrowding intensified and sanitary arrangements deteriorated as more foreigners were rounded up. Among Fred's new companions was the local English consul who had an acute heart condition. When he called a warder his request for a doctor was met with the door being slammed in his face.

Eventually a lack of space in the cells made it impossible to place any more prisoners in them. When a Frenchman arrived he was locked in a cupboard less than 3ft feet square with nowhere to sit. The desperate man could be heard banging on the cupboard where he remained for 21 hours until he was released and by which time he was half dead.

When interviewed in early September 1914, Fred said he "had quite made up my mind that I should be kept as a prisoner until the end of the war." In late October 1914, a vigorous press campaign in Germany demanded retaliation for the alleged internment of all Germans living in England. In fact, general internment in Britain did not take place until 13 May 1915 after the sinking of the Lusitania inflamed public opinion. On 31 October 1914, Germany issued an ultimatum to Britain that unless all German civilians were released by Bonfire Night then every Englishman in Germany would be interned. When the order was ignored then on 6 November all British subjects aged seventeen to 55 were arrested.

Most of the internees in Germany were then transferred to the civilian detention camp at Ruhleben, ('peaceful life' in English) a former racecourse just outside Berlin. Scarcely a section of British society was unrepresented including football with Steve Bloomer and John Cameron both incarcerated.

Most of the eventual 4,400 prisoners were packed into eleven stables. Each prisoner had a space 10 feet square, into which to fit themselves and all their belongings.

Germany nevertheless adhered to the Geneva Convention and the detainees at the camp administered their internal affairs. Consequently, over time a mini-society evolved and the detainees even organised their own internal police force to keep order.

Sport, football in particular, was to play a pivotal role in the life of camp detainees. League and cup competitions were organised and on 16 November 1914 Oldham Public Schools XI played Tottenham Scratch XI in the final of the first Ruhleben football competition.

Life at Ruhleben as such was bearable but it still marked the first instance in modern history of the mass internment of aliens. The prisoners had committed no crimes and were condemned without trial to four years' imprisonment.

Fred avoided Ruhleben because, to his surprise, a visiting doctor who came to his prison cell and examined him declared that he was not fit for military service and must be released.

Ellen Spiksley had remained free to roam around Nuremburg. Unable to speak German and with no food, money or water, she was fortunate when FCN, keen to help their former coach to be allowed to leave Germany, arranged for a car to take her to see the American consul in the city.

He in turn managed to persuade the local German military commander to see the Englishwoman. At first the commander was adamant that Ellen's husband and son must remain incarcerated and she was informed that the US Ambassador had arranged a train to Holland for American subjects stranded in Germany. The train was leaving shortly and Ellen was told that a car would take her to the station and a seat would be available for her to travel west. Ellen refused to go if her husband and son were to be forced to stay behind so she was told that she would be deported. At this point Ellen broke down in tears and, unable to stand seeing a grown woman cry, the hard-hearted commander reconsidered his decision and handed Ellen a signed order releasing her loved ones.

A German Count then took Ellen straight to Fred and Fred junior, both of whom were astonished when they walked out of prison to find Ellen greeting them before all three jumped in the car and were taken by the Count to the railway station to catch the departing train carrying American subjects. However, on arrival they were informed that no English people would be allowed on the train. As such they were forced to spend the night in a squalid nearby room before Fred went to the nearest police station where he was informed that all he could obtain was a pass to Lindau, nearly 400 miles further south on the German border close to neutral Switzerland. A party of thirteen British subjects, including the English consul with whom Fred had shared the police cell in Nuremburg, had come together and they caught the train to Lindau with fingers crossed that they would be able to cross the German border.

On their arrival, however, all of the men were informed they could go no further. The consul then intervened to tell the authorities that the police had released all the men as they were incapable of military service. It was thus agreed that all the men would need to undergo a further medical to see if this was true! The English consul himself immediately secured the necessary medical certificate confirming he was unfit for hostilities but not so a fit Fred Spiksley. Was he to remain stuck in Germany? The former footballer was told he would be re-examined by a doctor the following morning. He immediately hit "upon a plan to secure the certificate".

He had for many years suffered from an injury to his right knee and he felt that a liberal supply of very hot water would enable him to dislocate it. Fred rose early the following morning and spent two hours applying boiling hot water to the joint.

When Fred entered the surgery the doctor began by testing his muscles and found them in great condition. At 45 years of age the former England international was still as fit as a fiddle but when the doctor asked him if he could run then Fred said he could do so only for a short while as otherwise his right knee would dislocate and come out of its socket. When he was requested to demonstrate the former footballer did a little run across the surgery and pretended that his knee had dislocated. Fred was deliberately putting the knee out of joint. He then stood on his healthy left leg before putting the right knee in and out of the socket several times and on each occasion the joint cracked so loudly that the doctor immediately granted the patient confirmation that he was unfit to fight.

There was still some red tape to be overcome before German officials allowed Fred's party to pass and sail across Lake Constance to Switzerland. After landing in Switzerland the British stayed overnight in Saint Gallen before travelling via Zurich, Bern, Lausanne and Geneva to Lyon where just before they arrived they were held up for an hour as a trainload of wounded soldiers arrived from Saint Dieu after fighting a fierce battle. Fred spoke to some of the soldiers when they reached Lyon and they told him how several thousand Frenchmen and Germans had lost their lives. Seeing the French soldiers travelling in open trucks was a distressing sight and all the people, including Sir James Sive-Wright, in Fred's train tried their best to cheer them up and also gave all their food to the soldiers. This left the travellers with nothing to eat for two days. Fred, Ellen and Fred junior travelled on to Paris where they arrived on the day (30 August 1914) when bombs were dropped on the French capital for the first time during the war. The Spiksleys arrived home from Paris on 2 September and Fred was quickly interviewed about his experiences by a *Sheffield Independent* journalist and the story appeared in the paper on Friday 4 September 1914.

CHAPTER 24

AMERICA'S MISSIONARY
Developing the game in the USA, Mexico and Peru

ARRIVING BACK IN England, life was not easy for the Spiksley family especially as almost all their belongings were left in Germany. With no money or home, finding a job was essential. Fortunately, Fred managed to become a munitions inspector at Vickers in Sheffield, for 34 shillings a week (£1.70). The job was a fresh challenge for Fred but he quickly built up a good reputation in what was an important and necessary job during the war.

Sheffielders had rallied to the war cause in great numbers and 900 men had been accepted into the Sheffield City Battalion by 11 September 1914. It was on 12 May 1915 – just weeks after Sheffield United had beaten Chelsea 3-0 in the 1915 FA Cup final – that the battalion left for Staffordshire and after service on the Suez Canal they reported for front line duty at the Somme on 3 April 1916. On 1 July 1916, 248 Sheffield men were killed when Allied Forces attacked the German lines. One of many macabre elements of the war was that many of the armaments used by the Germans had been manufactured in Sheffield.

Altogether, 5,139 Sheffielders were killed during the First World War. They included civilians who experienced wartime Zeppelin raids aimed at Sheffield's industry. Bombs dropped on 25 September 1916 killed 28 people and injured nineteen.

The threat to civilians from the sky was replicated from under the sea when in 1915 the Germans declared the seas around the United Kingdom to be a war zone. On 7 May 1915 at around 2.15pm off the southern coast of Ireland, a German U-boat torpedoed, without warning, the British luxury ocean liner Lusitania, on voyage from America to Liverpool. The Germans suspected the boat of carrying ordnance and ammunition from America and the arguments raged for the rest of the war as to whether the ship was a legitimate target.

The Lusitania sank inside eighteen minutes with only 761 of the 1,959 passengers and crew surviving. With 128 Americans among those killed, the incident turned public opinion in the USA against Germany and ultimately contributed to the American entry into World War One in 1917. By then a number of other passenger ships had been sunk by German U-boats, including P&O's SS Persia that went down on 30 December 1915 with the loss of 343 lives.

Ellen and Fred would have been relieved to have got out of Germany, when reading a letter that came through their letterbox in the first week of May 1915. The letter was from one of their friends who was back in Germany, an English woman who had married a German and was free to remain in the country. The letter described a difficult life, and the Spiksleys must have been wondering what might have happened to them should Fred have been interned.

"My dear Mrs Spiksley, You don't know how I wish you were here with me; I seem to have nobody, and would give anything if only you could spend a couple of months with me. Things are dreadful here, and we haven't even bread enough to eat. Every ounce we buy is only obtainable by tearing a section stating the amount purchased off a card issued monthly by the town board and I'm just allowed 1/4lb per head per day, and although I've been three times to the authorities to say it is absolutely insufficient they won't allow me more. Flour we can only buy 1/4lb products per head per week, so I can't do much as it will hardly make a decent cake or sweet loaf. No bread or cakes made solely with white flour are allowed, and all semolina rolls must consist of 30% other ingredients such as potatoes, rye, wheat etc."

In another passage, Ellen's friend describes how greatly embittered her husband is against the English, regarding his part within the war, which is not disclosed, as a punishment for marrying an Englishwoman. He also says that England began the war and that the English must pay.

Life in England for the Spiksleys would have been more comfortable, but it was far from easy. Fred remained a bankrupt and money remained tight. In the summer of 1915, Vickers was approached by the War Office to find six volunteers willing to risk travelling to the US. They would work as ordnance officers and oversee military supplies bought by the British Government from American factories that were the source of many of the weapons used to fight the war. The conflict was to lead to an economic and industrial boom in the US and ultimately resulted in America replacing Britain as the world's most powerful nation.

The jobs would involve checking crates, consignments, weapons and ammunition bound for the Western Front. After what had happened with the Lusitania there was no great rush by anyone to apply for the posts. Fred Spiksley, though, desperately needed the money and the pay was attractive, especially as bonuses were on offer if shipment and delivery targets were met. He signed up for the trip and departed with five other Sheffield men on the SS Oduna that sailed from Liverpool's Princess Landing Stage on 7 August 1915.

Fred was one of three married men who made the trip, the other two being William Walker and Lewis Hague, both, like Fred, aged 35. The single men were Frank Barker, aged 30, William Henry Smith, 22, and John Barker, 20. When the Oduna steamed into Manhattan Harbour against a backcloth of New York skyscrapers the Statue of Liberty on Ellis Island would have been a sight to behold.

All six men had arrived with $50 in their pockets supplied by the War Office and were escorted to their lodgings which had been arranged by the Washington Steel and Ordinance Company. Fred was to stay with the Murphy Family in Newark, New Jersey.

Although, it is believed that Fred's job in America was intended to last the duration of the war, this would not turn out to be the case and after around a year overseas he returned to England.

Although Fred did not particularly enjoy working in the munitions factories, as he much preferred to be outside in the fresh air, it was a job he was evidently good at and with the necessity of bringing money in Spiksley returned to Vickers. It was reported in the *Daily Record* in 1917 that he had been a "very busy munitions worker for a long time past in Sheffield, and has built up a fresh record".

Money must have remained tight throughout war time, as it was also reported in the same paper that Fred was having to walk 37 miles a week in order to get to work. At least he could enjoy the fresh air! During his second period at Vickers Fred applied for his discharge from bankruptcy at the Lincoln County Court. Fred had been a bankrupt for almost eight years but had not recorded any misdemeanours during this period. However, Fred was left disappointed by the outcome, because although he succeeded in receiving a discharge, the judge suspended this for five years, meaning that Fred would effectively remain bankrupt until October 1921.

Flying over an Olive Grove

The Great War ended when an exhausted Germany signed the Armistice with the Allies on 11 November 1918. At the peace conference that followed in Paris in 1919 the victorious Allied leaders would state their desire to construct a post-war world that would ensure there would be no more similar devastating conflicts. However, the Versailles Treaty, by saddling Germany with heavy reparations, created resentment within large sections of the German population which, in part, paved the way for an even more explosive conflict little more than two decades later.

With munitions factories no longer equipped and with millions of soldiers set to be discharged, finding work was not easy and the Spiksleys did not have any savings. On 22 March 1919 it was reported in Sheffield newspapers that the former England football international was living back in Moscar, Sheffield. He was devoting his spare time to getting as fit as possible in order to enter 100 yards handicap events with the aim of capturing the prize money on hand for the winner and earning extra income from betting on himself to finish first.

At the same time, Fred and Ellen's relationship was floundering. On 25 November 1918 Ellen had opened a letter addressed to him from America. Ellen may have become suspicious of transatlantic letters arriving for Fred and her suspicions were to be confirmed. The letter turned out to be from Margaret Murphy from Newark, New Jersey, and the contents quickly revealed that a sexual relationship or liaison had been established between Fred and Margaret.

Rather than confront her husband it appears Ellen kept the contents of this letter secret for some considerable time. Regular training may have offered Fred not just an opportunity to win some money but also a chance to keep out of his wife's way. Tensions between Fred and Ellen would however continue to escalate until just before the start of the 1920–21 season when their relationship reached a point of no return. Fred moved out of the family home and returned to Gainsborough. William agreed to put him up and, as on previous occasions, Fred would help William with his under-the-counter bookmaking business. In his spare time, Fred resumed his training up on the hills in Thonnock Woods. His aim was not only to stay unnoticed by the long arm of the law but by members of the public who by warning bookmakers he was in fine condition would ensure reduced odds on him winning any race he entered.

On 20 November 1920, Fred was just setting off to Manchester on the early morning train when he received a summons to appear in the Sheffield Police Court where he was required to answer charges of desertion brought by his wife. He travelled to compete in the Manchester veterans 100 yards sprint handicap and after paying his stake money, collecting his number and discovering his handicap he went to the betting ring where he backed himself to win. What he didn't disclose was his real name and relying on no one recognising him he ran under the assumed name of Frederick Hayward (Fred Junior's middle name) and won, collecting thirty pounds in prize money and a very tidy sum from the bookies. It was a good day.

Three days later was not a good day. Charged with 'desertion and failure to look after his wife', the unrepresented Fred unwisely pleaded "not guilty". His American affairs were now set to be publicly aired after Ellen's lawyer, Harold Jackson, expressed his sorrow at the plea but promised to bring out some unpleasant home truths. The hearing's first part was occupied with establishing some basic details of the couple's relationship including the fact that husband Fred had left the marital home on 16 August 1920 since when he had failed to contribute to his wife's upkeep although he had contributed twelve pounds towards rent.

In the course of Ellen's testimony she explained that she had in her possession the November 1918 letter to her husband signed by Margaret that had come from Newark, New Jersey, where, coincidentally, Fred was billeted when working as a munitions inspector during the war. Margaret's terms were extremely endearing to her husband.

It turned out that another letter had arrived on 1 October 1920 at 118 Broomspring Road. Clearly Margaret must have been unaware that Fred had departed to Lincolnshire and it was now four years since the pair had clapped eyes on each other. Nevertheless this second intercepted letter was if anything more passionate and demonstrated that the pair must have been in correspondence with each other since Fred had returned in 1916. Furthermore it showed he was likely to be going back to North America as he had been lured back across the Atlantic to help establish the first recognisable football league in America – the America Soccer League.

"At last my darling the most wonderful news. I still can't believe it's true, and I shall not believe it until you reach me and I can hold you in my arms. I hope the days will pass quickly; this will be the happiest Christmas."

Mr Jackson then asked Fred if he was leaving for the US before Christmas but the reply failed to make any sense when he said he was "swinging the lead". Jackson asked if he was bluffing two women and Fred replied "Just one."

Jackson then asked the court chairman to grant an injunction preventing Fred Spiksley from leaving the country until he had been means-tested. It was stated the defendant had left his wife and failed to contribute sufficiently towards her support even though he was earning a good living as a bookmaker. Fred disputed this by claiming he had sent twelve pounds to his wife.

Under cross-examination, Fred quickly dropped his claim that he did not know Margaret, stating she was Margaret Murphy. Asked about his finances, Fred admitted working as a bookmaker and to having been paid £100 for writing his life story in the Dundee-based *Thomson Weekly News*. He also earned further limited income of a few pounds by being able to use his football knowledge to provide a critique of talented players for professional football clubs looking to sign new players. He admitted to being currently in negotiations with a football club in Mexico City to go there as a coach and produced a contract to demonstrate he was telling the truth. That certainly was not the case when he was asked if he had won £30 in a Manchester running handicap. He denied doing so.

In his summing-up the chairman of the bench said it was evident that the defendant had the resources to earn a livelihood and as such the duty of the bench was to make an order ensuring that Fred Spiksley provided for his wife. Accordingly, he was found guilty of desertion and there was an order made against him to pay Ellen Spiksley the sum of £2 a week.

In the event, Fred did not make it back to North America for Christmas 1920 but on 24 January 1921, the day before his 51st birthday, he sailed into New York aboard the SS Carmaria from Liverpool, to take up his role in establishing quality football in the US. There he would become a senior executive for the Pennsylvania Football Association. Football was most prominent in the New York metropolitan area and in Pennsylvania and the region's most successful side were Bethlehem Steel. Although there is no proof, there seem to be clear links between his new role in 1920 and his time as a munitions worker.

Writing for *Spalding's Athletic Annual* in 1921, Spiksley is clearly impressed by what he saw in the US. Indeed, he is often more complimentary of players from his time coaching abroad than he is of English football, believing that with the right training and management that teams in Germany and America would one day be able to match the best English teams. Speaking in 1921 about players in America, he said: "I could not help but admire the spirit with which these players went about their work. With the men that I have in my eye, I think I could build up a team that would do credit to their country in Olympic Games." This was not an opinion shared by his contemporaries back in England who at the time believed that the home nations would not be overthrown. Two years after Spiksley's death England would be embarrassed by the USA in the 1950 World Cup in Brazil.

Writing further, Spiksley was most impressed by the full backs and forwards in America, as well as the goalkeeping. "I saw more than one who would, with experience and coaching, make a name in Britain...The forward play, generally was to my mind the most satisfactory of all the lines and this showed great improvement with some teams as the season advanced, most notably with Robins Dry Dock. I was surprised with the aggressiveness, speed and skill that some of the forwards showed, and with a little steadying influence and more control of the ball they would in some instances compare with some of the great players in the old country. Their chief failures were those two essential arts – stopping a ball dead on the floor and heading."

Spiksley was quick to identify the main weaknesses of the American game, commenting on how the half-backs did not really understand their role and how to position themselves on the field so that they could link the play from back to front. This was something that he took upon himself to change as he coached different sides across the region.

In helping young American soccer players Spiksley had many pieces of advice. However, some of it sounds like the same advice handed down to him in 1887 by John Madden, who was establishing his legendary status in Prague at this time;

"Players who wish to become great must do a great deal of thinking, as in no sphere of life did man attain much prominence without such, and this stands in football... One selfish forward, no matter how good, can spoil the whole team, and I would advocate his services being dispensed with at once, as he is a really negative influence on the team's success... Forwards should shoot often and hard, and particularly when a decent opportunity presents itself. They may make mistakes, but the man that never made a mistake never made anything, and after all it is better to have tried and failed than to have never tried at all. Always endeavour to bring the ball to the feet and play the ball in the air as little as possible."

Although we do not know as much as we would like about what Fred did over the next three or so years we do know that he was, in February 1921, coach to Real Club Espana OD in Mexico City. Espana were Mexico City's premier football team at the time and would go on to win the Primera Fuerza title that year. Spiksley was photographed with an unidentified Mexican team, which is featured in this book, with a large trophy that may be for the Primera Fuerza.

In the 1970s Fred Spiksley junior was interviewed by the local Sheffield press. He eventually lived his life out in Sheffield, working for the electricity board. During the interview he describes how his father was considered football's first missionary. He said Fred would go out and help support fledgling football associations set up their infrastructure and teach the local teams how to play the 'English Way' This mostly involved a passing game with the ball being kept on the floor.

This version of Fred Spiksley's life as a travelling coach does seem to ring true to his time in America, where Spiksley, after initially starting work in Pennsylvania, had then travelled to Mexico City to work with numerous teams across the city. Fred would spend a brief time in Peru, making him the first person to coach football across three continents.

Flying over an Olive Grove

Spiksley would return to Mexico from Peru to complete his time in the Americas. On returning to England in the summer of 1924 Fred was interviewed by the Sheffield Telegraph and the journalist was clearly impressed with how fit and well he looked, writing: "I never saw him looking better. He has naturally put on weight, but today, now that he is in his 50s, he looks lithe and hardy as ever. Browned by a semi-tropical sun, and carrying not an ounce of superfluous flesh, he looks as though he is still able to put in a good sprint on the cinder path. In fact, some three years ago, shortly before he set out for Mexico, Fred had put out a challenge to beat any man in the country his own age in a sprint race. It is almost needless to say that the challenge was never taken up.

"Spiksley speaks highly of the reception he received in Mexico City. He was engaged by the management of the Reformers' Club, run by the white section of the population, composed both of Latins and Anglo-Saxons, among whom the dour Scottish element predominated.

"Spiksley's duty was to act as coach for the football section of this great club, which embraces most kinds of outdoor sport. The task was a strange one. Owing to the absence of twilight and the sudden descent of darkness over the earth, all the training had to be done before breakfast. Still, he found his pupils tractable and easy to teach, and it was not long ere he welded them into about the strongest side in the country. In fact, the old international states that if some of the team, notably a centre half back, were to make their appearance in English football, they would cause something like a sensation.

"After breakfast, Spiksley used to find time hung heavily on his hands, and he spoke to one of the chief officials of the club about looking for a suitable job for him. Well educated and always notable for strict attention to detail, Fred's thoroughness had not escaped attention and, when the post of head of the Dispatch Department in the Bank of Montreal, an important branch where there is a staff of 140, became vacant, he was unhesitatingly placed in the position which, by the way, he holds today. It is his proud boast that he has yet to make his first mistake.

"The worst of it is," said Spiksley, "that after training the team before breakfast, and then having to be on my feet all day in the bank, my legs feel inclined, occasionally, to become a little shaky before the day closes." Asked if he proposed returning, the reply was: "Well, I don't quite know yet. They have asked me to return, and perhaps I may, but as I have said, I don't quite know." It was palpable that now he is here, Fred has a hankering to remain".

Spiksley's method of freelancing his services to various football clubs and associations has made it difficult to pinpoint specific achievements and stories that could be included within the pages of this book. We do know that by 1924 Fred had coached in Sweden, Germany, Belgium, France, Switzerland, America, Mexico and Peru. This list would be further added to for after further periods in Germany and Switzerland he would spend a period of 1934 coaching football in Barcelona and would referee a match between Barcelona and CE Júpiter. Although it is very likely that Spiksley freelanced his expertise to the Spanish giants during his time in Barcelona, no definite link has yet been proved.

In 1924 what was missing from Spiksley's list of coaching achievements was a settled coaching role in English football. It is certain that he had worked with several English clubs on a part time basis and a 1924 cartoon drawn by Tottenham's Jimmy Seed, the future Sheffield Wednesday player and legendary Charlton Athletic manager, seems to substantiate this claim.

CHAPTER 25

A FINAL FLIRTATION
An underdog Cup run with Fulham 1924–26.

FRED SPIKSLEY'S BREAK into coaching in English football would come in 1924 when he was snapped up by a struggling Fulham side as new manager Andy Ducat sought success. The England international had retired from playing in May 1924. After successful stints with Arsenal and Aston Villa he played for Fulham between 1921 and 1924. Never cautioned, Ducat also played once for England at cricket.

Ducat had replaced the retiring Phil Kelso as Fulham manager in the summer of 1924. Playing in Division Two, the Cottagers had only just avoided relegation. With Fulham having heavy debts there was little money for the new man to invest in new players so another season of struggle seemed certain.

Ducat outlined his philosophy in a series of 'football tips' in *The Mercury* newspaper, which readers were urged to keep as "they will make you a better player". To help achieve this, and in a sign of the growing commercialisation of football, 'Andy Ducat Patent Boots' were available from the Biggleswade shop of former Luton Town and Fulham player William Albon. Ducat was following in the footsteps of Steve Bloomer who was the first footballer to have a pair of boots named after him.

Ducat inherited a squad packed with Scots, including George Aimer, Alec Chaplin, James Torrance and Henry Lafferty. Veteran centre-forward George Edmonds had scored the goals which had kept Fulham up. Seeking more goals, Ducat brought in William Prouse at inside-right and he scored in the opening League fixture at Bradford City that ended 1-1.

Fulham's indifferent start meant that when they drew 0-0 at home to Portsmouth on 4 October 1924 they had taken seven points from seven games. Off the pitch it was reported that Fred Spiksley had returned from his four-year football coaching role in Mexico. Within a week he had been appointed in a similar capacity at Fulham for a two-year period. According to the *Nottingham Evening Post* his duties included seeking out promising players and training them along scientific lines. The new Fulham coach outlined his philosophy in an article in the *Topical Times* of 25 October 1924 in which he stated "I honestly believe I can work the trick and restore football to its future glory." Key to any progress was the need for better ball control.

Fulham were the League's lowest scorers. Spiksley's arrival coincided with more goals being scored with six in the following three home matches that resulted in two wins and a draw.

There was also real pleasure when, on 6 December, Fulham beat Sheffield Wednesday 2-1 at home before an 18,000 crowd. Fulham thus rose to twelfth in the table and finished the season in that position. Only 41 goals were scored in 46 games. In the FA Cup, Fulham crashed out to eventual losing finalists Cardiff City.

The 1925–26 season started badly as Fulham were easily beaten 3-0 away to Sheffield Wednesday. Left half Bert

Barrett had come into the side and he was to go on and make 419 appearances and also play once for England. In December, 'keeper Ernie Beecham, signed from Hertford in the Spartan League, was given his debut against Blackpool. He went on to make 130 consecutive appearances before his run was halted when he broke his neck.

Eight of the first nine games of the season were lost with only a 1-0 victory against Stockport County at Craven Cottage putting points on the board. This result did enough, however, to ensure that when Fulham drew 0-0 with Bradford City on 19 December 1925 they stayed a point above bottom-placed Stockport. Only Clapton Orient had failed to score fewer goals than Fulham who had yet to get to grips with the offside law change introduced at the start of the season. Then called 'the one back system' it is best known today as the two-man offside rule. Alarmed by the shortage of goals, officials had changed the rules so that a player could only be offside if there were fewer than two rather than three players between him and the goal.

The 'experiment' was deemed to have worked as more goals were scored. In response the new Arsenal manager Herbert Chapman adopted the W-M formation of two full backs, a centre half, two half backs, two inside forwards, two wingers and a centre forward. As a consequence, out went the old straight line formation of five defenders and five forwards. The change did not meet with Fred Spiksley's approval and in August 1928 he wrote to *Athletic News* stating "The W formation is an apology for lazy or worn-out inside forwards" and arguing that it was easier for an attack to be neutralised if the outside forwards were shadowed by the wing halves. He urged a return to pre-1925 formations. It was an example of how Fred wasn't the most tactical of coaches and was better employed on improving a player's fitness and skills.

On 2 January 1926, Fulham took revenge for the opening-day defeat by beating Sheffield Wednesday 3-0 at Craven

Cottage. The defeated side had won their three previous matches and went on to win the next five with Jimmy Trotter in blistering form in front of goal; 37 League goals during the season helped his side capture the Second Division title at the end of the campaign. Fulham's two points against the champions proved vital as they were enough to ensure that Fulham finished in nineteenth place, two points above relegated Stoke City who had a superior goal average. With the General Strike only days away, Fulham had beaten Bradford City 2-0 at home on the final day of the season to avoid dropping down into Division Three South.

All of which made it all the more remarkable that Fulham almost made it into the last four of the FA Cup.

In the opening Cup match, Fulham drew 1-1 at Everton. Playing an open game, Fulham held on until half-time when Dixie Dean netted. However on 70 minutes, Teddy Craig cleverly steered the ball past Harry Hardy to equalise. Everton would have won the match if not for a magnificent late save from eighteen-year-old Ernie Beecham who was showered with congratulations when he reached the dressing room where he admitted to "having enjoyed every minute of the game".

A crowd of 20,176 attended the replay. Heavy snow and freezing temperatures made playing conditions difficult and Fulham were unfortunate when centre half Jock McNab's header hit the post. On 65 minutes the home side did take the lead when Bert White scored and although Alex Chaplin later left the field, Fulham held on to win with Beecham again being the hero following a series of fine saves topped off by a brilliant final-minute stop from Alec Troup. The youngster was chaired off the field by celebrating Fulham fans.

Fulham faced Liverpool in round four. With Edmonds unfit, Albert Pape led the line. Craven Cottage was packed with 36,381 inside and after Donald McKinlay failed to clear, Pape put his side ahead on three minutes and even though Dick Forshaw equalised, Frank Penn restored the home side's lead just before the interval. Pape finished off the scoring on 56 minutes. After that, Liverpool pressed but Beecham was in great form and was again chaired off the field by celebrating Fulham fans.

Fulham were away in round five to Notts County, where before a 28,000 crowd there was just three minutes remaining when Bill Prouse latched on to a perfectly-weighted ball from Jack Harris, who had been signed from Leeds United in the summer of 1925. Harris beat Albert Iremonger to set up a last eight tie with Manchester United, whom Fulham had beaten in the same round in 1908 to reach the last four, at the time their finest FA Cup run.

The game was played on Saturday 6 March 1926. It attracted a Craven Cottage crowd of 28,699 who saw Frank McPherson put the northern side ahead in the first minute. There was an equaliser almost immediately from Pape whose signature from Manchester United at the start of the season was only made on condition that he could live in Bolton and train during the week with Manchester United.

After that the game was a tight affair but when right full back Reg Dyer was forced off the field for treatment, Manchester United took advantage and Tom Smith netted to take his side through to a semi-final encounter against Manchester City that they subsequently lost 3-0.

Fulham's brave fight had come to an end and after such a poor League season it was no surprise that Ducat tendered his resignation as Fulham manager. He afterwards continued playing cricket for Surrey and suffered a fatal heart attack while batting for the Surrey Home Guard against Sussex Home Guard in 1942. In the wake of Ducat's departure, Fred Spiksley, whose two-year contract had ended, also left the Cottagers, who continued to struggle and were relegated at the end of the 1927–28 season.

On 16 March 1927, Ellen Spiksley of 118 Broomspring

Lane, Sheffield, the wife of Fred Spiksley, swore an oath saying the statements set forth in the petition of Ellen Spiksley were true to the best of her knowledge, information and belief and that there had been no collusion between her and her husband. Fred's address was given as 1 Fussball Club, Bahnhofstrasse 13, Nurnberg, Germany and he was listed as an athletics coach. The statements claimed Fred had deserted his wife for over two years without reasonable cause, "has frequently committed adultery" and "that from 1920 up to the present date he has frequently committed adultery with Lena Adams". Further "that from around May 1925 to around the month of June 1925 at 27 Third Cross Road, Twickenham in the County of Middlesex Fred Spiksley has committed adultery with the said Lena Adams". This was the period when Fred was working for Fulham as a coach.

This information was sent to Fred in Germany. He was instructed to "Take notice that you are required within eight days after service here to enter an application either in person or by your solicitor at the Divorce Registry of the High Court of Justice at Somerset House in the Strand and make answer to the charges in this petition and that in default of doing so the court will proceed to hear the said charges and if proved pronounce judgement in your absence."

The divorce petition was filed in court the following day and on 13 May the case was moved to Leeds Assizes where it was held before the Honourable Mr Justice Talbot on 22 July 1927. Fred Spiksley was not in court to defend himself and there would have been little point as he had clearly had a number of affairs and was no longer living with his wife. He was not even in the same country as her!

The marriage which was solemnised on 5 September 1895 was dissolved 'on reason that since the celebration of the marriage the respondent has been guilty of adultery'. A decree nisi was granted and finally made absolute on 13

Flying over an Olive Grove

March 1928. After over 32 years of marriage, Ellen and Fred
Spiksley were now officially free to go their separate ways.
Ellen was to later become an antique furniture dealer and
lived out the rest of her life in Sheffield, where she died in
December 1965.

CHAPTER 26

RETURN TO ZABO
Winning the German Championship with 1FC Nuremberg.

WITH MILLIONS OF casualties on both sides in World War One there appeared little chance in the immediate aftermath of the ending of hostilities of Fred being able to return to his pre-war role as coach to Football Club Nurnberg. (FCN). However, William Townley, scorer of the first hat-trick in an FA Cup final, had returned by 1919 to his post in charge at Bayern Munich and in April 1920 Stuttgart wrote to the secretary of Nottingham Forest asking if he could recommend "a man of the type of James Cowan, John Goodall, Johnnie Holt or Fred Spiksley. The idea that life in Southern Germany would be unpleasant for an Englishman is absolute piffle as indicated by the great popularity of Will Townley... a high salary and genial surroundings are guaranteed". Although the Forest secretary refused to assist with the request it was reported in a number of papers. How Fred became aware of the request is not known but he did not write to Stuttgart.

League football in Germany had been suspended between 1914 and 1918. When it resumed there were leagues covering each region with the top teams in each going forward to face one another in a knockout competition with the winners of the final being awarded the German championship. Football also became a mass spectator sport in Germany in the 1920s as many workers had more time off, including Saturdays.

FCN's hated local rivals, SpVgg Furth, won the championship in 1919 but, with the recruitment of Hungarians Petr Szabo and Alfred 'Spezi' Schaffer from MTK Budapest, FCN dominated the 1919–1920 championship and won it without losing a match. About 30,000 turned out to welcome the team on their return from the final. The championship was retained in 1920–1921 and was won again in 1923–4 and 1924–5.

FCN lost out to Furth in 1925–26 and many of their best players were ending their careers while the changes in the offside law demanded a much quicker style than that previously adopted by the club.

Only during the final matches in 1921 and 1922 had a special tactical coach been engaged in the person of former MTK centre half Dori Kurschner. Otherwise, captain Gustav Bark had taken the regular training seasons on Wednesdays and Saturdays when the players played for hours against one another.

Following the completion of his Fulham contract at the end of the 1925–26 season, Fred Spiksley telegraphed the FCN president Hans Schregele to remind him that at the onset of the Great War the then president, Leopold Neuberger, had promised he could return as the official football coach once the conflict had ended.

Whether he had inside knowledge about the desire of the German club to employ a coach, Fred chose the right time to make contact as it struck a chord with many club members, who would have remembered him guiding 1FCN to their famous 'kind of victory' against Spurs in

1914. Following discussions the management committee decided to engage him, initially for one year, at a monthly fee of 1,000 German marks.

With all the players being amateur, the training sessions started at 6.30pm with Mondays and Saturdays allocated to the youth team, Tuesdays and Thursdays to the first team and Fridays to all the other teams. First team matches were played on Mondays.

There was a successful start to the season as in all five pre-season friendlies, FCN beat their opponents and scored 36 goals while conceding only five. The day that Spiksley arrived in Germany he went straight to watch a 1FCN reserve team fixture. During the game a young player called Seppl Schmitt caught his eye and although Schmitt was just starting to break into the Nuremberg first team it was Spiksley who is credited with giving the teenager his first real chance to prove himself. After the match Spiksley hunted down the young Schmitt and on finding his man famously said; "Are you the little Schmitt?" Fred had realised that Schmitt was the young blood that was needed if he was to turn around the fortunes of an ageing squad. Schmitt would go on to win two German championships and become a club legend.

The competitive season started on Monday 6 September 1926 with a 7-0 thrashing at home of FC Bayreuth. FCN were in the Southern League and at the end of the League campaign they finished top of the group with a record of sixteen wins, one draw and just one defeat. They scored 64 goals and conceded only seventeen.

In the last-sixteen match, played at SpVgg Furth's ground on 8 May 1927, FCN made short work of Chemnitz and won 5-1 before beating Hamburger SV 2-1 in Hamburg.

The semi-final was held at the ASV ground in Nurnberg-Herrnhutte and, with Schorsch Hochsgang playing brilliantly, FCN qualified for the final by beating TSV Munchen 4-1.

Flying over an Olive Grove

Meanwhile, in the summer of 1927, Burnley had travelled to the continent to play three friendship games and after facing Dresden, where former Tottenham Hotspur manager John Cameron was now coach, they arrived in Nurnberg to face Fred Spiksley's side on 26 May 1927. The English side were billeted in the local Grand Hotel and a tour of the city that included the castle was organised for the 23-man party before they trained on the Zabo.

The home side that Burnley faced were: Heiner Stuhlfauth, Luitpold Popp, Georg Winter, Emil Koepplinger, Hans Kalb, Hans 'Bumbes' Schmidt, Baptist Reinmann, Georg Hochgesang, Seppl Schmitt,, Ludwig Wieder, Heiner Traeg.

Twenty-five thousand fans poured into the revamped Zabo ground when the stadium was opened an hour before kick-off but at the interval they were wearing long faces after the away side took the lead and held it to the break. The new coach had selected Seppl Schmitt and he notched two in the second period and with goals from Wieder and from Hochgesang it was the home side who triumphed 4-2 and captured the beautiful silver 'Cluberern Cup' that had been donated by Burnley's Georges Richart.

After the game, the executive committee of FCN held a banquet of honour for their visitors in the Richard Wagner Hall of the Grand Hotel.

In the other semi-final, played in Leipzig, SpVgg Furth, trained by Townley, were beaten 2-1 by Hertha BSC Berlin who would play the final in their home city as the match took place at the Grunewald Stadium. This had been built in 1913 to host the 1916 Berlin Olympic Games that subsequently did not take place. The stadium was knocked down in the 1930s to make way for the new Olympic Stadium that hosted the major athletics events in 1936.

The football final took place on 12 June 1927 and was attended by a crowd of 50,000 people of which just 1,200 were cheering for FCN.

FCN: Heiner Stuhlfauth, Luitpold Popp, George Winter, Emil Koepplinger, Hans Kalb, (captain) Hans 'Bumbes' Schmidt, Baptist Reinmann, Georg Hochgesang, Seppl Schmitt, Ludwig Wieder, Heiner Traeg.

Hertha Berlin: Goetze, Domscheid, Fischer, Leuschner, Tewes, Mueller, Ruch, Sobeck, Grenzel, Kirsey, Guelle.

Referee: Mr Willi Guyenz (Essen).

The game was notable for being the first German football match to be covered live and in full on national radio. In the lead-up to the contest, Hanne Sobeck, the Hertha captain, had predicted his side would stand a great chance of winning if the weather was hot and the ground was dry. The night before the match it rained heavily and right up to kick-off it continued to rain so that the playing surface was very wet and the conditions were cold, wet and miserable.

None of this stopped the masses of passionate Hertha Berlin fans belting out their club songs and anthems so that the visiting side could hardly hear their own band of hardy followers. With first teamers Carl Riegel and Anton Kugler injured, Fred Spiksley was forced to field two reserve team players in Koepplinger and Winter.

The noise of the Berlin fans was stilled on six minutes when Kalb, who played fifteen times for Germany, netted. Then the FCN captain produced a sterling performance by keeping quiet danger man Hanne Sobeck, who was renowned for his first touch. At one point the fans of the losing side even turned on their own player. When FCN sought a second goal they were thwarted by the offside tactics of Fischer and Domscheid. These so angered Traeg that when he continually showed his annoyance it led to the referee admonishing him. Traeg was on dangerous ground as he had been sent off when playing against Hamburg in the 1922 semi-final. That game ended with FCN having only seven players on the field.

Flying over an Olive Grove

At half-time in the 1927 final the score remained 1-0 in FCN's favour. During the break, the sun came out to warm the crowd and those in it supporting Hertha reminded Sobeck of his pre-match comments. However, it was FCN who forced the pace but they were grateful to Bumbes Schmidt when he cleared a shot that had beaten Stuhlfauth, a brilliant keeper who rivalled Spaniard Ricardo Zamora as the best in the world at the end of the 1920s. He was between the posts when Germany beat Italy for the first time in 1929. He made 21 appearances for his country.

Jolted at nearly conceding a goal, FCN launched a series of attacks and on 65 minutes a quick throw by Bumbes Schmidt to Ludwig Wieder saw the ball moved on to Heiner Traeg. Looking up, the outside left hit a first-time shot beyond Goetze and into the net to make it 2-0. The scorer then ran across to the Hertha hordes shouting out "We've won!"

Not quite, but the game should then have been over but first Wieder and then Kalb hit the Hertha woodwork before on 74 minutes the losing side were given an opportunity to reduce the arrears from the penalty spot when Popp fouled Sobeck in the area.

Domscheid's shot lacked pace and Stuhlfauth's save was an easy one. The 'keeper was especially popular among FCN fans and he ran a wine tavern called Sebaldusklause that Fred would frequent after training sessions in his desire to relax and get to know his players better. It was here that he met and fell in love with a young waitress, Rosi, whom he was to marry in 1929 and with whom he would spend the rest of his life.

Following the penalty save the game was meandering to a close when, on 80 minutes, Traeg took revenge for the kicking he had received throughout the game from Leuschner by booting the Hertha man with his left foot. The winger then abused the referee after he had rightly awarded a free-kick and was dismissed in what was his last game before retirement. Little good it did the losing side as FCN comfortably saw out the final ten minutes to deservedly win 2-0.

The *Berlin Tageblatt* paper summarised the proceedings accurately.

"Nurnberg's victory was due to greater self-belief and confidence instilled in the team by Fred Spiksley, the coach."

This confidence was on display when the 20:25 Football Special train containing the successful team left Berlin Anhalter railway station for home. The windows and doors were completely covered with big yellow posters announcing a victory party in the Apollo Theatre in honour of FC Nurnberg's fifth German championship.

The posters had been printed in Nurnberg before the match and when the train arrived back at Nurnberg station the team captain, Hans Kalb, was asked whether this was presumptuous and disrespectful to their opponents.

Kalb answered proudly: "Well surely you didn't think we were going all the way to Berlin for nothing did you?"

Despite the newspaper praise for the successful coach he remained unpopular with the amateur players who objected to what they felt was his rigorous and disciplined training methods. The players had even given Fred an unflattering nickname in the form of 'Fred Spiegelei' which translates as 'Fred Fried-Egg'. Perhaps it was his age, resentment that he was being paid a handsome salary or the fact he was English? Perhaps it was a combination of all three, but Fred had not been able to assert himself with the players and his contract was not extended by the FCN management committee who feared a backlash if they re-engaged him. Fred thus left the German city only weeks before the third annual rally of the Nazi Party in August 1927. This annual event later became world famous when the propaganda film 'Triumph des Willens' was made at the 1934 rally and showed Hitler greeting delegations from areas of Germinate cut off from the country under the Versailles Treaty.

With Fred gone, FCN employed Dr K Michalke and Hans Tauchert, men who were leaders of sporting exercises rather than coaches. Until August 1930, when Jeno Konrad was employed, the philosophy of the club remained that great successes could be achieved without a coach. It was not until 1935–36 that FCN again won the championship and the cup final.

Fred, aged 59, and Rose Reichel, a spinster twenty years younger, were married on 3 June 1929 at Paddington Register Office. Fred's occupation was listed as an athletics coach, while nothing was listed for Rose, whose father was Johann George Reichel and whose income was listed as by independent means. The couple were resident at the Beaumont Hotel, Princes Square, London at the time of their marriage.

CHAPTER 27

A FOCUS ON YOUTH
Passing on the secrets of his success.

AFTER DEPARTING GERMANY it was almost time for Fred to call time on his globe-trotting career as a football coach. However, he was to receive a final appointment as coach to Lausanne Sports. His time in Lausanne was a mixed one, the club were trying to establish themselves and how much Fred impacted on the club is difficult to gauge. Yet his time there would lead to a memorable encounter with Robert Alaway who, as an Eton schoolboy, had had his first encounter with football when in 1893 he was among the crowd at the 1893 Richmond international, witnessing Fred score his famous hat-trick.

Such impact did the game and his new hero – Spiksley – have on the youngster that he spent much of the rest of his life involved in the sport. In 1905 he founded the Middlesex Wanderers football club, who remain famous for their touring of the world. Alaway spent most of his life touring the globe with his football club and in 1948 released the book *Football All Round the World* in which he retells the tale of meeting Fred Spiksley some 35 years after his life-changing day at Richmond.

"My introduction to association football was with royalty; or rather, to be strictly accurate and respectful, it was in the company of royalty that I saw my first game – an international on the hallowed Richmond Athletic Ground between England and their historic foes, the Scots. I shall never forget it.

"Since then I have seen thousands of football matches in all parts of the world, graced by kings, emperors, princes, presidents and of course millions of the common kind. But an imperishable memory is that glorious spring afternoon of 1893 beneath the quiet trees beside the gentle flowing Thames.

"Apart from the spectacle of a real live duke and a princess, the outstanding personalities of this international were the immaculate English wingers – the late W I Bassett and Fred Spiksley. What players they were! With every respect to present-day players, these two were undoubtedly greatness personified. To see them both in action in the same game was indeed a schoolboy treat that loses none of its sweetness in old age. Both played a textbook game, with the highlight of the match three brilliant goals scored by Spiksley from the left wing, all within the space of about ten minutes. England won the game 5 goals to 2. Watching these players as a small boy I little thought that in after years I should have the great pleasure of knowing these men intimately...

"As for Spiksley, it was not until 35 years later that I saw this great figure of a man again; and that was at Lausanne in 1928. The Middlesex Wanderers had gone there to play Lausanne Sports FC, to whom Spiksley was the revered professional coach.

"At the reception after the match I told Spiksley that as a boy in stiff collar and Eton suit I had seen him score three goals for England. He had a remarkable memory for the games he played. Not only did he remember the Richmond international but nearly every movement of the game, and went through every one of them again while my eyes popped and my pulse quickened with renewed excitement. I had completely forgotten, but Spiksley reminded me, that the referee was J C Clegg, chairman of the Football Association, and that he took no notice of the fact that one of the players lost his football boots and turned out in black walking boots.

"At the same reception, one of my companions, R A Stephens, asked Spiksley: 'Do you remember scoring a goal from the junction of the halfway line and the touch line on the Spurs ground?' It happened years and years before but Spiksley remembered it distinctly. Indeed, he produced from his pocket-book a press cutting describing the phenomenon. Then said Stephens: 'I refereed that game. That is why I remember it so well.' And there at the foot of the report was printed: 'Referee: R A Stephens.'"

This is the only account that we have discovered of Spiksley's long distance strike at White Hart Lane, but evidence would suggest that it took place during a London Cup match while Fred was playing for Southern United, which means that Spiksley still had the timing in his legs to punch through the ball in the way we all remember David Beckham doing at Selhurst Park in 1996. Spiksley would have been about 35 when he scored the goal.

After his one-year contract with Lausanne Sports ended Fred returned to England, and although he was to spend some time in Barcelona in 1934, his return from Switzerland marked an end to his continual coaching around the world. When Fred was born in 1870 life expectancy for male children was just 39 years of age and on his return from Lausanne he was now well into his 50s. Despite his long involvement in football his finances remained unstable and he could not afford to retire. In 1929 he arranged with the London Evening News to contribute a series of practical hints in *How to Play Football*. It gave him the opportunity to share what he had learned from over 40 years' close study of the science and technology of football and was aimed at London teenagers eager to develop their footballing abilities.

As Fred matured as a coach he became increasingly aware of the importance of nurturing talented young players. When writing for *Spalding's Athletic Annual* during his time in America he was very vocal on how the USFA needed to do more to encourage and develop its talented youth:

"All the legislators in the world will not make players. You must act besides preach. Gentlemen interested must look out for plots of land where these boys can be taken to play. If an important match is in the vicinity, somebody with football at heart should take as many boys as wish to go to see the game. School officials should offer inducements and do all in their power to encourage them to play. The boys will soon see where the art of the game lies and will not be slow to pick up the main points. What they need is models to work up to.

"I would like to see some shield or cup offered for competition among the schools on the knockout principle. If the large towns would adopt this idea, you would have soccer footballers galore in a few years time. All clubs affiliated with the USFA should be compelled to contribute to a fund to encourage school football, and the allotment of this money to the various centres would then be in the hands of capable and impartial gentlemen."

In 1929 Fred expressed his disappointment at what he saw as the finer points of football having disappeared and at the lack of quality coaches. He felt that many footballers did not even know the correct part of the foot to kick the ball with – namely the outside – as in "my humble opinion, it is only the outside of the foot that that a football can be properly controlled with". He argued that muscles on the outside of the foot were stronger than the inside and consequently the use of the latter slowed down the time it takes for a ball to be passed to a teammate. The same was true for shooting at goal.

He recommended that young players should learn how to kick a tennis ball against the wall, that a left winger should control the ball with his right and vice versa. There were tips on how to trap the ball correctly, keeping your eyes on the ball, back heeling the ball, heading and swerving away from opponents – at which no-one he had witnessed was as good as Vivian Woodward. There was then advice for different positions, including playing in goal, at full back, in defence, wing half and up front. The articles were accompanied by a series of photographs of Spiksley demonstrating the various techniques, so that the young boys of London could practise them themselves.

Although Fred did not always believe that football was on a constant improvement projectile, there is no doubt that Fred was never stuck in the past and was constantly looking for ways to help improve the game. In the same year as his *Evening News* articles Fred Spiksley returned to Craven Cottage to record a film for *Pathé News*, who had first covered the FA Cup final in 1901 and then showed the newsreel in cinemas nationally. Cinema newsreels were silent until 1928, and Fred Spiksley's film was to become one of the earliest surviving films to combine motion picture with sound. The surviving footage is only 84 seconds long and it appears certain that what was recorded was longer as Fred Spiksley, wearing an England cap, jumper and track suit bottoms, can be clearly heard stating "This time I am going to demonstrate some further aspects of the game." Despite its brevity, it may well be the first ever football training film and it seems likely it was made to be taken into schools and be shown to youngsters in order to help them practise their skills.

Fred works with Fulham's Bert Barrett and Len Oliver, who as England internationals are shown wearing their international jerseys, and then are shown practising back heeling the ball with Fred stating "which is a very good trick". The former Fulham coach, whom the narrator describes as "the well-known football coach" then demonstrates himself the correct way to back heel the ball before Barrett and Oliver are filmed running down the wing as they first master and then pass the ball with the inside foot to one another. The surviving footage section of film is one of 85,000 films that British Pathé made freely available to the general public in 2014.

The film demonstrates that at nearly 60 years of age Spiksley was still forward thinking and eager to embrace the latest technologies to help nurture future talent. An advert for Spiksley's film in the *Sheffield Independent* 28 November 1929 describes how Spiksley uses a slow-motion camera to show the 'finer intricacies' of ball control. The video is available online.

King Edward VII School was built in the years 1837–1840 as the Wesley Proprietary Grammar School, later the Wesley College. It was designed by architect William Flockton who generally specialised in the design of churches.

When Sheffield became one of Britain's 330 local education authorities in 1902 the college was amalgamated with Sheffield Grammar School and became King Edward VII School in 1905. It was an all-boys school that was named after the reigning monarch and it had a history of preparing boys for entry to Cambridge and Oxford Universities. Girls were admitted to the school in 1969. Today it is a secondary school and language college.

The 1930s was the best decade for sport at King Edward VII as it had teams competing in all disciplines at inter-school level and many boys were competing for the house teams or playing for the school.

A Focus on Youth

The games committee set the framework, deciding the sports to be played and who would play them. The chairmanship of the sports curriculum was held between 1926 and 1938 by the headmaster, Mr Richard B Graham. Over the twelve years a new swimming pool and junior school were constructed and when he left the school magazine stated "the future historian will, we hope, remember to credit Mr Graham's term of office with record achievements in the scholastic field and some equally notable football seasons."

Mr Eric Simms, the history master, was responsible for the football teams at the start of the 1930s. His greatest innovation was to get the endorsement of his head to employ a professional football coach between September 1933 and November 1936. Fred Spiksley was chosen.

When the former Wednesday wide man arrived for his first day of coaching he was an old man of 63. He was wearing his best suit and a remarkably pristine bowler hat. Eric Simm had great pleasure in introducing the man who had won the FA Cup and after which Fred Spiksley explained his coaching background to the group and how he hoped to develop their ball skills and teamwork in order to collectively improve. He then placed his jacket carefully on the ground, removed his hat and proceeded to demonstrate the art of ball control using his hat as the ball. It was all a bit of fun but the boys were immediately thrilled by Fred's skills and smiled broadly.

It was now time for the hard work and soon Fred became a hugely positive influence on King Ted's football. The high standards he set were responsible for the brilliance of the first and second elevens.

One of King Ted's First XI was Eric Sivil who went on to become one of the best full backs to play for the school. Sivil's abiding memory of his coach was his insistence that the team must always keep their discipline and maintain the highest standards of sporting behaviour on the field of play. This reflected Fred's own playing career during which his only sending-off was later rescinded.

This insistence on high behaviour standards did, however, sometimes conflict with the other message that Fred Spiksley stressed. Eric Sivil was summoned into Richard Graham's office where the head told him that his late tackle on an opponent during the previous game was not the way to play football as "sport was not about winning". Whereupon Eric replied, "But Sir, Mr Spiksley had told us that football is all about winning."

Another of Fred's stars was Frank Melling who played at inside left for King Ted's First XI. Frank moved to London to work in the City and played for Corinthian Casuals as an amateur. When he returned to Sheffield he played for Wednesday in a wartime derby match against United at Bramall Lane. Watching was Fred Spiksley who was delighted to witness Malting scoring twice in an 8-2 success.

Fred's most successful coaching season with the school was 1933–34. The First XI, captained by Harold Pearson, won all twenty of their scheduled fixtures played against their traditional rivals from both public and grammar schools. The only defeat all season was against a men's club side. A total of 181 goals was scored, easily a record. Bob Gray knocked in 63. Best win of the season for King Ted's was 3-1 over the Repton Public School on Armistice Day. It was the first time that King Ted's had beaten Repton and they went on to win the return 5-2. Fred was also delighted when King Ted's beat Derby Grammar School 18-0 in 1934. It went some small way to avenging his worst day on a football field when on 21 January 1899 Derby had beaten Wednesday 9-0 with Steve Bloomer scoring six.

The remarkable achievements that Fred Spiksley inspired at King Ted's were recognised in a rather unusual way. The Ardath Tobacco Company included the King Edward VII school football team in their football cigarette photograph collection in 1935/36 alongside top football teams of the day such as Sunderland, Arsenal, Everton and the 1935 FA Cup winners Sheffield Wednesday, who, with Spiksley, Billy Beats and Tom Crawshaw watching on, beat West Bromwich Albion 4-2 in the final at Wembley.

The match was one of Wembley's finest but the game of the 1935 competition had featured Everton against Sunderland in the fourth round replay that the Toffees won 6-4 after extra-time. Fred Spiksley had last played top level football over thirty years earlier and yet in *the Guardian* match report by an 'Old International' he still featured – a sure sign of just how good he was on his day: "Old spectators saw Fred Spiksley come to life on 75 minutes as Cook ran upfield, balancing the ball on his head and dispatching it via Geldard to Stevenson, who made it 3-1."

Meanwhile, the *Sheffield Green Un* sports paper noted Spiksley's success with the youngsters in Sheffield. On 12 September 1936 it reported: "Fred Spiksley's great passion is his burning desire to coach young footballers. It is a pity that no club in the country has used his knowledge and football experience. The Sports Editor has previously questioned whether the current season's 'coaching stunts' and 'old teaching theories' were years behind Fred Spiksley's coaching methods and the development of ball play and his techniques that have been so successful throughout the world. When he recently visited us, Fred gave a few demonstrations of his tricks, flicks and pivoting with the body. They were very interesting not because of his clever execution alone, but also because there are no players in League football who can reproduce them – such simple manoeuvres and yet so obviously effective. England has never had a better outside left than Spiksley. What a tragedy that his services have not been used."

Fred maintained his links with King Edward's school and a local sports fanatic Mick Gill, who lived near the school as a child, later recalled how one Wednesday afternoon in 1946 two elderly neighbours, Charlie Briggs and Ernest Parry, returned home for tea in great spirits. The pair had witnessed a sprightly elderly man invited to advise some of the school students as they held a practice football match. His skills and athleticism had astounded everybody. The stranger turned out to be Fred Spiksley, aged 76, on a visit to family friends near Whiteley Woods.

In the mid 1930s, Gill, a young teenager, had met the former footballer while he was out walking with his dad and the pair had stopped for refreshments and to chat to two well-dressed men at the Hammer and Pincers pub at Bents Green. Afterwards, Gill's father told him he had been in the company of two famous men – Fred Spiksley and George Mooney. The latter was the leader of the Mooney Gang whose violent rivalry with the Park Gang over control of Sheffield's lucrative 'pitch and toss rings' saw one man murdered in the 1920s, two brothers hanged and many others imprisoned before the gangs were finally smashed by a Home Office-instigated flying Squad. Mooney twice went to prison but had retired for good from gang matters by 1936 and for the rest of his life he remained a well-known figure on northern racecourses as using a pseudonym he stood as a bookmaker. He was also a regular figure in the betting ring at Owlerton greyhound stadium that was constructed in 1929 and remains open today.

Mooney and Fred thus had a common gambling interest and it was while the latter was pursuing his passion for horse racing that he bumped into his former England colleague Steve Bloomer as he descended from the train at Derby Midland Station on his way to the local racetrack on Friday 19 November 1937. The pair had not met since before the war and Fred was shocked to see how unwell Bloomer was. A testimonial fund had raised sufficient for him to go cruising around Australia and New Zealand and Bloomer was going by train to Tilbury to board the luxury liner Otranto as the first part of the trip. Bloomer died three weeks after returning home in April 1938. His funeral took place on the afternoon of Wednesday 20 April 1938 at Derby Cathedral and was attended by numerous personalities from the world of football including Fred Spiksley.

CHAPTER 28

ONE FINAL BET
The perfect way to go.

LITTLE WAS REPORTED in the newspapers about Fred in the 1940s. It would be certainly interesting to know how he and his wife, a German national, faired during the Second World War, especially during the Blitz periods when many industrial locations in Britain were heavily bombed.

It would also be interesting to know how they fared financially and whether he claimed his state pension. He became entitled to this in January 1935 when he reached 65 but with Rosa many years younger than him it was not until 1948, when new laws were introduced, that he could have also claimed a dependent's addition for his wife.

Fred Spiksley died on Wednesday 28 July 1948 aged 78. The London Olympics were set to kick off and Britain sweltered in temperatures reaching well into the nineties. The England international told friends he was "feeling bad" before being overcome by the heat and falling dead in Tattersall's enclosure at Goodwood races on Ladies Day.

Fred's main love was always racing and so it was an appropriate ending although it meant he missed collecting his winnings from the bet he had placed on Aurelia to win the 3.10pm Goodwood Stakes run over two miles and three furlongs. Aurelia, who beat Billet and Whiteway in a ding-dong finish to win by a head at odds of 100-8, also had a Gainsborough connection as Aura, the dam of Aurelia, was by Dark Legend out of Ars Davina by Gainsborough.

Alan and Joyce Spicksley were on holiday in Great Yarmouth at the time and "I can recall seeing a newspaper board outside a shop stating 'Former England footballer dies at Goodwood Races.' My husband immediately knew it was Fred and went inside to buy the paper and confirm what he already knew."

Following a post mortem without an inquest the death was recorded at Chichester in West Sussex on 30 July 1948. Fred's occupation was recorded as a retired athletics coach.

It was reported that he had lived in London in recent years but had suffered indifferent health following a major internal operation. He left behind a widow, Rosa, who continued to live in the capital until 1960, when her name disappears from the electoral role, and one son, Fred junior, who lived until September 1978 and was chief electrician at the Neepsend Electricity Station, Sheffield.

He had four remaining relatives in Gainsborough including his sister-in-law, the urban district councillor Mrs Florence Spicksley, and his brother, William, who according to Joyce Spicksley was "owed a considerable sum of money by Fred at the time". Nevertheless, Fred, who did not make a will before he died, left to his wife, Rosa, assets of £477 12s 3d (£477.61), the equivalent of around £17,000 today. He also left behind to family members a number of possessions – including some expensive jewellery such as rings, necklaces and watches – that he had, according to Joyce Spicksley, "used as deposits to get funds from people to bet on the horses". Joyce herself has one of the rings.

It was over 45 years since Fred had played his last top-flight match for Wednesday and more than 50 years since he had performed internationally. Very few people still alive could possibly have seen the winger at his best.

Flying over an Olive Grove

Nevertheless, a week later a letter appeared in the *Gainsborough News* from C G Jennings of 16 Garnett Street, Cleethorpes, who stated that during his seven years working on the paper he had worked alongside Fred Spiksley when he was an apprentice compositor in the 1880s and 90s. The writer claimed he had seen every England international match and FA Cup final from 1897 till 1934 and "that with all due deference to (Stanley) Matthews wizardry, I shall always maintain Fred Spiksley, in possession of the ball, was the fastest forward I have ever seen, his phenomenal speed, his elusiveness and his shooting gifts made him the great player he became." Jennings commented on Fred's remarkable exploits at Richmond Park in 1893 when he inspired England to come from 2-1 down to beat the Scots 5-2.

ACHIEVEMENTS

Winner of every major trophy and honour available between 1887–1903
First player to score a hat-trick against Scotland.

More than 300 career goals.

The highest average goal ratio of any winger in the history of
English football.

Scorer of the fastest FA Cup final goal of all time – 20 Seconds
(Unconfirmed).

Hat-trick on England debut v Wales 1893.

Scored both goals in the 1896 FA Cup final in a 2-1 victory.

First player in history to receive a three-year contract.

Sheffield Wednesday's third leading goal scorer of all time across
all first team fixtures, with 170 goals.

Average of more than a goal a game for his local club;
Gainsborough Trinity – 131 goals in 126 matches.

First Wednesday player to score at Hillsborough.

Scorer of the first hat-trick at Hillsborough.

Professional playing career which lasted two decades.

Scored for every club he played for – Gainsborough Trinity,
Sheffield Wednesday, England, Glossop North End, Leeds City,
Southern United, Watford and the Corinthians.

Leeds City's first professional footballer and the man who provided
the necessary ambassadorial role in 1905 that helped Leeds gain
Football League status in 1905–06.

First Professional footballer to coach across three continents,
including England, Sweden, America, Mexico, Peru, Germany,
Switzerland, France and Spain.

One of Chelsea's first scouts.

Host of the first speaking football training film for young people

Managed 1FC Nuremburg when they captured the German
Championship in 1927,.

Fred Spiksley was one of the quickest players ever to play football,

The outside left played the game mainly with the outside of both
feet, believing this enabled him to pass the ball quicker and
more accurately,.

Bibliography

Reminiscences by Fred Spiksley, *Sheffield Football Special*, 1907

Twenty Years of Professional Football by Fred Spiksley, *Thomson's Weekly*, 1920

My Ideas About Football; Essentials For Success by Fred Spiksley, *London Evening News*, 1929

All of the above contributed significantly to *Flying Over An Olive Grove* and are known to be written by Fred Spiksley and not ghost written.

Sheffield Football

Blades and the Owls: A Pictorial History of the Sheffield Derby Matches – Keith Farnsworth

Football in Sheffield – Percy Young

One Hundred Years at Hillsborough – Jason Dickinson

Sheffield Football: A History Volume One 1857 – 1961 – Keith Farnsworth

Sheffield United: Champions 1897–98 – Nick Udall

Sheffield Wednesday – A Complete Record 1867 – 1987 – Keith Farnsworth

Sheffield Wednesday – The Complete Record – John Brodie and Jason Dickinson

The Origins of Sheffield Wednesday – Jason Dickinson

The Romance of The Wednesday 1867–1926 – Richard A. Sparling

The Wednesday Boys – A Definitive Who's Who of Sheffield Wednesday Football Club 1880–2005 – Jason Dickinson and John Brodie

Wednesday! – Keith Farnsworth

Football History

50 Years of Football 1884–1934 – Sir Frederick Wall

Association Football – Ernest Needham

Association Football – John Goodall

Association Football & The Men Who Made It – Alfred Gibson & William Pickford

Beastly Fury: The Strange Birth Of British Football – Richard Sanders

Behind The Glory: 100 Years of the PFA – John Harding

Goal-Post: Victorian Football Vol 1 & Vol 2. – Paul Brown

Golden Boot: Football's Top Scorers – Mark Metcalf And Tony Matthews

Bibliography

Herbert Chapman on Football – Herbert Chapman
Inverting the Pyramid: The History of Football Tactics – Jonathan Wilson
Origins of the Football League: The First Season 1888/89 – Mark Metcalf
Purnell's 1972 Encyclopedia of Association Football
The 1973 Hamlyn Book of World Soccer
The Ball Is Round: A Global History of Football – David Goldblatt
The FA Cup – Mike Collett
The Official Centenary History of the Football League and – *The Men Who Made It* – Simon Inglis
The People's Game – *The History of Football Revisited* – James Walvin
The Story of Association Football – J A H Catton [Tityrus]
The Victorian Football Miscellany – Paul Brown
Those Feet: A Sensual History of English Football – David Winner
Through the Turnstiles – Brian Tabner
TOR! The Story of German Football – Ulrich Hesse-Lichtenberger
Triumphs of the Football Field – Narrated By Archie Hunter

Biographies
Chaplin: His Life and Art – David Robinson
Chaplin: Stage by Stage – A.J Marriot
Colossus: The True Story of William Foulke – Graham Phythian
Football Wizard: The Billy Meredith Story – John Harding
Fred Karno: Master of Mirth and Tears – J. P. Gallagher
My Autobiography – Charles Chaplin
Remember Fred Karno?: The Life of a Great Showman – Edwin Alder
Steve Bloomer: The Story of Football's First Superstar – Peter Seddon

Club Histories
1 FC Nürnberg – Die Legende Vom Club. – Christoph Bausenwein, Bernd Siegler, Harald Kaiser
All Shook Up: Bury's Amazing Cup Story 1900 & 1903 – Mark Metcalf
Anfield Rising Liverpool: The First Decade – Brian Belton
Bolton Wanderers FC: The Official History 1877 – 2002 – Simon Marland
Das Club Lexikon 1FCN – Christoph Bausenwein, Bernd Siegler
Der Club – 100 Jahre Fussball – 1. FC Nürnberg – Christoph Bausenwein, Bernd Siegler, Harald Kaiser
Everton FC 1890/91: The First Kings of Anfield – Mark Metcalf
Everton FC: The Men From the Hill Country – Tony Onslow
History of Blackburn Rovers 1875–1925 – Charles Francis

Flying over an Olive Grove

Manchester – The City Years – Gary James
The Clarets Chronicles: The Definitive History of Burnley Football Club
    1888–2007 – Ray Simpson
Whu – Tony Hogg

Complete Record Books
Birmingham City – Tony Matthews; *Blackburn Rovers –* Mike
    Jackson; *Manchester City –* Gary James; *Middlesbrough –* Harry
    Glasper; *Sunderland –* Mike Gibson, Rob Mason and Barry
    Jackson; *Fulham –* Dennis Turner

Who's Who Books
Arsenal, Aston Villa, Everton, Liverpool, Manchester City, Stoke City,
    Wolverhampton Wanderers, WBA – Tony Matthews
Derby County – Gerald Mortimer
Newcastle United – Paul Joannou
Manchester United, Notts County – Garth Dykes *Preston North End –*
    Dean Hayes
Sunderland – Garth Dykes And Doug Lamming *Spurs Alphabet –*
    Bob Goodwin

Social History
A History of Sheffield – David Hey
Durham Miners Millenium Book – Dave Temple
Liberty's Dawn: A People's History of the Industrial Revolution –
    Emma Griffin
Ruhleben – A Prison Camp Society – J. Davidson Ketchum
Ruhleben Camp Magazine
The Age of Empire; 1875–1914 – Eric Hobsbawm
The Making of The English Working Class – E. P. Thompson
To Ruhleben and Back – Geoffrey Pyke
Who Owns Britain – Kevin Cahill
Yesterday's Britain – Reader's Digest

Websites
Ancestry.com
The British Library The National Archives

Newspapers
Gainsborough News; London Evening News; Sheffield Daily Telegraph
    (Inc. The Green-Un) Sheffield Evening Telegraph; Sheffield
    Independent; The Athletic News; The Cricket and Football Field;

390

Bibliography

Thomson's Weekly Sports
Other Newspapers
*Aberdeen Journal; Birmingham Daily Post; Black And White Budget;
Daily Record; Derby Daily Telegraph; Dundee Courier; Dundee
Evening Post; Edinburgh Evening News; Evening Dispatch; Football
Post; Fulham Chronicle; Glasgow Herald; Hull Daily Mail; Illustrated
London News; Illustrated Sporting & Dramatic News Kirkcaldy
Guardian; Lancashire Evening Post; Leeds Mercury; Leicester
Chronicle ; Lincolnshire Chronicle Lincolnshire Echo Liverpool
Mercury; Lloyd's Weekly Newspaper London Standard Manchester
Courier Manchester Guardian Morning Post; Northern Echo;
Northants Evening Telegraph Nottingham Evening Post Nottingham
Guardian; Pall Mall Gazette; Reynold's Newspaper; Sheffield Star;
Stamford Mercury; Sunday Post; Sunderland Daily Echo Tamworth
Herald; The Daily Graphic; The Era; The Express; The Express On
Sunday; The Graphic; The Illustrated London News The Sentinel
(Stoke-on-Trent) The Sketch; The Sporting Life; The Times; Windsor
Magazine; Western Morning News Wrexham Advertiser Yorkshire
Post; York Herald*

Picture Credits
National Archives, British Pathé, National Football Museum,
Bonham's, Sheffield Library, Sheffield Wednesday Football
Club, Swedish Football Association, 1. FC Nuremberg Museum,
Gainsborough Heritage Association, Spiksley Family, Andy
George, Denis Clareborough, John Brodie, Tom Crawshaw, Roy
Massey.

ABOUT THE AUTHORS

Mark Metcalf

Mark Metcalf is a football author with a passion for books on the formative years of the game. He has written books on Charlie Hurley, Stan Anderson, Frank Swift, the 1960 FA Cup, the First League season 1888–89, Everton 1890–91, Bury 1900–03, Manchester United 1907–11, Barnsley 1910–12, Sunderland 1912–13 and 1935≠37, England's top scorers and the rivalry between Liverpool and Manchester United.

Mark also works as a freelance journalist, particularly for the Big Issue North magazine and the publications of Unite the union. Mark has previously worked with the Manchester United Disabled Supporters Association on two books charting their achievements. In 2013 Mark, with the assistance of his friend Robert Boyling, ended the 125 year mystery on who scored the first League goal on 8 September 1888.

Mark has travelled the world watching football and remains a Sunderland fan with a fondness also for Halifax Town, Bradford Park Avenue and Brighouse Town.

Clive Nicholson

Clive Nicholson was born in 1981 and is a member of the Spiksley family. After graduating from Kingston University in 2003 with a BA (hons) in Illustration. Clive subsequently trained to become an art and design teacher and has worked at Archbishop Holgate's School in York for eleven years. He now lives near Leeds with his partner Karen and their two children Megan and Freddie. This book represents over two decades of research that Clive undertook with his father; Ralph.

Ralph Nicholson

Ralph Nicholson was born in 1950 and grew up in Newark-on-Trent. After leaving school at the age of eighteen he embarked on a successful career at Barclays Bank that was to last over 35 years. When not researching the life of Fred Spiksley he is often found volunteering in a small Staffordshire village, where he lives with his wife Lynda.